Antidocetic Christology in the Gospel of John

Antidocetic Christology in the Gospel of John

An Investigation of the Place
of the Fourth Gospel
in the Johannine School

UDO SCHNELLE

Translated by
Linda M. Maloney

FORTRESS PRESS
MINNEAPOLIS

Dedicated to

Georg Strecker

in gratitude

Translated from the German *Antidoketische Christologie im Johannesevangelium.*
Copyright © Vandenhoeck & Ruprecht 1987.

Interior design: The HK Scriptorium, Inc.

Library of Congress Cataloging-in-Publication Data

Schnelle, Udo.
  [Antidoketische Christologie im Johannesevangelium. English]
  Antidocetic Christology in the Gospel of John / Udo
Schnelle : translated by Linda M. Maloney.
    p.   cm.
  Translation of: Antidoketische Christologie im Johannesevangelium.
  Includes bibliographical references and index.
  ISBN: 0-8006-2592-7 (alk. paper)
  1. Bible. N.T. John—Theology.   2. Jesus Christ—Person and
offices—Biblical teaching.   3. Jesus Christ—History of doctrines—
Early church, ca. 30–600.   I. Title.
BS2625.5.S3613   1992
226.5′06—dc20   92-9073
                                                           CIP

Manufactured in the U.S.A.   1-2592

96   95   94   93   92   1   2   3   4   5   6   7   8   9   10

Contents

Preface

The present work was accepted by the theological faculty of the University of Göttingen in fulfillment of the requirements for the *Habilitation*. It has been lightly edited for publication. I am grateful to Hartmut Stegemann for his valuable advice, and once again I extend my special thanks to Georg Strecker. Through the years in which we have worked together, he has always allowed me the freedom to try out new paths in Pauline and Johannine exegesis, and his own work has stimulated my thinking in significant ways. He sees the goal of New Testament study not in the more or less original reproduction of results that have long been acknowledged but in the thorough and persistent investigation of new questions and new insights in order to arrive at a more comprehensive historical and theological understanding of the New Testament. I feel myself united with him in this task, and as a small token of my thanks, I dedicate this book to him.

Udo Schnelle

Translator's Preface

For the most part, I have followed the text of the NRSV for English translations of the Bible; occasionally, and particularly in the translation of individual phrases that are the focus of the author's comments at a given point, I have rendered the Greek text into English to correspond to the German translation or to provide a very literal reading, when this seemed necessary to assist the reader in following the author's interpretation.

I wish to express my appreciation to the editors at Fortress Press for the opportunity to translate Professor Schnelle's book. It is my hope that the translation will expand the English-speaking audience for this significant contribution to Johannine studies.

LINDA M. MALONEY

Abbreviations

DLZ	*Deutsche Literaturzeitung*
EdF	Erträge der Forschung
EH	Ergänzungsheft
EHS	Europäische Hochschulschriften
EHS.T	Europäische Hochschulschriften. Theologie
EKK	Evangelisch-katholischer Kommentar zum Neuen Testament
EKL	*Evangelisches Kirchenlexicon*
EtB	Études bibliques
EvTh	*Evangelische Theologie*
EWNT	*Exegetisches Wörterbuch zum Neuen Testament*
FRLANT	Forschungen zur Religion und Literatur des Alten und Neuen Testaments
FThSt	Freiburger theologische Studien
FTS	Frankfurter theologische Studien
FzB	Forschung zur Bibel
GCS	Griechisch-christliche Schriftsteller
GNT	Grundrisse zum Neuen Testament
GTA	Göttinger theologische Arbeiten
HC	Hand-Commentar zum Neuen Testament
HNT	Handbuch zum Neuen Testament
HNTC	Harper's New Testament Commentaries
ICC	International Critical Commentary
JAC	*Jahrbuch für Antike und Christentum*
JBL	*Journal of Biblical Literature*
JJS	*Journal of Jewish Studies*
JPTh	*Jahrbücher für protestantische Theologie*
JSHRZ	Jüdische Schriften aus hellenistisch-römischer Zeit
JSJ	*Journal for the Study of Judaism*
JSNT	*Journal for the Study of the New Testament*
JThS	*Journal of Theological Studies*
Jud.	*Judaica.* Zürich
KEK	Meyers kritisch-exegetischer Kommentar über das Neue Testament
KNT	Kommentar zum Neuen Testament
KuD	*Kerygma und Dogma*
LSSK.T	Publications de la Société des sciences et des lettres d'Aarhus. Série de théologie.
MSSNTS	Society for New Testament Studies, Monograph Series
MThS	Münchener theologische Studien
NA[26]	Nestle, Eberhard, Erwin Nestle, and Kurt Aland. *Novum Testamentum Graece.* 26th ed. Stuttgart, 1979.
NCeB	New Century Bible
NGWG.PH	Aus den Nachrichten der königlichen Gesellschaft der Wissenschaften zu Göttingen. Philologisch-historische Klasse
NHL	*Nag Hammadi Library*
NT	*Novum Testamentum*
NT.S	Novum Testamentum. Supplements
NTA	Neutestamentliche Abhandlungen
NTD	Das Neue Testament deutsch
NTS	*New Testament Studies*

ÖTK	Ökumenischer Taschenbuchkommentar zum Neuen Testament
QD	Quaestiones Disputatae
RAC	*Reallexikon für Antike und Christentum*
RGG	*Religion in Geschichte und Gegenwart*
RNT	Regensburger Neues Testament
RVV	Religionsgeschichtliche Versuche und Vorarbeiten
SBB	Stuttgarter biblische Beiträge
SBL DS	Society of Biblical Literature, Dissertation Series
SBS	Stuttgarter Bibelstudien
SF	Studia Friburgensia
SGV	Sammlung gemeinverständlicher Vorträge und Schriften aus dem Gebiet der Theologie und Religionsgeschichte
SHR	Supplements to Numen
SJTh	*Scottish Journal of Theology*
SNT	Schriften des Neuen Testaments
StANT	Studien zum Alten und Neuen Testament
StCh	Studia ad Corpus Hellenisticum Novi Testamenti
StEv	*Studia evangelica*
StNT	Studien zum Neuen Testament
StTh	*Studia theologica.* Lund, et al.
SUC	Schriften des Urchristentum
SUNT	Studien zur Umwelt des Neuen Testaments
TB	Theologische Bücherei
TDNT	*Theological Dictionary of the New Testament*
ThBeitr.	*Theologische Beiträge*
ThBl	*Theologische Blätter*
ThDiss.	Theologische Dissertationen
ThHK	Theologischer Handkommentar zum Neuen Testament
ThJb	*Theologisches Jahrbuch.* Gütersloh
ThLZ	*Theologische Literaturzeitung*
ThR	*Theologische Rundschau*
ThViat	*Theologia Viatorum*
ThZ	*Theologische Zeitschrift*
TRE	*Theologische Realenzyklopädie*
TThZ	*Trierer theologische Zeitschrift*
TU	Texte und Untersuchungen
TynB	*Tyndale Bulletin*
VF	*Verkündigung und Forschung*
WdF	Wege der Forschung
WMANT	Wissenschaftliche Monographien zum Alten und Neuen Testament
WUNT	Wissenschaftliche Untersuchungen zum Neuen Testament
ZBK NT	Zürcher Bibelkommentare, Neues Testament
ZKG	*Zeitschrift für Kirchengeschichte*
ZNW	*Zeitschrift für die neutestamentliche Wissenschaft und die Kunde der älteren Kirche*
ZSTh	*Zeitschrift für systematische Theologie*
ZThK	*Zeitschrift für Theologie und Kirche*
ZWTh	*Zeitschrift für wissenschaftliche Theologie*

1
Introductory Considerations on Method in Johannine Research

For all theological and historical questions, the answers obtained always present new problems; this is particularly the case for the Fourth Gospel. There is a remarkable discrepancy here between the intensive research being done on the Gospel, as indicated by the number of publications, which is growing with the speed of an avalanche,[1] and the lack of any fundamental consensus. Whereas there is a comparatively great measure of agreement in the exegesis of the Pauline corpus or of the Synoptic Gospels regarding methodology and basic historical presuppositions,[2] consensus concerning both of these is lacking in Johannine study. The reason for this lies primarily in the object itself; the Fourth Gospel's theological and historical complexity is a barrier to any kind of one-sided or single-strand attempt at explanation. In reading John, one is quickly overcome with the feeling "of being surrounded by nothing but riddles and mysteries, as if the author wanted to say many more and very different things than are conveyed by the surface meaning of the words themselves; at every turn one feels oneself called upon to search for buried treasures."[3] Besides the object itself, the principal reasons for the lack of consensus in Johannine exegesis are a dearth of reflection on method and vague definitions of the religious-historical phenomena in the

---

[1] Malatesta's bibliography, *St. John's Gospel 1920–1965,* which appeared in 1967 and covered the whole literature on John between those years, contained about 3,100 titles. For the period 1966–1971 (really to 1973), Thyen lists some 1,030 titles in his survey of research (*ThR* 39). Again, Becker notes around 130 titles in the period 1978–1980 (see "Aus der Literatur," *ThR* 47).

[2] There is widespread acceptance of the two-source theory as an explanatory model for the literary relationships of dependence in the Synoptic Gospels, and of the use of form and redaction criticism, on that basis, as the authoritative methodology. Paul's origins in Hellenistic Judaism and Jewish Christianity are not disputed, and there is also a considerable measure of agreement on the number of "genuine" Pauline letters (1 Thessalonians, 1 and 2 Corinthians, Galatians, Romans, Philemon, Philippians). Johannine research is far from reaching even such a minimal consensus!

[3] W. Heitmüller, *Johannes,* 9.

1

vicinity of which, or in the midst of which, the Fourth Gospel is supposed to have been composed. Anyone who wishes to make an adequate approach to the Fourth Gospel is therefore compelled to embark on an intensive discussion of methodology—not only to justify one's own approach within the current state of research but primarily because in no other New Testament writing does methodology exercise so strong a preconditioning influence on the results of research.

What follows is a critical description of only those methods in Johannine research that are important in the modern and most recent discussion. The aim is not to offer a complete survey of the history of research but to give examples of methodological problems as illustrated by selected studies. In testing and evaluating these methods, we are less interested in detailed critical exegesis (which is to be found in chaps. 3, 4, and 5) than in basic issues: uncovering unspoken methodological presuppositions, working out problems in the development of particular methods, indicating some questionable historical and religious-historical presuppositions, and formulating methodological and hermeneutical inquiries.

1.1 Johannine Literary Criticism

For some time, literary criticism—the discussion and isolation of sources, and the elaboration of secondary or redactional levels and bases for shifting the order of text segments—has been *the* methodology for Johannine research. It seems to be too often forgotten that all the relevant literary critical problems in the Fourth Gospel were already listed by Julius Wellhausen and Eduard Schwartz.[4]

Wellhausen presumed that John 18:1 should follow 14:31,[5] and that chapters 15–17 were the later contribution of a redactor who was very close to 1 John.[6] He saw the difficulties in the order of chapters 5–7 as also due to a redactor and suggested that the sequence of chapters should be 4, 6, 5, 7.[7] He considered the eucharistic passage John 6:51-59 an addition to the text,[8] struck out ὕδατος καί in 3:5,[9] and thought that both the sacramental

---

[4] Both of these scholars clearly name the problems that have determined Johannine exegesis until now. A comprehensive description of Johannine research, something that at the present time is regrettably still lacking, would demonstrate this. Schürer offers a preliminary overview of research in the nineteenth century in "Über den gegenwärtigen Stand der johanneischen Frage" (1899). For Johannine research in the twentieth century, see Howard, *Fourth Gospel;* and Menoud, *L'Évangile de Jean d'après les recherches récentes.* Kysar offers a good description of more recent research in *The Fourth Evangelist and His Gospel.*

[5] See Wellhausen, *Erweiterungen,* 1.

[6] Ibid., 12.

[7] Ibid., 15–19; see also his *Evangelium Johannis,* 105.

[8] Wellhausen, *Erweiterungen,* 32.

[9] Ibid., 18.

references in 19:34, 35, 37 and the eucharistic passage were the work of the author of 1 John.[10] Wellhausen described the tensions between the eschatological saying in 5:21-24 and that in 5:25-29,[11] as well as the apparent misplacing of the race to the grave between 20:1 and 20:11.[12] Finally, he considered the Thomas pericope to be secondary,[13] and he also recognized the problems raised by John 21.[14] These literary-critical analyses led Wellhausen to the thesis of a basic document that was the "original creation of a distinctive personality,"[15] and was distinguished theologically by the absence of sacraments or of any expectation of the parousia.[16] Because the passages that expand and improve the text reveal differences among themselves, Wellhausen supposed that not just one editor, but a number (!) of "epigones"[17] or "imitators" had worked over the basic document.

E. Schwartz's *Aporien im vierten Evangelium* are individual studies paralleling the work of Wellhausen that were prepared and published in an ongoing dialogue with him. Although they do not yield a comprehensive interpretation of the Fourth Gospel, they still represent a series of very important literary-critical analyses.

We can mention here only the most important of Schwartz's numerous observations. Beginning with the question whether the Beloved Disciple was part of the original Gospel,[18] Schwartz analyzed John 13 and the Johannine passion story, concluding that the Beloved Disciple entered the Gospel in chapters 13, 18, and 19 through the hand of an early editor[19] and that in John 21 a later interpolator made a secondary identification of this Beloved Disciple with John of Ephesus.[20] Schwartz saw in the earlier editor the presbyter of 2 and 3 John,[21] who is also supposed to be the author of 1 John, a conclusion derived from the identical theological tendencies in the revision of the Gospel and of 1 John (especially as regards the sacraments). The later interpolator, who attempted to assimilate the Gospel to the Synoptics,[22] is to be sought in the chiliastic circles of Asia Minor, which are known primarily through Papias.[23] He not only made major changes in the Gospel (including

---

[10] Ibid., 30ff.
[11] See *Evangelium Johannis*, 26.
[12] Ibid., 91.
[13] *Erweiterungen*, 27ff.
[14] *Evangelium Johannis*, 96ff.
[15] Ibid., 102.
[16] Ibid., 125.
[17] Ibid., 100.
[18] Schwartz, *Aporien* I, 342.
[19] Ibid., 346ff., esp. 345.
[20] Ibid., 362–63.
[21] Ibid., 371.
[22] Ibid., 356, and frequently elsewhere.
[23] Ibid., 368.

the insertion of John 1:14!)[24] and in 1 John, but it was his identification of the unknown presbyter with John of Ephesus that gave rise to the notion of the "writing"[25] apostle John and thus ensured the inclusion of the Johannine writings in the canon. It seems, Schwartz would admit, that it is not often possible to decide "whether a passage in the Gospel that is related to the letters is the work of the author of the letters or that of the later interpolator,"[26] but this admission does not deter him from attributing a large number of passages to the later interpolator.

Schwartz also ascribes to this interpolator the contradictory chronology of journeys to the feasts in chapters 5–7; the interpolator is supposed to have made radical changes in the original order of events for the sake of anti-gnostic polemic.[27] In the "real" Fourth Gospel, which can no longer be reconstructed but which comes from a "cool, humanely creative evangelist,"[28] Jesus was not in Jerusalem before chapter 7. His first journey was described in chapters 7–10, reaching its high point in the healing of the man born blind and its nadir in Jesus' flight from the Jews (10:39).[29] According to Schwartz, we have here a glimpse of "the outlines of a poetic composition showing the life of Jesus as a tragedy and using the preliminary failure of the hero as a retarding moment in order to furnish the peripeteia with redoubled power."[30] This "creation" and also the original Lazarus pericope were destroyed by the later, anti-gnostic interpolator, in order to give the pericope of Jesus' entry into Jerusalem the same prominent position in the Fourth Gospel that it holds in the Synoptics.[31] Finally, Schwartz worked out a considerable number of secondary additions in all the important parts of the Gospel,[32] suggested that the evangelist had suppressed the baptism by John, and disclosed the supposed aporiae in the prologue, especially the secondary character of 1:14.[33]

For Schwartz, John the evangelist was "an ἀρεταλόγος [aretalogist] of the finest kind; it is not his fault that redactors have left us only pitiful, tattered scraps of the wreath of stories he so artfully wove."[34]

> [John was a] highly individual poet . . . who undertook to compose a completely new hymn over the ἀρεταί [mighty deeds] of his God. He has

---

[24] Ibid., 367.
[25] Ibid., 372.
[26] Ibid.
[27] See Schwartz, *Aporien* II, 118, 122, 140; *Aporien* III, 149.
[28] Schwartz, *Aporien* III, 178.
[29] Ibid., 165.
[30] Ibid., 166.
[31] Ibid., 176.
[32] Ibid., 184ff.; see also *Aporien* IV, 498ff., 504ff., 514ff.
[33] *Aporien* IV, 532ff.
[34] Ibid., 516.

no interest in the hopes of ancient times; his Jesus is not the mistreated servant of YHWH, abandoned by his own disciples and subjected to a shameful sentence. He is a hero who courageously seeks out the enemy (the Jews) and goes heroically to his death, freely renouncing the protection of his own followers.[35]

It was only the redactors and above all the later interpolator who turned this work of art into the heap of rubble whose individual parts can probably still be subjected to analysis but whose original shape is irrevocably lost. The classical methods of literary criticism (attention to tensions, breaks in the text, faulty logic, redactional connections, doublets, contradictions, inconsistencies, additions that disturb the flow of the text, different theological positions) were fully applied to the Fourth Gospel by Wellhausen and Schwartz, and their observations are still the basis for all literary-critical work on that Gospel. Literary-critical theses that have been put forward since their time do not rest on new insights but are all deductions based on analogical reasoning.[36]

Both of these scholars proceeded on the assumption that the evident disorder in the Gospel can be traced to one or more redactors close to 1 John, who attempted to assimilate the Fourth Gospel to the Synoptics. By analogy with large portions of Jewish and early Christian literature, the Gospel as it stands was seen as the end product of a literary process

> that took place in a series of steps. The basic document furnished only the outline and in extent was far outdistanced by the additions. Thus it cannot be regarded as the real Gospel of John, but only as an ingredient within it. It has by no means been preserved intact and complete, and it is not possible to discern with certainty what was the original and what are the various stages of redaction.[37]

Wellhausen was thus quite aware of the problematic character and the limitations of his procedure, and his commentary on John is to be regarded more as a sketch of the problems than as a solution to them. Schwartz too states with resignation that the chaos in the Fourth Gospel makes any "reconstruction of the earliest form of the Gospel impossible" and that "one is easily tempted, in a weary and dispirited mood, to lay down the critical knife and to leave these fragments in the confusion and disorder to which revision has reduced them."[38] "A judgment on the original Gospel as a whole is difficult, if not impossible."[39]

---

[35] Ibid., 557–58.

[36] A clear indication of this is the renaissance of Wellhausen's thesis of a Johannine "basic document." This theory has been revived in different forms by Richter, Langbrandtner, and Thyen (see section 1.2 below).

[37] Wellhausen, *Evangelium Johannis,* 6–7.

[38] Schwartz, *Aporien* IV, 497.

[39] Ibid., 557.

Both these exegetes, educated in the study of the Old Testament and ancient literature, made use of literary criticism as a means to historical insight, for they suspected that beneath the present disorder of the Fourth Gospel there was an orderly original, and they regarded that original as particularly valuable from both a historical and a theological point of view. They did not find that original, and they were able to trace neither the extent nor the theological tendencies of the individual revisions. Ultimately their analyses ended in a *non liquet:* the full extent of the chaos was revealed, but a theologically or historically persuasive explanation for the present shape of the Gospel could not be given.

This was the task undertaken by Rudolf Bultmann in his commentary on John. He reconstructed the pre- and post-history of the Fourth Gospel and arrived at an impressive solution for the literary and theological problems, a solution that has had an abiding influence. He began his reflections with the hypothesis that a redactor had not only attempted to bring new order to the original Gospel of John, which had been mutilated and thrown into disorder by external agents,[40] but had also made additions in order to soften some theological statements that this redactor considered doubtful.[41] In Bultmann's view, this redactor did not succeed in restoring the original text, and he himself undertook this task in his role as exegete. The object of interpretation is not the Gospel in its final form; instead, it is a text purified of all additions and restored to its original order.[42] Like Wellhausen and Schwartz, Bultmann also sought to reconstruct the "real" Gospel of John, using the methods of literary criticism. But in contrast to the other two, he gave the literary-critical phenomena a theological and historical explanation that was plausible within the framework of his presuppositions.

If the unsatisfactory order of the text and the theological tensions within individual sections (especially as regards sacraments and eschatology) were traceable to an "ecclesiastical" redactor, other unevennesses were due to the evangelist's use of written sources. On the basis of stylistic and linguistic peculiarities, plus the numbering of miracles in 2:11 and 4:54, Bultmann posited a signs source, a source containing revelatory discourses, and a pre-existing passion account.[43] It is now generally recognized that in the framework of his passion story John has redacted traditions.[44] A source of revelatory

---

[40] See Bultmann, *John* 17 n. 2. Even before Bultmann, Faure had stated his opinion that "we are dealing with an unfinished work, an incomplete draft" ("Zitate," 117).

[41] On this point, see the list of passages in Smith, *Composition and Order,* 213–38.

[42] See the reconstruction of the "Bultmann" Gospel of John in Smith, *Composition and Order,* 179–212. Cf. also Haenchen, *John* 1:48–50, for justified criticism of Bultmann's methodological procedures.

[43] The texts of the supposed sources are printed in Greek in Smith, *Composition and Order,* 23–34 (revelatory discourses), 38–44 (semeia source), and 48–51 (passion source).

[44] On this, see especially Dauer, *Die Passionsgeschichte im Johannesevangelium.* Before Bultmann it was primarily Dibelius, in "Die alttestamentlichen Motive in der Leidensgeschichte des

discourses is rejected at the present time, and rightly so;[45] however, many exegetes still affirm the existence of a signs source.[46]

The strength of Bultmann's interpretation of John undoubtedly lies in the intensive interaction of historical and theological interpretation. The literary-critical phenomena are explained in the context of a theological conception, a process that adds to their plausibility. The apparently different theological standpoints of the source documents, the evangelist "John," and the "ecclesiastical" redactor, in turn, are established through the application of literary-critical methods. At the center of the exegesis is not the Gospel of John as we have it but the creative power of the exegete who succeeds in untangling the snarl by explaining the diachronic and synchronic structure of the Gospel in terms of two three-level theories of tradition and redaction, locating it within the history of religion and of theology (gnostic savior myth and "ecclesiastical" redaction), and finally subjecting it to the method of interpretation adopted by the exegete himself (demythologizing and existential interpretation).

The three most important literary-critical analyses of the Gospel of John had this in common: they suggested the existence of the original "real" Gospel behind the final form as we have it, and they attempted to reconstruct, order, and interpret that original. But did this original form, which can be reconstructed primarily by the application of the methods of literary criticism, ever exist at all?[47] Alone, the presumption of a "better" meaning of the text and of tensions within the order of the text that can be evaluated by literary criticism is not sufficient to allow us to restore the original form of the Gospel of John by rearranging some passages and removing others that are thought to be secondary.[48]

Since a real explanation for the original causes of the "disorder" cannot be given, the responsibility for all the supposed breaks in the text, which the exegetes themselves detect in the course of their search for source documents and revisions, is laid at the door of an unknown redactor, or several such. Here it is the subjective sensibility of the individual exegetes, their delight in reconstruction and combination, and their theological imagination that play the dominant role, as is clearly evident from the numerous, highly complicated

Petrus- und Johannesevangeliums" (first published in 1918), who had posited a written source behind the passion story in John.

[45] See, e.g., Käsemann, "Neutestamentliche Fragen," 25; Haenchen, "Aus der Literatur zum Johannesevangelium," 305–6; Schnackenburg, John 1:51–52; Conzelmann, Grundriß, 354–55.

[46] See chapter 3 below.

[47] See the insightful methodological notes in Dodd, Interpretation, 289–90.

[48] See Smith, Composition and Order, 175; Thyen, "Aus der Literatur," ThR 39, 294. For a critique of Bultmann's hypothesis of a rearrangement of pages, see Haenchen, John 1:50; Schnackenburg, John 1:41-44; Brown, John 1:xxvi–xxviii; Kümmel, Introduction, 171–72.

and sometimes mutually exclusive theories of the origins of the Gospel of John.[49]

A reordering of the text is justified only when the impossibility of the order as given is established at both the literary-critical and the theological level. But this proof at both levels has not been offered for the Gospel of John! Therefore we must hold to the fundamental methodological rule that the exegete's first duty is to interpret the Gospel as it now stands.[50] In doing so, one must proceed from the working hypothesis that the final form of the Gospel is not the result of accidents or failed attempts at reconstruction, but that the Gospel of John, like the others, is based on a considered plan that it is our task to discover. Certainly we need to keep in mind that this plan does not correspond to the technical and logical demands that are imposed on texts today. In view of these fundamental considerations, the problems of Johannine literary criticism as source criticism become apparent, in their practical consequences as well: since there are no parallel traditions,[51] we can draw only on indications within the work itself. In this process, the subjective judgment of the exegete has a weight that is not really subject to methodological evaluation or correction.

Moreover, linguistic and stylistic features must be almost wholly excluded as criteria for decision, with the result that tensions in the content of the work furnish almost the only bases for literary-critical judgment. But the answer to the question of what is to be regarded as a contradiction in content or theology is dependent primarily on the subjective judgment of the exegete.

The studies of E. Schweizer and E. Ruckstuhl have shown how problematic are the numerous hypotheses of divisions in and revisions of the text based on peculiarities of language and style. Whereas Ruckstuhl very quickly concludes from the stylistic unity of the Gospel to its literary unity,[52] Schweizer is somewhat more cautious in saying that stylistic criticism does not demonstrate the falsity of all literary-critical analyses; "but it has been shown that, if there is any truth in them, the various levels must have been very thoroughly revised. Therefore, as long as no better and more objective characteristics of the individual sources are given than heretofore, we may not treat them as other than unprovable hypotheses."[53]

---

[49] See merely the summary of new theories of the Gospel's origin in Kysar, *Fourth Evangelist*, 38–54.

[50] See Thyen, "Aus der Literatur," *ThR* 39, 308; Haenchen, *John* 1:80, 87.

[51] Becker points to the Sayings Source (Q) as a support for the plausibility of a Johannine source criticism ("Aus der Literatur," *ThR* 47, 295). But there is a decisive methodological difference here! The Sayings Source can be reconstructed as a support for Synoptic source criticism only because there is a double tradition. In John, on the contrary, there are no double traditions, so we are left simply with data within the work itself. As a result, it is very difficult to escape the dangers of methodological circular reasoning.

[52] See Ruckstuhl, *Einheit*, 218–19.

[53] E. Schweizer, *Ego Eimi*, 105. Besides Schweizer and Ruckstuhl, we should mention especially the work of Noack, *Zur johanneischen Tradition*. Noack primarily employs the arguments of stylistic criticism in an attempt to refute Bultmann's theory of sources.

Thus, methodological considerations require us to reject literary criticism as source criticism, since it does not inquire about the compositional unity of a book and the theological concepts on which it is based but seeks for the supposed original form of the work, looking for extensive, redacted written sources and secondary revisions. Nevertheless, this is not a rejection of a kind of literary criticism that, taking as its premise the compositional and theological unity of a work, searches out the traditions made use of by the author.[54] This form of literary criticism, applied primarily to limited units of text, is on the contrary an indispensable precondition for a redaction-critical approach that poses, integrates and expands questions in religious and tradition history and matters of form criticism. This is not to deny that the Fourth Gospel had a subsequent history (see John 5:4; 7:53 — 8:11; 21), nor that there is serious evidence of the reordering of text units and of secondary revisions; but for the methodological reasons given, neither of these, nor both together, legitimate extensive literary criticism.

1.2 Redactional Levels in John's Gospel

One variant of older literary-critical theories has become highly important in current Johannine research: namely, the thesis that there are a number of literary layers (or redactions) in the Gospel of John. This approach is represented among German-speaking exegetes especially by W. Langbrandtner, H. Thyen, and, with different accents, G. Richter. It attempts, by making use of literary-, form-, tradition-, and redaction-critical methods, both to trace the history of the development of the Fourth Gospel and to describe the precise theological intentions of the individual layers.

W. Langbrandtner, in his remarkable study, not only attempts to present an exact reconstruction of the different layers in the Gospel of John and to interpret them theologically, but beyond all that, he undertakes to locate the Johannine literature on a broad scale within the scope of religious history. His methodological approach is literary-critical. He hopes in this

---

[54] Methodological objections to distinguishing sources and to extensive literary criticism have always existed in Johannine exegesis. In older literature, see Overbeck, *Johannesevangelium,* 244–45; Jülicher, *Einleitung,* 312ff.; Windisch, "Erzählungsstil," 200-201; Howard, *Fourth Gospel,* 95–172; Streeter, *The Four Gospels,* 377; Bauer, *Johannesevangelium,* 250. In recent Johannine exegesis there are an increasing number of voices that reject extensive literary criticism: see Strathmann, *Johannes,* 9–10; Hoskyns, *The Fourth Gospel,* 66; Schnackenburg, *John* 1:72–74; idem, "Entwicklung und Stand," 16ff.; Barrett, *John,* 15–26; Schneider, *Johannes,* 23–27; Kümmel, *Introduction,* 210–17; Blank, *Johannes* 1:22ff.; Wengst, *Bedrängte Gemeinde,* 18ff.; Smalley, *John,* 97ff.; Leidig, *Jesu Gespräch,* 1–14; Lindemann, "Gemeinde und Welt," 136–38; Wilckens, "Der eucharistische Abschnitt," 248. Carson offers a critical analysis of recent source theories for the Gospel of John in "Current Source Criticism of the Fourth Gospel," 411ff.

way "to be able to create [for himself] an initial basis from which it will be possible to trace the development of theological thought in the Johannine communities and thus give a preliminary sketch of the history of Johannine Christianity."[55] Hence Langbrandtner, using the literary-critical arguments that have been reasonably well known at least since Bultmann, reconstructs a Johannine "basic document" essentially containing texts in which a sharp cosmological dualism is articulated as the basis for an a-sacramental, conventicle-type Christianity dedicated to a realized eschatology. In the gnostic dualism that is determinative for the whole movement, two spheres, mutually exclusive in their very essence, stand opposed to each other: a heavenly realm above and an earthly realm below.[56]

This dualistic foundation has inevitable consequences for christology, soteriology, cosmology, and anthropology: Jesus, as God's unique word of revelation, brings God's will to human beings and at the same time realizes it, by his *anodos,* moving from the lower to the upper sphere. Those who decide for Jesus are immediately saved. Through faith, they receive a share in the superior, heavenly realm and are thus freed from earthly mortality and death. A community of nature and of destiny is created between the Revealer, who is simultaneously the revelation, and the believers. The sole and unique form of the saving event is faith; there are no mediating agents, and thus the miracle stories in their earthly magnitude can only be understood as reverse reflections (like photographic negatives) of true faith in the Revealer, which is directed to the heavenly sphere alone. The Jesus of the Johannine "basic document" is, by his very nature, disengaged from the world and all things earthly.

According to Langbrandtner, the theology of the Johannine "redaction" is characterized primarily by a shift in this dualistic conception. The cosmological and soteriological dualism of the "basic document" is transformed into a this-worldly opposition between the community and the world; the natural result is that cosmology loses its soteriological significance.[57] Now soteriology centers on ecclesiology, the concept of Jesus' sacrificial death, sacramentalism, and future eschatology. Within christology, the mutual exclusivity of the two spheres is ruptured (John 1:14!) and the bodiliness of the earthly as well as the risen Jesus acquires a soteriological function. The sacraments are guarantees of salvation; Peter is the guarantor of the church's unity; and the Beloved Disciple watches over the "purity" of the church's teaching.[58] The community missionizes, demands correct ethical behavior, and regards itself as being, through the Paraclete, a continuing locus of divine revelation.

---

[55] Langbrandtner, *Weltferner Gott,* viii.
[56] Ibid., 84ff.
[57] Ibid., 107.
[58] Ibid., 111.

The purpose of Langbrandtner's work is nothing less than an integration of two contrary tendencies in previous Johannine interpretation. Whereas the basic document corresponds to the gnostic interpretation of John by E. Käsemann and L. Schottroff, the theology of the redaction more closely resembles a conservative interpretation of John as represented by R. Schnackenburg, among others. But the primary influence on Langbrandtner's work is Rudolf Bultmann's commentary on John: the results of his literary-critical analysis correspond to those of Bultmann throughout, and Langbrandtner's "redaction" differs substantially from Bultmann's ecclesiastical redaction only in its title. The methodological objections raised in section 1 above against an extensive use of literary criticism as source criticism are thus applicable also to Langbrandtner's work. After establishing an initial standpoint, he proceeds schematically and with great confidence to assign chapters, verses, and even individual words to the basic document or to the redaction.

Beyond this method of source criticism, there are other fundamental methodological objections to be raised against Langbrandtner's analysis. His attempt to get behind the existing literary form of the Gospel of John and to reconstruct a basic document fails primarily because "the literary structure" of this basic document as "the decisive determinant of all its details is irrevocably lost to us."[59] It is not possible, on the basis of the Gospel as it now exists, to reconstruct layers running through it and to place them convincingly in form-critical categories. Add to this the fact that the evangelist treated the given traditions with great freedom, and it "is from the outset hard to believe that [the evangelist] relied on the sequence of a 'basic document' over long stretches of text."[60] The basic document is an ideal construct!

Even if there could have been a basic document, the question arises: Why did the redactors adopt and publish it if their aim was to correct and reinterpret the theology of this basic document?[61] Why should redaction undertake a "reinterpretation"[62] of the basic document and not simply set forth its own theology? Could it be at all certain that hearers and readers of the Gospel would recognize its subtle "reinterpretation?" Why did this redaction regard as theologically compatible what to modern exegesis seems

---

[59] Thyen, "Entwicklungen," 267 n. 25; see also his "Brüder," 536. Langbrandtner of course raises the problem of the literary form of the "basic document" (see his *Weltferner Gott,* 103–4), but he is able only to determine that Jesus' discourses and conversations "resemble tractates with no surrounding context" (p. 104) similar to gnostic revelatory discourses.

[60] Bauer, *Johannes,* 249–50.

[61] See Schnackenburg, "Entwicklung und Stand," 17–18. Langbrandtner can only suppose at this point that the basic document may have "been a part of the traditions of the Johannine community that could not be surrendered."

[62] The concept of "reinterpretation" is central for Langbrandtner but is nowhere precisely defined, so that it remains questionable what hermeneutical concept would, in the mind of the redactor(s), have been connected with this procedure.

contradictory and quite incompatible?[63] Beyond these questions it is doubtful whether a "theology of the redaction" can be reconstructed at all, because
it is lifted out of sections, verses, and individual words that never existed in
any literary connection and, according to the purpose of the redaction, are
only to be understood in the context in which they now exist.[64] Finally, there
is no acute christological conflict to be found in the Gospel of John—in contrast to the Johannine letters—against the background of which the supposed
method of redaction could be understood.

As far as can be determined from his publications to date, the special
feature of Thyen's interpretation of John is his attempt to recognize in the
author of John 21 the "real" fourth evangelist.[65] Inasmuch as the author of
this chapter has "thoroughly and penetratingly"[66] revised and altered a "basic
document" that must be regarded as "naïvely docetic" in its christology[67] and
that is independent of the Synoptics in its tradition history[68]—so much so
that that basic document can no longer be precisely reconstructed—the title
"evangelist" belongs to him alone. Thyen rejects all source theories and
attempts to make the author of the basic document responsible for difficulties
in the Gospel of John. For him, as for F. Spitta earlier,[69] the solution of all
the problems lies in the final redaction of the Fourth Gospel. Therefore (as
F. C. Baur had already said!)[70] John 20:30-31 is not the real ending of the
book but is only a "summary 'conclusion'"[71] employed to make John 21
resemble an "epilogue," in conscious correspondence to the "prologue." "This
is deliberate structuring and not literary clumsiness."[72]

In John 21 the readers are told the identity of the guarantor of the tradition, the truthful witness and the author of the Gospel of John: it is the
Beloved Disciple.[73] For Thyen, the Beloved Disciple is both a literary figure
and a historical person within the Johannine circle.[74] Thyen sees in him the
πρεσβύτερος of 2 and 3 John.[75] The fourth evangelist has fashioned the

---

[63] For many exegetes, theological systems are only imaginable in a "pure form"; that is, they
must be completely without internal contradictions, and not even nuances are permitted. This
axiom is applied to the New Testament texts, and the "pure form" of theological and literary
"layers," corresponding to the established demands, is constructed according to this principle.

[64] See also Thyen, "'Niemand hat größere Liebe,'" 478.

[65] See Thyen, "Johannes 13," 356; idem, "Entwicklungen," 267, 282, 288; idem, "'Das Heil
kommt von den Juden,'" 164.

[66] Thyen, "Entwicklungen," 282.

[67] Ibid., 268 n. 28, 285, 292.

[68] Ibid., 289 n. 79.

[69] See Spitta, *Johannesevangelium,* 16.

[70] See Baur, *Composition,* 188–91.

[71] Thyen, "Entwicklungen," 260.

[72] Ibid.

[73] Ibid., 262.

[74] Ibid., 293.

[75] Ibid., 296.

Beloved Disciple as a literary memorial to him. Thyen sees the concrete occasion for this in an acute christological schism within the Johannine circle (see 1 John 2:18ff.) that caused the author of John 21, the disciple of the presbyter (who had unexpectedly died) to undertake a thorough revision of the "naïvely docetic basic document"[76] by inserting the passages about the Beloved Disciple[77] (John 1:14-18,[78] 6:48ff.,[79] 13:34-35[80]) and the sections of futurist eschatology.[81] In addition, he rearranged sections of text and introduced a great number of "reinterpretations" modeled on the Synoptics.[82] Since many members of the Johannine community (under the influence of Diotrephes)[83] had adhered to the docetic heresy, a direct confrontation with them was unavoidable. In this conflict, the πρεσβύτερος, clothed in the literary form of the Beloved Disciple, served as a guarantor of tradition, thus contributing to "combatting the docetic heresy and overcoming the schism."[84]

The cornerstone of Thyen's theories is John 21.[85] This is his starting point in unfolding his thesis of a comprehensive redaction of the Johannine basic document; in this way he avoids the difficulties involved in a precise reconstruction of sources. Here also, on the basis of the Beloved-Disciple passages, which are supposedly introduced by the author of John 21, he finds the concrete historical background for this redaction. But is John 21 really a deliberately placed epilogue written by the person Thyen dubs the "fourth evangelist?" John 20:30-31 is still good evidence against it! These two verses, composed by John, are obviously the conclusion of a book and represent the original ending of the Gospel of John.[86] In closing, John indicates that his portrayal is selective, applies the motif of "things that cannot be spoken," which is so frequently found at the end of ancient books, and finally, in v. 31, states the purpose of his Gospel. Moreover, John 21:25 clearly refers to 20:30. In addition, the expression ἐν τῷ βιβλίῳ τούτῳ [in this book], unique to John, indicates that this is a consciously formulated conclusion to the book. Thyen makes a virtue of necessity in positing as deliberate what has previously been properly regarded as the sign of a subsequent addition. The authors of chapter 21 needed only to strike out 20:30-31 or insert the

---

[76] Ibid., 292.

[77] Ibid., 274ff. The thoroughly secondary character of the "Beloved Disciple texts" was proposed earlier, especially by Schwartz, *Aporien* I, 342ff.

[78] See Thyen, "Entwicklungen," 273.

[79] Ibid., 277.

[80] Ibid., 280.

[81] Ibid., 269 n. 29.

[82] Ibid., 288.

[83] Thyen is inclined at this point to accept the well-known thesis of Bauer; see "Entwicklungen," 298.

[84] Thyen, "Entwicklungen," 296.

[85] See earlier Smith, who states that John 21 "is the key and cornerstone for any redactional theory" (*Composition and Order,* 234).

[86] See the thorough analysis in section 3.8.1 below.

addition before those verses to obtain a smooth transition and a rounded composition. But they did not do so!

Unique features of language and style do not prove the secondary character of John 21,[87] but there are a considerable number of arguments for it, based on content. In chapter 21 it appears that the missing epiphanies in Galilee are appended, and Jesus' appearances to his disciples in 20:19-29 are ignored. It is remarkable that, *after* the disciples have been given the Spirit and sent forth, Jesus has them return to Galilee, to their old tasks as fishers—something not mentioned in this Gospel before—so that he can appear to them again in that locale.[88] In addition, the redactional verse 20:29 utterly excludes any further appearance,[89] since in this macarism John states something that from that point on applies to later generations in distinction from the eyewitnesses: they are to believe without having seen. In contrast to this pastorally motivated conclusion of the narratives in the Fourth Gospel, the additional appearances in chapter 21 seem out of place.[90]

The enumeration in 21:14 is further evidence that this chapter is a subsequent addition, because it presupposes the appearances in 20:19-23, 24-29. The sons of Zebedee appear only in 21:2, and we must inquire why it is only at this point that we learn that Nathanael comes from Cana.[91] Finally, in 21:24-25 the authors of chapter 21 and probably the editors of the whole Gospel reveal themselves.[92] Their testimony about the Beloved Disciple[93] follows seamlessly on vv. 1-23, but it is impossible on the lips of John the evangelist. It strongly emphasizes the character of John 21 as an addition supplied by a post-Johannine redaction.[94]

Beyond this, we find articulated in chapter 21 an intensified ecclesiological interest that has altered in character since chapters 1–20. This can be demonstrated in, among other things, the depiction of the Beloved Disciple. The authors of chapter 21 present the Beloved Disciple as a historical person

---

[87] See Bultmann, *John*, 700; Barrett, *John*, 576ff.; Reim, "Johannes 21," 331. Important *hapax legomena* are παιδία [children] in 21:5 as an address to the disciples and ἀδελφοί [brothers and sisters] in 21:23 as a designation for Christians.

[88] See Haenchen, *John* 2:222.

[89] See section 3.8.2 below.

[90] See Bultmann, *John*, 701.

[91] Ibid.

[92] Thyen silently ignores the plural in v. 24b and speaks throughout of "an" author or composer (see "Entwicklungen," 275, 277, and frequently elsewhere).

[93] Only the "Beloved Disciple" can be meant here; see Schnackenburg, *John* 3:372.

[94] Among those who regard chap. 21 as secondary are Bultmann, *John*, 700–706; Haenchen, *John* 2:229ff.; Pesch, *Fischfang*, 39; Becker, *Johannes* 2:634ff.; Gnilka, *Johannesevangelium*, 156ff.; J. Schneider, *Johannes*, 327; Wikenhauser, *Johannes*, 286. On the other side, those who consider chap. 21 original include Bauer, *Johannes*, 234–35; Ruckstuhl, *Einheit*, 134ff.; Smalley, *John*, 95–97; Reim, "Johannes 21"; Minear, "John 21"; Schlatter, *Johannes*, 363; Jülicher, *Einleitung*, 312; Brown, *John* 2:1077ff. (epilogue); Barrett, *John*, 576–77 (appendix); Lightfoot, *John*, 337ff. (appendix); Dodd, *Interpretation*, 431; Heitmüller, *Johannes*, 180 (appendix).

whose death, which has just occurred, has caused confusion in the community. Apparently there was a saying of the Lord (vv. 22b, 23c: αὐτὸν θέλω μένειν ἕως ἔρχομαι [that he remain until I come]) at the basis of the tradition that this disciple would not die (v. 23a). Many in the Johannine community therefore expected the parousia within the lifetime of the Beloved Disciple.[95] This hope had not been fulfilled, and the problem had to be dealt with theologically. The authors of chapter 21 faced the altered situation by countering this personal legend about the Beloved Disciple circulating in the community and the eschatological expectations accompanying it with a relativizing interpretation of the Lord's saying (v. 23b,c).[96] They also corrected or expanded in two ways the picture of the Beloved Disciple as found in chapters 1–20. On the one hand, the Beloved Disciple, the guarantor of the Johannine tradition, was made the author of the whole Gospel (v. 24a). It is true that even in chapters 1–20 his immediate access to Jesus is a guarantee of the truth of the Johannine witness to Christ (see especially John 19:34b-35, as well as 13:21-30; 18:15-18; 19:25-27), but the composition of the Fourth Gospel, which is now attributed to him, is an intensification of this motif. On the other hand, v. 24 equates the Beloved Disciple and the evangelist, John, though there are no indications of this in chapters 1–20.[97]

In John 21 the relationship between Peter and the Beloved Disciple is corrected. In John 1–20, Peter has no special importance. He is not the first to be called (see John 1:40ff.: Andrew brings him to Jesus); instead, he is only one among many disciples mentioned by name (Andrew in 1:40; 6:8ff.; 12:22; Philip in 1:43ff.; 6:5ff.; 12:22; 14:8; Nathanael in 1:45-51; see also Mary, Martha, and Lazarus in 11:12). The appearance stories in chapter 20 say nothing about a "*protepiphania Petri* [first appearance to Peter]."[98] In contrast, the special relationship of the Beloved Disciple to Jesus is repeatedly emphasized.

In the redactional section John 13:23-26a,[99] the Beloved Disciple lies on the breast of Jesus (κόλπος only in 13:23 and 1:18, where Jesus is in the bosom of the Father!) and Peter has to ask him for the name of the betrayer. It is true that he does not receive an answer; that is, the central motif of this section is not the uncovering of the

---

[95] See Schnackenburg, *John* 3:370-71.

[96] With Schnackenburg (*John* 3:371) the correction of the personal tradition about the Beloved Disciple offered here is to be found in an altered interpretation of μένειν [remain].

[97] It is not possible to take the witness motif in 19:35 in connection with 19:26 (where it is only the Beloved Disciple who remains under the cross) as an equation of the Beloved Disciple with John the evangelist, for witness is not authorship!

[98] See Lorenzen, *Lieblingsjünger,* 93–94.

[99] For a demonstration of the redactional character of 13:23-26a, see Lorenzen, *Lieblingsjünger,* 15 n. 21. The opposing view is taken by Bultmann (*John,* 479–80) and Hartmann ("Osterberichte," 206 n. 1). Thyen sees at this point also the redactors of chap. 21 at work ("Entwicklungen," 276ff.); for a critique, see Schnackenburg, *John* 3:13–14.

betrayer but the contrasting of Peter and the Beloved Disciple.[100] While Peter is clearly reduced to an auxiliary role at this point, the Beloved Disciple functions as a hermeneut for Jesus, as Jesus is the hermeneut of the Father (John 1:18).[101]

The unique relationship between Jesus and the Beloved Disciple is further expressed in 19:25-27. In vv. 26-27, the work of the evangelist,[102] the Beloved Disciple and the mother of Jesus are directed toward each other, with the result that the Beloved Disciple appears as the true witness beneath the cross and the earthly successor of Jesus, to whose protection Mary is to entrust herself.[103] If she is the exemplary representative of believers of all ages,[104] this furnishes a further indication of the elevated status of the Beloved Disciple: Jesus' last words are addressed to him, and it is to him that the community is entrusted after Jesus' departure. He is authorized by Jesus himself to be the only legitimate interpreter and transmitter of Jesus' message and probably the recognized leader of the Johannine community as well. The contrast to the installation of Peter in the office of shepherd, in John 21:25-27, is unmistakable![105]

The preeminence of the Beloved Disciple over Peter is reflected also in John 20:2-10.[106] In a tomb tradition that originally spoke only of Peter (v. 3a: ἐξῆλθεν [he set out]),[107] the evangelist inserts within the framework of an extensive redactional

---

[100] See Lorenzen, *Lieblingsjünger,* 17.

[101] Against Thyen, who makes the unfounded assertion that "a direct competition between Peter and the Beloved Disciple is not evident" ("Entwicklungen," 280).

[102] See Lorenzen, *Lieblingsjünger,* 23–24; Schnackenburg, *John* 3:275; Dauer, *Passionsgeschichte,* 196–200 (extensive demonstration of the redactional character of vv. 26-27); Bultmann, *John,* 666; Kragerud, *Lieblingsjünger,* 27; Wilkens, *Entstehungsgeschichte,* 84–85. Thyen disagrees ("Entwicklungen," 283). He also ascribes v. 25 to the redaction and attributes the lack of mention of the Beloved Disciple in v. 25 to the "effective technique" of the author of John 21.

[103] Schnackenburg, *John* 3:281: "The disciple accepts Mary into his own circle: that is what the evangelist intends, that is the point of what he is saying."

[104] See Schürmann, "Jesu letzte Weisung," 20ff. Dauer essays some different interpretations of Mary (*Passionsgeschichte,* 318ff.).

[105] Against Thyen, who states: "Still, the juxtaposition of Mary and the Beloved Disciple in this scene clearly shows that the depiction is not shaped by any kind of competition with Peter" ("Entwicklungen," 284). The evangelist could not go against tradition by placing Peter beneath the cross (see Bultmann, *John,* 484 n. 4), which would, in any event, not eliminate the motif of competition, since the place here assigned to the Beloved Disciple nullifies a Petrine claim to leadership, drawn from traditions that were certainly known to the Johannine community (cf. Mark 1:16, 29 – 3:16, and frequently elsewhere: Peter as the first disciple called, and having a leading position in the list of apostles; 1 Cor. 15:5; Luke 24:34: first resurrection appearance; Matt. 16:18: installation in the pastoral office). The authors of chap. 21 also understood this and applied their correction accordingly.

[106] There is a general consensus that the evangelist inserted the race to the tomb (vv. 2-10) in the story of Mary Magdalene's visit to the grave and the appearances there (vv. 1, 11-18). Wilkens gives the reasons (*Entstehungsgeschichte*).

[107] Schnackenburg (*John* 3:305) and Hartmann ("Osterberichte," 200) think that Peter and Mary Magdalene originally returned to the tomb; for a critique, see Lorenzen, *Lieblingsjünger,* 32 n. 32. Luke 24:12 (see also Luke 24:24) should be regarded as furnishing the tradition-historical background for the story as we have it in John: see the list in Lorenzen, *Lieblingsjünger,* 27 n. 10.

editing (vv. 2, 3b [καὶ ὁ ἄλλος μαθητής (and the other disciple)] . . . 4, 5b [οὐ μέντοι εἰσῆλθεν (but he did not go in)], 6, 8, 10)[108] the person of the Beloved Disciple as ὁ ἄλλος μαθητὴς ὃν ἐφίλει ὁ 'Ιησοῦς [the other disciple, the one whom Jesus loved].[109] The motive for this is undoubtedly to be found in the rivalry between Peter and the Beloved Disciple; the latter is clearly given prominence not only in the race to the tomb (v. 4: προέδραμεν [outran]; v. 8: πρῶτος [first]) but especially in v. 8.[110] In contrast to Peter, who is an important witness of the Easter event because of his careful observation (v. 7),[111] the Beloved Disciple accurately interprets the situation, becomes the first Easter witness, and is also the first to attain to full faith in Jesus' resurrection.[112] This extraordinary and exemplary faith again illustrates the special relationship of the Beloved Disciple to Jesus. Moreover, the Beloved Disciple (like Peter) emphatically establishes the reality of Jesus' death and bodily resurrection; in this an antidocetic tendency is apparent.

John 18:15-18, like 20:3, 4, 8, speaks of an ἄλλος μαθητής [another disciple] (v. 15: ἄλλος μαθητής, ὁ δὲ μαθητὴς ἐκεῖνος; v. 16: ὁ μαθητὴς ὁ ἄλλος). Although Peter and the other disciple follow their Lord to the house of the high priest, only Jesus and the ἄλλος μαθητής, and not Peter, who is mentioned first in the text, enter the courtyard. This disciple, in contrast to Peter, has the privilege of acquaintance with the high priest and free access to his court. He must return to the gate in order to arrange for Peter's admission. The motif of competition between the ἄλλος μαθητής and Peter, evident in the priority accorded the former,[113] the numerous parallels to John 20:2-10 (where, again, in v. 2 Peter is named first, but in vv. 4 and 8 the Beloved Disciple comes before him), and the redactional character of vv. 15b-16,[114] all make it probable that the ἄλλος μαθητής is no one other than the Beloved Disciple.[115] He follows his captured Lord, and no gate can prevent him from doing so.

---

[108] For the reasoning in each case, see Lorenzen, *Lieblingsjünger,* 29–36. Langbrandtner (*Weltferner Gott,* 30–32), Thyen ("Entwicklungen," 288ff.), and Hoffmann (*TRE* 4:506) regard John 20:2-10 as the work of those who redacted chap. 21. They make light of the motif of competition between Peter and the Beloved Disciple and wrongly deny an antidocetic tendency on the part of the evangelist John.

[109] The designation of the Beloved Disciple as ὁ ἄλλος μαθητὴς ὃν ἐφίλει ὁ 'Ιησοῦς [the other disciple, the one whom Jesus loved] is a reference to John 13:23 (18:15-16); 19:26. Concerning the shift from ἀγαπᾶν to φιλεῖν [both meaning "love"], cf. John 3:35 with 5:20; 11:3 with 11:5; 14:24 with 16:27. See also Lorenzen, *Lieblingsjünger,* 30 n. 22.

[110] See Kragerud, *Lieblingsjünger,* 29-30; Lorenzen, *Lieblingsjünger,* 25-26; Schnackenburg, *John* 3:313–14.

[111] Of course, the Beloved Disciple also sees the linen cloths in v. 5b, so that Peter's only advantage over him is in seeing the head cloth.

[112] Against Bultmann, *John,* 684, who thinks that Peter also comes to believe when he sees the empty tomb.

[113] See Haenchen, "Historie und Geschichte," 61 n. 15; Kragerud, *Lieblingsjünger,* 26; Wilkens, *Entstehungsgeschichte,* 81; Lorenzen, *Lieblingsjünger,* 50; Cullmann, *The Johannine Circle,* 72.

[114] See Lorenzen, *Lieblingsjünger,* 49ff.

[115] Among those who argue for this identification are: Strathmann, *Johannes,* 239; Kragerud, *Lieblingsjünger,* 25-26; Wilkens, *Entstehungsgeschichte,* 81; Brown, *John* 2:822; Lorenzen, *Lieblingsjünger,* 51; Cullmann, *The Johannine Circle,* 71; Thyen, "Entwicklungen," 281; Langbrandtner, *Weltferner Gott,* 44-45. (For Thyen and Langbrandtner, of course, the author of

He even makes it possible for Peter to approach Jesus, but Peter then shamefully denies the Lord.

The testimony to the reality of Jesus' death by the outflowing of αἷμα καὶ ὕδωρ [blood and water] in John 19:34b-35 is to be seen as being in continuity with 19:25-27 but in sharp contrast to 18:15-18. This scene, introduced by John the evangelist[116] in a preexisting context, has a clearly antidocetic tendency, articulated not only in the sacramental αἷμα καὶ ὕδωρ but also in the person who testifies to the event. In favor of the identification of the unknown witness with the Beloved Disciple is 19:26-27, where he is the only witness under the cross in addition to the women.[117] Since John knows of no other male witness beneath the cross besides the Beloved Disciple, it would be remarkable if he were not thinking of him.[118] Evidently, 19:25-27 is a preparation for the scene, so that here the Beloved Disciple need not even be mentioned individually. He remains as a true witness beneath the cross, while Peter denies Jesus!

Finally, the Beloved Disciple is also to be surmised behind the unnamed disciple in John 1:35-42, who, together with Andrew, is the first to be called. After the witness of the Baptizer (vv. 19-28) and Jesus' first appearance (vv. 29-34), John has included two successive stories about disciples (vv. 35-42 and 43-51), each of which is clearly divided into two sections (vv. 35-39, 40-42; vv. 43-44, 45-51). Although the call of the two anonymous disciples of John in vv. 35-39 is essentially based on a pre-Johannine narrative,[119] the identification of one of the disciples with Andrew in v. 40 must be attributed to the evangelist. Although this verse is not tightly anchored in its context,[120] it has some characteristic marks of Johannine style,[121] and the description of Andrew as the brother of Simon Peter anticipates data from v. 41.[122] On the other hand, the testimony of Andrew and the bestowal of the name on Simon in vv. 41-42

---

chap. 21 is responsible for this identification.) On the contrary, an identification is rejected by Bultmann, *Johannes*, 369–70; Dodd, *Tradition*, 86ff.; Lindars, *John*, 548; Roloff, "'Lieblings-jünger,'" 131–32; Dauer, *Passionsgeschichte*, 72–75; Schnackenburg, *John* 3:234–35.

[116] For argumentation, see the extensive exegesis of John 19:34b-35 in section 4.3 below.

[117] Among those who consider the witness in 19:35 to be the Beloved Disciple are Hoskyns, *Fourth Gospel*, 533; Kragerud, *Lieblingsjünger*, 140; Bauer, *Johannesevangelium*, 266; Roloff, "'Lieblingsjünger,'" 132; Schnackenburg, *John* 1:93–94; Brown, *John* 2:936; Lorenzen, *Lieblingsjünger*, 58; Bultmann, *John* 678–79 ("ecclesial redaction"); Thyen, "Entwicklungen," 186; Langbrandtner, *Weltferner Gott*, 34. (Thyen and Langbrandtner also see in 19:34b-35 the work of the author of chap. 21.)

[118] In addition, the Beloved Disciple has appeared at every important point in the passion story up to this time.

[119] The only parts that are certainly redactional are τῇ ἐπαύριον [the next day] (v. 35; cf. 1:29, 42; 6:22; 12:12), πάλιν [again] (43 times in the Gospel of John) in v. 35a, and the οὖν [then]-*historicum* in v. 39. The partitive ἐκ in v. 35 may also be Johannine; for a thorough explanation, see Lorenzen, *Lieblingsjünger*, 40ff., especially 40 n. 10.

[120] See Lorenzen, *Lieblingsjünger*, 42.

[121] Simon Peter (Ruckstuhl, *Einheit*, Appendix, no. 24), partitive ἐκ (Ruckstuhl, no. 45), asyndeton (Ruckstuhl, no. 6).

[122] See Lorenzen, *Lieblingsjünger*, 42. Dodd (*Tradition*, 306) and Hartmann ("Osterberichte," 209) also consider v. 40 redactional.

are to be regarded as traditional,[123] while, on the other hand, Jesus' calling of Philip[124] in v. 43 is redactional.[125] As in v. 40, the disciple is mentioned in advance of the following narrative, and through v. 44, which is also redactional, Andrew, Peter, and Philip are placed in relationship to one another before another traditional vocation narrative follows in vv. 45ff.[126] With vv. 40 and 43-44, John has connected three traditional narratives of the calling of disciples (vv. 35-39, 41-42, 45ff.) and identified one anonymous disciple of John the Baptizer with Andrew. In the other nameless disciple, who remains deliberately unmentioned in v. 44, we must conclude that the evangelist is pointing to the Beloved Disciple, who, in the proper sense, first appears in chapter 13 but who is a true witness of the Christ-event from the very beginning.[127] He is called before Peter, who is only brought to Jesus by his brother, Andrew.

In chapters 1–20, the Beloved Disciple, as the true witness and hermeneut of Jesus, is the guarantor of the Johannine tradition from the outset. He is appointed by Jesus himself as his earthly successor, and he is the first to achieve true Easter faith. He is constantly placed before Peter, who, in sharp contrast to the Beloved Disciple, does not remain faithful to his Lord but denies him.[128] This picture changes in chapter 21. Here Peter is the central figure in the group of disciples, as hinted in vv. 1-14 and emphatically expressed in Peter's appointment to the pastoral office (vv. 15-17).

In vv. 1-14, the authors of chapter 21 have combined an appearance tradition with another traditional story about a catch of fish (cf. Luke 24:13-35).[129] The uppermost redactional layer, seen in vv. 1 and 14, is indicated by the conjunctive particles μετὰ ταῦτα [after these things] and πάλιν [again] in v. 1, the repeated φανεροῦν [appeared] in v. 1 and v. 14, and also the enumeration in v. 14, referring to 20:19-23, 24-29.[130] It is possible that the indication of place, ἐπὶ τῆς θαλάσσης τῆς Τιβεριάδος [by the sea of Tiberias], is traditional,[131] but the narrative proper begins only with the list of disciples in v. 2. The original list contained only Peter and the sons of Zebedee; the redaction added Thomas (cf. 20:24-29), Nathanael (cf. 1:49), and the other two

---

[123] For the reasoning, see Lorenzen, who accurately observes that v. 41 probably had Ἀνδρέας [Andrew] instead of οὗτος [he] (Lieblingjünger, 43). On the text-critical problems in v. 41 (πρῶτος/πρῶτον), see Barrett, John, 181–82.

[124] See Haenchen, John 1:165.

[125] See Lorenzen, Lieblingsjünger, 43ff., including the debate with Boismard and Schnackenburg, who regard v. 43 as post-Johannine, which would mean attaching v. 44 to v. 42, so that the second disciple in vv. 37-39 would be Philip. But in that case, we should expect πρῶτος rather than πρῶτον in v. 41! In addition, τῇ ἐπαύριον and the parallel to v. 40 point to John as the author.

[126] See Lorenzen, Lieblingsjünger, 44ff.

[127] Among those who argue for this identification are Kragerud, Lieblingsjünger, 19ff.; Hoskyns, Fourth Gospel, 180; Wilkens, Entstehungsgeschichte, 35 n. 122; Hahn, "Jüngerberufung," 184–85.

[128] Against Brown, Donfried, and Reumann, who deny any rivalry between Peter and the Beloved Disciple (Peter in the New Testament, 138).

[129] For a discussion of the problems, see Schnackenburg, John 3:345–47.

[130] See Pesch, Fischfang, 88; Schnackenburg, John 3:351–52; Becker, Johannes 2:639.

[131] See Schnackenburg, John 3:345–47.

disciples, to attain the number seven.[132] If vv. 2, 3, and 4a are part of the report of the catch of fish, the comment in v. 4b makes sense only in the context of the appearance tradition.[133] On the other hand, v. 5 is part of the redaction, as suggested by the *hapax legomena*, παιδία [children] (cf. 1 John 2:13, 18), προσφάγιον [lit. "anything to eat," usually translated in this verse as "fish"], and the tensions with v. 9 (where the meal is, in miraculous fashion, already prepared, whereas in v. 5 the disciples cast their net for fish so that they may eat).[134] Verse 6 belongs wholly to the fishing tradition, while v. 7, on the other hand, is attributable to the redaction.[135] As in 20:8, the Beloved Disciple gives a correct assessment of the situation in v. 7a, whereby the redaction establishes a connection with the portrayal of the Beloved Disciple in chapters 1–20 but at the same time prepares for the juxtaposition of the two disciples in vv. 20-22. As soon as Peter hears that it is the Lord, he leaps into the lake in order to reach Jesus before all the other disciples. The basis of vv. 8-9 lies in the appearance story, which, like the Emmaus pericope, included a meal scene.[136] Verse 10 represents a redactional connection between the large catch of fish and the appearance tradition: some of the fish that have just been caught are now to be eaten, even though in fact the meal is already prepared (cf. v. 9).[137] Verse 11 is the conclusion of the story of the catch of fish. Here it is Peter alone who brings the great number of fish to land, without bursting the net. The number, 153, confirms the magnitude and reality of the miracle; it symbolizes fullness and universality.[138] At the same time, the net represents the church, which contains everyone, and Peter is the one shepherd who gathers together the children of God. The meal scene in vv. 12-13 is the end and high point of the appearance tradition. At the meal the disciples recognize that this is the Lord (cf. Luke 24:30ff.), who continues his community with them even after Easter. The introduction in v. 12a (cf. vv. 5a and 10a) belongs to the redaction, as does the strange wavering between wanting to ask and knowing, necessitated by the recognition on the part of the "Beloved Disciple" in v. 7.[139]

The Beloved Disciple in 21:7 has the gift of correctly recognizing Jesus, a motif that was evidently rooted in the tradition and could not be overlooked by the post-Johannine redaction. On the other hand, it is clear that the events focus on Peter:[140] (1) it is at his initiative that the disciples go fishing (v. 3); (2) he leaps into the lake in order to reach the Lord before anyone else

---

[132] See Pesch, *Fischfang,* 91; Schnackenburg, *John* 3:352; Becker, *Johannes,* 1:637–38; against R. Fortna, who attributes all personal references to his "source" (*Gospel,* 89–90).

[133] See Pesch, *Fischfang,* 94; Schnackenburg, *John* 3:353.

[134] See Pesch, *Fischfang,* 95; Becker, *Johannes* 2:637.

[135] See Schnackenburg, *John* 3:355; Becker, *Johannes* 2:640–41. Pesch differs: he assigns v. 6 to the story of the catch of fish, but v. 7 he thinks is part of the appearance tradition (*Fischfang,* 95ff.).

[136] See Schnackenburg, *John* 3:356. He correctly surmises that the ἄλλοι μαθηταί in v. 8a and the last part of the verse (σύροντες [dragging] etc.) are traceable to the redaction.

[137] See Pesch, *Fischfang,* 99; Schnackenburg, *John* 3:356; Becker, *Johannes,* 2:641.

[138] On various interpretations of the number 153, see Schnackenburg, *John* 3:357–58.

[139] See Schnackenburg, *John* 3:358–59.

[140] In terms of tradition criticism, this is to be attributed to the story of the catch of fish, which in all probability was primarily a tradition about Peter.

(v. 7b); (3) he alone draws the overflowing net to land (v. 11). This heavy emphasis on the person of Peter is a means by which the redactors prepare for the subsequent dialogue between Peter and the Risen One.

Within the dialogue, Peter is brought to the foreground in a variety of ways:[141] with the comparative πλέον [more] in v. 15, the post-Johannine redaction emphatically introduces the motif of competition between Peter and the other disciple (cf., to the contrary, Mark 9:33-37; 10:35-40, 41-45), in order to underscore the preeminence of Peter. Jesus' threefold question and Peter's sorrow in v. 17 refer back to his promise of discipleship (John 13:36-38) and his threefold denial (18:15-18, 25-27). The purpose is to rehabilitate Peter. Finally, Peter's installation in the pastoral office makes him the earthly successor of Jesus; what God had entrusted to Jesus (John 10) Peter now receives. The interest of the post-Johannine redaction is unmistakable: to retain the connection with the special function of the Beloved Disciple within the Johannine school, though to a limited degree, but at the same time to place Peter clearly in the foreground. This is especially evident in the conversation between Jesus and Peter about the Beloved Disciple in 21:20-22. Whereas in chapters 1–20 the Beloved Disciple, in contrast to Peter, had direct access to Jesus, at this point Jesus and Peter talk about the destiny of the Beloved Disciple, who himself remains silent.

H. Thyen's attempt at a new interpretation of the course of the Fourth Gospel's development on the basis of John 21 failed because of the secondary nature of that chapter.[142] It is not a "purposeful epilogue" but a later addition, as is proved by the conclusion of the book in 20:30 and the numerous material differences between chapters 1–20 and chapter 21. Nor is the person of the Beloved Disciple an element of unity, since all the Beloved-Disciple texts in chapters 1–20 are from John the evangelist, who deliberately places this central figure of the Johannine school in the foreground, whereas in chapter 21 the post-Johannine redaction is emphatically interested in the preeminence of Peter. Also questionable, both historically and hermeneutically, is Thyen's suggestion that the author of John 21 should be regarded as the fourth evangelist. Since it appears that Thyen deliberately avoids a reconstruction of any basic document that is supposed to have been available to the fourth evangelist, it is not clear how extensive the evangelist's literary and theological activity might have been and whether he deserves the title "evangelist." Finally, this conceptual shift makes it even less clear than before what is to be regarded as pre-Johannine tradition, what is "genuinely" Johannine, and what is post-Johannine redaction.

---

[141] For the exegetical details not treated here, see Schnackenburg, *John* 3:360–67. He properly emphasizes the shaping of vv. 15ff. by the post-Johannine redaction and understands the scene with Peter "from the internal conditions of the Johannine school" (p. 360). He thus correctly rejects Brown's opinion (*John* 2:1111) regarding a connection with Luke 5:8, 10.

[142] For a critique of Thyen, see Bergmeier, *Glaube als Gabe,* 205–12.

In addition to Rudolf Schnackenburg, the person within the Catholic tradition who has most advanced Johannine research through his own independent proposals is Georg Richter. His starting point is John 20:31. Here the evangelist states the purpose of his Gospel, and this "must continually be called upon as a guideline for interpretation."[143] The Gospel is not a missionary document for Jews or Gentiles. Its intent is to show that Jesus of Nazareth is the Messiah and Son of God. "It is on the basis of this aim, as stated by the evangelist himself, that an understanding of the whole and of its parts has to be worked out."[144] Therefore, for Richter, 20:31 is both a theological and a literary-critical guideline. What does not accord with the purpose of the Gospel as here stated cannot be attributed to the evangelist but must belong to other layers of the Gospel of John.

Richter finds the oldest layer of the Fourth Gospel in a "Jewish-Christian basic document," whose christology broadly agrees with that of later Jewish Christian groups (e.g., the Ebionites).[145] Jesus is presented in the messianic christology of the basic document as an eschatological prophet like Moses, who legitimates himself through signs and wonders. Jesus is Messiah by God's designation, not because of his divine origin. He is not the Son of God, but only a human being, the son of Joseph of Nazareth (John 1:45, 46; 6:42). The basic document included, among other things, a description of the Baptizer that differed from that of the Synoptics, a "semeia [signs] source,"[146] and narratives of the passion and Easter that differed from those in the Synoptics, in that statements about the resurrection are omitted in favor of others referring to Jesus' exaltation.[147]

After some time, a group within the community that saw in Jesus not the Prophet-Messiah but the Son of God turned against the prophetic Messiah christology of the basic document. "The representative, and probably the leading personality in this group, was the Fourth Evangelist."[148] Jesus' heavenly origins and his divinity were now the condition of salvation rather than faith in his messiahship. The circle surrounding the evangelist separated from the Jewish Christian parent community and worked over the basic document in order to present the new, "high" christology as that preached by Jesus himself and as the only one corresponding to the will of

---

[143] Richter, "'Bist du Elias?'" 12.

[144] Ibid.

[145] Richter offers a brief summary of the theology of the "Jewish-Christian basic document" ("Der Vater und Gott Jesu," 266–68). Explicit indications of the agreements with Ebionite christology may be found in his "Präsentische und futurische Eschatologie," 355 n. 41.

[146] See Richter, "Semeia-Quelle," 287.

[147] See Richter, "Der Vater und Gott Jesu," 266ff. Richter thinks that the author of the basic document consciously eliminated statements about the resurrection that were contained in his tradition. His concern was with Jesus' being taken up into heaven, in parallel with Moses' assumption into heaven; this was his way of demonstrating Jesus' messiahship.

[148] See Richter, "Zum gemeindebildenden Element," 404.

God. If the basic document understood Jesus as merely a human being, the evangelist laid full emphasis on Jesus' heavenly origins and divine sonship. One possible result of this was the false impression that the evangelist taught a docetic christology.

Thus an antidocetic revision of the Fourth Gospel became necessary.[149] The "antidocetic redactor," who was the same person as the author of 1 and 2 John, emphasized Jesus' having come in the flesh, his corporeality (from him come, among other passages, John 1:14-18; 19:34-35; 1 John 4:2-3; 5:6; 2 John 7), and corrected many statements of the Docetists in the realms of anthropology, christology, eschatology, and ethics. He thus rejected the sharp dualism of the Docetists, proclaimed the salvific importance of Jesus' death (1 John 1:7; 2:2) and of the Eucharist (John 6:51c-58), taught a resurrection of the dead at the last day (John 5:28-29; 6:39b, 40c, 44c), and combatted the docetic teachers' claim to sinlessness (1 John 1:8) as well as their ethical libertinism (see John 13:34-35; 15:10, 12-14; 1 John 2:29; 4:7-8; and frequently elsewhere).

Like Langbrandtner, Richter is also largely dependent on Bultmann for his literary criticism. What Bultmann regarded as the work of the "ecclesiastical redactor" is generally attributed by Richter to the "antidocetic redactor." Both see the Son-of-God christology and present eschatology as central features of the evangelist's theology. Like Bultmann, Richter posits the existence of a "semeia source," though he regards it as part of his Jewish Christian basic document. Richter's originality lies in his evaluation of the literary-critical evidence. He is motivated by a desire to locate the precise place of the individual literary layers of the Gospel of John in the history of early Christian theology, in the debates with contemporary Judaism, and in the conflicts within the Johannine school. However, at this point his argumentation is very hypothetical. The existence of an ebionitically colored Jewish Christian basic document cannot be proved. Neither can we reconstruct it with literary precision, nor can we imagine that in an early stage of Johannine theology Jesus was revered only as a human being and not as the Son of God. In addition, the attribution of all the antidocetic passages, which are certainly present in the Fourth Gospel, to a late "antidocetic redactor" is questionable. Why should John the evangelist not have had an interest in Jesus' corporeality and the salvific significance of his death, and also in sacraments, ethics, and ecclesiology?

In his method, Richter ignores the questions of form and tradition criticism. He excludes the possibility that tensions within the text are traceable not to extensive literary revisions but to a process of growth within the tradition. Literary criticism is the basic method employed to establish the

---

[149] See Richter, "Präsentische und futurische Eschatologie," 357–58; idem, "Zum gemeinde-bildenden Element," 409–10.

reasons why individual sections of the text should be assigned to one or the other of the three layers. But if a text can be integrated in the postulated theology of one layer, this remains true even if there are no literary indications for its location. Richter also leaves unanswered the question why the individual redactors took over previous documents whose theology was contrary to theirs, instead of laying them aside and presenting nothing but their own specific theology.

Important to all three of the proposals described are two theories about the origins of the Gospel of John that can be mentioned here only in passing. W. Wilkens thinks "that the Gospel went through a process of development beneath the hand of one and the same evangelist, from a basic gospel to the present form of the Gospel as we have it."[150] Wilkens's "basic gospel" contained primarily narrative material, especially Jesus' miracles and parts of the passion narrative.[151] It was then redacted by the evangelist, with the insertion of extensive discourse material.[152] Finally, the evangelist arranged the Gospel anew, from the point of view of the Passover: by using the "Passover outline formula" (John 2:13; 6:4; 11:55) and adding new materials, he introduced the framework of the Passover as a compositional principle for the Gospel. Thus the Fourth Gospel became a "Gospel of the passion."[153]

R. E. Brown, following Wilkens, posits five stages in the development of the Gospel of John:[154] (1) material on Jesus' words and discourses independent of the Synoptics;[155] (2) development and shaping of this mainly oral tradition within the Johannine communities;[156] (3) collection of the material into a first draft of the Gospel by the evangelist;[157] (4) reworking and writing of a new version of the Gospel by the evangelist, occasioned by contemporary events;[158] (5) final reworking by a redactor close to the evangelist, who added, among other elements, 6:51-58; 3:31-36, and chapters 11 and 12.[159]

The theory of Brown, in particular, leaves a good deal of elasticity for explaining tensions within the Fourth Gospel. However, his methodology has a crucial weakness: because he consciously avoids a precise literary-critical reconstruction of the individual layers, the assignment of material to different layers cannot be verified. But a suggested process of development of a literary work through several stages must be verifiable by literary-critical methods if it is to be persuasive!

Common to all the proposals described is the tracing of the present form of the Gospel of John to a rather lengthy literary process, in the course

---

[150] Wilkens, *Zeichen und Werke*, 9.

[151] See Wilkens, *Entstehungsgeschichte*, 32–93.

[152] Ibid., 94–122.

[153] Ibid., 123–70. For a critique of Wilkens, see Schnackenburg, *John* 1:68–70.

[154] For the agreements between Wilkens and Brown, see Kysar, *Fourth Evangelist*, 38–54, esp. 49.

[155] See Brown, *John* 1:xxxiv.

[156] Ibid., xxxiv–xxxv.

[157] Ibid., xxxv–xxxvi.

[158] Ibid., xxxvi.

[159] Ibid., xxxvi–xxxvii.

of which a changed theological situation was directly reflected in a literary "layer" subject to reconstruction. Then an attempt is made to determine with precision both the complex final form of the Gospel and the individual literary and theological stages along the way.

The following methodological and historical objections must be raised against this procedure: (1) The basic document presupposed by most exegetes cannot be precisely reconstructed either by methods of form criticism or by those of literary criticism. (2) It is doubtful whether the theologies of the individual "redactions" can be discerned at all, since they are lifted from short sections of text—verses and individual words that never stood in any literary connection with one another and that, according to the wishes of their author, are to be understood only in the context in which they now exist. (3) Why did the individual redactors take over the earlier document(s), if they did not agree with their theology? Why did they not simply present their own theologies? (4) In the Gospel of John we can discern neither an *acute* conflict with contemporary Judaism nor an *immediate* christological controversy within the Johannine school, so that the existence of the proposed historical beginning points for individual literary layers cannot be proved. (5) It is methodologically questionable to conclude directly from presumed theological differences to different groups or authors representing those points of view.[160] To do so is to draw historical conclusions directly from literary material. (6) John 21, as a secondary addition, cannot serve as the starting point for redactional theories concerning chapters 1–20.

1.3   John and Contemporary Judaism

Under the influence of Rudolf Bultmann's interpretation of John, the questions of the place in religious history and the concrete historical background of the Fourth Gospel were for a long time answered in terms of the Gospel's relationship to gnosis.[161] In the most recent research, however, the older thesis[162] that John is to be understood exclusively against the background of the Judaism of the period has recovered a great deal of influence. The starting point is the *opinio communis* that there is one point at which the concrete historical situation of Johannine Christianity becomes especially

---

[160] See Schnackenburg, "Entwicklung und Stand," 17.

[161] For the present state of research on the problem of John's Gospel and gnosis, see the admirable essays of Fischer, "Der johanneische Christus," and of Tröger, "Ja oder Nein zur Welt: War der Evangelist Johannes Christ oder Gnostiker?" See also Kohler, *Kreuz und Menschwerdung,* 142–58, a penetrating description of the differences between Johannine and gnostic theology.

[162] Cf. only Schlatter, "Sprache und Heimat des vierten Evangelisten" (1902), and his *Johannes* (1930).

clear: the expulsion from the synagogue, threatened or prophesied in John 9:22; 12:42; and 16:2 with the singular terminology ἀποσυνάγωγος γίνεσθαι (or ποιεῖν) [to "cause to be" or "put" out of the synagogue] is thought to refer to the formulation and introduction of the "heretics' blessing" (בִּרְכַּת הַמִּינִים) in the Eighteen Benedictions by Schmuel the Small, something that is supposed to have happened at the Synod of Yavneh, under Gamaliel II, between 85 and 90 C.E.[163] Since Yavneh is also regarded as the place at which the decisive separation between Jews and Jewish Christians occurred, this same conflict is reflected in the Gospel of John; that is, the Fourth Gospel is to be understood as a witness to the definitive separation of Jewish Christianity from the synagogue, and essential points in its theology are to be interpreted in terms of that historical locus.

J. L. Martyn and K. Wengst, in particular, defend the thesis that the Gospel of John is read correctly only if it is understood as a document of *acute* conflict between Jewish Christianity and "orthodox" Judaism, a writing by a Jewish Christian for other Jewish Christians. According to Martyn, the Gospel of John was written in a Hellenistic city of the Jewish diaspora, probably in Alexandria.[164] Jews were being converted to the Christian faith, and after some time a controversy arose between Jewish Christians and Jews over the salvific significance of Jesus. The Fourth Gospel is a witness to that controversy. On the one hand, it furnishes traditions about the life and activity of Jesus of Nazareth, but on the other hand it reports the acute conflict between the Johannine community and the Jews in the evangelist's own time.[165] In the Gospel of John, a drama is being played out on two levels — the time of Jesus and the situation of the evangelist and his community. Thus, in the different parts of the text a distinction must be made between two temporal levels and historical situations. For Martyn, the situation of the community is reflected most clearly in chapters 3, 5, 6, 7, and 9. Understanding the text as a witness both to Jesus' activity and to the current situation of the community is made possible through the Paraclete, who continues the work of Jesus. Martyn illustrated his approach especially in John 9, referring v. 22, with 12:42 and 16:2, to the *birkat hammînîm,* in order to obtain a concrete historical point of departure.[166] The Gospel of John is thus a (Jewish) Christian reaction to the events at Yavneh, and many of its statements can therefore be *directly* evaluated in historical terms. "Thus the Fourth Gospel affords us a picture of a Jewish community which has been (recently?) shaken up by the introduction of a newly formulated means for detecting those Jews who want to hold a dual allegiance

---

[163] Cf. only Brown, *John* 1:lxxxv (first edition of the Gospel around the year 80, before the introduction of the excommunication); also his *Ringen um die Gemeinde,* 34ff.; Lindars, *John,* 35; Becker, *Johannes* 1:43; Smalley, *John,* 83; Schnackenburg, *John* 2:250; Schulz, *Johannes,* 145; Barrett, *John,* 93; Martyn, *History and Theology,* 31f.; Wengst, *Bedrängte Gemeinde,* 48ff.; Leistner, *Antijudaismus,* 50–51; Pancaro, *Law,* 245ff.; Thyen, "'Das Heil kommt von den Juden,'" 180–81; Trilling, "Gegner Jesu," 198; Onuki, *Gemeinde und Welt,* 31ff.; Wiefel, "Scheidung," 226; Grässer, "Polemik," 86; Whitacre, *Polemic,* 7ff.; Blank, "Irrlehrer," 168.

[164] See Martyn, *History and Theology,* 73 n. 100.

[165] Ibid., 30.

[166] Ibid., 37ff.

to Moses and to Jesus as Messiah."[167] The precondition for Martyn's interpretation is an equality of value and a seamless continuity between the work of Jesus and that of the Paraclete. But that is not what the Fourth Gospel teaches; for here too the cross and resurrection, as the exaltation of Jesus Christ, constitute *the* saving event. They are the ground and basis for the work of the Paraclete, which cannot be understood simply as a fully equivalent continuation of the life of Jesus. To the extent that there is a qualitative difference between Jesus and the Paraclete, there cannot be two equally valid levels of interpretation in the Gospel of John.

For Wengst, also, the exclusion from the synagogue attested in John 9:22; 12:42; and 16:2 is "a problem that currently threatens the community of John's Gospel."[168] He sees behind the Fourth Gospel a Greek-speaking, predominantly Jewish Christian community, living as a minority in a Jewish-dominated world, which up to this time had not separated from the synagogue and was now suffering as a result of the measures decided on at Yavneh. Moreover, Wengst knows exactly where this threatened community lives: in the southern part of the kingdom of Agrippa II, more precisely in the "country of Gaulanitis and Batanea, northeast of the Jordan."[169]

There are both historical and theological objections to the exclusive application, very popular in Johannine exegesis, of ἀποσυνάγωγος in John 9:22; 12:42; and 16:2 to the *birkat hammînîm* and a consequent interpretation of the Fourth Gospel in Jewish Christian terms.

First, it is dubious historical procedure to accept data from Jewish history that have for a long time been questioned within the field of Jewish studies.[170] Although a precise dating of the decisions at Yavneh is impossible,

---

[167] Ibid., 40–41. In agreement with Martyn's position are, among others, Smith, "Johannine Christianity," 238; Kysar, "Community and Gospel," 362ff.; Brown, *Community*, 174. Martyn's thesis was anticipated by Wrede, *Charakter und Tendenz*, 40ff. Martyn developed his approach most fully in his essay "Glimpses into the History of the Johannine Community." Here he distinguishes three phases in the history of the Johannine community that are reflected on the literary level in the Gospel: (1) a messianic group within the synagogue; (2) exclusion from the synagogue and persecution; (3) building of an independent Jewish Christian community.

[168] Wengst, *Bedrängte Gemeinde*, 52.

[169] Ibid., 97. On pp. 82ff., Wengst portrays Agrippa II as the representative of Jewish orthodoxy, in whose domain—particularly because of supposed relationships "between the learned men at Yavneh and leading Jews in Agrippa II's military and governmental circle" (p. 89)—the decisions of Yavneh were quickly and thoroughly carried out. All that we know of Agrippa II speaks against this thesis: his private life (the relationship with his sister, Berenice), his coinage (the coins all carry the image of the reigning Roman emperor), and his relationship to Rome; for a thorough account, see Schürer, *History* 1:471–83. Schürer concludes that Agrippa II "was altogether more attached to the Roman than to the Jewish side" (p. 475). In addition, it is questionable whether, in the second half of the first century C.E., it is possible to speak matter-of-factly of "Jewish orthodoxy," as Wengst does. (See the critical remarks in Aune, "Orthodoxy in First Century Judaism.") Finally, the conflicts with the Jews that can be glimpsed in the Gospel of John need not have been limited to a particular region; they could as easily have happened in Asia Minor as in Syro-Palestine.

[170] See Stemberger, "Synode," 14; on the history of research within Jewish studies, see Schäfer, "Synode," 56–57.

the effects of those decisions in practice should not be taken lightly; however, the authority of Yavneh probably did not extend far beyond Palestine.[171] Add to this the question: Against whom was the *birkat hammînîm*, formulated at Yavneh, really aimed? In the rabbinic tradition the *birkat hammînîm*, except for the eulogy, has not been preserved; there is only (in *b. Ber.* 28b-29a) a report of the fact of its formulation by Schmuel the Small.[172] We are thus dependent primarily on two manuscripts from the Cairo Geniza, written some eight hundred to nine hundred years after Yavneh.[173] Here alone are the נוֹצְרִים [*noṣerim*] mentioned together with the מִינִים [*minim*].[174] A reconstruction of the oldest text version of the *birkat hammînîm* does not allow for the different traditions;[175] all that can be worked out is a common structure showing that the insertion of the *birkat hammînîm* in an already existing benediction[176] "was directed both against hostile rulers and against various groups of heretics that, according to changing current needs, could be designated by different termini."[177]

If we consider the wide variations in the textual tradition, the mention of the נוֹצְרִים only in very late manuscripts and the fact that the concept of the נוֹצְרִים does not appear in the tannaitic literature,[178] it is very likely that הַנוֹצְרִים entered part of the tradition only at a later period,[179] perhaps even after Christians had become the ruling group.[180] The מִינִים certainly does not refer in the first instance to Jewish Christians; on the contrary, it can be shown that in older rabbinic texts this term always refers to Jews, and in more recent texts (after 180–200 C.E.), its reference is "no longer to heretics within

---

[171] See Stemberger, "Synode," 15–16.

[172] The text is printed in Schäfer, "Synode," 55.

[173] See Maier, *Auseinandersetzung,* 137–38.

[174] Ibid., 241 n. 403. Maier also mentions a textual witness from the year 1426.

[175] On the individual text variants, see especially Schäfer, "Synode," 57ff.; further, see Maier, *Auseinandersetzung,* 136–37; K. G. Kuhn, *Achtzehngebet,* 23–24; Billerbeck, *Kommentar* 4/1:208–49.

[176] Schäfer thinks that a desire for the elimination of hostile rulers was at the heart of the original benediction and that it was expanded at Yavneh to include the מִינִים ("Synode," 64 n. 35). The prayer was then later modified to meet current needs. On the original meaning of the prayer against the heretics, see also Flusser, "Schisma," 230ff.

[177] Schäfer, "Synode," 60.

[178] See Kimelman, "Birkat Ha-Minim," 233.

[179] Among those who consider the mention of נוֹצְרִים as *not* original are Hoennicke, *Judenchristentum,* 388–89; Friedländer, *Bewegungen,* 223; Avi-Yonah, *Geschichte,* 141–42; Maier, *Auseinandersetzung,* 137ff.; Schäfer, "Synode," 60; idem, *Geschichte,* 254; Kimelman, "Birkat Ha-Minim," 232ff.; Urbach, "Self-Isolation," 288; Charlesworth, "Prolegomenon," 269; Katz, "Issues," 63–68, 74; Flusser, "Schisma," 229–30; Fischer, *Urchristentum,* 131. Of course, Martyn, like many others, regards מִינִים and נוֹצְרִים as original (*History and Theology,* 58ff.).

[180] This is suggested by Maier, *Auseinandersetzung,* 138–39.

Judaism, but to those outside Judaism who hold 'other beliefs,' . . . mainly Christians."[181]

The content of the *birkat hammînîm* was a plea that God might destroy hostile rulers and heretics,[182] but by no means did it have as its primary purpose the removal of Jewish Christians from the synagogue.[183] "The original purpose of the Birkat ha-minim was probably not the exclusion of the *minim* from divine worship, no more than its desire for the expulsion of Rome indicated an intention to expel Romans from the worshiping assembly."[184] Instead, the introduction of the *birkat hammînîm* was a Jewish proceeding directed against all groups that posed a threat to Jewish unity.[185] Besides, we must ask whether, at the time the decisions were being made in Yavneh, Jewish Christians in Palestine (!) were very important to learned Jews.[186] Finally, it is doubtful whether, at the time of Yavneh, one can really speak of such a thing as a Jewish "orthodoxy"[187] that was proceeding against heretics according to a considered plan.

Nothing in the ancient church witnesses speaks against this interpretation. Justin does report that the Jews in their synagogues cursed those who believed in Christ (*Dial.* 16.4: καταρώμενοι ἐν ταῖς συναγωγαῖς ὑμῶν τοὺς πιστεύοντας ἐπὶ τὸν Χριστόν; see also *Dial.* 47.4; 93.4; 95.4: Christians are cursed and, on occasion, even killed; 96.2; 117.3; 133.6), but he was not thinking of the *birkat hammînîm*.[188] This is clear from *Dial.* 137.2, where Justin says the leaders of the synagogues teach that Christ is to be ridiculed after (!) the prayer (Συμφάμενοι οὖν μὴ λοιδορῆτε ἐπὶ τὸν υἱὸν τοῦ θεοῦ, μηδὲ Φαρισαίοις πειθόμενοι διδασκάλοις τὸν βασιλέα τοῦ Ἰσραὴλ ἐπισκώψητέ ποτε, ὁποῖα διδάσκουσιν οἱ ἀρχισυνάγωγοι ὑμῶν, μετὰ τὴν προσευχήν [Assent, therefore, and do not ridicule the Son of God; do not obey the Pharisaic teachers, and do not scoff at the king of Israel, as the rulers of your synagogues teach you to do after the prayers]). If the *birkat hammînîm* were intended here, the ridiculing

---

[181] K. G. Kuhn, "Giljonim," 39; see also Maier, *Auseinandersetzung,* 141; and Katz, "Issues," 73–74.

[182] Maier names three groups against whom the *birkat hammînîm* is directed: (1) hostile rulers (Rome); (2) internal enemies, in particular those who, from a Pharisee's point of view, were heretics; (3) *minim,* which does not, in the first instance, refer to Jewish Christians (*Auseinandersetzung,* 136–37). Maier points out that in the rabbinic texts most of the references to *mînîm* have nothing to do with Jewish Christians; they are directed at "those with an anti-rabbinic attitude and Jews with a syncretistic and assimilative orientation" (p. 141). Moreover, the fact that, besides מִינִים, there are other *termini* in the talmudic tradition (see the list in Maier, p. 137), is against the interpretation of מִינִים as referring to Jewish Christians.

[183] See especially the critique by Schäfer ("Synode," 61), directed at Elbogen, who saw the *birkat hammînîm* as the decisive step in the separation of Judaism and Christianity.

[184] Maier, *Auseinandersetzung,* 140.

[185] See Schäfer, "Synode," 60; Stemberger, "Synode," 18; idem, *Das klassische Judentum,* 18; Maier, *Auseinandersetzung,* 140.

[186] See Schäfer, "Synode," 60–61; Stemberger, "Synode," 17.

[187] See n. 169 above.

[188] See Hoennicke, *Judenchristentum,* 387–88; Schürer, *History* 2:462–63; Kimelman, "Birkat Ha-Minim," 233–34; against Conzelmann, *Heiden — Juden — Christen,* 282 n. 347.

(not expulsion or cursing!) of Christ would have to have been spoken during the prayer, not after it.

Like Justin, Origen also mentions in general terms that Christ is cursed by the Jews (*In Ps.* 37 [36] hom. 2.8; *In Matth.* 16.3), but there is no evidence that he is thinking of the *birkat hammînîm*.[189] It is only Epiphanius and Jerome who can be regarded as the earliest serious witnesses for a version of the *birkat hammînîm* in which, besides the *mînîm*, (Jewish) Christians are cursed. Thus Epiphanius says that the Nazarenes are cursed three times daily in the synagogue (*Panarion* 29.9: τρὶς τῆς ἡμέρας φάσκουντες ὅτι ἐπικαταράσαι ὁ θεὸς τοὺς Ναζωραίους [saying thrice daily that God should utterly curse the Nazarenes]).[190] Jerome also mentions a thrice-daily cursing of the Nazarenes in the synagogue, and he clearly understands "Nazarenes" to mean all Christians (*In Amos* 1.11-12: usque hodie in synagogis suis sub nomine Nazarenorum blasphemant populum christianum [to this day they in their synagogues blaspheme the Christian people under the name of Nazarenes];[191] *In Esaiam* 5.18-19: usque hodie perseuerant in blasphemiis et ter per singulos dies in omnibus synagogis sub nomine Nazarenorum anathematizent uocabulum Christianum [to this day they persist in blasphemies, and day by day, in all the synagogues, they anathematize the word "Christian" under the name of "Nazarenes"]).[192] Jerome reports about the Ebionites that "usque hodie per totas Orientis synagogas inter Iudaeos haeresis est, quae dicitur Minaeorum, et a Pharisaeis huc usque damnatur: quos uulgo Nazaraeos nuncupant [down to this day, throughout all the synagogues of the East, that heresy (known as the Minaean) persists among the Jews and is utterly condemned by the Pharisees; they are commonly called Nazarenes]" (*In ep.* 112.13 to Augustine).[193] This association of *mînîm* and Nazarenes in the second half of the fourth century cannot establish an early date for נוֹצְרִים, since both Jerome and Epiphanius are thinking of the state of things in *their own* time. Moreover, we need to be conscious of the church fathers' use of language, for whereas in the last text cited there is nothing explicitly said about a cursing of the *mînîm* and the Nazarenes in the synagogue, in the other passages Ναζωραῖοι or Ναζαρηνοι on the lips of the Jews expressly or possibly refers to Christians as a whole.[194]

Thus the *birkat hammînîm* should in no way be regarded as a definitive barrier drawn between Jewish Christianity and Judaism; instead, it is to be seen as primarily an action taken within Judaism. The really effective historical separation between Judaism and Christianity had already taken place prior to this and was due to the constantly increasing influence of Gentile Christianity.[195] Moreover, the idea that the purpose of the *birkat hammînîm* was to separate Jewish Christians from the synagogue presumes that Jewish

---

[189] See Kimelman, "Birkat Ha-Minim," 236–37.

[190] Quoted from Klijn and Reinink, *Patristic Evidence,* 174.

[191] Ibid., 218.

[192] Ibid., 220.

[193] Ibid., 200. See Caroline White, *The Correspondence (394–419) between Jerome and Augustine of Hippo* (Lewiston, N.Y., 1990) *ad loc.*

[194] See Maier, *Auseinandersetzung,* 138–39.

[195] This process is reflected also in the break between Gentile and Jewish Christians; the reasons are given by Fischer in *Tendenz,* 88–93.

Christians were still taking an active part in synagogue worship and would have been cursing themselves in reciting the *birkat hammînîm,* although this cannot be demonstrated historically.[196]

The Gospel of John cannot be interpreted as a witness to Jewish Christianity. On the contrary, it reflects both a historical and a theological distance from Judaism. The threat of expulsion from the synagogue reported in John 9:22; 12:42; and 16:2 is not an acute problem for the evangelist; instead, this is a retrospective glance,[197] if not a purely literary means for depicting the unbelief of the Jews in its full compass.[198]

The distance that already exists between the Fourth Gospel and Judaism is clearly evident from the Gospel's understanding of the law. Key to that understanding is the Pauline-sounding v. 17 of the Johannine prologue.[199] Is the parallelism of the two parts of that sentence to be understood antithetically or synthetically? In favor of an antithethical interpretation is the exclusive meaning of the paired concepts, taken up from John 1:14, of ἡ χάρις καὶ ἡ ἀλήθεια [grace and truth].[200] The word χάρις, which appears only in the prologue, should be interpreted christologically: the incarnation of the Preexistent One is grace (1:14) and becomes grace for believers (1:16). Ἀλήθεια is also exclusively christological in Johannine usage. Jesus not only says what is true (see 8:45-46; 16:7) and sends the "Spirit of truth" to his own (see 14:17; 15:26; 16:13), but he *is* the truth (14:6). There is no salvation-historical continuity between Moses and Jesus; Christians live in grace and truth, not under the law. Moses is thus devalued (see also 6:32; 7:22), where the divine legitimation given to Moses is clearly disparaged). The law belongs to the Jews (see 7:19; 8:17; 10:34), while the Christians, by contrast, have left the stage of a religion of law behind them (see 4:20ff.). The problem of "law versus grace," which was so important for Paul, has in the eyes of the fourth evangelist been solved long since, so that this evangelist can, with a remarkable complacency, assign Jews to the sphere of the law and Christians to the unique realm of grace and truth.[201] It is possible that in v. 17 the evangelist is also writing a polemic against an application to the Torah of the

---

[196] See Stemberger, "Synode," 19; Hare, *Jewish Persecution,* 55; Maier, *Auseinandersetzung,* 140.

[197] See Luz, *Gesetz,* 125; Haenchen, *John* 2:39.

[198] See the exegesis of the three texts in section 3.6.2 below.

[199] See Luz, *Gesetz,* 119.

[200] With H. J. Holtzmann, *Theologie* 2:401; Luz, *Gesetz,* 119; Becker, *Johannes* 1:85–86; Barrett, *John,* 169; Dodd, *Interpretation,* 93; Bultmann, *John,* 79; Hübner, *EWNT* 2:1172; Grässer, "Polemik," 79; Gutbrod, *TDNT* 4:1083–84; von Campenhausen, *Bibel,* 64–65; Bornkamm, "Paraklet," 81; Zeller, "Paulus und Johannes," 176; against Jeremias, *TDNT* 4:872–73; Schnackenburg, *John* 1:277 n. 1; Brown, *John* 1:16; Loisy, *Le quatrième Évangile,* 193; Thyen, "'Das Heil kommt von den Juden,'" 173; Pancaro, *Law,* 534ff. Pancaro characteristically treats the first occurrence of this word in the Gospel at the end (!) of his work, in order to apply his solution of the problem to this text also.

[201] See Becker, *Johannes* 1:84.

prologue's fundamental statements about the Logos, as we see especially in rabbinic Judaism's adoption of wisdom traditions.[202] Even in John 1:17 it appears that Johannine christology, with its absolute claim to be the possessor of revelation, leaves no room for an independent theological significance of the law, no matter how limited.

The two individual passages in which Jesus enters into direct conflict with the law (breaking the Sabbath in 5:9c; 9:14, 16) are due to Johannine composition.[203] The evangelist uses the breach of the Sabbath merely as an excuse, in each case, for the subsequent conflict dialogue between Jesus and the Jews, and thus as a means of exacerbating the conflict. The breach of the Sabbath, as such, plays no role in the content; it is purely a matter of style and its theological importance exists only insofar as it illustrates the falsity of the fundamental attitude of the Jews. With the law in their hands, they accuse Jesus, but the truth is that the Son of man is judging them; only the man born blind is saved, because he believes in Jesus (see 9:35-41). Here it is clear what role John assigns to the law: it is merely a negative or positive auxiliary argument in a debate whose primary orientation is christological.[204]

This situation is further clarified by the passages in which the law is called upon to witness to Jesus (see 7:19, 23; 8:17; 10:31-39; 15:25). Thus the Jews rely on the law in making a specific accusation of blasphemy against Jesus (19:7; cf. 5:18; 8:58), but John refutes it by calling upon the law (see the reference to Ps. 82:6 in John 10:34). The law itself, that is, the Scripture, testifies in Jesus' favor. This idea is reflected in a special Johannine terminology: while νόμος [law] always refers to the law of the Jews—"your law" in a negative sense (see 7:19; 8:17; 10:34; 15:25; 18:31; 19:7),[205] γραφή [Scripture] always appears in a positive sense, on the lips of Jesus or of the evangelist (see 2:22; 5:39; 7:38, 42; 10:35; 17:12; 19:24, 28, 36-37; 20:9), and refers to the Scriptures, insofar as they testify to Jesus' messiahship.[206] John the Baptizer (5:33), and even Moses himself (1:45; 5:45-47), whose disciples the Jews are (9:28), confirm Jesus' divine origin and mission. The Scriptures can be rightly understood only in the light of Easter (2:22; 12:16; 20:9); through the Father's testimony for the Son, the law is fulfilled (8:17-18). The Scriptures can in no way be abolished by Jesus, because they witness to his divinity (10:35-36).

For John, the law can be read only in light of Jesus: he is at the same time the content and the goal of the law, and also Lord both of the law and

---

[202] See Billerbeck, *Kommentar* 2:353ff.; Kittel, *TDNT* 4:134–36; cf. Luz, *Gesetz,* 155 n. 191. For an equation of ἀλήθεια with νόμος in the Old Testament, in wisdom literature, in apocalyptic, and at Qumran, see Pancaro, *Law,* 95ff.

[203] See the analysis in section 3.6.2.

[204] See especially the good observations of Luz, *Gesetz,* 119–28.

[205] See the similarly reserved formulations in Mark 7:9, 13; Matt. 4:23; 9:35; 10:17; 12:9; 13:54.

[206] See Luz, *Gesetz,* 120; W. Schrage, *Ethik,* 288.

of the Scriptures. By thus laying claim to the Old Testament as a support for the christology of the Fourth Gospel, the evangelist asserts that the Jews are untrue to their own identity when they reject the revelation in Christ. If the meaning of the Scriptures can be discerned only in light of Jesus, then from the Johannine point of view all those who point to their privileged status as Jews and do not convert to Christ are in error. Therefore only Nathanael is an "Israelite" in the true sense, for he acknowledges Jesus as Son of God and king of Israel (1:47-49). Nicodemus is called a "teacher of Israel" (3:10) because he takes up the cause of Jesus (19:39) and accuses the Sanhedrin of abusing the law. Jesus, finally, is "king of Israel" (1:49; 12:13), but not "king of the Jews" (see Pilate's question in 18:33 and Jesus' answer in 18:37!). The unbelieving Jews, on the other hand, can even be called children of the devil (8:44) if they stubbornly refuse to acknowledge the Christ and thereby fail to realize their very identity as Jews.

It is precisely because, for this evangelist, Jesus is the measure of the Scriptures, that the content of the Old Testament commandments is of no consequence for his ethics.[207] John's deliberate use of the word ἐντολή [command or commandment] to refer to Jesus' specific ethical commands (see 10:18; 12:49, 58; 13:34; 14:15, 21; 15:10, 12) indicates what is new in this christocentric ethic. Here we can recognize how formally the fourth evangelist treats the law—in contrast to someone like Paul. On the one hand, he takes it over as a christological argument, but on the other hand, this does not imply that the content of the law has any special relevance. On the contrary, christology fully usurps the function of the law and robs it of its theological importance as the vehicle of revelation and as ethical norm. The really important thing for John is one's relationship to Jesus himself, that is, faith (1:7, 50; 3:15, 18, 36; 6:29, 40; and frequently elsewhere). Therefore a reference to the law may be regarded as convenient in terms of the history of religion and even as necessary from the perspective of contemporary history, but theologically it is quite superfluous.[208] The Old Testament is so sharply subjugated to the service of a christocentric conception of things that its independent witness is silenced; it serves now only as an auxiliary argument and a rhetorical device, with the result that its function is, at the most, that of pointing to something else.

This description of the Johannine concept of the law, although necessarily brief, still makes it clear that it is impossible to regard the Fourth Gospel as primarily a witness to Jewish Christianity. If observance of the law is a notable characteristic of a Jewish way of life and, next to the confession of Christ, *the* mark of Jewish Christian theology,[209] then the Gospel of John,

---

[207] See Luz, *Gesetz*, 124.

[208] Against Luz, who thinks "that the claim made on the Old Testament as a witness for Christ is of fundamental importance" (*Gesetz*, 127).

[209] See Strecker's definition in "Judenchristentum und Gnosis," 262–63; also the review of

in light of the concept of the law that has been sketched above, cannot be called Jewish Christian. For John, the law has neither soteriological nor ethical importance: this finding speaks decidedly against a Jewish Christian interpretation of the Fourth Gospel.

The breadth of the distance between the Gospel of John and Judaism is evident not only from the concept of law but from the translations of Hebrew and Aramaic words found in the Gospel (1:38, 41, 42; 4:25; 5:2; 9:7; 11:16; 19:17; 20:16, 24) and the reserved way in which it speaks of the feasts (2:13; 5:1; 6:4; 7:2, 11; 11:55) and customs (2:6; 4:9; 18:20; 19:40, 42) of "the Jews."

The gulf between the Fourth Gospel and Judaism is evident also in the Johannine use of Ἰουδαῖος.[210] What strikes one first is the frequency of the word's appearance in comparison with the usage of the Synoptics (195 occurrences in the New Testament overall; of those, 71 in John, 5 in Matthew, 6 in Mark, 5 in Luke, and 79 in Acts). This points to a usage that results from theological reflection. Of the 71 instances, 34 occur in scenes of conflict between Jesus and "the Jews" and thus have an anti-Jewish tendency (1:19; 2:18, 20; 3:25; 5:10, 16, 18; 6:41, 52; 7:1, 11, 13, 15, 35; 8:22, 48, 52, 57; 9:18, 22; 10:24, 31, 33; 11:8, 54; 13:33; 18:12, 14, 31, 36; 19:7, 31, 38; 20:19). But John can also speak neutrally of the crowds that are present as Ἰουδαῖοι (10:19; 11:19, 31, 33, 36, 45; 12:9, 11; 18:20, 38; 19:12, 14, 20, 21), or mention and explain the customs and practices of "the Jews" (see the passages listed above), or distinguish the Jews from those who are not Jews (18:33, 35, 39; 19:3, 19, 21). The evangelist uses the word in a positive sense when he speaks of the Ἰουδαῖοι who believe in Jesus (8:31; 11:45; 12:11). In 4:9, Jesus himself is called Ἰουδαῖος, and 4:22 emphasizes the importance of the Jews in the history of salvation, although this is immediately relativized (v. 23).[211]

This survey shows that we may not begin by positing a uniform (negative) Johannine usage. The Jews are not simply *massa damnata* as such. Instead, the context determines the meaning in each case. Still, it is notable that nearly half the occurrences of the term are found in the context of

---

research by G. Lüdemann, *Paulus* 2:13–52. Strecker sees the confession of Christ and a "Jewish structure of theology and way of life," whose prime characteristic is the observance of the law, as the constitutive signs of Jewish Christianity. It is revealing that interpretations of John's Gospel as Jewish Christian in character—including those of Martyn and Wengst—do not attempt a precise definition of Jewish Christianity (though I think such a definition is indispensable); thus they silently presuppose a genetic definition.

[210] See Bauer, *Johannesevangelium,* 31.

[211] For a categorization of the Johannine use of Ἰουδαῖος, see the folding table in the appendix to Leistner, *Antijudaismus* (neutral and negative use of οἱ Ἰουδαῖοι); see also Mussner, *Traktat,* 282–88; Kuhli, *EWNT,* 2:479–80; Grässer, "Polemik," 78–79; Wiefel, "Scheidung," 223–24; Fuller, "'Jews,'" 32. There is an extensive review of research on the various interpretations of Ἰουδαῖος in the Fourth Gospel in Schram, "The Use of Ioudaios," 145–204; see also von Wahlde, "Johannine 'Jews,'" 34–38.

conflicts between Jesus and his opponents. The "Jews" are against Jesus from the outset (2:18); they mutter against him (6:41; 7:12), persecute him (5:16), seek to kill him (5:18; 7:1, 19; 8:22-24), want to stone him (8:59; 10:31, 33; 11:8), and appear as the most important opponents at his trial (18:36, 38; 19:7, 12, 20). Their main complaint against Jesus is that he makes himself equal to God (5:18; 10:33; 19:7). The disciples (20:19), the parents of the man born blind (9:22), and Joseph of Arimathea (19:38) are afraid of the Jews. Ultimately, the Jews are said to be children not of Abraham (see 8:33-40) or of God (see 8:41-43, 45-47), but of the devil (8:44).[212]

The correspondence between this picture of "the Jews" and Johannine statements about "the world" has always been apparent.[213] The "world" rejects Jesus (1:10; 3:19) and hates him (7:7). It cannot know God (17:25) and cannot receive the Spirit of truth (14:17). Like Jesus (8:23), the disciples are not ἐκ κόσμου [of or belonging to the world] (15:19; 17:14, 16) and therefore must bear the world's hatred (15:18-19; 17:14; see also 16:20, 33). Finally, the world is the realm of the Adversary (ἄρχων τοῦ κόσμου [the ruler of this world], 12:31; 14:30; 16:11), whose power, though already broken, is still not without its effects. The differentiation of individual groups of Jews is sharply reduced, in comparison with the Synoptics.[214] This, together with the overwhelmingly negative and schematic use of Ἰουδαῖος in the conflict scenes and the almost synonymous usage of Ἰουδαῖος and κόσμος, justifies the conclusion that "the Jews" serve primarily as a Johannine paradigm for the crisis of the world in the face of revelation.[215] It is probable that contemporary conflicts may have influenced the portrayal, but they are not its primary motive.[216] Instead, the argument is shaped by the absolute claims of

---

[212] See Kuhli, EWNT, 2:479; Wiefel, "Scheidung," 223. On the question of the extent to which "the Jews" refers to the Jewish authorities, see von Wahlde, "Johannine 'Jews,'" 41–42.

[213] See Bultmann, John, 295; Grässer, "Polemik," 88–89; Wiefel, "Scheidung," 221ff.; Baumbach, "Gemeinde und Welt," 123–24. On the other hand, Trilling wishes to place sharp limits on the synonymous uses of "Jews" and "world" ("Gegner Jesu," 206).

[214] Only in 1:19 do we read of priests and levites; the "high priest" is mentioned 10 times (7:32, 45; 11:47, 57; 12:10; 18:3, 35; 19:6, 15, 21); 5 times we find the combination of "chief priest and Pharisees" (7:32, 45; 11:47, 57; 18:3); and the Pharisees are mentioned 19 times overall. This relative frequency, however, does not justify the notion that John is here giving a historically correct portrayal of the Judaism of his time, shaped by the Pharisees. The use of Ἰουδαῖος sketched here is christologically, not historically, oriented; this against Wengst, Bedrängte Gemeinde, 40ff.

[215] See especially Bultmann, John, 86–87; and his Theologie, §44 (2:26–32); Grässer, "Polemik," 89-90; Bauer, Johannes, 28–29. On the problem of the supposed Johannine "antiJudaism," see the judicious reflections of Mussner, Traktat, 281ff.; Hahn, "'Die Juden' im Johannesevangelium," 430ff.

[216] Against Trilling, who, on the basis of the usual interpretation of 9:22; 12:42; and 16:2, presumes that current conflicts were the background for the Johannine portrait of events ("Gegner Jesu," 202ff.).

Johannine christology; the Jews are not described empirically, as a real group of people, but serve as representatives of the unbelieving world. They reject the truth that has appeared in Jesus Christ; they are not converted; they persist in unbelief and enmity.

The Gospel of John cannot be read as a conscious witness to Jewish Christian theology. It may well be that there are ideas and traditions in the Gospel that were influenced by Jewish Christianity,[217] but these do not reflect the historical or theological viewpoint of the evangelist. That is to be found, rather, in the Gospel's specific christological concept, pointing to a considerable distance from Judaism. This concept will be investigated in the chapters that follow.

---

[217] Against Thyen, who sees the Johannine community as a Jewish Christian minority threatened by an immediate exclusion from the synagogue, their Jewish heritage in dispute ("'Das Heil kommt von den Juden,'" 181ff.). Significantly, Thyen neglects to give a definition of Jewish Christianity or to analyze the Johannine view of the law.

2

Redaction Criticism as a Method for Johannine Exegesis

Neither an extensive application of literary criticism as an analysis of sources nor the thesis of wide-ranging layers consistent in their literary origins and in their theology is adequate to describe the literary form and theological stance of the Fourth Gospel, for the methodological and historical reasons just described. The same is true of an approach based on precisely determinable historical data or a supposed religious-historical context as clues to the construction of the Johannine theology. The Gospel of John may not be regarded as an archaeological dig, from which, depending on one's methodological approach, "sources," literary layers, or historically determinable stages of development can be excavated. Instead, it must be approached as the conscious and deliberate literary and theological work of an outstanding early Christian theologian. Beginning from this positive presupposition, we will attempt to apply the method of redaction criticism, heretofore well tested in the exegesis of the Synoptics, to the Fourth Gospel in a more comprehensive manner than has been done thus far. To the extent that the aim of redaction criticism is "the explanation of the work in its present form,"[1] that it presupposes form and tradition criticism as well as the history of religions and regards the evangelist as the "spokesperson for the community,"[2] it appears particularly well adapted for the exposition of so theologically and historically complex a work as the Fourth Gospel.

2.1 Redaction Criticism in Previous Johannine Exegesis

Redaction criticism is *the* acknowledged method of Synoptic exegesis. Starting with the two-source theory, together with the literary-critical and

---

[1] Conzelmann, *Theology of St. Luke,* 1.
[2] Strecker, "Redaktionsgeschichte," 23.

form-critical analyses of K. L. Schmidt, Martin Dibelius, and Rudolf Bultmann, it inquires about the points of view from which the individual evangelists chose and organized their material.[3] Whereas form criticism concentrated primarily on the forms of individual units and their history, redaction criticism has focused mainly on the last stage of the tradition, the editing by the final redactor of the individual pericopes and their integration into a complete theological conception. If the compositional shape and overall theological statement of the Gospels are due to the final redactor, then the evangelists can no longer be regarded simply as transmitters and collectors of material.[4] They must be taken seriously as independent theologians and literary figures.

Redaction criticism must be understood as a logical continuation of form- and tradition-critical inquiry.[5] Where form criticism inquires primarily about the laws according to which oral tradition was handed down and its rootedness in the life of the early communities, redaction criticism is interested in the integration of the tradition within a total, superimposed compositional context and in the theological motives that guide the composition. Thus, redaction and tradition are not to be seen as opposites. Even at a preredactional level, we can discern a tendency to combine traditions (e.g., the Sayings Source, the passion account, collections of parables),[6] so that redaction criticism should be understood as a method already inherent in form and tradition criticism. Thus, redaction criticism combines diachronic and synchronic approaches.

The often-asserted primacy[7] of synchronic text analysis over diachronic is very questionable, from both a linguistic and a hermeneutical point of view. E. Coseriu, in his fundamental work on the relationship of synchrony and diachrony from the point of view of linguistics, shows that the two aspects may not be understood as an antinomy. The nature and the development of language should not be regarded as opposites, for "language functions synchronically and is built up diachronically. But these concepts are neither antinomies nor contradictions, since the process of development of a language affects its functioning."[8] Coseriu rejects an identification of synchrony with "language as such"[9] as part of a mistaken theory of knowledge. He emphatically points out that history is the realm in which language comes to be and goes through its process of change. "To put it another way, only history can give a full account of the dynamic reality of language, by regarding it as a 'system in process,' one which, in every moment of its development, is the realization of a tradition. But the history of language may not be seen as 'external history.' It is 'internal history':

---

[3] For surveys of the history of research, see Rohde, *Die redaktionsgeschichtliche Methode;* and Strecker, "Redaktionsgeschichte," 9–20.

[4] Thus, still, Dibelius, "Zur Formgeschichte der Evangelien," 210.

[5] Against Marxsen, who sees a contradiction between form and redaction criticism (*Mark,* 18ff.).

[6] Against Marxsen, who states that "the traditional material scatters in every direction!" (*Mark,* 17).

[7] E.g., Theobald, "Primat," 161; Culpepper, *Anatomy,* 5ff.

[8] Coseriu, *Synchronie, Diachronie und Geschichte,* 237.

[9] Ibid., 220.

the investigation of language itself as historical object. It must both include so-called historical grammar and permit it to dissolve fully within itself."[10]

To the extent that biblical texts are the result of and witness to a history, of which they give an account, the question of their own historicity as texts quite naturally arises.[11] They can be rightly analyzed and interpreted only if their own statement is taken seriously, a statement that is the outgrowth of a particular historical occurrence which they describe in dramatic fashion. The premise of the historicity of biblical texts is not a precondition imposed from outside; it can and must be established from the texts themselves by the methods of a disciplined literary, form, and tradition criticism. Both the concrete literary shape and the theological statement of all New Testament texts require a method that, beginning with the form of the text as it stands, investigates both the history of the material (diachrony) and its editing and interpretation by the final redactor (synchrony). This method is redaction criticism. By being alert to the coherence of the text, redaction criticism avoids the principal weakness of classical literary criticism. Because it inquires about the prior history of a text, redaction criticism at the same time avoids the essential defect of a structural analysis that looks only at the final form of the text. Redaction criticism should not be limited to the Synoptic Gospels; it is to be applied wherever a New Testament author has placed existing text units in a new compositional context.[12]

Redaction criticism in the classical sense, as used in Synoptic exegesis, has not yet been adequately applied to the Fourth Gospel. Previous redaction-critical works on the Gospel of John are entirely dependent on theories of sources and layers. Rudolf Bultmann is to be regarded as the precursor of redaction criticism of the Gospel of John, as he is for redaction criticism as a whole.[13] In his commentary on John he highlights the theology of the evangelist to a considerable degree, in contrast to the evangelist's sources. R. Fortna[14] and W. Nicol,[15] who regard their works expressly as redaction-critical analyses, proceed, as do many other exegetes, on the assumption of a "semeia source." They attempt to demonstrate this source with the aid of literary-, form-, and tradition-critical methods, and then to isolate from it the evangelist's redaction. This approach gives too little scope to the compositional and theological abilities of John the evangelist, for in this view he finds a "gospel" or a "source" already at hand, which on the one hand he adopts and on the other hand sharply criticizes. In addition, the positing of

---

[10] Ibid., 240.

[11] See Luz, "Erwägungen," 503.

[12] See Strecker and Schnelle, *Einführung,* 120ff. Against Rohde, who thinks that redaction criticism can be used only for the Synoptic Gospels and the Acts of the Apostles (*Redaktionsgeschichtliche Methode,* 14).

[13] See Bultmann, *History of the Synoptic Tradition,* Part 3, "The Editing of the Traditional Material," 319–67.

[14] Fortna, *Gospel,* 1–15; idem, "Christology in the Fourth Gospel: Redaction-critical Perspectives."

[15] Nicol, *Semeia,* 3ff.

a pre-Johannine "semeia source" will be shown, in chapter 3 below, to be untenable.

The theories of W. Wilkens, R. E. Brown, W. Langbrandtner, H. Thyen, and G. Richter about layers and redactions in the Fourth Gospel also presume written, connected "models," "basic documents," or "sources" that were revised by the evangelist and/or the redactor(s), sometimes more than once. We have already demonstrated the methodological problems that result from this procedure: because neither the supposed models nor the revisions can be precisely demonstrated from the text, these suggestions remain at the level of improbable hypotheses.

Because these exegetes, who represent theories of redactional layers or sources in the Fourth Gospel, also use the term "redaction criticism," a certain terminological inconsistency has intruded. In the present book, redaction criticism is consciously understood in the previously described classical sense used in Synoptic exegesis.[16] Thus, redaction criticism includes both the method and the object to be investigated.[17]

One central aspect of redaction criticism has thus far been mentioned only in passing: the evangelists were not simply individual authors or theologians; they wrote the Gospels as members of their communities and for the sake of those communities, so that early Christian communities, with their traditions and problems, entered into the writing of the Gospels.[18] This is especially true in the case of John, and the three letters of John and John's Gospel in particular are proof of the extensive literary and theological productivity of a group in early Christianity who can justly be called the "Johannine school," an expression that describes the community within which the letters of John and the Gospel of John were written.[19] The importance of that school's existence, as a context for understanding the letters and the Gospel, must be considered before the methodological approach that underlies the present study can be fully formulated.

---

[16] Schnackenburg thinks otherwise ("Zur Redaktionsgeschichte des Johannesevangeliums," 90–91). He distinguishes the redaction criticism of the Gospel of John (=theories of layers) from the redaction-critical method (=redaction criticism as a method in Synoptic exegesis). This is inappropriate, because the concept of redaction criticism arose in Synoptic exegesis and designates an exegetical method.

[17] The literature makes some distinction between redaction criticism [*Redaktionskritik*] as a method, and redaction history [*Redaktionsgeschichte*] as an object of investigation. I consider this distinction artificial, since there can be no method without a corresponding object.

[18] See Strecker, "Redaktionsgeschichte," 23ff.

[19] The Revelation of John is thoroughly different in style, theology, and tradition from the other Johannine writings and thus should not be attributed to the Johannine school in the narrower sense: Conzelmann correctly observes: "It [Revelation] is not to be considered in distinguishing 'Johannine' theology" (*Grundriß*, 351). See further the more recent work of Müller, *Offenbarung des Johannes*, 46–52: "Instead, tracing the tradition history of the characteristic ideas in Revelation shows that its author could have come from Jewish Christian groups in Syro-Palestine that had no immediate relationship to the so-called 'Johannine' circle (Gospel and letters)" (p. 49). See also Roloff, *Offenbarung des Johannes*, 19–20.

2.2 The Johannine School

On the basis of the research of W. Bousset[20] and W. Heitmüller,[21] the existence of a Johannine school can be regarded as certain. Beyond this broad and largely unquestioned consensus among scholars, however, we need to ask what characteristics of a "school" can be found in the Johannine writings.

2.2.1 Criteria for the Existence of a Johannine School

1. The *theological agreements* among the three Johannine letters and the Gospel of John point to the existence of a Johannine school. We will mention only a few common central ideas:[22]

- the unity of Father and Son (2 John 9; 1 John 1:3; 2:22ff.; 4:14; John 5:20; 10:30; 14:10; etc.)
- the incarnation of Jesus Christ (2 John 7; 1 John 4:2; John 1:14)
- the dualism of God and the world (2 John 7; 1 John 2:15-17; 4:3-6; John 14-17)
- "being born (or begotten) of God" (1 John 2:29; 3:9; 4:7; John 1:13; 3:4ff.)
- the "knowledge" of God (1 John 2:3-5, 13-14; 3:1, 6; 4:6-8; John 1:10; 8:55; 14:7; 16:3; etc.)
- "remaining" in God, in Jesus, in the truth and in the teaching (2 John 2:9; 1 John 2:6, 24, 27; 4:12-16; John 8:31; 14:10, 17; 15:4-10)
- water and the blood of Jesus Christ (1 John 5:6-8; John 19:34-35)
- the love commandment (2 John 4–6; 1 John 2:7-8; John 13:34-35)
- "belonging to the truth," "knowing the truth" (2 John 1; 3 John 3, 8; 1 John 2:21; 3:19; John 8:32; 18:37)
- "being from God" (3 John 11; 1 John 3:10; 4:1-6; John 8:47)
- keeping the commandments (1 John 2:3-4; 3:22, 24; 5:3; John 14:15, 21; 15:10)

2. Another indication of a Johannine school may be found in the *common linguistic features* in the three Johannine letters and the Gospel.[23] They point beyond the idiolect of the individual authors to a sociolect of the Johannine school. Especially indicative are favorite Johannine words that appear very often in the letters and in the Gospel but are less frequent in the

---

[20] Bousset, *Jüdisch-christlicher Schulbetrieb,* 316.

[21] Heitmüller, "Zur Johannes-Tradition," 189ff.

[22] See Windisch, *Johannesbriefe,* 109–10; H. J. Holtzmann, "Problem," II, 133.

[23] The characteristic set of concepts in the Johannine writings must be seen as an expression of the specifically Johannine "way of seeing"; see Mussner, *Sehweise,* 80ff.

other New Testament writings.[24] Equally instructive is the rare use or absence in the Johannine writings of words that are otherwise frequent in the New Testament.[25] Finally, there are the many common expressions and formulae that testify to an independently developed set of concepts and reflect the Johannine sociolect.[26]

3. The existence of a Johannine school is clearly attested by *John 21.* In v. 24b, the author of this secondary additional chapter and perhaps also the editor of the whole Gospel introduce themselves with καὶ οἴδαμεν ὅτι ἀληθὴς αὐτοῦ ἡ μαρτυρία ἐστίν [and we know that his testimony is true]. They make the Beloved Disciple the author of the Gospel of John and designate his relationship to Peter in a new fashion. The mere existence of this addition and the "we" in v. 24b, which is certainly to be understood not as an editorial "we" but as a plural *communicis,*[27] are indications of a Johannine school.

4. The *ecclesiological terms* in the Johannine letters and the Gospel of John also point to a Johannine school. In 3 John 15, the presbyter chooses οἱ φίλοι [the friends] as the self-designation of his community and applies this title also to the addressees. "Undoubtedly the term φίλοι here in this connection with the salutations has a share in the exclusiveness of the Johannine communities."[28] Lazarus is Jesus' friend (John 11:11), and in John 15:14 Jesus says to the disciples: ὑμεῖς φίλοι μού ἐστε [you are my friends] (cf. also v. 15). Finally, John 15:13 introduces the fundamental principle, widely known throughout the ancient world,[29] that it is the highest duty of friends to give their lives for one another. The Johannine texts, the rich treasury of uses of φίλος in the whole of ancient literature,[30] and the use of this word as a self-designation in the Epicurean school[31] make it probable that φίλος was also a common title in the Johannine school.[32]

---

[24] For example: ἀγαπᾶν, ἀλήθεια, ἀληθής, γεννᾶν, γινώσκειν, ἐντολή, ζωή, κόσμος, μαρτυ-ρεῖν, μένειν, μισεῖν, περιπατεῖν, πιστεύειν, τηρεῖν.

[25] Here we may mention ἀπόστολος, γραμματεύς, δέχεσθαι, δύναμις, ἐλπίς, ἐπαγγελία, ἕτερος, εὐαγγελίζειν, εὐαγγέλιον, κηρύσσειν, παραβολή, παρακαλεῖν, πίστις, πιστός, προσ-έρχεσθαι, προσεύχεσθαι, πρόσωπον, σοφία.

[26] See the list in H. J. Holtzmann, "Problem," II, 131ff.; see, in addition, the lists in Brooke, *Johannine Epistles,* 11ff.; and Brown, *Epistles of John,* 755–59.

[27] See especially Harnack, "Das 'Wir' in den Johanneischen Schriften," 642–43. Harnack, arguing against T. Zahn, points out that the "we" in the Johannine writings is not evidence of the author's status as an eyewitness, but can only be understood against the background of a Johannine circle in Asia Minor. Zahn, on the contrary, evaluates even ἐθεασάμεθα [we have seen] in John 1:14 as evidence that the author of the Fourth Gospel was an eyewitness to the life of Jesus (see Zahn, *Johannes,* 82).

[28] Stählin, *TDNT* 9:166.

[29] See the references in Stählin, *TDNT* 9:153 nn. 64ff.

[30] Ibid., 146–54.

[31] References in Culpepper, *Johannine School,* 108 n. 48.

[32] Ibid., 272.

Similarly, τεκνία or τέκνα (θεοῦ) [children; child (of God)] seems to have been a frequent form of address within the Johannine school. (For τεκνία, see 1 John 2:1, 12, 28; 3:7, 18; 4:4; 5:21; John 13:33; for τέκνα [θεοῦ], see 2 John 1:4, 13; 3 John 4; 1 John 3:1, 2, 10; 5:2; John 1:12; 11:52).[33] Believers are τέκνα θεοῦ because they are born or begotten of God (see 1 John 2:29; 3:9; 4:7; 5:1, 4, 18; John 1:12). As a title of honor, τέκνα θεοῦ is also the expression of a strong consciousness of election, for in 1 John 3:9, 10 the terminology shifts between "children of God" and "born of God." The members of the Johannine school are convinced that God's seed is and abides in them. Another term closely related to τέκνα is παιδία. In 1 John 2:14, 18 it serves as an address to the community; in John 21:5 Jesus calls the disciples παιδία.

Another title of honor in the Johannine school is ἀδελφός [brother, sister]. Gaius is praised by the Presbyter because, in contrast to Diotrephes, he welcomed itinerant brethren (see 3 John 3:5, 10). In the Gospel, the departing Jesus calls his disciples and followers "brothers" (20:17; cf. 21:23). It is probably no accident that up to this point in the Gospel ἀδελφός was used only in the sense of physical relationship (1:40, 41; 2:12; 6:8; 7:3, 5, 10; 11:2, 19, 21, 23, 32). It is only when he is about to die that Jesus institutes and legitimates ἀδελφός as an honorable title in the Johannine school.

5. The *ethical statements*[34] in the letters and in the Gospel also speak in favor of the existence of a Johannine school. They are for the most part to be seen not as universalist but as applying to the group. At the center stands the commandment to love the brethren (2 John 4–6; 1 John 2:7-11; John 13:34-35), which is clearly prior to that of love of neighbor. In 1 John, love of the brothers and sisters is the essential characteristic and sign of Christian existence (see 1 John 3:11-18; 4:7-21), extending to the demand to give one's life for them (1 John 3:16). Love of the brethren even appears as a criterion for love of God, for only those who love their brothers and sisters, whom they see, can also love God, whom they do not see (1 John 4:20). In the Gospel of John, ἀγάπη, ἀγαπᾶν, and φιλεῖν [all three meaning "love"] designate, in the first place, the reciprocal relationship among the Father, the Son, and the members of the community. The Father "loves" the Son and those who are his own; the Son "loves" the Father and his own; his own, in turn, "love" the Son and one another (3:35; 5:20, 42; 8:42; 10:17; 13:1; 15:9-17; 16:27; 17:20-26). The concentration of the Johannine community's ethics on their own group remains unmistakable.

---

[33] On τέκνα θεοῦ, see especially Schnackenburg, *Johannesbriefe*, 175–83.

[34] For an introduction to the difficult problems of Johannine ethics, see Schrage, *Ethik*, 280–301. There is no disagreement among scholars about the primary direction of Johannine ethics toward the behavior of the group. What remains controversial is the question whether the Johannine conception leaves any room at all for material ethical instructions and for some sort of openness to the world, whatever form that might take.

Passages like John 13:12-20; 1 John 2:6; 3:3, 7, 16 speak clearly against the interpretation of Johannine ethics as those of a natural community, which is suggested by E. Käsemann and M. Lattke,[35] following M. Dibelius.[36] In these texts there is an explicit demand, based on the exemplary actions of Jesus, that the disciples behave in like manner. The challenge to a concrete form of social behavior toward the brethren in 1 John 3:17, 18 is also resistant to any interpretation in the direction of an ethic of principle.

Both the letters (1 John 2:2; 4:9, 14) and the Gospel (3:16; 10:17; 12:25; 15:13) contain universalist statements that contravene a literal and spiritual interpretation of Johannine ethics, explode any purely sectarian ethic, and show that love of the brethren can be understood as a model for love of neighbor. Nevertheless, this ethic must be understood primarily as that of a group: the object of love is, first of all, the brother or sister, not the world.

6. A further indication of the existence of a Johannine school is the depiction of Jesus as *teacher*.[37] In no other Gospel is Jesus so often addressed as ῥαββί [Rabbi] (John, 9 times; Mark, 3; Matthew, 4),[38] and Jesus' teaching work is repeatedly mentioned (6:59; 7:14, 28; 8:20; 18:20). Nicodemus calls Jesus a teacher come from God (3:2). God personally teaches Jesus (8:26, 28); Jesus' teaching is ἐκ θεοῦ (7:16, 17). Jesus teaches his friends everything he has received from the Father (15:15; cf. 17:26), so that the Johannine school appears as the place in which the revelation of the Father to the Son is handed on and preserved. The Johannine Christians regard themselves as διδακτοὶ θεοῦ [those taught by God] (6:45).

Jesus knows the Scriptures, although he was not educated in them (John 7:15). The Johannine school studies Scripture as a witness to Jesus (see John 5:39, 46). Often the disciples feel themselves "reminded" of Jesus' words and the words of Scripture (see John 2:17, 22; 12:16; 20:9). In addition, the twelve direct citations of the Old Testament and the introductory formula γεγραμμένος or γέγραπται [it is (or was) written] (see John 2:17; 6:31, 45; 8:17; 10:34; 12:14-16; 15:25) point to a study of the Old Testament that is christologically oriented.

The Johannine school observes, preserves, and protects Jesus' words (1 John 2:5; John 8:51-52, 55; 14:23, 24; 15:20; 17:6) and commandments (1 John 2:3, 4; 3:22, 24; 5:3; John 14:15, 21; 15:10), for Jesus heard them from the Father and handed them on to the disciples (John 14:24; 17:8). The term τηρεῖν [keep, observe] appears in the Johannine writings more often (25 times) than in any other book of the New Testament; thus, the use of τηρεῖν τὸν λόγον [keep the word] and τηρεῖν τὰς ἐντολάς [keep the commandments]

---

[35] See Käsemann, *Jesu letzter Wille*, 122ff.; Lattke, *Einheit*.
[36] See Dibelius, "Joh 15,13," 173ff.
[37] See Culpepper, *Johannine School*, 273ff.
[38] See also ῥαββουνί [my teacher] in Mark 10:51; John 20:16.

points to a catechetical tradition within the Johannine school.[39] Jesus' ῥήματα [words] are also from God (John 3:34; 14:10), and he has handed them on to the disciples (John 17:8). He promises them that every request will be fulfilled, ἐὰν μείνητε ἐν ἐμοὶ καὶ τὰ ῥήματά μου ἐν ὑμῖν μείνῃ [if you abide in me, and my words abide in you] (John 15:7; see also 6:68).

The Johannine school is not only aware that it possesses divine revelation and traditions, but it is also certain of receiving divine instruction in the present time, since the παράκλητος [paraclete] (John 14:26) or χρῖσμα [anointing] (1 John 2:27) teaches and reminds them. This clearly presupposes the existence of a school within which not only are the Johannine traditions about Jesus handed on and interpreted but also new truths guaranteed by the "Paraclete" or "Anointing" are formulated. The challenges of opponents call for reflection on the tradition, intensive discussion within the school, and statement of the school's own position. It is, of course, the essence of false teaching that it does not abide in the traditional teaching (2 John 9, 10) and in the true confession of faith (2 John 7; 1 John 2:22-23; 4:2-3).

7. The central characteristic of ancient schools is that they trace their existence to a *founder*.[40] R. A. Culpepper sees the founder of the Johannine school in the Beloved Disciple and thinks "that the role of the BD is the key to the character of the community."[41] He finds broad correspondence between the functions of the Beloved Disciple and those of the Paraclete and concludes from this that the community identified the Beloved Disciple with the Paraclete. "Just as Jesus had been the first Paraclete for the original group of the disciples, so the BD had been the first Paraclete for the Johannine community."[42] After the unexpected death of the founder of the school, who had been regarded as the incarnation of the Paraclete, a distinction was made between the Paraclete and the Beloved Disciple, so that an identification of the Holy Spirit with the Paraclete might secure the Paraclete's continuing activity.

If the Beloved Disciple was the founder of the Johannine school, he must have had a fixed place in the existing tradition. Our analysis showed, however, that all the passages about the Beloved Disciple were the redactional additions of the evangelist.[43] This result speaks decisively against Culpepper's thesis, especially since he does not make any attempt at a real exegesis of the corresponding passages. Nor does the equation he postulates of the Beloved Disciple with the Paraclete find any foundation in the text. If that identification had really existed in the Johannine school, it would necessarily

---

[39] See Riesenfeld, *TDNT* 8:144–45.
[40] See Culpepper, *Johannine School,* 264ff.
[41] Ibid., 265.
[42] Ibid., 269.
[43] See section 1.2 above.

have left at least some traces in the Johannine writings. But this is the case neither in the Gospel of John nor in 1 John, where, significantly, Jesus is equated with the Paraclete (2:1). Finally, the Beloved Disciple would have to appear also in the Johannine letters, especially since the conflicts with opponents that are portrayed there would call for a reference to the founders of the community.[44]

G. Strecker gives a new answer to the question of the founder of the Johannine school. He traces the school to the Presbyter of 2 and 3 John.[45] The two short Johannine letters are not unimportant late Johannine writings; they mark the beginnings of Johannine theology. As original writings of the founder of the Johannine school, they were included in the canon, and they should be regarded as highly important for the origin and development of Johannine theology.[46] Strecker sees in the Presbyter of 2 and 3 John the πρεσβύτερος ᾽Ιωάννης [presbyter (elder), John] of Papias, which lends greater plausibility to his thesis, since in that case a historical personality who was known in early Christianity is made the founder of the Johannine school, whereas the picture of the Beloved Disciple is a composite of idealizing, typifying, and historical motifs.

If it is 2 and 3 John that represent the beginnings of the Johannine tradition, and not some source or basic document supposed to lie behind the Gospel, this has the additional methodological advantage that it obviates all the problems of extensive literary criticism associated with redactional theories and other suppositions about layers in the Gospel, as described in chapter 1 above.

The closest parallel to the Johannine school in early Christianity is the school of Paul.[47] H. Conzelmann showed that Paul, in cooperation with his associates, founded a school in the Jewish wisdom tradition, in which "theology as training in wisdom" was taught. The school is supposed to have been located at Ephesus.[48] The discussions within the Pauline school were recorded in (among other writings) texts preliminary to the composition of a letter; these ideas were then integrated into the letter. "Among possible texts are, for example, 1 Cor 1:18ff.; 2:6ff.; 10:1ff.; 11:2ff.; 13; 2 Cor 3:7ff.; Rom 1:18ff.; 7:7ff.; 10:1ff."[49] We may surmise that breaks and seams in the letters of Paul are traceable to the incorporation of traditions from the school and are not evidence of different "letters" or "letter fragments." The members of the Pauline school would have been the apostle's many associates, who functioned as co-senders of the letters and delivered them in person. The Deutero-Pauline letters can also be

---

[44] Culpepper attempts to meet this decisive counter-argument with a reference to the expression ἀπ᾽ ἀρχῆς in 2 John 6; 1 John 2:7, 24; 3:11, which he sees as a reference to the Beloved Disciple (*Johannine School,* 288).

[45] See Strecker, "Die Anfänge der johanneischen Schule," 39.

[46] Ibid., 39ff.

[47] Surprisingly, Culpepper seems to suppose that there was a "Jesus school" (*Johannine School,* 215–46), but at no point does he mention the Pauline school.

[48] See Conzelmann, "Paulus und die Weisheit," 179.

[49] Conzelmann, "Die Schule des Paulus," 86.

understood in the framework of a Pauline school, since their authors were either students of Paul or were influenced by the school of Paul.[50]

There are remarkable analogies to the Gospel of John in the *Letter of Barnabas,* which is close to it both chronologically and geographically.[51] Apparently the author of the *Letter of Barnabas* did not make use of unitary source documents but incorporated "a great many individual pieces of tradition."[52] Thus, attention to form and content shows, for example, *Barn.* 2.1; 2.4–3.6; 4.1-5.4; 5.5-7, 11b-13f.; 6.1-4; 7.3-5; 9.4-6; 16.1-2, 6-10 to be preexisting pieces of tradition that were brought together by the letter writer.[53] The independence of the fragments of tradition in *Barnabas* 2–16 and the observation that the author of the letter was probably a teacher[54] permit the conclusion that the traditions in the letter arise out of an "educational enterprise."[55] "In [the letter], the individual pieces are handed on and, in the same process, further developed. The author, as teacher, also participates in the process of tradition by editing, varying, adding, expanding, and even by the independent creation of new pieces."[56]

2.2.2   *The Writings of the Johannine School*

It is very important for an understanding of the Johannine school to know whether the writings stemming from it were all written by the same author. If the existence of only one author can be demonstrated, the whole literary production is traceable to a single outstanding theologian and must be understood, in all essentials, as a unit. If, on the other hand, the individual writings permit the conclusion that several authors were at work, we must suppose that we are dealing with a lively literary and theological productivity in the Johannine school that was not at all uniform and perhaps even filled with tensions. The question of chronological order should also be discussed, for it tells us something about the place of the writings in the history of the Johannine school.

2.2.2.1   The Question of Authorship

We should begin our inquiry with 2 and 3 John, since here, with ὁ πρεσβύτερος, we find the only identification of an author in the Johannine writings. Both of these documents should be regarded as real letters,[57] having all the

---

[50] Ibid., 88ff.

[51] Stegemann (review of Prigent, *Testimonia,* 149–50) and Wengst (*Barnabasbrief,* 115ff.) date the *Letter of Barnabas* between 130 and 132 and locate it in western Asia Minor.

[52] Wengst, *Barnabasbrief,* 121.

[53] For an extensive analysis of the traditions in *Barnabas* 2–16, see Wengst, *Barnabasbrief,* 17–53.

[54] Ibid., 119.

[55] This was first proposed by Bousset, *Schulbetrieb,* 312–13; most recently by Wengst, *Barnabasbrief,* 122–23.

[56] Wengst, *Barnabasbrief,* 122.

[57] Against Bultmann, who sees the letter form of 2 John as fictional (*Johannine Epistles* 1, 107); cf., in contrast, Schnackenburg, *Johannesbriefe,* 295; and Haenchen, "Neuere Literatur zu den Johannesbriefen," 299–300. The only one among the newer commentators who agrees with Bultmann is Schunack, *Die Briefe des Johannes,* 108–9.

features of an ancient private letter.[58] The identification of the sender with the same title, the language, and the agreements in the form of the letters make it certain that both are by the same author. But what does ὁ πρεσβύτερος mean?[59] Linguistically, the most probable interpretation would be "the old one, the venerable"—someone who has a special status because of his age and experience.[60] However, the contest between the Presbyter and the opponents gives no indication that his authority rests on his great age.[61]

Another possibility is that ὁ πρεσβύτερος refers to the official of a local church community who has special authority because of his office. It must be said against this thesis, upheld primarily by E. Käsemann,[62] that the office of presbyter was exercised, in early Christianity, only within a collegial group (see, e.g., 1 Tim. 4:14; Titus 1:5). Moreover, this would be a unique instance of the use of the title ὁ πρεσβύτερος without the person's name. An official status cannot really be demonstrated either for the Presbyter or for Diotrephes.

Therefore, ὁ πρεσβύτερος is an honorable title for "a specially valued teacher."[63] The Presbyter must have been an outstanding figure within the Johannine school, perhaps even its founder, for this is the only explanation for the preservation and acceptance of 2 and 3 John in the canon. There is no reason not to identify the Presbyter of 2 and 3 John with that ὁ πρεσβύτερος Ἰωάννης whom Papias mentions as one of the guarantors of his tradition, while clearly distinguishing him from John the son of Zebedee (Eusebius *Eccl. Hist.* 3.39.4). Neither the Presbyter of the letters of John nor the πρεσβύτερος Ἰωάννης of Papias is an officeholder; instead, he is a bearer of tradition.[64] As the agent and/or founder of the Johannine tradition, the Presbyter of 2 and 3 John enjoyed great respect, and as a special bearer of tradition he appears in Papias's account as well.[65]

---

[58] Cf. the letters printed in Deissmann, *Light from the Ancient East*, 192–97.

[59] Haenchen ("Neuere Literatur zu den Johannesbriefen," 282–311) gives a description of the suggested solutions of Harnack, Bauer, and Käsemann, with a critical discussion of the problem. See also the summary of research in Brown, *Epistles of John*, 108–9.

[60] The extreme age of the Presbyter is emphasized especially by Wendt, *Johannesbriefe*, 7–8.

[61] See Bornkamm, *TDNT* 6:670.

[62] Käsemann sees in the Presbyter a man "who heads his own community group and center of missionary activity and is highly active in church politics, seeking to establish bases for his organization in other communities" ("Ketzer und Zeuge," 177). For a critique of Käsemann, see Bornkamm, *TDNT* 6:671 n. 121.

[63] Bornkamm, *TDNT* 6:671; see also Schnackenburg, *Johannesbriefe*, 306.

[64] See Vielhauer, who shows that Papias regarded the πρεσβύτεροι as agents of tradition (*Geschichte*, 763).

[65] Körtner's suggestion (*Papias von Hierapolis*, 197–201) that 2 and 3 John are pseudepigraphic writings and that the designation of the sender as ὁ πρεσβύτερος is fictional must be rejected. Körtner offers as a basis only the opinion of Bultmann that 2 John is a fictional letter, which quite rightly has been almost universally rejected in recent research. Körtner, differing from Bultmann, applies the same idea to 3 John. He thinks that no current conflict is being described in this letter and that it is not even certain whether Gaius and Diotrephes were still

Papias received the oral tradition he so highly prizes from students of the Presbyter, whom he questioned about traditions from the apostles. This is the meaning of the expression εἰ δέ που καὶ παρηκολουθηκώς τις τοῖς πρεσβυτέροις ἔλθοι, τοὺς τῶν πρεσβυτέρων ἀνέκρινον λόγους . . . [and whenever anyone came who had been a follower of the presbyters, I inquired into the words of the presbyters . . .] (Eusebius *Eccl. Hist.* 3.39.4). The chain of traditon is thus: apostles — presbyters (=disciples of the apostles) — students of the presbyters — Papias.[66] The relationship between the first group of the Lord's disciples (the apostles) and the second group (Aristion and John the Presbyter) is difficult to determine. While the difference in tense (εἶπεν [had said] for the apostles, λέγουσιν [were still saying] for Aristion and John the Presbyter) allows the conclusion that Aristion and John the Presbyter were still alive in Papias's own time,[67] it must be questioned whether Papias knew both of them. Eusebius insists that this is so (*Eccl. Hist.* 3.39.7) in order to ensure the credibility of the Papias tradition he is presenting (see *Eccl. Hist.* 3.39.15, 16, 17). This seems likely in Papias's own statement as well, because, in the second indirect question, the relative pronoun ἅ [what] recapitulates the interrogative τί [what], while τέ [and] and the new predicate, λέγουσιν, mark a new beginning.[68] Then Papias would have received traditions directly from Aristion and John the Presbyter and would have to be called their disciple.

H. Windisch, C. H. Dodd, R. Schnackenburg and R. E. Brown, among others, think that the Presbyter of 2 and 3 John is also the author of 1 John.[69] Their principal argument is the uniform style of all three Johannine letters. But the agreements in style could stem from the sociolect of the Johannine school; moreover, there are characteristic differences in style between 2 and 3 John, on the one hand, and 1 John, on the other.

The expression ἐχάρην λίαν [I was overjoyed] (cf. Phil. 4:10) occurs only in 2 John 4 and 3 John 3, and the only occurrences of περιπατεῖν ἐν ἀληθείᾳ [to walk in the truth] are in 2 John 4 and 3 John 3, 4. Only in 2 John do we find the expressions ἐκλκητῇ κυρίᾳ [elect lady] (2 John 1), τὴν ἀλήθειαν τὴν μένουσαν ἐν ἡμῖν [the truth that abides in us] (2 John 2), παρὰ 'Ιησοῦ Χριστοῦ τοῦ υἱοῦ τοῦ πατρός [from Jesus

---

alive at the time the letter was written. This argumentation must be described as purely speculative, since Körtner maintains his thesis against both the form and the content of 2 and 3 John in a very one-sided manner.

[66] See Heitmüller, "Zur Johannes-Tradition," 195; Haenchen, *John* 1:9–10.

[67] See Larfeld, "Das Zeugnis des Papias," 387. Grammatically, both τί 'Ανδρέας . . . and ἅ τε 'Αριστίων . . . [what Andrew . . . and what Aristion . . .] are indirect questions, in which the relative pronoun ἅ replaces the interrogative τί, "a linguistic usage that can be found both in classical authors and in biblical Greek" (Larfeld, "Zeugnis," 387). Two subordinate clauses were needed because the two generations mentioned by Papias did not permit a common predicate.

[68] But it is also grammatically possible that both indirect questions refer to the handing on of traditions by students of the presbyters and that Papias, in that case, had not known Aristion or John the Presbyter personally; see Heitmüller, "Zur Johannes-Tradition," 195; Larfeld, "Zeugnis," 387.

[69] Schnackenburg, *Johannesbriefe,* 298; Brown, *Epistles of John,* 19; Windisch, *Johannesbriefe,* 143; Dodd, *Johannine Epistles,* lxviii–lxxix.

Christ, the Father's son] (2 John 3), ἐν ἀληθείᾳ καὶ ἀγάπῃ [in truth and love] (2 John 3), and βλέπετε ἑαυτούς [be on your guard (lit., look to yourselves)] (2 John 8). *Hapax legomena* within the Johannine school that are found in the two shorter letters include: μέλαν [ink] (2 John 12; 3 John 13; otherwise only 2 Cor. 3:3), κάλαμος [pen] (3 John 13); ἔλεος [mercy] (2 John 3), μισθός [reward] (2 John 8), ἀγαθοποιεῖν [to do good] (3 John 11), εὐοδοῦσθαι [prosper, be successful] (3 John 2), and κακοποιεῖν [to do evil] (3 John 11). *Hapax legomena* in the New Testament are φιλοπρωτεύων [preferring to place (himself) first] (3 John 9) and χάρτης [paper] (2 John 12).

If 1 John is also the work of the Presbyter, how can we explain the fact that in this writing ὁ πρεσβύτερος does not appear as the sender? Apparently the author of 2 and 3 John deliberately dons the honorable title of ὁ πρεσβύτερος, in the sense of a special agent of tradition, in the context of his conflict with the opponents. It serves as an expression of his dignity and ensures the authority of his words. Why should the Presbyter give up the honorable title that is his, especially in 1 John, where the conflict with opponents reaches its climax?[70] The form of 1 John also speaks against the authorship of the Presbyter, for, whereas 2 and 3 John are stylistically correct private letters to individual communities or persons, 1 John lacks all the characteristics of a letter. It is a circular to communities of the Johannine school, in the form of a homily. This is evident from the constantly shifting dogmatic and paraenetic sections and the address to the community as τεκνία (2:1, 12, 28; 3:7, 18; 4:4; 5:21), ἀγαπητοί (2:7; 3:2, 21; 4:1, 3, 11), or παιδία (2:14, 18).

Finally, the Johannine dualism is found only in a rudimentary form in 2 and 3 John, and there are evident shifts in content: (1) In 2 John 4-6, the love commandment is not a new one but something given "from the beginning." By contrast, in 1 John 2:7-11 the love commandment is dialectically described both as something given from the beginning and, at the same time, as a new commandment. In addition, only 1 John 2:10-11 speaks explicitly of a command to love the *brothers and sisters*. (2) While in 2 John 7 the word ἀντίχριστος [Antichrist] appears in the singular, 1 John 2:18 takes a historical stance, introducing both the singular and the plural, ἀντίχριστοι. (3) According to 2 John 7, the opponents refuse to acknowledge Ἰησοῦν Χριστὸν ἐρχόμενον ἐν σαρκί [Jesus Christ *come* in the flesh], while in 1 John 4:2, with a view to the opponents, the confession demanded is of Ἰησοῦν Χριστὸν ἐν σαρκὶ ἐληλυθότα [Jesus Christ as *having come* (perfect tense) in the flesh].

---

[70] Those who argue for a common authorship of all three letters have no persuasive answer to this question. Schnackenburg remarks: "It is not surprising that the author of 1 John, who has presented himself to his readers in 1:1-3 as a well-known personality, should introduce the two shorter letters with a brief ὁ πρεσβύτερος" (*Johannesbriefe*, 298). To this we must object that the prologue of 1 John can scarcely be understood as the introduction of a known personality. It is thoroughly ecclesiastical in its intent. Brown solves the problem with the statement "that II John is a letter where identification is required, while I John is not" (*Epistles of John*, 17).

The linguistic independence of 2 and 3 John, their form (that of an ancient private letter), the title of the sender (ὁ πρεσβύτερος), and the material differences from 1 John point to different authors for 2 and 3 John and for 1 John.[71]

E. Käsemann also considers the Presbyter of 2 and 3 John to be the author of the Gospel of John. "The Presbyter is a Christian Gnostic, with the really unimaginable coolness to write a gospel of the Christ whom he experienced, and whom he inserts into the world of Gnosis."[72] Reversing W. Bauer's thesis,[73] Käsemann sees Diotrephes as a monarchical bishop, and the author of 2 and 3 John as a presbyter who has been excommunicated because of his gnostic heretical teaching.[74] The Gospel of John proves the thesis, for it contains what from the point of orthodoxy is "heretical, gnostic teaching," which has led to the Presbyter's excommunication; this means that he must also be the author of the Gospel.

But Diotrephes does not appear as a "monarchical bishop" in 3 John, nor is anything said about the Presbyter's excommunication. This places Käsemann's presumed contrast of heresy and orthodoxy on very uncertain ground.[75] Both of the presuppositions for his theory have to be regarded as unproved, since only the designation of the Presbyter as a heretic permits Käsemann to make the connection back to the Gospel of John and to classify it as a gnostic writing.

It is very important for an understanding of the Johannine school to know whether the Gospel of John and 1 John are by the same author. There is, in the first place, linguistic evidence against this identification, for important concepts in the Gospel are missing from the letter (γραφή [scripture], δόξα [glory], δοξάζειν [to glorify], ζητεῖν [to seek], κρίνειν [to judge], κύριος [lord], νόμος [law], πέμπειν [to send], προσκυνεῖν [to bow down in worship], σῴζειν [to save], χάρις [grace]). On the other hand, some of the central theological terms in the letter are not found in the Gospel (ἀντίχριστος [Antichrist], ἐλπίς [hope], ἱλασμός [sacrifice], κοινωνία [fellowship], σπέρμα [θεοῦ] [seed, i.e., offspring (of God)], χρῖσμα [anointing]).[76] In construction and style as well, the letter reveals its linguistic independence,[77] all of which permits the conclusion that "[t]he language of the letter, despite many echoes of the Gospel, permits us to suppose that it had a different author."[78]

---

[71] Among those who argue for different authorship of 1 John and 2 and 3 John are Bultmann, *Johannine Epistles*, 1, 10; Balz, "Johannesbriefe," 159; Wengst, *Johannesbriefe*, 230–31.

[72] Käsemann, "Ketzer und Zeuge," 178. On the identity of the authors of the letters and the Gospel, see especially p. 174 n. 23.

[73] See Bauer, *Rechtgläubigkeit und Ketzerei*, 97.

[74] See Käsemann, "Ketzer und Zeuge," 173–74.

[75] For a critique of Käsemann, see Haenchen, "Neuere Literatur zu den Johannesbriefen," 295ff.

[76] See H. J. Holtzmann, "Problem" II, 137.

[77] See the extensive demonstration in H. J. Holtzmann, "Problem" II, 135ff.; see also Dodd, *Johannine Epistles*, xlvii ff. There is a critical overview of the history of research on this topic in Haenchen, "Neuere Literatur zu den Johannesbriefen," 238–42.

[78] Haenchen, "Neuere Literatur zu den Johannesbriefen," 242.

In addition, there are specific theological concepts that are found only in the letter: in 1 John 2:1, and nowhere else, Jesus Christ is identified with the παράκλητος. Although future eschatology cannot be eliminated from the Gospel, it is clear that the governing ideas are those of present eschatology. In contrast, future eschatology dominates in 1 John, as can be seen from the concepts (unique to the Johannine school) of παρουσία [coming, i.e., (second) coming (of Christ)] (1 John 2:28) and ἐλπίς (1 John 3:3). Jesus is called ἱλασμός [atoning sacrifice] only in 1 John 2:2; 4:10 (see also the statements about atoning death in 1 John 1:7, 9; 3:5), and the only occurrences of χρῖσμα in the whole New Testament are in 1 John 2:20, 27. In contrast to the Gospel of John (which has eighteen citations of the Old Testament or echoes of Old Testament texts), there is not a single such citation in 1 John, and the only reference of any kind to the Old Testament is in 1 John 3:12 (Cain). In addition, the central ethical problem, the sinlessness of Christians (see 1 John 1:8-10; 3:4-10; 5:16-18) is not found in the Gospel. Finally, 1 John presupposes a different situation from that of the Gospel.[79] The letter struggles vehemently against a christological heresy that has broken out in the author's own community (see 1 John 2:19), while the Gospel reveals no evidence of an *acute* conflict.

Language, theological worldview, and difference of situation all indicate the probability that 1 John and the Gospel are the work of different authors.[80]

2.2.2.2 Temporal Priority

To a remarkable degree, contemporary exegesis takes it as a given that the Gospel of John — or, more precisely, the "sources" on which it is based — forms the starting point for the Johannine school.[81] The three letters are supposed to have followed the Gospel, and on the one hand to connect with the Gospel but on the other hand to "dilute" the radical views of John the evangelist in the context of early Catholicism and make them useful for their own situation. In contrast, G. Strecker, like H. H. Wendt before him,[82]

---

[79] For Bultmann (*Johannine Epistles,* 1) this is the decisive argument against an identity of authorship between the letter and the Gospel.

[80] Among those who argue for different authors are Bultmann, *Johannine Epistles,* 1; Schnackenburg, *Johannesbriefe,* 335; Haenchen, "Neuere Literatur zu den Johannesbriefen," 282; Wengst, *Johannesbriefe,* 24–25; Dodd, *Johannine Epistles,* vi; Balz, *Johannesbriefe,* 160; Brown, *Epistles of John,* 30; Conzelmann, "'Was von Anfang war,'" 211; Klein, "'Das wahre Licht scheint schon'"; H. J. Holtzmann, "Problem" II, 136ff. Among those who advocate the theory of identical authorship are Kümmel, *Introduction,* 445; Wikenhauser and Schmid, *Einleitung,* 623; Schunack, *Johannesbriefe,* 108.

[81] Cf. only Robinson, "The Johannine Trajectory," 232–68. He sees the "semeia source" as the starting point for the construction of Johannine theology and tries to reconstruct the "trajectory" of the Johannine writings from there.

[82] See Wendt, *Johannesbriefe,* 107. Bousset sees Revelation as the oldest writing of the Johannine school (*Offenbarung,* 44). Following it, from the same author (=the Presbyter) would come 2 and 3 John. Finally, disciples of the Presbyter would have written the Gospel and 1 John.

correctly sees 2 and 3 John as the oldest documents of the Johannine school.[83] Between the two shorter letters, 2 John has temporal priority, since 3 John 9 apparently refers to 2 John.[84]

It is often objected, against this observation, that 3 John 9 must refer to a letter of recommendation for itinerant missionaries and that 2 John is not such a letter.[85] It is true that the expression ἔγραψά τι τῇ ἐκκλησίᾳ [I have written something to the church] indicates only that the Presbyter has written to the community at some time in the past. But it is only in v. 10b that reference is made again to the itinerant missionaries, so that the rejection of Diotrephes in v. 9b can refer to the Presbyter and his theological position, with its inherent claim to authority, as described in 2 John.[86]

If 2 and 3 John mark the beginning of the Johannine school and its theology, there still remains the question of the relationship between 1 John and the Gospel. In the twentieth century,[87] this question has been almost universally answered by pointing out that 1 John continues the Gospel. The arguments for this position require critical examination.

1. Many exegetes see in the prologue of the letter, 1 John 1:1-4, a clear reference to the prologue of the Gospel.[88] Here the ἀρχή [beginning]-concept is especially important, since, according to Conzelmann, "[t]he beginning of the letter refers to John 1:1; this furnishes an answer to the question whether ἀπ᾽ ἀρχῆς points to the beginning of all things or to the beginning of the church."[89] Conzelmann presumes, at this point, what in fact needs to be demonstrated: the priority of the Gospel. In addition, he overlooks the characteristic difference between the use of ἀρχή in the prologue of the letter and in that of the Gospel. In the whole Johannine corpus, ἐν ἀρχῇ appears only in John 1:1, 2 and designates the being of the preexistent Logos with God at the absolute beginning, before the creation of the world. In contrast, ἀπ᾽ ἀρχῆς in 1 John 1:1 describes the *whole* saving event, including the incarnation, public activity, death, and resurrection of Jesus in its significance for

---

[83] See Strecker, "Die Anfänge der johanneischen Schule," 34.

[84] Ibid., 37.

[85] See Schnackenburg, *Johannesbriefe,* 326; Dodd, *Johannine Epistles,* 161; Brooke, *Johannine Epistles,* 187–88; Kümmel, *Introduction,* 447; Bultmann, *Johannine Epistles,* 108; Wengst, *Johannesbriefe,* 248; and others.

[86] Among those who argue that 3 John 9 refers to 2 John are Zahn, *Einleitung* 2:581; Wendt, *Johannesbriefe,* 23; Dibelius, *RGG*² 3:348; Jülicher and Fascher, *Einleitung,* 235.

[87] Among those in the nineteenth century who argued for the temporal priority of 1 John were Huther, *Briefe des Apostel Johannes,* 34–35; Bleek, *Einleitung,* 588; Pfleiderer, "Beleuchtung der neuesten Johannes-Hypothese," 419ff.; Hilgenfeld, *Einleitung,* 737; B. Weiss, *Briefe des Apostels Johannes,* 8–9. In the twentieth century this position is represented primarily by Wendt, *Johannesbriefe,* 1–7; Büchsel, *Johannesbriefe,* 7; Appel, *Einleitung,* 197; and Strathmann, *EKL* 2:364.

[88] Cf. only Bultmann, *Johannine Epistles,* 8; Brown, *Epistles of John,* 149ff. On the other hand, Wendt decidedly rejects an interpretation of 1 John 1:1-4 in terms of John 1:1 ("Der 'Anfang,'" 38–42).

[89] Conzelmann, "'Was von Anfang war,'" 208.

the community (4 times "we"!), without even the slightest reference to the creation. In no way is there any talk of the absolute beginning here, as Conzelmann thinks.[90] It may be that existence "in the beginning" is somehow included, but that in itself does not exhaust the ἀπ᾿ ἀρχῆς in 1 John 1:1. Instead, the deliberate accent on the visibility and reality of the saving event seems already aimed at the opponents who are being combatted in 2:22-23; 4:1-3.[91] In that case, as in 1 John 2:24, ἀπ᾿ ἀρχῆς at the beginning of the letter would also relate to the Johannine tradition as a center of critical judgment against false teachers. In the same way, ἀπ᾿ ἀρχῆς in 2 John 5, 6; 1 John 2:7, 13, 14;[92] 3:11 is to be interpreted in terms of the Johannine tradition as basis and critical norm for the preaching of the Johannine school.[93] But at no point is it apparent that this "tradition" means the Gospel of John![94] Not even a reference to the Logos hymn (which is *pre*-Johannine and therefore cannot be introduced as evidence for the temporal priority of the Gospel) can be strictly proved.

It may be doubted whether περὶ τοῦ λόγου τῆς ζωῆς [concerning the word of life] in 1 John 1:1 refers to John 1:1-14, since the roundabout expression in the letter (where an accusative would be expected) is too unlike the absolute ὁ λόγος, which appears only in the prologue of the Gospel. In the latter, the emphasis is placed on the existence of the Logos with God before all things came to be, the mediation of creation by the Logos, rejection by the unbelieving world, and incarnation. But in 1 John 1:1, the stress lies on the apposition τῆς ζωῆς, as 1 John 1:2 shows. The Logos has the saving gift of life within itself: this is an idea that could have arisen within the Johannine school, quite independently from John 1:1-18 (cf. 1 John 2:7), considering that λόγος appears 39 times in the Gospel (without counting John 21:23), and 6 times in 1 John, while ζωή is found 36 times in the Gospel and 13 times in 1 John. Similarly, the use of θεᾶσθαι [look at] (6 times in the Gospel, 3 times in 1 John) in John 1:14//1 John 1:1, and the comparable expressions ἦν πρὸς τὸν θεόν [(it) was with God], and ἦν πρὸς τὸν πατερά [(it) was with the Father] in John 1:1, 2//1 John 1:2 cannot prove a *literary* dependence of the letter's prologue on the prologue of the Gospel.[95] In addition, κοινωνία

---

[90] Ibid.

[91] See Schnackenburg, *Johannesbriefe,* 57-58. I differ with Brown, who believes that the prologue of the letter is a "reinterpretation of the GJohn Prologue, done in order to refute adversaries who are distorting the meaning of the GJohn Prologue" (*Epistles of John,* 178).

[92] Here I disagree with Conzelmann, who thinks that 1 John 2:13, 14 also refer to the ἀρχή pure and simple ("'Was von Anfang war,'" 208).

[93] In 1 John 3:8 (cf. John 8:44), ἀπ᾿ ἀρχῆς refers to the devil as the original opponent of God.

[94] I differ with Conzelmann, "'Was von Anfang war,'" 211. He writes: "I believe that one can only understand the expressions in the letter by supposing that the author is already thinking of the Gospel of John as an established authority."

[95] Among those who argue for a literary dependence of the prologue of the letter on John 1:1-18 are Bultmann, *Johannine Epistles,* 8; Schnackenburg, *Johannesbriefe,* 51; Balz, *Johannes-*

in 1 John 1:3 (twice) introduces a concept that is not found in the Gospel (of the 19 occurrences in the New Testament, 13 are in Paul and 4 in 1 John).

Undoubtedly, the prologue of the letter and the prologue of the Gospel arise out of the same traditional roots in the Johannine school. But it cannot be proved that John 1:1-18 was the literary model for 1 John 1:1-4.

2. G. Klein sees a fundamental shift between letter and Gospel in the historicizing of the opposite terms φῶς and σκοτία in 1 John 2:8b. Whereas the Gospel contains only an existential notion of time, 1 John introduces a chronological notion, something that speaks clearly in favor of the temporal and material priority of the Gospel.[96] In addition, the transfer of the attribution of "light" to God in 1 John 1:5, according to Klein, is connected with that transformation of the concept of time. Because the christological sayings about light in the Gospel (8:12; 9:5; 12:35, 46, etc.), which were to be understood existentially, could now be misunderstood in a chronological sense, "the transfer of the attribute of 'light' from Jesus to God represents an appropriate updating of the language."[97] Klein also sees a tendency to historicizing and ecclesial application in the use of ἐσχάτη ὥρα [the last hour] in 1 John 2:18, since this refers to the appearance of the false teachers, that is, to "an empirical fact in the history of the church."[98] Finally, according to Klein, the "old" and "new" commandments in 1 John 2:7-8 are evidence of an altered view of time: "the commandment is 'old' because the history of the church has already been going on for some time; it is 'new' because the church's history as a whole marks a new phase in the history of the world."[99] In Klein's view, 1 John articulates "the theological discovery of the continuum of time" in the Johannine school.[100] If the Gospel is interested only in the eschatologically qualified present, 1 John deals with the problem of the extension of the time.[101]

Though the christological shaping of the contrast between light and darkness in the Gospel is unmistakable, no contrast to 1 John can be drawn from it, for there too God's being as "light" is manifested in the Son. The content of the ἀγγελία [message] in 1 John 1:5 is Jesus Christ, as is clearly evident from the preceding prologue to the letter and from the statement in

---

briefe, 167; Brown, Epistles of John, 176ff. Undecided are Windisch, Johannesbriefe, 108; Wengst, Johannesbriefe, 38–39.

[96] See Klein, "'Das wahre Licht scheint schon,'" 282ff.; see, earlier, Brooke, Johannine Epistles, xxiv; Conzelmann, TDNT 9:349–55.

[97] Klein, "'Das wahre Licht scheint schon," 288. In the case of 1 John 1:5, Klein overlooks the fact that the equation of God and light could be, from the point of view of tradition history, older than the christological interpretation in the Gospel (John 8:12; etc.), for in the history of religions an identification of God with light is frequently found; see Conzelmann, TDNT 9:329 n. 134, 331, 335ff., 335 n. 187, 351 n. 341.

[98] G. Klein, "'Das wahre Licht scheint schon,'" 302.

[99] Ibid., 306.

[100] Ibid., 316.

[101] Ibid. 325.

1 John 1:7b of the reason why the believers walk in the light (cf. 1 John 3:23; 5:1, 5). The victory of light over darkness, grounded on the revelation of God in Jesus Christ, is, both in the Gospel and in 1 John, a fact already established in faith, which acquires an eschatological and chronological quality. It is final and unsurpassable, yet at the same time, it happens for the faithful within history. In the Gospel also, a decision between light and darkness is presupposed (3:19) and corresponds to the ethical demand to be children of light (12:35-36).

If in 1 John the accent falls more on the chronological and ethical level, that is occasioned by the specific situation of the letter, and not by fundamental theological shifts. The form of the Gospel as a representation of the *vita Jesu* (true of John's Gospel also!) calls for a concentration on christology, whereas the letter is written in conflict with opponents and therefore demands a preservation of the true confession of faith within historical time and a corresponding standard of ethical behavior. The interpretation of 1 John 2:8b must proceed from this basis. Light's banishing of darkness, here temporally conceived, takes place in the context of a struggle that is threatening the community. In essence, the power of darkness has already been broken by the appearance of the light, but the completion of this victory within history is yet to come. Light and darkness are understood as two principles, which means that a simple equation of the "true light" with Christ is impossible.[102] Still, there can be no doubt that, from the point of view of the author of the letter, the "true light" means Christ. While a mentality shaped by the historical situation and directed toward the future dominates the letter, the Gospel is governed by a concentration on the *vita Jesu* that is likewise chronologically oriented, since Jesus is the light for the world and for the disciples as long as he remains in the world (12:35: ἔτι μικρὸν χρόνον τὸ φῶς ἐν ὑμῖν ἐστιν [the light is with you for a little longer]; cf. 8:12; 9:5). The differences between the Gospel of John and 1 John are undeniable, but they consist of variations in the form and in the historical situation presupposed by each of the documents and are not rooted in any far-reaching change in thinking between the Gospel and the letter.

In addition, criticism must be leveled at the presuppositions in Klein's interpretation of John because, following Bultmann, he recognizes only an "existential" concept of time in the Gospel, but no chronological concept.[103] Even the prologue of the Gospel contains statements relating to time, and not only to nature,[104] and both Johannine eschatology and the idea of the Paraclete testify to a chronological concept of time. It is characteristic of the fourth evangelist to collapse the temporal levels, as we see in John 5:25 in

---

[102] This is emphasized by Schnackenburg, *Johannesbriefe*, 113.

[103] See Klein, "'Das wahre Licht scheint schon,'" 287, and frequently elsewhere. For the critique of Klein, see also Kümmel, *Introduction*, 445.

[104] See the exegesis of the prologue in 5.1 below.

the expression ἔρχεται ὥρα καὶ νῦν ἐστιν [the hour is coming, and now is].[105] The eschatological events already have a present reality, and the future extends into the present (see John 3:3, 5, 18; 4:23; 5:25, 29; 6:27ff.; 10:9; 11:24, 25; 12:25, 32; 14:2-3; 17:24). Even the exclusion of the future-apocalyptic sayings in the Gospel of John does not alter this observation, since the passages that are above literary-critical suspicion (John 4:23; 5:25; 16:32; cf. 1 John 2:18: ἀντίχριστος ἔρχεται, καὶ νῦν [!] ἀντίχριστοι πολλοὶ γεγόνασιν [antichrist is coming, and now many antichrists have come]; cf. also Rom. 13:11) presume an interleaving of times, a knowledge of present and future, and therefore also a chronological conception of time. Without question, Johannine eschatology is shaped by the *praesentia Dei* in the incarnate Logos, and thus by the presence of salvation. But that does not make future-eschatological sayings unnecessary, for the separation between good and evil, salvation and destruction, that has been accomplished in the encounter with Jesus must be carried forward and confirmed by the judgment.[106] It is precisely this unique perspective of the evangelist located within two time frames that proves his knowledge of the importance of time.

The consciousness that the Johannine school exists in time and history is clearly articulated in the concept of the Paraclete.[107] The Paraclete appears in the post-Easter situation[108] as the present Christ, "as the re-presentation of the glorified Jesus in his earthly community of disciples."[109] The appositional definition of the Paraclete as πνεῦμα τῆς ἀληθείας [spirit of truth] (John 14:17; 15:26; 16:13) in itself indicates the Paraclete's eminent importance for the church, and this is evident also in the functions assigned: the Paraclete will be with the disciples forever (14:16), teaching and reminding the community (14:26), witnessing to Jesus (15:26), overcoming the world (16:8), declaring to the disciples the things that are to come (16:13: τὰ ἐρχόμενα ἀναγγελεῖ ὑμῖν [(he/she) will declare to you the things that are to come]), and glorifying Jesus in the community (16:14). The Johannine school is conscious of being within a temporal continuum, and the idea of the Paraclete is nothing but the Johannine solution to the problems connected with that situation. Thus, it is not 1 John that first marks the entrance of the Johannine school into "the history of the church."[110]

---

[105] See Haenchen, *John* 1:253, and frequently; Bühner, "Denkstrukturen," 224–25.

[106] See, in this sense, Stählin, "Zum Problem der johanneischen Eschatologie," 225ff.; Barrett, *John*, 67–70; Wilkens, *Zeichen und Werke*, 163–65. Blank has demonstrated the unity of the *locus classicus*, John 5:19–30 (*Krisis*, 109–82).

[107] For the literary-critical problems in the Paraclete sayings, which cannot be treated here, see Wilckens, "Der Paraklet und die Kirche," 186–90. In this good analysis he emphasizes the literary unity of the farewell discourses and thus the unity in content of the Paraclete sayings.

[108] The coming of the Paraclete is tied to the departure of Jesus (John 16:7b).

[109] Wilckens, "Der Paraklet und die Kirche," 193.

[110] Against Klein, who considers the historicizing of time and the dogmatizing of revelation to be exclusive characteristics of 1 John ("'Das wahre Licht scheint schon,'" 317).

3. E. Schweizer sees in the ecclesiology of 1 John "a logically more advanced stage"[111] than in the Gospel, since the unity of the church in 1 John has become much more problematic.[112] Undoubtedly, the appearance of false teachers has made community harmony a problem for 1 John. On the other hand, the strong emphasis on the unity of the church in the Gospel of John (see 10:16; 11:50-52; 17:20-24) shows that there too community life is in danger. However, it is impossible to discern a fundamental shift that would establish the temporal priority of the Gospel. Instead, it can be shown that there are a great many agreements in the ecclesiology of the two documents: the existence of the Johannine school is owing to the love of God that has been revealed in the sending of the Son (see 1 John 4:9, 14; John 3:16). Both in 1 John (see 2:29; 3:9; 4:7; 5:1, 4, 18) and in the Gospel (1:13; see also 6:37, 44; 17:2), membership in the community is understood as being born of God and thus as purely the action of God and God's gracious gift. The characteristic mark of the Johannine community is love for the brothers and sisters, which constitutes the center of Johannine ethics (see 1 John 2:7-11; 3:14-18; 4:7-21; 5:1-2, and frequently elsewhere; John 13:34-35; 15:12-17).

The disciples are called to "abide" (μένειν) in Jesus or in God (1 John 2:6, 24b, 28; 3:6; 4:12-16; John 15:4-6), in the word or commandment (1 John 2:14; 2:24a; 3:24; John 8:31; 15:7), in love (1 John 2:10; 4:16; John 15:9, 10), and in the Spirit (1 John 2:27; John 14:17). Like Paul, the Johannine school recognizes the notion of a mutual "indwelling," as expressed in the Johannine formulae of immanence[113] (see 1 John 3:24; 4:13, 16b; John 6:56; 15:4-7). The Spirit is the ground of Christian existence (1 John 2:27; 3:24; 4:13; 5:6-8; John 3:5) and preserves it in the present and in the future (1 John 2:20, 27; John 14:26; 15:26-27; 16:12-15). Finally, neither the letter nor the Gospel says anything about offices, and there is no multiplicity of gifts of the Spirit, as there is in Paul.

4. Again, it is not possible to found the notion of a temporal priority of the Gospel on the idea of the Paraclete, which instead favors a prior composition of the letter. In 1 John 2:1 it is exclusively Jesus Christ who is identified with the Paraclete, but in the Gospel the concept of the Paraclete is extended. What dominates here is the equation of the Paraclete with the πνεῦμα ἅγιον [holy spirit] or πνεῦμα τῆς ἀληθείας (see John 14:17, 26; 15:26; 16:13). Ecclesial functions are connected with this, and these are now accomplished by the Paraclete.[114] If 1 John was written in connection with, and subsequent to, the Gospel, it would be hard to explain why the letter writer did not take up the ecclesial functions of the Paraclete, although in that case the letter would mark the entrance of the Johannine school into ongoing

---

[111] E. Schweizer, "Der Kirchenbegriff," 266.
[112] Ibid.
[113] See Schnackenburg, *Johannesbriefe*, 105–10.
[114] See the listing under point (2).

time and thus into the history of the church. Instead, he makes use of the χρῖσμα idea in his conflict with the opponents (1 John 2:20, 27). Finally, John 14:16 contains a reference back to 1 John 2:1, for here Jesus asks the Father to send an ἄλλος παράκλητος and thus indirectly designates himself as a Paraclete.

5. Frequently, the differences in eschatology between the Gospel of John and 1 John are treated as proof of an earlier composition of the Gospel. The "genuine" Johannine conception of a present eschatology is seen in the Gospel, and then it is possible to recognize the "re-apocalypticizing" in 1 John as merely an accommodation to the dominant future eschatology of early Christianity.[115]

Two fundamental methodological objections should be made to this view: (a) A genuine contradiction between the eschatological statements of the Gospel and 1 John exists only if, following Bultmann, all the Gospel passages representing a future eschatology (with the possible exception of 14:2) are regarded as secondary, from the standpoint of literary criticism. But this is a *petitio principii,* since an interpretation of the Gospel that is, to say the least, disputed is made the basis for evaluating the eschatology of 1 John. The fact that within the Johannine school a combination of future and present eschatology was conceivable, is apparent from the existing version of the Gospel of John! One should seriously consider whether what is frequently thought to be due to a post-Johannine redaction, namely, the taut interweaving of two eschatological perspectives, could not possibly have been the work of the evangelist. In support of it are, not least, the texts already cited (John 4:23; 5:25; 10:9; 12:25, 32; 14:2-3; 17:24), which literary criticism cannot eliminate. (b) In the history of early Christian theology there was from the beginning a coexistence between present and future eschatology. Both conceptions can be shown to exist throughout the Pauline school, to name the most prominent example (see only 1 Thess. 4:13-18; 1 Cor. 4:8; Rom. 6:3-4; 13:11-12; Col. 2:12; Eph. 2:5-6; 2 Tim. 2:18; 2 Thess. 2:1-12). The types of eschatology that formed the starting point, from the perspective of the history of tradition within the Johannine school, must therefore be established by detailed exegesis and without allowing an overarching interpretation of Johannine theology to prejudice the results. From the point of view of tradition criticism, the future-eschatological statements in 1 John (see 2:18, 28; 3:3) could represent an early stage of the Johannine school. This possibility cannot be eliminated by positing an accommodation to common Christian ideas.

6. The suggestion that many passages in 1 John can be understood only against the background of the Gospel is not a methodologically cogent

---

[115] See Brooke, *Johannine Epistles,* xxi.

argument for the priority of the Gospel.[116] Since it cannot be shown that there is any quotation from the Gospel in 1 John, and since at no point is there even a reference to the supposedly earlier writing, such a procedure yields nothing but a posterior confirmation of an already existing conclusion.

7. The possible mention of an earlier writing in 1 John 2:14 does not apply to the Gospel, since here the reference can only be to a letter.[117] Perhaps 1 John 2:14 is a reference to 2 John, as H. H. Wendt suspected.[118]

8. Many exegetes see the love commandment in 1 John 2:7-8 as an allusion to John 13:34-35.[119] But this interpretation is not at all decisive, because 1 John 2:7 clearly relates to the identical formulation in 2 John 5. Whereas in the latter the reference to the commandment "from the beginning" is directed against the "go aheads" mentioned in v. 9, in 1 John 2:7 the commandment is "old" because it was given to the community at the time of its foundation and has remained since that time as the constitutive content of its preaching.[120] The commandment is "new" because it is the teaching of the Revealer,[121] which gives it an eschatological quality (cf. 1 John 2:8b!). The author of 1 John expands the tradition of 2 John dialectically: on the one hand, he emphasizes the traditional character of the commandment, and, on the other hand, he interprets it as a "new" commandment of love for the brothers and sisters (cf. 1 John 2:9-11) in the specific situation.

Thus the arguments proposed in the literature for a temporal priority of the Gospel are not persuasive. In 1 John there is no quotation from the Gospel,[122] and the often-suggested shifts in theological emphasis between the Gospel and the letter are either nonexistent or rest on a particular interpretation of the Gospel that prejudices the desired result. But there is one fundamental point of divergence between the letter and the Gospel: only the letter presupposes an *acute* christological dispute with opponents within the community. This conflict is a secure methodological starting point from which to clarify the chronological order of the letter and the Gospel.

R. Bultmann and R. E. Brown also employ this methodological criterion for determining the order of letter and Gospel. Bultmann states succinctly: "The Gospel of John and 1 John are directed against different fronts. Whereas the Gospel is opposed

---

[116] Against Brooke, who states: "Many passages in the Epistle seem to need the help of the Gospel in order to become intelligible" (*Johannine Epistles*, xxii–xxiii).

[117] See Schnackenburg, *Johannesbriefe*, 125.

[118] Cf. Wendt, "Beziehung," 140–46; idem, *Johannesbriefe*, 3–4.

[119] See only Schnackenburg, *Johannesbriefe*, 111; Wengst, *Johannesbriefe*, 76; Balz, *Johannesbriefe*, 177; Brown, *Epistles of John*, 264; Brooke, *Johannine Epistles*, xxvi.

[120] Bultmann also sees in 1 John 2:7 a reference to the false teachers in 2 John 9 (*Johannine Epistles*, 27).

[121] In 1 John 2:8a, ἐν αὐτῷ refers to Christ.

[122] See Brown, *Epistles of John*, 33. This very finding testifies against the thesis of Painter, according to which a different interpretation of the Gospel was the source of the conflict between the author of 1 John and his opponents ("'Opponents,'" 49ff.).

to the 'world,' or to the Jews who are its representatives, and therefore to non-Christians, the false teachers who are opposed in 1 John are within the Christian community and claim to represent the genuine Christian faith. This shows that 1 John originates in a period later than the Gospel."[123] Here Bultmann presumes that an intracommunity conflict necessarily represents a later stage in the development of a theological school. Brown adduces this as an argument for the priority of the Gospel: "If there were already Johannine christological extremists (as attested in I John), would the evangelist have dared to present the prototype of the Community, the Beloved Disciple, as superior even to Peter in his perception of Jesus?"[124] Brown sees in the Beloved Disciple a companion of the historical Jesus[125] and the founder of the Johannine school. Both of these proposals have been refuted by our analysis of the Beloved Disciple texts. Brown's second argument, that "the silence of GJohn about inner-Johannine conflict is hard to explain, if such a conflict had already occurred,"[126] is also unpersuasive, since the Gospel is not at all silent about the christologically motivated intra-Johannine conflict.[127]

If the opponents who are challenged in the letter refer in a recognizable manner to the Gospel, or if the letter writer does so in combatting them, that would speak in favor of the priority of the Gospel. But if the Gospel presupposes this very conflict and engages it theologically, the letter would have chronological priority.

To clarify this problem, we first need to define the teaching of the opponents in 1 John. In doing so, we may adduce only those texts in which the author of 1 John clearly engages the opponents' thought or attacks it, either by naming the opponents directly as ψεύστης, ἀντίχριστος, or ψευδο-προφῆται [liar, antichrist, false prophets], or by rejecting their theology by means of positive or negative confessional formulae. Antithetic formulations, possible allusions, warnings, and moral defamation are, however, not adequate criteria for the description of opposing positions.[128]

The opponents are frequently seen as being representatives of some kind of ethical libertinism (see 1 John 1:5-10; 3:4-24; 4:20-5:3).[129] K. Wengst, in particular, constructs the anthropology of the opponents on the basis of antithetical formulae: he regards them as Gnostics who thought themselves sinless because their essential being was quasi-divine. In the first place, it is a very questionable methodological beginning to infer the opponents' statements on the basis of antithetical formulae *alone* and then to reconstruct them.[130] Second, the first person plural in 1 John 1:8, 10 indicates that

---

123 Bultmann, *Johannine Epistles,* 1.

124 Brown, *Epistles of John,* 34.

125 See Brown, *Ringen um die Gemeinde,* 27.

126 Brown, *Epistles of John,* 35.

127 See chapters 3–6 below.

128 On this point, see the good methodological reflections of Berger, "Die impliziten Gegner," 373ff. He correctly criticizes subjective reconstructions of "opponents" or their "teachers" and calls for a clear methodological system (see esp. pp. 392–94).

129 See R. Schnackenburg, *Johannesbriefe,* 16; K. Wengst, *Häresie und Orthodoxie,* 38ff.

130 See Berger's critique of Wengst ("Die impliziten Gegner," 381 n. 59).

the question of sinlessness was a problem *within* the community.[131] Wengst's interpretation of the first person plural as "impersonal: 'one'"[132] is arbitrary, especially since there is no visible reference to the opponents in 1 John 1:5-10. Finally, 1 John 3:9 is clear evidence against the thesis that the opponents thought themselves sinless. Here the author of 1 John claims sinlessness for the Christians of the Johannine school. If 1 John 1:5-10 referred to the opponents, in 1 John 3:9 the author of the letter would be applauding exactly the thing that he had denied of the opponents earlier![133]

The opponents, who had once belonged to the community (cf. 1 John 2:19),[134] denied, from the point of view of the author of the letter, the soteriological identity between the earthly Jesus and the heavenly Christ (see 1 John 2:22: Ἰησοῦς οὐκ ἔστιν ὁ Χριστός [Jesus is not the Christ]; see also the identity statements in 1 John 4:15; 5:1, 5).[135] Evidently, for the opponents only the Father and the heavenly Christ were relevant for salvation, but not the life and death of the historical Jesus of Nazareth. For the author of 1 John, on the contrary, anyone who teaches the work of the Son falsely does not have the Father.[136]

The statement in 1 John 4:2 about the incarnation (cf. 1 John 1:2; 3:8b) allows us to conclude that the opponents contested that the preexistent Christ had become flesh.[137] Again it is clear that the atoning death of the

---

[131] Windisch sees this correctly (*Johannesbriefe*, 111). The statements of 1 John on sin, sinlessness, and second repentance (see esp. 1:6–2:2; 3:4-10; 5:16-17) are to be regarded as entirely paraenetic, and not dogmatic. It is a question of a community problem, which the author attempts to solve in light of the tension between sinlessness as an eschatological reality and sinfulness as a reality in the community's life. The distinction between a "sin that is mortal" and a "sin that is not mortal" simply serves to sharpen the imperative by underscoring in an unmistakable manner the seriousness of the moral demand to love the brothers and sisters.

[132] Wengst, *Häresie und Orthodoxie*, 39 n. 74.

[133] Wengst avoids this problem simply by claiming that 1 John 3:9 (like 3:6) is quoting the opponents (*Häresie und Orthodoxie*, 44).

[134] It is the *opinio communis* among scholars that 1 John is fighting against only one set of opponents; see Schnackenburg, *Johannesbriefe*, 16.

[135] See Bultmann, *Johannine Epistles*, 38–39; Balz, *Johannesbriefe*, 183; Wengst, *Johannesbriefe*, 112; Brown, *Epistles of John*, 352; Windisch, *Johannesbriefe*, 127–28; Haenchen, "Neuere Literatur zu den Johannesbriefen," 274. If 1 John 2:22 is viewed in isolation, it could also refer to Jewish denial of Jesus' messiahship, though this is certainly excluded by 1 John 2:19 – this against Weiß, who sees the denial of Jesus' divine sonship as the characteristic feature of the opponents' teaching ("Die 'Gnosis' im Hintergrund und im Spiegel der Johannesbriefe," 343); thus also, more recently, Whitacre, *Johannine Polemics*, 131.

[136] Ὁ Χριστός [the Christ] and ὁ υἱὸς τοῦ θεοῦ [the Son of God] have the same meaning here; see Schnackenburg, *Johannesbriefe*, 157.

[137] See Bultmann, *Johannine Epistles*, 62; Windisch, *Johannesbriefe*, 127; Wengst, *Johannesbriefe*, 169; Balz, *Johannesbriefe*, 195–96; Brown, *Epistles of John*, 50ff.; Dodd, *Johannine Epistles*, xix. R. Schnackenburg sees no antidocetic tendency in 1 John 4:2 and asks whether Ἰ. Χρ. ἐν σαρκὶ ἐληλυθότα is an incarnational formula at all (*Johannesbriefe*, 221). Minear also denies that 1 John 4:2 contains a statement about the incarnation ("Idea of Incarnation," 300–301).

historical Jesus of Nazareth (see 1 John 1:9; 2:2; 4:10) had no salvific significance for them. They make a strict distinction between the heavenly Christ, who alone is relevant for salvation, and the earthly Jesus; for the letter writer, on the contrary, everything depends on the identity of the two. But how did the opponents conceive the relationship between the earthly Jesus, whose mere existence they, as Christians, could not deny, and the heavenly Christ? At this point 1 John is silent, but there is nothing to prevent our supposing that the opponents saw Jesus Christ, in his essence, as exclusively God, who, in an earthly appearance, could have only an apparent body that was not important for salvation. In that case, they would have advocated a docetic christology. In favor of this interpretation is 1 John 4:3, where we should read καὶ πᾶν πνεῦμα, ὃ λύει τὸν Ἰησοῦν ἐκ τοῦ θεοῦ οὐκ ἔστιν [and every spirit that dissolves Jesus is not from God].[138] The opponents "eliminated Jesus from their teaching, denied the human side of the Redeemer."[139]

Excursus: What is Docetism?

A consideration of the problem of docetism is necessary not only for the sake of a more precise identification of the opponents who appear in 1 John. Ever since E. Käsemann (following F. C. Baur,[140] A. von Harnack,[141] G. Baldensperger,[142] and H. Lietzmann[143]) described the christology of the fourth evangelist as "naïve docetism,"[144] the notion of docetism has been of critical importance for an assessment of the whole of Johannine theology.

Methodologically, the starting point for an analysis of early Christian docetism lies in the letters of Ignatius, in which this christology is truly palpable for the first time.[145] Moreover, these letters are very close in content and in time to the Johannine writings.[146] Ignatius accuses his opponents of denying the corporeality of Jesus Christ. They do not acknowledge that the Lord has a body (Ign. *Smyrn.*n. 5.2: μὴ ὁμολογῶν αὐτὸν σαρκοφόρον [not acknowledging him to be flesh-bearing]). The vehemence with which Ignatius emphasizes the bodiliness of Jesus Christ shows that this is the central

---

138 Among those who advocate the reading λύει are Schnackenburg, *Johannesbriefe,* 222 (with extensive argumentation); Bultmann, *Johannine Epistles,* 62; Brown, *Epistles of John,* 494–96; Zahn, *Einleitung* 2:577; Weigandt, "Doketismus," 104; Wengst, *Häresie und Orthodoxie,* 17 n. 14; Müller, *Geschichte der Christologie,* 60.

139 Weigandt, "Doketismus," 105.

140 Baur, *Kritische Untersuchungen,* 233, 286, 291, 373.

141 Harnack, *Dogmengeschichte,* 1:215.

142 Baldensperger, *Prolog,* 171.

143 Lietzmann, *Geschichte der Alten Kirche,* II, 117.

144 Käsemann, *Jesu letzter Wille,* 62.

145 See Weigandt, "Doketismus," 57.

146 See only Bauer, *Johannesevangelium,* 244; Bultmann, *John,* 29 n. 6. Passages comparable to the Gospel of John include, for example, Ign. *Rom.* 7.2, 3; *Magn.* 7.2; *Phld.* 7.1.

point of controversy. Jesus Christ was really born of the virgin Mary, baptized by John, and under Pontius Pilate was really nailed to the cross in the flesh for us (Ign. *Smyrn.* 1.1; cf. *Trall.* 9.1). Jesus Christ is both flesh and spirit, begotten and unbegotten, God appearing in the flesh (ἐν σαρκὶ γενόμενος θεός), from Mary and also from God, first capable of suffering and then incapable of suffering (Ign. *Eph.* 7.2). Finally, Ignatius even believes that Jesus Christ is in the flesh *after* the resurrection (*Smyrn.* 3.1).

For the opponents, Jesus Christ only appeared to suffer. Ignatius says of them: λέγουσιν, τὸ δοκεῖν πεπονθέναι αὐτόν [they say he only appeared to suffer] (Ign. *Trall.* 10; cf. *Smyrn.* 2; 4.2). In contrast, Ignatius strongly emphasizes the suffering and death of Jesus (see Ign. *Eph.* 7.2; 20.1; *Trall.* 9.1; 11.2; Ign. *Rom.* 6.1; *Smyrn.* 1.2; 6.2). If Jesus Christ appeared on earth only "τὸ δοκεῖν," if he did not really suffer, then the opponents must also deny his resurrection. This is the only explanation for the insistence with which Ignatius, with an eye to these opponents, emphasizes the resurrection of Jesus Christ in the flesh (see *Smyrn.* 1.2; 3.1; 7.1; *Trall.* 9.2; *Eph.* 20.1; *Magn.* 11). If the opponents deny the resurrection, then the Eucharist is also emptied of meaning and the grace of Christ is reduced (Ign. *Smyrn.* 6.2), so that it is only logical for the opponents to absent themselves from the eucharistic celebration (see Ign. *Smyrn.* 7.1; further 6.2).[147]

What should we call the αἵρεσις opposed by Ignatius (*Eph.* 6.2; *Trall.* 6.2)? Because the opponents dispute the fleshly existence of the earthly Jesus Christ, his real suffering, and his resurrection, because they draw consequences from this for the Eucharist, and because the key word "τὸ δοκεῖν [appearance]" enters the picture, the teaching deserves the name of "docetism."[148] Apparently, the whole earthly existence of Jesus Christ is regarded as δόκησις [fancy],[149] Jesus Christ came only as an appearance and was not born. It cannot be proved that the opponents only rejected the passion of Jesus Christ, without devaluing his whole activity. We cannot detect even a temporary connection between the heavenly Christ and the earthly Jesus. Jesus Christ, in the opinion of the opponents, only appeared "τῷ δοκεῖν."

It is only this form of monophysite christology, in which the Redeemer is exclusively divine in nature—and consequently it is not he himself but only

---

[147] Because Ignatius is evidently combatting judaizers as well (see *Magn.* 8–11; *Phld.* 5–9), people who advocate observing the Sabbath (*Magn.* 9.1) and even place the Old Testament writings above the gospel (*Phld.* 8.2), it has often been supposed that there are two heresies in the picture. (For the history of research, see Rohde, "Häresie und Schisma," 229–30; Barrett, "Jews and Judaizers," 134ff.) Although it is possible to see docetism and Judaism as "two sides of the same heretical phenomenon" (Bauer, *Briefe des Ignatius,* Trall, 240; Barrett also argues for a single group of opponents in "Jews and Judaizers," 152), the two aspects are really combined only in the letter to the Magnesians, a fact that, in my opinion, points rather to two heresies. See also Bauer and Paulsen, *Briefe des Ignatius,* Trall, 65; Schoedel, *Ignatius,* 118.

[148] See only Bauer, *Briefe des Ignatius,* Trall, 239–40; Weigandt, "Doketismus," 57–58; Bauer and Paulsen, *Briefe des Ignatius,* Trall, 64–65; Schoedel, *Ignatius,* 20, 230ff.

[149] See Bauer, *Briefe des Ignatius,* Trall, 239.

his δόκησις that appears on earth—that P. Weigandt, in his fundamental study, calls "docetism."[150] In this, he correctly opposes the heuristically unfruitful use of "docetism" in the sense of a collective concept within the history of dogma for all kinds of gnostic christology.[151] Apart from the letters of Ignatius, Weigandt also finds a docetism thus defined—the consequence of which was a complete emptying of the earthly existence of Jesus Christ—in Satornilius, Cerdon, Marcion and the *Acts of John*.[152]

Satornilius worked in Antioch soon after Ignatius's death. Irenaeus describes his teaching in this way: "salvatorem autem innatum demonstravit et incorporalem, et sine figura, putative autem visum homine [he has also shown that the Savior was without birth, without body, and without figure, but was, by supposition, a visible human being]" (*Adv. Haer.* 1.24.2). The Redeemer was unborn, bodiless, without form, and only appeared to human senses (see also Pseudo-Tertullian *Haer.* 1.4; Hippolytus *Ref.* 7.28.1–5).

---

[150] See Weigandt, "Doketismus," 16, 18. Since Weigandt's dissertation was not published and therefore is not easily available, we must say that the state of research on the problem of docetism is unsatisfactory. Orbe (*Christología Gnóstica* 1:380–421), Grillmeier (*Jesus der Christus* 1:187–89), and Rudolph (*Gnosis,* 179–84) apparently were not able to consult Weigandt's work. Orbe calls only the Valentinians docetists and traces the *Acts of Peter,* of *John,* and of *Thomas* to them. A broader conception of docetism than that of Weigandt is represented by Slusser, "Docetism." Brox writes: "At the moment when the 'how' of the obviously human form of Jesus Christ became something other than the real Incarnation, namely δόκησις, only an appearance of whatever and however substantial type, the teaching was docetic" ("'Doketismus,'" 309). On the problem of docetism, see also Knox, *Humanity and Divinity of Christ,* 26ff., 94ff.; Tröger, "Doketische Christologie in Nag-Hammadi-Texten"; Rudolph, *Gnosis,* 179–84. A noteworthy typology of docetism can be found in Bauer, *Briefe des Ignatius,* Trall, 239. Bauer distinguishes three forms of docetism: (1) It was not Christ who was crucified but someone else in his place (Basilides, according to Irenaeus *Adv. Haer.* 1.24.4). (2) A distinction was made between the human being, Jesus, and the "Christ above," who united with Jesus at his baptism and left him again before the passion. (3) Bauer calls "perfected docetism" the teaching of those who "completely [dissolve] the earthly existence of the Lord into appearance."

[151] See the discussion in Weigandt, "Doketismus," 4–19; he examines seven "types" of gnostic christology and distinguishes them carefully from one another. He also points out that Simon Magus, Basilides, Valentinus, and Cerinthus cannot be called docetists in the strict sense. This point is also made regarding Basilides by Hauschild, "Christologie und Humanismus," 82; and for Simon Magus by Lüdemann, *Untersuchungen,* 81ff. Like Weigandt, Brox now also emphasizes with reference to the Nag Hammadi documents that gnosis and docetism are in no way identical and not necessarily mutually related ("'Doketismus,'" 312–14). "There are good reasons, though not decisive, within the text for calling the false teachers in the Johannine letters docetists (1 John 2:22; 4:2-3; 5:1, 6). But the basis for a supposition that they are Gnostics is far weaker. By all appearances, non-gnostic docetic christologies were not a rarity in the early second century" (p. 313).

[152] See Weigandt, "Doketismus," 28, 82–86. Denker regards the *Gospel of Peter* as an early witness to docetism; he states that it represents "a christology with docetic consequences. The Lord sweeps over the earth as a being in angelic form. His sufferings exist only in the imagination, in people's fantasies, but not in reality" (*Die theologiegeschichtliche Stellung des Petrusevangeliums,* 126). Denker surmises that the *Gospel of Peter* originated in the circles of Ignatius's opponents.

Because Christ did not appear *substantia corporis* [in bodily form], he only appeared to suffer.[153]

Cerdon, Satornilius's contemporary, lived and taught after 140 in Rome. Irenaeus reports that Cerdon was Marcion's teacher. According to Pseudo-Tertullian (*Haer.* 6.1), Cerdon taught that Jesus Christ was not born of a virgin; he was not born at all. He came to earth as the son of God but did not appear *in substantia carnis* [in fleshly substance]. On earth he existed only as a phantasm, and therefore he did not suffer. Epiphanius also describes Cerdon's docetic christology at length (*Panarion* 41.1.7-8; see also Irenaeus *Adv. Haer.* 2.32.4; *Fil. Haer.* 44.2). Cerdon distinguished between a *deum malum* [evil god] and a *deum bonum* [good god], corresponding to the gnostic ἄγνωστος θεός [unknown god] and πατήρ [father] (Pseudo-Tertullian *Haer.* 6.1; Epiphanius *Panarion* 41.1.3). Although according to these witnesses Cerdon's teaching should clearly be called docetic, it must be noted "that Irenaeus, Tertullian and Hippolytus know nothing of the christology of this heretic, while Justin, Clement of Alexandria and Origen never even mention Cerdon."[154]

It is much disputed among scholars whether Marcion was a Gnostic.[155] Nevertheless, there can be no doubt that there were docetic features in his christology. Marcion taught that Jesus Christ was not born but appeared suddenly from heaven in the fifteenth year of the reign of Tiberius. He came directly from heaven *in hominis forma* [in human form] (Irenaeus *Adv. Haer.* 1.27.2). According to Tertullian's version, this was only *per imaginem substantiae humanae* [through an image of human substance] (*Marcion* 3.10.2). Jesus Christ had no body at all; instead, he was a *phantasma carnis* [phantasm of flesh] (*Marcion* 4.42.7). Marcion also disputed the reality of the passion of Jesus Christ; because the Redeemer was not really a human being and had no fleshly body, he was not really crucified, did not really die, was not really buried, and did not really rise from the dead (Tertullian *De carne* 5.2-3,9). Christ suffered only *putative* (Tertullian *Marcion* 3.8.4), only δοκήσει (Epiphanius *Panarion* 42.12.3), only τῷ δοκεῖν (Hippolytus *Ref.* 10.19.3). Consequently, there was no bodily resurrection of the dead (Irenaeus *Adv. Haer.* 1.27.3; Tertullian *Marcion* 3.8.6-7; 5.7.4; etc.). The Eucharist was necessarily devalued; Marcion interpreted *hoc est corpus meum* [this is my body] to mean *figura corporis mei* [image of my body] (Tertullian *Marcion* 4.40.3) and used bread and water as elements for the

---

[153] For further information on Satornilius's system, see Epiphanius *Panarion* 23.1.10; *Fil. Haer.* 31.6; see also Weigandt, "Doketismus," 64–65.

[154] Weigandt, "Doketismus," 66.

[155] Whereas Harnack definitely refused to see Marcion as a Gnostic and emphasized his differences from Gnosticism (*Marcion,* 196 n. 1), B. Aland attempts to demonstrate both Marcion's agreements with and differences from gnosis ("Marcion"). I am relying on the description of Weigandt, "Doketismus," 67–73, which I consider very good.

Lord's Supper (Epiphanius *Panarion* 42.3.3). It is true that, for Marcion, the soteriological meaning of the death of Jesus Christ was not diminished, because the Redeemer did not come to save human bodies; therefore, he needed only to be seen in an apparent body.[156]

Weigandt regards the *Acts of John* as the only testimony to docetic christology from a docetic source.[157] *Acts of John* chap. 104 proclaims the fundamental idea of docetic christology: since God is unchangeable, and Christ is God, he cannot have become human. Therefore Christ may not be preached and worshiped as a human being who appeared on earth. *Acts of John* sees Christ as an exclusively divine being; it says of him: "I saw him . . . not like a man at all" (chap. 90), and "who was made human [apart from] this body" (chap. 103).[158] Sometimes the Redeemer has a material body; "at other times again, when I felt him, his substance was immaterial and incorporeal, and as if it did not exist at all" (chap. 93). In the *Acts of John*, Christ, both "earthly" (chaps. 88–93) and "risen" (chaps. 82, 87), is polymorphous. He appears as a boy and a man, an old man and a youth, sometimes big, sometimes small. It was not Jesus who hung on the cross (chap. 99), and he did not suffer the things that would be said of him (chap. 101). Consequently, the Eucharist has no salvific importance; it is only a prayer of thanksgiving celebrated with bread (chaps. 46, 84-86, 109-110). Weigandt sees a monophysite christology in docetism.[159] God, as Christ, does not enter into a loose union with the man Jesus, making Jesus a *vehiculum* for Christ and having a subordinationist, diphysite christology in the background. Instead, Jesus Christ is, in his essence, only God, and his physical appearance can be only a phantom, for God is unchangeable. Thus, if "the Redeemer is envisioned as God alone, he cannot come into the world, because he is outside it. The union with the human being is then achieved through a typically Greek idea of δόκησις, so that the Redeemer who appears on earth is only a deceptive image. That is docetism. . . ."[160]

In particular, the parallels between the opponents against whom both Ignatius and Polycarp write (see Pol. *Phil.* 7.1) allow us to conclude that the

---

[156] See Weigandt, "Doketismus," 70; B. Aland, "Marcion," 438ff.

[157] See Weigandt, "Doketismus," 83–96. Brox disagrees: he does not regard the *Acts of John* as docetic ("'Doketismus,'" 309–10). For an opposing view, see Schäferdiek, "Herkunft und Interesse," 267. Schäferdiek emphasizes that the *Acts of John* represents a "docetic christology of glory." [Translator's note: For the English translation I have followed Schäferdiek, "Acts of John," in Hennecke-Schneemelcher, *New Testament Apocrypha* 2:188–259.]

[158] See Schäferdiek, "Acts of John," 226. The Greek text presented by Lipsius and Bonnet, (*Acta,* 202) and by Junod and Kaestli (*Acta,* 215), αὐτῷ τοῦ ἀνθρώπου γινομένου τούτο τοῦ σώματος, is hard to understand; James's correction (αὐτῷ τῷ ἀνθρώπῳ γενομένῳ [ἐκτὸς] τούτου τοῦ σώματος), which is given in both text editions and accepted by Schäferdiek, is to be preferred. See also Weigandt, "Doketismus," 84 n. 221.

[159] Weigandt, "Doketismus," 147ff.

[160] Ibid., 148.

enemies in 1 John also taught a docetic christology.[161] Here also the corporeality of the Son of God is denied. The heavenly Christ alone is relevant
for salvation; the existence of the earthly Jesus, by contrast, has no soteriological function. The opponents understood themselves as representing a
monophysite doctrine. They attributed to the Redeemer a single, divine
nature, which by its very essence cannot be capable of suffering. Therefore,
from the perspective of the author of the letter, a division between the
historical Jesus of Nazareth and the heavenly Christ is constitutive for their
soteriology.

The opponents' rejection of a salvific meaning for the passion of Jesus
can be seen in 1 John 5:6b. When the letter writer emphasizes here that Jesus
Christ came οὐκ ἐν τῷ ὕδατι μόνον ἀλλ᾽ ἐν τῷ ὕδατι καὶ ἐν τῷ αἵματι [not
with the water *only* but with the water and the blood], we may conclude that
the opponents probably derived some soteriological significance from the
baptism of Jesus but not from his death on the cross.[162] Apparently baptism
was highly important in the Johannine school as the locus of the gift of the
Spirit (see 1 John 2:27; 3:24; 4:1-3, 13; John 1:33; 3:5). The opponents based
their own status as pneumatics on baptism, while rejecting the cross and
therefore probably the Lord's Supper as well. In contrast, the author of
1 John emphasizes the salvific significance of baptism *and* the Eucharist
(1 John 5:7, 8).

It is true that in 1 John 5:6 there is no explicit mention of the sacraments, but the author's argumentation is directed toward vv. 7-8, according
to which, from a Johannine point of view, the saving event and its representation in the sacrament cannot be separated, since water and blood are the
elements of the sacraments.[163] The statement of v. 7 already resonates in v. 6!

---

[161] See H. J. Holtzmann, *Johanneische Briefe*, 236–37; Windisch, *Johannesbriefe*, 127 (Cerinthus); Bultmann, *Johannine Epistles*, 62; Balz, *Johannesbriefe*, 157; Dodd, *Johannine Epistles*,
xix; Brooke, *Johannine Epistles*, xlv ff. (similarity to Cerinthus); Weigandt, "Doketismus,"
103ff. (But Weigandt wavers strangely in his argumentation: on the one hand, he emphasizes
that 1 and 2 John oppose docetism [pp. 105, 107], and on the other hand he writes that 1 and
2 John were written "to warn about all kinds of christological errors" [pp. 103–4]). See also
Brown, *Epistles of John*, 65ff. (Cerinthus); Bogart, *Orthodox and Heretical Perfectionism*,
128–29; Langbrandtner, *Weltferner Gott*, 376–77; Müller, *Geschichte der Christologie*, 59–63;
Schunack, *Briefe des Johannes*, 75 (prelude to thoroughly developed docetic ideas). Schnackenburg advances a cautious argument: he sees the greatest similarities to the opponents of Ignatius
(*Johannesbriefe*, 15–21). Weiss argues against a docetic interpretation ("Die 'Gnosis' im Hintergrund und im Spiegel der Johannesbriefe," 343). He thinks that the opponents are Gnostics who
worshiped an "eon-Christ"; Schneider also sees the opponents as Gnostics (*1. Johannesbrief*,
138). Painter proposes that the opponents are former pagans influenced by ideas from the
mystery cults, who first entered the Johannine community after Johannine Christianity had
broken away from the synagogue ("'Opponents,'" 65ff.).

[162] See Schnackenburg, *Johannesbriefe*, 258.

[163] See Langbrandtner, *Weltferner Gott*, 380–81. Against Bultmann, *Johannine Epistles*,
80–81; Nauck, *Tradition und Charakter*, 147; Wengst, *Johannesbriefe*, 207; Schnackenburg,
Johannesbriefe, 257–58. Schunack interprets αἷμα and ὕδωρ in v. 6a exclusively in terms of the

The sacramental meaning of ὕδωρ and αἷμα in v. 8 results from a trans-formation of meaning between v. 6 and v. 8.[164] If in v. 6 ὕδωρ and αἷμα are that to which the Spirit witnesses, they appear in v. 8 as witnesses themselves; that is, in the sacraments of baptism and the Eucharist the saving event is made present by the Spirit and witness is thereby given.

1 John 5:6 often serves as the principal foundation for the thesis that the christology of the opponents is to be connected with or identified with that of Cerinthus.[165] According to Irenaeus,[166] Cerinthus, a native of Asia Minor, taught that the world was created not by the first God but by an unknown power separated from God. Jesus was born not of a virgin but rather from his natural parents, Mary and Joseph. Never-theless, he was superior to all others in righteousness, insight, and wisdom. "Et post baptismum descendisse in eum ab ea principalitate quae est super omnia Christum figura columbae; et tunc annuntiasse incognitum et virtutes perfecisse; in fine autem revolasse iterum Christum de Iesu et Iesum passum esse et resurrexisse: Christum autem impassibilem perseverasse, existentem spiritalem" [And after (his) baptism, Christ descended upon him in the form of a dove from the Supreme Ruler, and that then he proclaimed the unknown and performed miracles. But at last Christ again departed from Jesus, and then Jesus suffered and rose again; but Christ remained impassible, inasmuch as he was a spiritual being].

Epiphanius summarizes Cerinthus's christology with the remark, οὐ τὸν Ἰησοῦν εἶναι Χριστόν [Jesus is not Christ] (*Panarion* 28.1.7). The uniqueness of Cerinthus's teaching lies in his cosmogony (separation of Father God and Demiurge) and the acceptance of a temporary union between the pneumatic Christ and the man Jesus. But we cannot call this an adoptionist christology, because the spiritual Christ later departs from the man Jesus. Weigandt accurately describes the christology of Cerinthus as "clearly subordinationist as well as diphysite and diprosopic; the man Jesus and the God Christ remain at all times separate from one another in their natures and persons."[167] Therefore, for Weigandt, Cerinthus is not to be counted among the docetists.

---

historical data about Jesus' baptism and death on the cross (*Briefe des Johannes*, 94). Klos sees ὕδωρ and αἷμα in v. 6 as a saving gift stemming from the death of Jesus, a gift that gives life (ὕδωρ) and removes sins (αἷμα) (*Sakramente*, 78–79). For this view, see Thüsing, *Erhöhung*, 168; Brown, *Epistles of John*, 577–78; Venetz, "'Durch Wasser und Blut gekommen,'" 354.

[164] Against Wengst, who denies that the meaning shifts (*Johannesbriefe*, 210). Correctly: Schnackenburg, *Johannesbriefe*, 261–62; Klos, *Sakramente*, 80–81; Thüsing, *Erhöhung*, 169–70; Nauck, *Tradition und Charakter*, 147–48; Houlden, *Johannine Epistles*, 128–29.

[165] See especially Wengst, *Häresie und Orthodoxie*, 24ff.; Brown, *Epistles of John*, 65ff.; Blank, "Irrlehrer," 174ff.

[166] Irenaeus *Adv. Haer.* 1.26.1 (=Hippolytus *Ref.* 7.33.1-2; 10.21.2-3). Irenaeus's report is the only certain basis on which Cerinthus's system can be reconstructed. Descriptions of Cerinthus as a chiliast (Eusebius *Eccl. Hist.* 3.28.1ff.) and a Judaist or Ebionite (Epiphanius *Panarion* 28) should be regarded as secondary. Wengst gives a description and discussion of all the relevant texts (*Häresie und Orthodoxie*, 24–34); see also Brown, *Epistles of John*, 766–71. Blank's sup-position ("Irrlehrer," 176) that Cerinthus's christology was "a problematic and heretical mis-interpretation of Johannine shekinah-christology that was rightly rejected by the Johannine community" cannot be proved from the text.

[167] Weigandt, "Doketismus," 17.

There are undeniable agreements between the teaching of Cerinthus and the supposed christology of the opponents in 1 John (e.g., separation between the heavenly Christ and the earthly Jesus, and special value placed on Jesus' baptism). But there are also major differences. Evidently, the constitutive element in Cerinthus's system was his cosmogony, something that cannot be established for the opponents in 1 John. In addition, the distinction between a pneumatic, impassible Christ and the man Jesus, who served the heavenly Christ as a *temporary* vessel, cannot really be derived from 1 John 2:22; 5:6.[168] Therefore it is not advisable to associate the opponents in 1 John too closely with the theology of Cerinthus.

The author of 1 John combats the opponents with the traditions taught by the Johannine school—which, in his eyes, are legitimate (cf. ἀπ' ἀρχῆς in 1 John 1:1-4; 2:7-8; 3:11)—but not with the Gospel of John! While the opponents, in effect, divide the figure of the Redeemer, the author of the letter emphasizes the soteriological unity of the earthly Jesus and the heavenly Christ (see 1 John 2:22; 4:2, 9, 15; 5:1, 5). Confession of faith is set against false teaching. Whereas the bodily appearance of the Redeemer is in the final analysis irrelevant for the opponents, for the author of 1 John it is of the highest importance (see 1 John 2:6; 3:3-4; 4:17). Against the pneumatic self-understanding of the dissidents, 1 John sets the anointing of the community (cf. 1 John 2:20, 27), which instructs its recipients concerning truth and falsehood.[169]

The initial question about the chronological relationship of 1 John and the Fourth Gospel can be answered if the relationship of the Gospel to the false teaching opposed in 1 John can be clarified. If it is true that important aspects of the christology of the Fourth Gospel reveal antidocetic features and thus a conscious reaction to false teaching, the chronological priority of 1 John must be considered probable. An answer to this problem will be possible only after the analyses in the following chapters.

---

[168] See Schnackenburg, *Johannesbriefe,* 258.

[169] The points of contact in the Gospel of John for the theology of the opponents proposed by Wengst are not persuasive. According to him, they would have derived their (Cerinthian) christology from John 1:29-34; 19:30 (see Wengst, *Häresie und Orthodoxie,* 24; see also Hofrichter, *Nicht aus Blut,* 158–59, agreeing with Wengst). Even the proposed closeness to Cerinthus is questionable, and Cerinthus could have developed his christology out of Mark 1:9-11. In John 19:30 it is emphasized that Jesus understood even his death as a conscious act (see Schnackenburg, *John* 3:284). A separation of the pneumatic Christ from the earthly Jesus can scarcely be derived from this text. Nor are the other points of contact (John 1:13; 3:6; 10:36; 14:7a; 17:25 as bases for the pneumatic-gnostic self-understanding of the opponents; see Wengst, *Häresie und Orthodoxie,* 43, 45, 53) anything more than a subjective collection of passages to support the exegete's existing theses. If the reconstruction of the opponents' statements from 1 John is hypothetical, the derivation of their theology from the Gospel of John must be called pure speculation, especially since there is no passage in 1 John regarding the opponents that can be regarded as even a remote reference to the Gospel. Wengst's methodology is arbitrary: he simply associates verses from the Gospel with a questionable reconstruction of the opponents' christology and then adds the opponents' interpretation of these verses! (p. 53).

2.3   Starting Point and Method of this Book

The preceding investigations have shown that we should expect to find multiplicity rather than uniformity within the Johannine school. The varying authorship of the Johannine writings, the theological and linguistic differences, and the handing on of traditions and the theological discussion discernible within the school permit us to conclude that within the Johannine communities there were a considerable number of well-formed, theologically differing traditions as well as fixed, preformed units.[170] John the evangelist confirms this when, at the end of the Gospel, he remarks that he could write of other σημεῖα [signs] that are not recorded in this book (20:30-31).[171] He has even more traditions at his disposal, which he has not integrated into the Gospel.[172] The Fourth Gospel represents only a selection of the material available to John. The evangelist even gives the criterion for selection, in v. 31: ταῦτα δὲ γέγραπται ἵνα πιστεύητε ὅτι 'Ιησοῦς ἐστιν ὁ Χριστὸς ὁ υἱὸς τοῦ θεοῦ [but these are written so that you may come to believe that Jesus is the Christ (Messiah), the son of God]. It is not historical but exclusively theological perspectives that guide John in the selection and presentation of the material. The aim is to induce faith in the readers or hearers of the Gospel; they are no longer eyewitnesses (20:29), and yet they are to be included in the saving event that stretches from the incarnation to the glorification of Christ.

The evangelist reveals himself as a critically selective author who shapes his narrative in light of theological considerations, and who writes a Gospel for a later generation of early Christians on the basis of a wealth of oral and written traditions at his disposal. The criteria for the choice and arrangement of material, which are of central interest for redaction criticism, are stated by John himself in 20:30-31; therefore, redaction criticism must be considered the appropriate method for analyzing the Gospel of John. According to the evangelist's own testimony, the Fourth Gospel can be regarded as an "etiology of the Johannine group"[173] or an "account of the "life-situation of the Johannine community"[174] only in a very restricted sense; although the history of the Johannine school left its traces in the Gospel, that history is relevant for John, according to the criteria mentioned in 20:30-31, only in light of the stated theological and christological criteria. The

---

[170] I believe there must have been a number of Johannine communities: see Schnackenburg, "Die johanneische Gemeinde," 35ff.

[171] For a demonstration of the redactional character of John 20:30-31, see section 3.8.1 below.

[172] Cf. Cullmann, *Early Christian Worship,* 38; Haenchen, *John* 2:212.

[173] Meeks, "Funktion," 279.

[174] Brown, *Ringen um die Gemeinde,* 23. Cf., in contrast, the accurate remark of Strathmann (*Johannes,* 23): "In his account, it is not historicism that John reveres, but the principle of kerygmatic stylization."

evangelist is far removed from the idea of presenting a portrait of events, tendencies, and developments in the Johannine school that could be evaluated in historiographical terms as those are presently applied, so that every statement of the Gospel would allow us to conclude to a historically verifiable situation or group.

Instead, it is the task of a redaction-critical analysis of the Gospel of John to describe the traditions and their reworking by the evangelist, as well as the total redactional concept that governed this process. Undoubtedly, the history of the Johannine school will be evident from John's use of traditions. But it cannot be deduced by means of a methodologically uncontrolled and immediate inference from isolated passages in the text to historical situations. Rather, it is reflected in the evangelist's redactional concept.

In John, tradition and redaction should not be viewed as historical or material opposites, as has been the practice of many exegetes working from theories of sources.[175] Why should the evangelist have incorporated traditions that contradicted his own theology? This obvious question is not answered by a reference to fidelity to tradition, because John made a selection from the available material, which means that he did not need to incorporate traditions that worked against his own theology. The fourth evangelist worked traditions from the Johannine school into his Gospel to illustrate his specific theological conception. Thus, redaction and tradition are to be seen as interdependent; the evangelist affected, by his editorial work, how a tradition was to be understood, and at the same time he developed his theology to a considerable extent out of the tradition. Therefore, the starting point for analysis must be the text as it now exists. The literary and material tensions in the text are pointers to the *pre*history of the text as we now have it.

It is more difficult to separate redaction and tradition in John than in the Synoptics. There is a nearly complete absence of parallel traditions, and the overall uniformity of the language and worldview of the Gospel of John provide additional difficulties for this methodology. Nevertheless, the tools of a limited form of literary criticism can also be applied to John, in order to distinguish the traditional material from its redactional treatment.[176] Formal and theological tensions; contradictions, seams, and breaks in sentence construction and in the sequence of events; and missing references to context and differing uses of language permit conclusions about redaction and tradition, as do observations based on form criticism, tradition criticism, and the history of religions. Linguistic analysis alone gives no convincing

---

[175] As a typical example, let me mention only Haenchen, *John* 2:212: "The Evangelist himself had used the old 'gospel' [=*semeia* source]. . . . He had understood it in an entirely different sense, to be sure, than its author [!], but he believed firmly—one ought not to doubt that—that Jesus had really performed all these great miracles."

[176] For this point, see the efforts of Schille, "Traditionsgut im vierten Evangelium," 77ff.; Schnackenburg, "Tradition und Interpretation im Spruchgut des Johannesevangeliums," 72ff.

proof of the redactional or traditional character of a text, but in combination with other methods it is an indispensable method for Johannine exegesis.

A redaction-critical analysis of the Gospel of John should investigate the evangelist's reception and integration of heterogeneous traditions from the Johannine school. In the following chapters this methodology will be carried out in three areas that are foci of interest for the christology of the Fourth Gospel: the miracles of Jesus, the sacraments, and the prologue.

3

The Visible Christ:
Miracles and Johannine Christology

There are three good reasons for beginning our investigation with the Johannine miracle stories: (1) They present an especially good opportunity to demonstrate how John integrates traditional material in his Gospel and interprets it in doing so. The separation of redaction and tradition as a starting point for any redaction-critical examination can be carried out in an exemplary manner in this important part of Johannine theology, and on a broad textual basis. (2) The Johannine miracle stories are of decisive importance for the interpretation of Johannine christology, because, according to John 10:41, the working of miracles is the distinguishing feature of Jesus as Messiah.[1] (3) Moreover, the miracle stories are extremely important for an understanding of the Gospel as a whole, since ποιεῖν σημεῖα [doing signs] marks the beginning (2:11), the turning point (12:37), and the end (20:30) of Jesus' activity,[2] and it may have been the miracle stories that made it possible for the Fourth Gospel to be included in the canon, thus rescuing it from oblivion.[3]

3.1 John 2:1-11

3.1.1 Context

As in the Gospel of Mark (see 1:21-28), so also in John, Jesus' public activity begins with a miracle. The whole portrayal to this point is directed toward this miracle, for in it is visibly revealed what was described in mythical terms by the prologue and what the disciples are promised, in John

---

[1] See Hofbeck, *Semeion,* 72. For a demonstration of the redactional character of John 10:41, see section 3.8.3.1 below.

[2] See Nicol, *Semeia,* 115.

[3] This is the suggestion of Schwartz, "Aporien" IV, 588.

1:50-51, they are to see: Jesus' δόξα [glory]. The promise to Nathanael in John 1:50c, μείζω τούτων ὄψῃ [you will see greater (things) than these], indicating something future, finds its visible fulfillment in Jesus' first great deed of power in Galilee;[4] Jesus' second great work follows immediately, in Jerusalem (2:14-17) and is also connected with the key word σημεῖον [sign] (2:18, 23).[5] The miracle at Cana is not only the introduction to chapters 2–4 in the strict sense but is also the beginning of the revelation of the δόξα of the Preexistent One in space and time; it unveils the essence of the Son of God, whose whole activity John can designate as ποιεῖν σημεῖον (12:37; 20:30). As the "first sign," it anticipates further manifestations of the glory of Jesus Christ.[6]

3.1.2   Redaction and Tradition

Except for the time designation τῇ ἡμέρᾳ τῇ τρίτῃ [on the third day], v. 1 belongs to the tradition.[7] This phrase indicates that the evangelist is not continuing an enumeration including 1:29, 35, and 43,[8] but instead is emphasizing that the promise in 1:50-51 was quickly fulfilled.[9] It may be that in this phrase John is referring at the same time to the morning of the resurrection, an interpretation that is suggested by vv. 2, 4c, 19, and 20.[10] The indication of place, Κανὰ τῆς Γαλιλαίας [Cana of Galilee], was a fixed part of the narrative, together with the mother of Jesus.[11] Another indication of traditional material is the unusual singular γάμος [wedding],[12] a word that appears in the Gospel of John only in this story. Also part of the original narrative was the brief exposition in v. 2 (καλέω [call, invite] only here and

---

[4] See Schnackenburg, *John* 1:323; Becker, *Johannes* 1:108; Haenchen, *John* 1:82.

[5] See J. Schneider, *Johannes,* 79.

[6] See Schnackenburg, *John* 1:323.

[7] See Bultmann, *John,* 114 n. 3; J. Schneider, *Johannes,* 80; Becker, *Johannes* 1:107. Against Schwartz, "Aporien" IV, 512; Wilkens, *Zeichen und Werke,* 31; Heekerens, *Zeichen-Quelle,* 68, who also assign v. 1b to the redaction because the mention of Mary in the Fourth Gospel is supposed to be redactional in every instance; see n. 16 below.

[8] In order to arrive at the time scheme of a single week (so Barrett, *John,* 189), John 1:40-42 must be counted as one day, even though John has not made that clear; see Schnackenburg, *John* 1:325–26; Becker, *Johannes* 1:330–31.

[9] See Becker, *Johannes* 1:107. Schnackenburg sees "the third day" as simply a round figure (*John* 1:326).

[10] See Bultmann, *John,* 114 n. 3; Dodd, *Interpretation,* 300; Wilkens, *Entstehungsgeschichte,* 41. A reference to Exod. 19:10-11, as suggested by Olsson (*Structure and Meaning,* 102–3) and Heekerens (*Zeichen-Quelle,* 72) cannot be established on the basis of the text.

[11] The place referred to is Khirbet Kana, fourteen kilometers north of Nazareth: see Dalman, *Sacred Sites and Ways,* 101.

[12] Normally, the plural γάμοι was used for weddings; see *BAGD,* 151.

in John 1:42);[13] the mention of the disciples should certainly not be regarded as secondary.[14]

The highly compact narrative style of v. 3 matches that of the whole pericope. It is not said why the wine supply has failed, and Mary's words to Jesus serve only to prepare the way for the miracle.[15] There are no indications of redactional activity;[16] on the contrary, the Johannine *hapax legomena* ὑστερεῖν [to fail, be wanting] and οἶνος [wine] (only in John 2:1-11 and the redactional reference in 4:46) favor the traditional character of the verse. The reason for Jesus' aloof response in v. 4b[17] is given in v. 4c: οὔπω ἥκει ἡ ὥρα μου [my hour has not yet come]. The remarkable parallelism between this language and that in 7:30 and 8:20 (οὔπω ἐληλύθει ἡ ὥρα αὐτοῦ [his hour had not yet come]) and the talk about the hour of Jesus' glorification, which is so important for John (12:23, 27-28; 17:1), the hour that testifies to Jesus' sending from the Father (13:1; 7:30; 8:20), the hour of Jesus' acceptance of the passion (12:27), and the hour that is coming (4:21, 23; 5:25; 16:2, 4, 25)[18] establish the redactional character of v. 4c.[19] This means not only the hour of the wonder-worker[20] but primarily the hour of the passion and

---

[13] All suggestions about who might have invited Jesus are purely hypothetical; according to Brown, it was Nathanael! (*John* 1:98).

[14] Against Wellhausen, *Evangelium Johannis,* 13; Bultmann, *John,* 114.

[15] See Bultmann, *John,* 116; Haenchen, *John* 1:172; Becker, *Johannes* 1:108.

[16] Against Schwartz, "Aporien" IV, 512; Wilkens, *Zeichen und Werke,* 31; Fortna, *Gospel,* 31–32; Boismard and Lamouille, *Jean,* 101–2; Heekerens, *Zeichen-Quelle,* 67ff., who consider vv. 3-5 (and v. 1b) redactional. The primary argument for this is Schwartz's apodictic opinion that the mother of Jesus could not give orders to the household servants and that she plays no role in the Gospel of John elsewhere and must therefore be secondary here also. Within the narrative, the dialogue between Mary and Jesus serves to prepare for the miracle, and therefore the mention of the mother of Jesus should be regarded as original.

[17] For this formula of refusal in the Old Testament, see Judg. 11:12; 2 Sam. 16:10, 19:23; 1 Kings 17:18; 2 Kings 3:13; 2 Chron. 35:21; in Hellenism, see Epictetus, *Diss* 1.1.16, 22.15, 27.18; 2.19.16; in the New Testament, see Mark 1:24, 5:7; Matt. 8:29; Luke 4:34; 8:28. It is unclear why, in light of such a widespread use of τί ἐμοὶ καὶ σοί [what (is that) to me and you], O. Betz ("Das Problem des Wunders," 40) and Leidig (*Jesu Gespräch,* 251) see this very formula as a primary proof of their thesis that there is a tradition-historical connection between 1 Kings 17:9ff. (the widow of Zarephath) and John 2:1-11.

[18] As a simple expression of time, we find ὥρα in 1:39; 4:6, 52, 53; 16:3; 19:14, 27.

[19] See Strathmann, *Johannes,* 58; Haenchen, "Johanneische Probleme," 93 1; Dodd, *Tradition,* 226; Ruckstuhl, *Einheit,* 197, 204 (characteristic stylistic elements are ὥρα with a personal pronoun [No. 18] and γύναι [woman] as address to Jesus' mother [No. 27]); Schnackenburg, *John* 1:328–29; Rissi, "Hochzeit," 87; Fortna, *Gospel,* 31–32; Wilkens, *Zeichen und Werke,* 31; Nicol, *Semeia,* 31 (beyond the suggestions of Ruckstuhl, Nicol names οὔπω [not yet] as characteristic element No. 70 and ὥρα, in the sense of the hour already determined for Jesus by God, as element No. 67); Olsson, *Structure and Meaning,* 100; Teeple, *Origin,* 171.

[20] Against Bultmann, *John,* 117; Haenchen, *John* 1:173; Becker, *Johannes* 1:107. If v. 4c referred to Jesus' wonder-working activity, we would be faced with the difficulty that, immediately after refusing, he works the miracle; cf. Spitta, *Johannesevangelium,* 69.

glorification of the Son of God.[21] As in 7:6, 8, οὔπω separates the time before the passion from the time of the passion; in no sense does it merely emphasize the sovereignty of the miracle worker who personally chooses the moment in which to demonstrate his power.

Whereas all of v. 5 must be assigned to tradition, the expression κατὰ τὸν καθαρισμὸν τῶν Ἰουδαίων [for the Jewish rite of purification] in v. 6 is probably the work of the evangelist.[22] The isolated placing of the participle κείμεναι [standing] indicates on the linguistic level that, as in Mark 7:3-4, we are looking at an inserted commentary. In addition, there is a difficulty in the content, because according to v. 7 the jars are empty, which makes it questionable whether they were really used for ritual purposes.[23] In contrast, the rest of v. 6, as well as vv. 7 and 8, belong to the original narrative, as indicated both by the New Testament *hapax legomena* (μετρητής [liquid measure ca. 10 gallons], ἀρχιτρίκλινος [chief steward]) and the Johannine *hapax legomena* (λίθιναι ὑδρίαι [stone water jars]) and by χωρεῖν [have or make room for] (only here in the sense of "containing,"), γεμίζειν [to fill] (otherwise only in 6:13), ἀντλεῖν [to draw out] (also in 4:7, 15), and γεύεσθαι [to taste] (otherwise only in 8:52). In v. 9, καὶ οὐκ ᾔδει . . . τὸ ὕδωρ [and did not know . . . the water] should be read as a parenthesis.[24] It interrupts the narrative and reveals itself as Johannine redaction through formal (see 2:16, 22; 6:6b; 12:16; 20:9) and material parallels (contrast of knowing and not knowing; πόθεν [from where]; see 3:8; 4:11; 7:27; 8:14; 9:29; 19:9).[25] By contrast, all of v. 10 should be seen as part of the original story. (In the Gospel of John, μεθύσκεσθαι occurs only here.) At this point, in accordance with proper miracle-story style, the steward of the feast confirms the fact of the miracle.[26]

---

[21] See Bultmann, *John*, 121; Thüsing, *Erhöhung*, 94; Schnackenburg, *John* 1:328–31; Hofbeck, *Semeion*, 94ff.; Lindars, *John*, 129; Olsson, *Structure and Meaning*, 43ff.

[22] See Fortna, *Gospel*, 32; Boismard and Lamouille, *Jean*, 101–2; Becker, *Johannes* 1:107. Wellhausen refers the expression to the editor of the "basic document" (*Evangelium Johannis*, 13). Heekerens considers all of v. 6 redactional (*Zeichen-Quelle*, 70-71).

[23] See Becker, *Johannes* 1:107.

[24] See Blass-Debrunner-Funk §442, 20.

[25] Cf. Schmidt, "Der johanneische Charakter," 35; Bultmann, *John*, 118 n. 5; Fortna, *Gospel*, 33; Wilkens, *Zeichen und Werke*, 31; Becker, *Johannes* 1:107. Heekerens also regards v. 9a (τὸ ὕδωρ οἶνον γεγενημένον [the water that had become wine]) as a redactional insertion (*Zeichen-Quelle*, 70). But this observation is a precondition for the point of the story in v. 10!

[26] Against Rissi, who considers v. 10 secondary ("Hochzeit," 78). He thinks that ὑστερή-σαντος οἴνου [the wine being lacking, deficient], as the original reading in v. 3, says only that there was no wine at all for the wedding. Then the longer reading, represented by, among others, the first hand of Sinaiticus, attempts to rectify the resulting contradiction to v. 10. In addition, Rissi considers the "rule for wine" an ad hoc construction for which there are no parallels in the ancient world. Finally, the point of the narrative is supposed to be the contrast between water and wine, not between bad wine and good wine. Against Rissi we must object that the shorter reading in v. 3 does not necessarily say that there had been no wine before this moment (see Wilkens, *Zeichen und Werke*, 31 n. 12). Moreover, it is possible that the longer reading,

Verse 11, which is crucial for understanding the miracle story, should be attributed entirely to the Johannine redaction.[27] This conclusion is based primarily on linguistic evidence: (1) Sentences beginning with a preliminary ταῦτα [this] are typically Johannine (1:28; 6:6, 59; 8:20; 9:22; 10:6; 12:16; 19:36). The closest parallel to 2:11 is 12:37: τοσαῦτα . . . σημεῖα.[28] (2) The expression ποιεῖν σημεῖα is redactional, apart from the major miracle stories, in 2:23; 6:14, 30; 7:31; 10:41; 12:18, 37, and a redactional origin should be posited in 3:2; 4:54; 9:16; 11:47; 20:30.[29] (3) In the Gospel of John and 1 and 2 John, ἀρχή [beginning, first] occurs 18 times, and of those occurrences only in John 1:1, 2 can a tradition be presumed. In the present instance, ἀρχή describes both Jesus' first miracle and the beginning of Jesus' public ministry as a whole. (4) The place designation Κανὰ τῆς Γαλιλαίας was taken over by the evangelist from v. 1.[30] (See the note in John 4:46a, which is also redactional.) (5) A central concept in the Johannine view of revelation is φανεροῦν [manifest, make visible] (18 times in the Gospel of John and 1 John; the closest parallel is John 17:6).[31] (6) In addition, δόξα [glory] (19 times in the Gospel of John) and πιστεύειν εἰς [to believe in] (36 times in the Gospel of John) are also undoubtedly Johannine.[32] (7) John took οἱ μαθηταὶ αὐτοῦ [his disciples] from v. 2. Μαθητής in the plural with a

---

as given by the first hand of Sinaiticus, is original (so Fortna, *Gospel,* 30–31; Boismard and Lamouille, *Jean,* 100; Heekerens, *Zeichen-Quelle,* 64; cf., to the contrary, Metzger, *Textual Commentary,* 201). In any case, at this point we need to raise the methodological question whether highly uncertain text-critical decisions should determine the interpretation. Rissi's attempt simply to declare useless all the parallels adduced by Windisch ("Die johanneische Weinregel") must also be called into question. But what speaks most decisively against Rissi is the form-critical observation that v. 10 establishes the reality of the miracle: it has the function of confirming that a miracle has taken place. Since the indirect description of the process of the miracle is characteristic of a "gift miracle," v. 10 is an indispensable constituent element of the form.

[27] Against Schottroff, *Der Glaubende,* 245; Richter, "Semeia-Quelle," 284; Becker, *Johannes* 1:107 (who assign all of v. 11 to the "source"). Bultmann attributes v. 11b to the evangelist (*John,* 115), but see *Johannes* EH, 20, where Bultmann says that the whole of v. 11 except οἱ μαθηταὶ αὐτοῦ [his disciples] is traditional. The assignment of v. 11b to the evangelist is found also in Schnackenburg, *John* 1:334; Wilkens, *Zeichen und Werke,* 30; Schulz, *Johannes,* 47; Heekerens, *Zeichen-Quelle,* 75; Boismard and Lamouille, *Jean,* 101–2. Fortna (*Gospel,* 37), Nicol (*Semeia,* 31), and Teeple (*Origin,* 172) regard v. 11b as redactional, but v. 11 a,c as traditional.

Against Fortna (*Gospel,* 35–36) and Heekerens (*Zeichen-Quelle,* 26–27) one should read (with NA[26]) ἐποίησεν ἀρχὴν τῶν σημείων [he did the first of the signs] (p[66c] p[75vid] A B L et al.).

[28] See Olsson, *Structure and Meaning,* 262 n. 26.

[29] For the reasoning supporting this point, see section 3.8 below.

[30] See Fortna, *Gospel,* 36–37.

[31] In Nicol's work, φανεροῦν is characteristic No. 72.

[32] See Schnackenburg, *John* 1:336 n. 2; πιστεύειν εἰς is Ruckstuhl's characteristic No. 42.

possessive pronoun following occurs 34 times. Thus on the linguistic level there is no reason to reject the evangelist's authorship even of parts of v. 11.[33]

As regards content, two arguments (the numbering of the miracle in v. 11a and the concept of faith in v. 11c) are repeatedly cited[34] to prove that v. 11 is at least partly traditional. Of course, in such cases the existence of a "signs source" is presumed—a presupposition that cannot be sustained on the basis of John 2:1-11 and therefore should not determine the interpretation a priori. In addition, it can be shown that both the enumeration and the relationship between signs and faith are traceable to John.[35]

The background of the Cana pericope in the tradition and in the history of religions can no longer be defined with certainty. It cannot be traced to the Old Testament idea of the wedding as the beginning of the messianic age,[36] nor is a pagan traditional background (Dionysus cult), as posited by Bultmann, probable, as the thorough study by H. Noetzel has shown.[37] Again, a sacramental interpretation according to which

---

[33] E. Schweitzer has some good reasons for calling John 2:1-10 an "erratic block" (*Ego Eimi*, 100). The series of *hapax legomena*, unique in the Fourth Gospel, justify this assessment of vv. 1-10, but not of v. 11, which Schweitzer is careful not to include in the text he is describing. For the Johannine flavor of v. 11, see also Ruckstuhl, *Einheit*, 110.

[34] See only Fortna, *Gospel*, 37.

[35] See section 3.1.3 below and the excursus, "Miracle Stories in John's Gospel."

[36] Against Jeremias, *Jesus als Weltvollender*, 21–29; Heekerens, *Zeichen-Quelle*, 97; Brown, *John* 1:105; for a critique, see also Broer, "'Ableitung,'" 109.

[37] Noetzel, *Christus und Dionysos*; his position has been generally accepted, but see Linnemann, "Hochzeit zu Kana," 415ff.; Jeremias, *Theology* 1:88; Becker, *Johannes* 1:110–11; Koester, *Introduction* 2:184; Broer, "'Ableitung,'" 111ff.

Noetzel's principal argument against Bultmann (*Christus und Dionysos*, 27) is that it is not reported anywhere "that Dionysos changed water into wine." Particularly problematic in Bultmann's interpretation is his statement that "[t]here can be no doubt that the story has been taken over from heathen legend and ascribed to Jesus" (*John*, 118). This posits not only a religious-historical analogy, but a tradition-historical connection to the Dionysus cult, which is hardly probable. The only parallel that can be perceived between the Dionysus cult and John 2:1-11 is the abundance of wine.

Noetzel frequently emphasizes that there are neither Jewish nor pagan Hellenistic parallels for the changing of water into wine. Not even Philo asserts that the Logos changes water into wine. According to *All.* 3.82, the Logos reflected in Melchizedek bestows on the soul wine in place of water (ἀντὶ ὕδατος, οἶνον προσφερέτω). In *Som.* 2.249, the Logos is called οἰνοχόος τοῦ θεοῦ [God's cup-bearer]. On the other hand, too little attention has been paid to Philostratus *Vita Apol.* 6.10 (suggested long ago by Wettstein, *Novum Testamentum* 1:847). I believe this to be the only place in which the motif of water changed into wine can be found; see also Petzke, *Apollonius*, 178; Bauer, *Johannesevangelium*, 47. It is said of Apollonius, "And yet it would be just as easy for him to convulse the whole mountain of Parnassus, and to alter the springs of the Castalian fountain so that it should run with wine. . . ." The further texts introduced by Broer ("'Ableitung,'" 114–19; especially Pliny *Nat. Hist.* 2.231; Lucian *Ver. Hist.* 1.7; Philostratus *Imag.* 1.14) do not contain transformation motifs that are in any way as clear as that in Philostratus *Vita Apol.* 6.10. It would appear that the transformation motif that is central in John 2:1-11 appears only in the pagan Hellenistic context, but not in the Old Testament or in ancient Judaism!

the marriage feast at Cana would be a reference to the eucharistic meal has no real basis in the text; it rests on association of motifs (wine as element of the Lord's Supper) and ultimately comes close to being an allegorical interpretation.[38] A dependence on the Elias tradition is frequently suggested (Jesus as Elias *redivivus*), but the suggestion is not persuasive because the genuine parallels are too few.[39]

The miracle at Cana is Johannine special material characterized by a spare narrative style and a total concentration on the reality of the miracle and the power of the wonder-worker. Form-critically, the pericope is a "gift miracle"[40] in the classic style (vv. 1-2, exposition; vv. 3-5, preparation for the miracle; vv. 6-8, indirect description of the miraculous event; vv. 9-10, concluding confirmation of the miracle). Parallels in the "gift miracle" form can be found in Luke 5:1-11; John 6:1-15 par.

3.1.3   Interpretation

The Johannine understanding of the Cana miracle is unfolded in v. 11: in this miracle, Jesus reveals his δόξα, and through the miracle his disciples come to believe in him. As the *doxa* of Jesus reveals itself and becomes visible in the incarnation (1:14), so the miracle is not only an indication of the *doxa*, but an expression of the *doxa* itself (cf. 11:4, 40; 12:41). In no way is the earthly *doxa* of Jesus merely an anticipatory image or indication of the *doxa* present in Jesus' preexistence and exaltation. Instead, the one *doxa* of Jesus manifests itself in different ways.[41] Jesus never departed from the one *doxa* with the Father. Even during his earthly activity, the Father was always with him (8:54; 16:32), and at the end Jesus returns to the *doxa* with the Father

---

[38] Against Bauer, *Johannesevangelium,* 46–47; Strathmann, *Johannes,* 58–59; Cullmann, *Early Christian Worship,* 70; idem, *The Johannine Circle,* 16–17; Rissi, "Hochzeit," 87ff.; Heekerens, *Zeichen-Quelle,* 73; Léon-Dufour, *Abendmahl und Abschiedsrede,* 344.

[39] Against Betz, "Das Problem des Wunders," 38ff.; Leidig, *Jesu Gespräch,* 255–56; Reim, *Hintergrund,* 207–8, 218; Nicol, *Semeia,* 53, 55, 67; Boismard and Lamouille, *Jean,* 104. Linnemann ("Hochzeit zu Kana," 40ff. and Broer ("'Ableitung,'" 107–10) give an extensive critique of attempts to derive the story from Old Testament and Jewish sources.

[40] See Theissen, *Miracle Stories,* 103–6; Bauer speaks of an "extravagant miracle" (*Johannesevangelium,* 46).

[41] The basic monograph on the Johannine concept of *doxa* is still Thüsing, *Die Erhöhung und Verherrlichung Jesu im Johannesevangelium.* Thüsing distinguishes two stages in Jesus' glorification: (1) the earthly work of Jesus, extending until his "hour," with its accent on Jesus' obedience (see p. 100), and (2) Jesus' work beyond the "hour," marked by the effects of his exaltation. This appears "as Jesus' rule, through faith, over human beings whom the Father draws to him, as the giving of life and as judgment, and finally as the work of the Paraclete" (p. 101). Blank ("Krisis," 268–76) accurately criticizes Thüsing. Blank emphasizes that Thüsing's two stages cannot be sharply distinguished from one another; instead, the passion and cross already represent the beginning of Jesus' glorification. There is only one work of revelation, salvation, and glorification. "Consequently, the two stages, as proposed by Thüsing, must be abandoned because they are inadequate to the unity of Johannine thought" ("Krisis," 269 n. 11). For further critique of Thüsing, see Schnackenburg, *John* 2:402–3; Hofbeck, *Semeion,* 98ff.; Riedl, *Heilswerk,* 77.

(17:5).[42] The distinction between preexistent (17:5b,c, 24cd; 12:41), earthly visible (1:14cd; 2:11b; 11:4, 40), and postexistence *doxa* (17:1b, 5, 10b, 22, 24c)[43] is appropriate for describing the temporal dimensions and mutually supportive aspects of the Johannine notion of *doxa,* but it cannot deny the substantial unity of the Johannine *doxa* concept. Insofar as *doxa,* for John, means nothing other than Jesus' divinity, which he had before the foundation of the world, now revealed in his earthly activity (especially in the miracles!) and demonstrated in the event of the cross, in which he both fulfilled the Father's *doxa* and made the gift of *doxa* available to the community, we must maintain the unity in principle of Johannine *doxa* theology.

If, therefore, preexistence *doxa* and postexistence *doxa* are identical (17:5), and if, at the end of his work, the Son is glorified by the Father (13:31a, 32; 17:1a, 5; etc.) and the Father by the Son (13:31b; 17:1b, 4), and if the glorification of Jesus makes possible the gift of the Spirit (7:39) and the bestowal of *doxa* on the disciples (17:22; see also 17:24; 16:14), then the miracle, like the incarnation, is the locus of the epiphany and glorification of the Son, and thus also of the Father (2:11; 11:4, 40; 12:41; 17:4).

With the word φανεροῦν, John designates this deed of power as a revelatory event, for in the Fourth Gospel this concept characterizes both the revelatory work of the fleshly Jesus as a whole (see 1:31; 3:21; 17:6), and his miraculous deeds in particular (see 2:11; 7:3-4; 9:3).[44] The revelation of *doxa* in miracles evokes faith. This process is fulfilled for the disciples in an exemplary fashion in this first miracle. Here John demonstrates, using a completely nondualist terminology, how he interprets the relationship between miracles and faith: it is not faith that sees the miracle; rather, faith is brought into being through the revelation of the *doxa* of the Incarnate One in the miracle.[45] Since the miracle is the locus of revelation of the *doxa* of the fleshly Jesus, it can lead to faith. Here the christological intent of the evangelist is visible: John is interested neither in miraculous faith nor in a diminishment of the miracle; his only interest is in depicting the *doxa* of the Incarnate One and thereby showing the reality of the incarnation. John emphasizes this fact—that the Word has really become flesh—in a twofold way in the Cana miracle: Like all Johannine miracles, the event at Cana can scarcely be surpassed in its material consequences; it effects demonstrable changes in space and time (the wine can be tasted by the "neutral" steward of the feast), and it points to the fleshly existence of the miracle worker. But at the same time, in its very massiveness, the miracle is the locus of revelation

---

[42] See Hegermann, *EWNT* 1:839.

[43] See Riedl, *Heilswerk,* 129.

[44] In addition, in John 21:1, 14 φανεροῦν describes the revelations of the Risen One, and in 1 John 2:28; 3:2 the revelation of the one who is to come.

[45] Against Hofbeck, for whom the revelation of the glory is "visible only to the eyes of faith" (*Semeion,* 102). Thus also Walter, "Auslegung überlieferter Wundererzählungen," 97.

of the *doxa* of the Incarnate One, for the reality of incarnation contains both aspects: visibility in space and time, and illumination of the δόξα of the Pre-existent One, which causes faith.

In addition, John uses the concept of δόξα to connect Jesus' miracle working with the beginning and end of his whole activity: incarnation and glorification. The miracles are not an episode in the life and activity of the fleshly Jesus; they certainly are not restricted to being mere indicators, nor are they to be understood symbolically.[46] Rather, in them is manifested the one *doxa* of Jesus, which first became visible for all in the incarnation and will also be visible in the hour of his death. This gives us a basis from which to explain the redactional additions in v. 1 (τῇ ἡμέρᾳ τῇ τρίτῃ) and in v. 4c (οὔπω ἥκει ἡ ὥρα μου): Jesus' "hour" is that of his final glorification (12:23, 16),[47] and the illumination of the *doxa* in the miracle is not only an indication of the incarnation but is also always a pointer to the passion that is to come. The concept of *doxa* makes it possible for John to connect incarnation, miracle working, and passion, to set forth his *theologia crucis* at the very beginning of Jesus' public activity, without creating tensions between the *doxa* of preexistence, miracle, and exaltation. The Johannine insertion of κατὰ τὸν καθαρισμὸν τῶν Ἰουδαίων in v. 6 reveals a certain distance from Judaism (cf. Mark 7:3-4); the abundance of wine, in contrast to the Jews' water jars, points to a surpassing of the old order of salvation through the Christ-event (cf. 1:17). With πόθεν ἐστίν [where (it) came from], the parenthesis in v. 9 receives a christological dimension (cf. 7:27; 8:14; 9:29-30; 19:9): the miracle witnesses to the divine origin of the miracle worker.

The Cana pericope is of special importance, both for the Johannine conception of miracles and for Johannine theology as a whole. John has Jesus' public ministry begin with a miracle story that, through its highly condensed narrative style and the material nature of the miracle itself, draws attention solely to the one who accomplishes the miracle. The evangelist picks up in v. 11 this total concentration on the miracle worker. Here he describes not only the place and effect of Jesus' first miracle, but by means of the *doxa* concept he brings miracle, incarnation, and glorification into relationship with one another and emphasizes the centrality of Jesus' miracle-working activity: in the miracles there stands revealed the one *doxa* of the Preexistent and Exalted One, the *doxa* that evokes faith.

---

[46] Against Bultmann, *Theology* 2:44: "They [sc. σημεῖα] are pictures, symbols."

[47] Thüsing opts not to interpret the revelation of the δόξα in 2:11 as δοξασθῆναι, since in his opinion the verb is primarily connected with the "hour" of glorification (*Erhöhung*, 240ff., 321–22). But it is precisely that connection that is effected in 2:1-11 by the redactional addition in v. 4c!

3.2 John 4:46-54

3.2.1 Context

The first part of Jesus' public activity ends as it began: with a miracle in Cana. The express reference to the wine miracle in 4:46a shows that, in the evangelist's composition, chapters 2–4 constitute a unit.[48] Although after the first miracle Jesus' symbolic action of cleansing the temple had awakened Jewish enmity against him and strengthened the faith of the disciples (2:22), the crowd believed in him because of the miracle (2:23). As at the outset he showed himself, in contrast to Jewish officialdom and to the Samaritans, as the one who brings rebirth, everlasting life, and living water, so the circle of Jesus' first official appearance closes with the healing of the son of a royal official. In 2:11 it was the disciples, in 2:23 the people of Jerusalem, and in 4:39 a Samaritan woman who came to believe; now, in 4:46-54 it is a Gentile[49] who believes in Jesus because of a σημεῖον. In addition, the thrice-repeated ζῆν [to live] in 4:50, 51, 53 ties the miracle story to the preceding conversation between Jesus and the Samaritan woman. If Jesus appeared there as the one who gives living water and everlasting life (4:10, 11, 14, 36), now the healing of the son of a βασιλικός [royal official] can be understood as an illustration of these fundamental truths.

3.2.2 Redaction and Tradition

The itinerary in v. 46a is the work of the evangelist.[50] This is evident from the express reference to the wine miracle,[51] the Johannine style (οὖν, πάλιν, Κανὰ τῆς Γαλιλαίας), and the second reference to the place in v. 46b. This v. 46b, which was part of the original story, raises the question whether

---

[48] See Barrett, *John,* 246; Schnackenburg, *John* 2:282–83.

[49] The word βασιλικός can mean a man of royal descent, a royal official, or even a soldier in the royal service (see the instances in Bauer, *Johannesevangelium,* 77). The evident relationship of this story to that of the centurion from Capernaum makes the last interpretation the most likely, so that in John also the man is a Gentile; this position is now represented also by the work of Wegner, *Hauptmann,* 57–72 (with an extensive presentation of the material), and Mead, "βασιλικός," 69ff. Most of the commentators interpret βασιλικός as referring to a Jew. This overlooks the fact that John never says that clearly at any point. It should be admitted, however, that the father's origin no longer has the significance in John that it had in the Synoptic tradition.

[50] See Bultmann, *John,* 206; Wilkens, *Zeichen und Werke,* 33; Schnider and Stenger, *Johannes und die Synoptiker,* 66ff.; A. Dauer, *Johannes und Lukas,* 51–52; Fortna, *Gospel,* 39; Teeple, *Origin,* 180; Schnackenburg, *John* 1:470; E. Schweizer, "Heilung," 407; Wegner, *Hauptmann,* 22. On the other hand, Becker assigns v. 46a to his "semeia source," founding his assertion simply on a reference to John 2:1, 11 (*Johannes* 1:185).

[51] For the Johannine stylistic element of the backward reference, see 1:30; 6:65; 13:33; 15:20; 16:15; 18:9.

the healing at a distance originally took place in Capernaum in the Johannine tradition also and was transferred to Cana by the evangelist through the insertion of v. 46a. In favor of this is John 2:12, a verse that has no proper meaning in its present context but would be an ideal introduction to 4:46b.[52] In that case, Jesus would have gone to Capernaum with his family and done the healing there. The evangelist would have had a double tradition, as in chapter 6, with one miracle story taking place in Cana, the other (as in the Synoptics) in Capernaum. John separated the two miracle stories and transferred the second miracle to Cana as well, in order to finish Jesus' first public appearance with a "ring composition," and because Cana was very important to him as a special place of Jesus' activity.[53] If the story took place at Capernaum in the Johannine tradition also, a large part of v. 47a (ἐκ τῆς ᾿Ιουδαίας εἰς τὴν Γαλιλαίαν [from Judea to Galilee], καταβῇ καί [come down and]) must be assigned to the redaction, since Jesus' coming from Judea into Galilee presumes the present context.[54]

There is a broad consensus on the redactional character of v. 48;[55] however, the interpretation of the verse is disputed. Is John, with the singular σημεῖα καὶ τέρατα [signs and wonders],[56] rejecting an interpretation of miracles that sees them merely as this-worldly demonstrations of power and legitimations of the wonder-worker?[57] Does he mean to criticize faith that is based merely on miracles, in order to demonstrate his own understanding of the traditional story or its concept of miracles?[58] These explanations, which are

---

[52] See Schnider and Stenger, *Johannes und die Synoptiker*, 66ff.; Bultmann, *John*, 206; Dauer, *Johannes und Lukas*, 52–53.

[53] See Kundzins, *Topologische Überlieferungsstoffe*, 22ff.

[54] See Bultmann, who considers ἐκ τῆς ᾿Ιουδαίας εἰς τὴν Γαλιλαίαν and καταβῇ καί redactional (*John* 206); Fortna, *Gospel*, 39–40. Schnider and Stenger think, with some justice, that "going down" in vv. 49, 51 is also redactional (*Johannes und die Synoptiker*, 68). Schnackenburg holds the passage from ἀκούσας to Γαλιλαίαν in v. 46b, καταβῇ καί in v. 47b, and ἤμελλεν γὰρ ἀποθνῄσκειν in v. 47c to be redactional (*John* 1:466, 470); so do Teeple, *Origin*, 180–81 (though the latter assigns καταβῇ καί [come down and] to the "source" and thinks that ἠρώτα [asked, begged] is an addition by the evangelist); Heekerens suggests an influence from Luke 7:3 (*Zeichen-Quelle*, 53–54). Dauer considers v. 47a redactional and v. 47b traditional (*Johannes und Lukas*, 55–59).

[55] See Schwartz, "Aporien" IV, 511; Bultmann, *John*, 206; Becker, *Johannes* 1:186; Haenchen, *John* 1:234; Schottroff, *Der Glaubende*, 248ff.; Barrett, *John*, 247; E. Schweizer, "Heilung," 407; Schnackenburg, "Traditionsgeschichte," 60–61; Brown, *John* 1:196; Lindars, *John*, 203; Fortna, *Gospel*, 41; Nicol, *Semeia*, 28–29; Schnider and Stenger, *Johannes und die Synoptiker*, 69; Dauer, *Johannes und Lukas*, 59–63; Wegner, *Hauptmann*, 25–26. From the point of view of the language, ἐὰν . . . οὐ μή (Ruckstuhl, No. 44) and οὖν-*historicum* (Ruckstuhl, No. 2) point to Johannine redaction. The shift to the second person plural is also striking.

[56] On the tradition history of this Old Testament expression (Isa. 8:18, 20:3; Jer. 39:20; Deut. 4:34; Exod. 7:3; Wis. 8:8 LXX), see especially Stolz, "Zeichen und Wunder."

[57] This is the pointed conclusion of Schottroff, *Der Glaubende*, 248ff.

[58] So especially Haenchen, "Johanneische Probleme," 88–89; idem, *John* 1:83, 234; Nicol, *Semeia*, 29; Bultmann, *John*, 206–8; Schulz, *Johannes*, 80–81; Schnackenburg, *John* 1:466; Schnider and Stenger, *Johannes und die Synoptiker*, 69; Schweizer, "Heilung," 411ff.; Hahn,

generally accepted in the literature, overlook the fact that here, as in 2:4, the request for the miracle is first rejected, but then the miracle is actually performed and immediately evokes faith.[59] Verse 48 is not an expression of a specifically Johannine critique of miracles; in the rejection of σημεῖα καὶ τέρατα John is in accord with the Synoptic tradition. The Synoptics are also acquainted with the rejection of requests for signs (cf. Mark 8:11-12; Matt. 12:39-42; 16:1-2, 4; Luke 11:16, 29-32; cf. also 1 Cor. 1:22), and the motif of the indifference of the miracle worker in the face of suffering is found in the Synoptic miracle tradition as well (see Mark 6:48; 7:27).[60] Like 2:4, 4:48 is not to be seen as an expression of a Johannine criticism of miracles. John does not reject the miracle as such but only the *demand* for signs and wonders.[61] The evangelist's only response to a simple demand for signs is to point to the death and resurrection of Jesus Christ (cf. John 2:18-22).

L. Schottroff interprets the Gospel of John consistently in the framework of a gnostic dualism, in which a God far removed from the world and a godless world are sharply opposed.[62] She also sees this determinative dualism in the Johannine miracle stories, in which John distinguishes between a "right" miracle faith, whose object is Jesus as the heavenly revealer, and a "wrong" miracle faith, which sees Jesus only as the miracle-man "who brings this-worldly healing."[63] Seeing Jesus correctly means recognizing both his heavenly origin and the opposition between God and the world. On the other hand, this-worldly demonstrations of power by a miracle worker cannot lead to the right faith, because in that case the absolute opposition between God and world goes unrecognized. L. Schottroff finds an example of this interpretation of miracles in John 4:48.[64] This verse is her proof of a Johannine critique of miracles directed "against a this-worldly interpretation of the miracles and the miracle worker."[65] In saying this, she ignores the fact that what is articulated in 4:48 is not a critique of miracles in principle. Instead, as in 2:4, the Johannine Jesus first rejects the simple demand for a miracle, in order to accomplish it afterward. Moreover, there is no dualistic theology in 4:46-54 (nor in 2:1-11); the text instead contradicts Schottroff's analysis, because faith follows immediately on the miracle (v. 53).[66] John 4:46-54 is not a proof of a dualistically oriented Johannine view of miracles. Instead, Schottroff inserts into this text the gnostic dualism of a distant God and a godless world, which is her key to interpreting the Fourth Gospel.

"Glaubensverständnis," 54–55; and Fortna, who speaks of a Johannine rejection of miracles as a basis for faith (*Gospel,* 41).

[59] See Langbrandtner, *Weltferner Gott,* 73.

[60] See Theissen, *Miracle Stories,* 60.

[61] Among those who opt against a comprehensive and fundamental Johannine critique of miracles in v. 48 are Barrett, *John,* 247; Wilkens, *Zeichen und Werke,* 33–34; Langbrandtner, *Weltferner Gott,* 73–74; Heekerens, "Zeichen-Quelle," 80ff.

[62] See Schottroff, *Der Glaubende,* 228ff.

[63] Ibid., 252.

[64] Ibid., 263ff.

[65] Ibid., 256.

[66] See also Langbrandtner, *Weltferner Gott,* 73; Thyen, "Aus der Literatur," *ThR* 39, 235 n. 1.

Verse 49 continues the story from v. 47b; its function is to restore the flow of the story that was interrupted by v. 48. Therefore v. 49a is certainly to be attributed to Johannine redaction,[67] and possibly also the father's second request in v. 49b, this time formulated as direct address.[68] Verse 50 was also part of the original narrative, for it describes Jesus' necessary reaction to the father's repeated plea.[69] The motif of the father's trust (πιστεύειν should be translated as "trust"; cf. Matt. 8:13) is, in different forms, a part of all the variants of this story and was part of the pre-Johannine tradition.[70] The sequence ὁ υἱός σου ζῇ—ἐπίστευσεν [your son will live . . . he believed] is striking; it is repeated in v. 53b. While in v. 50b "belief" refers to an unconditional trust in Jesus' promise, the absolute πιστεύειν in v. 53b is the expression of faith based on the miracle that has now been witnessed; this is clearly an intensification.

In vv. 51 and 52, which are part of the tradition,[71] it is, in contrast to the Synoptics, the servants who, "assisted by the motif of the 'hour,'"[72] testify to the healing that has occurred. In v. 53a there are a considerable number of characteristic elements of Johannine language and style (γινώσκειν [know], πατήρ [father], οὖν-*historicum*, reference to a saying of Jesus—cf. John 5:11-12; 7:33ff.; 16:16-19; etc.) that might suggest redaction.[73] On the other hand, the motif of validation of the wonder-worker, which dominates v. 53a, is one of the fixed formal elements of healings done at a distance. It is expressly noted that the miracle occurred at the hour when the wonder-worker spoke the word that effected the miracle (cf. Mark 7:29; Matt. 8:13; Ber 34b Bar).[74] This form-critical observation speaks in favor of v. 53a as part of the tradition. The reaction to the verification of the miracle is depicted in v. 53b: the βασιλικός and his whole household (cf. Acts 10:2; 11:4; 16:15, 31; 18:8) come to believe; that is, they become Christians.[75] As in 2:11, seeing

---

[67] See Fortna, *Gospel,* 41.

[68] So Bultmann, *John,* 206; Wilkens, *Zeichen und Werke,* 33; Haenchen, "Johanneische Probleme," 88; idem, *John* 1:234–35; Schnider and Stenger, *Johannes und die Synoptiker,* 69; Becker, *Johannes* 1:186; Heekerens, "Zeichen-Quelle," 67; Dauer, *Johannes und Lukas,* 63.

[69] On the motif of Jesus' miraculous foreknowledge, see section 3.4.2 below.

[70] Against Fortna, *Gospel,* 42; Schnider and Stenger, *Johannes und die Synoptiker,* 70; and Dauer, who attributes v. 50b to John (*Johannes und Lukas,* 65–66). Correctly: Barrett, *John,* 248.

[71] Except for 13:24 (where the text tradition is uncertain), πυνθάνομαι [to inquire] occurs only here. Against Boismard and Lamouille, who consider v. 51 redactional (*Jean,* 146).

[72] Theissen, *Miracle Stories,* 188. The "motif of the hour" is hinted at already in Matt. 8:13 and is a stylistically appropriate continuation of v. 51. This form-critical observation speaks against all attempts to see v. 52 (and 53a) as redactional: against Schwartz, "Aporien" IV, 511; Wilkens, *Zeichen und Werke,* 34; Heekerens, *Zeichen-Quelle,* 60ff.

[73] Among those who argue for redaction are Fortna, *Gospel,* 43; Wilkens, *Zeichen und Werke,* 34; Heekerens, *Zeichen-Quelle,* 60.

[74] See Bultmann, *History of the Synoptic Tradition,* 225.

[75] See Barrett, *John,* 248; Fortna, *Gospel,* 43; Dodd, *Interpretation,* 185.

the miracle results immediately in belief. It is not faith that beholds the miracle; instead, faith comes to be as a result of the miracle.[76] The dependence of faith on the seeing of the miracle is already present in the tradition, but it is adopted by the evangelist and has been shown to be redactional in 2:11. It leaves no room for a dualistic theology.

We must credit v. 54 entirely to Johannine redaction.[77] This is indicated by the structure, parallel to 2:11, and by the Johannine πάλιν [again] and ἐλθών [coming], as well as the expression ἐκ τῆς Ἰουδαίας εἰς τὴν Γαλιλαίαν [from Judea to Galilee], which presupposes the present context.[78] The overworked argument concerning the enumeration of the miracles is just what does *not* testify to a "source," since δεύτερον [second] merely says that the healing of the son of a βασιλικός was Jesus' second miracle *in Cana*. For the same reason there is no tension between 4:54 and the summary statement about miracles in 2:23 (and 4:45), which does not refer to miracles in Cana.

3.2.3   *John 4:46-54 in Relationship to Matthew 8:5-13/Luke 7:1-10*

Now that the Johannine tradition has been reconstructed, our first task is to investigate the parallel traditions in the Synoptics before we can give a concluding interpretation of the second miracle at Cana. The following agreements show that there is a common tradition behind all three narratives:[79] (1) A Gentile holding a high position in the service of King Herod Antipas approaches Jesus and requests the healing of one of his dependents. (2) The sick person is in Capernaum. (3) Jesus accedes to the request. (4) The petitioner trusts Jesus. (5) Jesus works the miracle without visiting the house of the sick person. (6) The healing takes place when Jesus speaks the effective word.

But, in addition to these common features, there are some serious differences: (1) In John, the principal action takes place not in Capernaum but in Cana. (2) The Synoptic ἐκατόνταρχος [centurion] has become a βασιλικός [royal official] in John. (3) Matthew calls the sick person παῖς

---

[76] See Langbrandtner, *Weltferner Gott,* 73.

[77] Against Bultmann, *John,* 209; Haenchen, *John* 1:235–36; Fortna, *Gospel,* 44; Schulz, *Johannes,* 81; Nicol, *Semeia,* 28; Becker, *Johannes* 1:186; Schnackenburg, *John* 1:470; E. Schweizer, "Heilung," 407; Heekerens, *Zeichen-Quelle,* 63; Teeple, *Origin,* 181; Lindars, *John,* 205; Dauer, *Johannes und Lukas,* 71–72; Wegner, *Hauptmann,* 29–30, who, especially with reference to the enumeration and the supposed contradiction to 2:23, want to assign all of v. 54 or at least v. 54a to the tradition, or to a "semeia source." In favor of the redactional character of 4:54 (and 2:11), in my opinion, is the observation that, in the rabbinic and the pagan miracle traditions, this type of summarizing verse is placed at the beginning of the narrative. (See the references in Theissen, *Miracle Stories,* 128.)

[78] Wilkens also considers v. 54 redactional (*Zeichen und Werke,* 34–35).

[79] For the agreements and differences, see Schnider and Stenger, *Johannes und die Synoptiker,* 57; Schnackenburg, *John* 1:472; Haenchen, "Johanneische Probleme," 82ff.; idem, *John* 1:236–38; Dauer, *Johannes und Lukas,* 39–44; Wegner, *Hauptmann,* 18ff.

[child]; in Luke he is a δοῦλος [servant], and in John he is called υἱός [son]. (4) The details concerning the sick person also vary. Matthew speaks of lameness, John of a fever, and in Luke the δοῦλος is at the point of death. (5) In Luke, in contrast to Matthew and John, it is not the centurion himself who requests the healing but two messengers from him. (6) The centurion's statement of faith, which is central to the narratives in Matthew and Luke, is missing from John. (7) Matthew integrates a saying of Jesus into the story of the centurion of Capernaum; Luke has the saying in a different context, and it is entirely lacking in John. (8) In John, the establishment of the fact of the miracle is more fully described than in the Synoptics.

A tradition-critical explanation of this situation must begin with the Q material, as probably the oldest level of tradition that can be reconstructed. The present position of the pericope in Matthew and Luke still shows that in Q also it was placed just after the Sermon on the Plain or Sermon on the Mount.[80] At the beginning, Matthew is closer to Q than is Luke.[81] This is seen from the designation of the boy as παῖς, which is found also in Luke 7:7b;[82] from the immediate appearance[83] and direct address of the centurion; from the father's description of the illness; and finally from the description of the sickness with the term παραλυτικός [paralyzed].[84] In Q, the description of the illness was followed by Jesus' readiness to undertake the healing (cf. Matt. 8:7). At the center of the Q tradition was the centurion's statement of faith (Matt. 8:8-9/Luke 7:6b, 7b, 8).[85] It was followed by Jesus' closing words (Matt. 8:10/Luke 7:9) as "the real point of the whole anecdote."[86] The established fact of the miracle concluded the narrative (Matt. 8:13/Luke 7:10).[87]

Except for the controversy over Beelzebul (Matt. 12:22-23 par.), the narrative of the centurion of Capernaum is the only miracle story in Q. Although the Sayings Source mentions Jesus' miracles (see Matt. 11:5, 21-22 par.), it seems to have remained aloof from the miracle tradition as a whole.[88] This is apparent in the very fact of its inclusion of a healing at a distance, in which, since it is a special form of the miracle tradition, miraculous elements are almost entirely absent and all the weight lies on the dialogue

---

[80] See Strecker, *Weg der Gerechtigkeit,* 99.

[81] Ibid.; Schulz, *Q,* 236ff. The detailed analysis of the word statistics, which cannot be repeated here, will be found in Schulz's work.

[82] See Schulz, *Q,* 236 n. 400; Schnider and Stenger, *Johannes und die Synoptiker,* 60–61. On the other hand, Haenchen thinks that δοῦλος was already part of a pre-Lukan tradition ("Johanneische Probleme," 84–85).

[83] See Strecker, *Weg der Gerechtigkeit,* 99.

[84] See Schulz, *Q,* 237.

[85] For the details, see Schulz, *Q,* 238–39.

[86] Ibid., 243.

[87] Both verses have been thoroughly redacted, but they agree in their content, to the extent that the verification of the miracle was the end of the story. See Schulz, *Q,* 239–40.

[88] Ibid., 240.

between the petitioner and the wonder-worker, as well as on the wonder-working word (cf. Mark 7:24-30).[89] Here too the dialogue between Jesus and the centurion constitutes the center of the narrative; it emphasizes the unheard-of faith of a Gentile in Jesus' miraculous power.[90] The centurion's confession of faith is applied in Jesus' λέγω ὑμῖν [I say to you] saying, the real climax of the narrative. It is true that this saying does not surrender the primacy of Israel; the pericope is "written from the standpoint of Israel."[91] Jesus does not enter a Gentile's house. Instead, the unconditioned faith of the centurion is the exception, the "ideal case" that shames Israel.[92]

It is different in Matthew: his inclusion of vv. 11-12 (Luke 13:28-29)[93] introduces an anti-Jewish accent into the original story. The exemplary faith of the centurion demonstrates Israel's unbelief; this presages the rejection of the chosen people. It is not the heirs of the kingdom who will be with Abraham, Isaac, and Jacob, but the "many" will be called and the heirs will be dismissed.[94] From the evangelist's point of view, the faith of the centurion of Capernaum predicts, even in the lifetime of Jesus, what in the time of the Gentile Christian Matthew is already past: the rejection of Israel and the transfer of the βασιλεία [kingdom] to "another people" (see Matt. 21:33-46).[95]

Luke has reshaped the Q version of the story much more thoroughly than Matthew. His redaction produced the description of the situation in v. 2, the designation of the sick person as δοῦλος, the dramatic depiction of the illness, the two sets of messengers in vv. 3-6a, and the shape of the final verse.[96] Especially by the introduction of the second group of messengers, Luke shifts the focus of the narrative from the dialogue between Jesus and the centurion to a description of the sequence of events that is studded with dramatic elements.[97] Luke's interpretation of the Q material is particularly

---

[89] On the great similarity between Mark 7:24-30 and John 4:46-54, see Dodd, *Tradition,* 188–95.

[90] See Haenchen, "Johanneische Probleme," 83: "This faith, and not Jesus' deed of healing, is really the center of the story."

[91] Strecker, *Weg der Gerechtigkeit,* 100.

[92] Haenchen, "Johanneische Probleme," 83.

[93] The form transmitted by Luke may be the original; for details, see Strecker, *Weg der Gerechtigkeit,* 100.

[94] Ibid., 101.

[95] See Haenchen, "Johanneische Probleme," 83–84.

[96] For a thorough analysis, see Busse, *Die Wunder des Propheten Jesus,* 144–50 (with discussion of the literature). Haenchen regards the two sets of messengers as a "failed revision" of the Q tradition by Jewish Christian circles at a pre-Lukan stage of development ("Johanneische Probleme," 84ff.); Dauer also considers the two sets of messengers pre-Lukan (*Johannes und Lukas,* 93–94). This idea is inaccurate, because both the language and the theological interest point to Lukan redaction; for the details, see Busse, *Die Wunder des Propheten Jesus,* 142ff.; and Schnider and Stenger, *Johannes und die Synoptiker,* 60–63. This criticism applies also to Theissen, who wishes to assign only the second set of messengers to Luke (*Miracle Stories,* 183).

[97] See Busse, *Die Wunder des Propheten Jesus,* 150ff.

evident in the motif of the two sets of messengers, which echoes the ancient form for petitioning.[98] Here the centurion is presented as a God-fearing friend of the Jewish people (cf. the centurion Cornelius in Acts 10), who thinks himself unworthy to ask Jesus to heal his slave. Therefore he sends Jewish elders and friends to make the request in his stead. The fact that the emphasis in Luke's story lies on the centurion's humility is ultimately illustrated by the deliberate contrast between vv. 4b-5 and vv. 6b-7. Although the elders expressly indicate that they find the centurion worthy, he himself, through the mouths of his friends, emphasizes his unworthiness. Luke uses the example of the centurion of Capernaum to show what real humility is: deprecation of oneself, combined with complete trust and unconditioned faith in Jesus (cf. Luke 18:9-14).[99]

What is the relationship between the pre-Johannine tradition and the three variants of the narrative that have been discussed here? First, we can draw the negative conclusion that the principal themes in the Synoptic traditions (Q: dialogue between Jesus and the centurion; Matthew: the problem of church versus Israel; Luke: the centurion as example of humility) played no part in the form of the story available to John. In the pre-Johannine tradition, the accent is entirely on the process at the end of the narrative by which the fact of the miracle is established. The dialogue between Jesus and the βασιλικός is sharply reduced, and the theological interest concentrates on the description of Jesus' miraculous power, which produces faith. The central interest of the narrative has shifted from the exposition to the conclusion. This very different arrangement leads us to conclude that, although the pre-Johannine tradition and the Synoptic variants all described the same event, there is no literary dependence. If there were, then the substantial differences among the individual narratives would be unexplainable.[100] The very minor agreements in vocabulary are further evidence against literary dependence.

Bultmann supposed that John the evangelist, by inserting vv. 48-49, had "suppressed an original dialogue, which must have corresponded to Mt 8:7-10."[101] But the manner of the Johannine insertion in vv. 48, 49a rather suggests that the evangelist already had a fixed tradition that he was redacting without eliminating any elements of the model before him.[102]

Therefore, we should conclude that John's model document had received its present form in the course of an independent process of Johannine tradition and that the interest of the Johannine communities transmitting it

---

[98] Ibid., 152–53.

[99] Ibid., 155–60; Schnider and Stenger, *Johannes und die Synoptiker,* 78–79.

[100] See Haenchen, *John* 1:236; Schnider and Stenger, *Johannes und die Synoptiker,* 64; Dauer, *Johannes und Lukas,* 120–21.

[101] Bultmann, *John,* 206.

[102] See Haenchen, *John* 1:236–37.

is still visible: the use of the absolute πιστεύειν in v. 53 in the sense of "becoming a Christian" suggests missionary terminology.[103] The missionaries of the Johannine communities campaigned on the basis of the superior miraculous powers of their Lord.[104]

3.2.4 Interpretation

John deliberately closes the first cycle of Jesus' public activity with a second miracle at Cana. This "ring composition" not only reveals the compositional talents of the fourth evangelist but at the same time establishes Jesus' miracle-working abilities as central to his public activity: the miracle visibly demonstrates the divinity of the wonder-worker and evokes faith in the Son of God. Both aspects, already apparent in 2:1-11, are also found in this miracle story.

The evangelist emphasizes the impressiveness of Jesus' second miracle in particular by shifting this healing-at-a-distance to Cana, since the increase in distance underscores the greatness of the miracle. In addition, he adapts a variant tale from his tradition about the centurion of Capernaum, drastically shortening the expositional motifs and placing all the emphasis on the establishing of the truth of the miracle at the end of the story. This also serves to underscore the magnitude of the miraculous deed.

The idea that faith comes about in the face of and because of a miracle, which is also central for John, was already present in the tradition (especially v. 53), so that the evangelist had no need to put a redactional stress on it, as he did in 2:11. There is no expression of a specifically Johannine critique of miracles in v. 48; on the contrary, as in 2:4, Jesus first rejects the request for a miracle in order to fulfill it immediately afterward. In 4:46-54 we do not find a supposed basic dualistic concept in Johannine theology involving a godless world and a God far removed from it. Instead, the evangelist emphasizes, as in 2:1-11, that faith depends on seeing the miracle.

Excursus: Miracle Stories in John's Gospel

Since the work of A. Faure,[105] the enumeration of the miracles in John 2:11 and 4:54, taken together with 20:30, has been an important argument

---

[103] Cf. Acts 11:14; 16:15, 31; 18:8; 1 Cor. 1:16.

[104] See Schnider and Stenger, *Johannes und die Synoptiker*, 80.

[105] See Faure, "Die alttestamentlichen Zitate," 107–12. The precursors of the thesis of a "semeia source" in the broader sense are Wendt and Spitta. Wendt distinguishes between an original discourse level and later narrative material, including the miracle stories (*Schichten im vierten Evangelium,* 35ff.). Spitta includes 2:1-11; 4:46-54; 21:1-14, because of the enumeration of miracles, among those passages in the Gospel that were later inserted by the author of John 21 into a "basic document" (*Johannesevangelium,* 16, 63–70). In 1915, J. M. Thompson

for the thesis that John worked into his Gospel a "semeia source" or a whole gospel of miracles.[106] In the opinion of many exegetes, this proposal is supported also by the summary mention of miracles in 2:23 and 4:45, which apparently contradict the numbers in 2:11 and 4:54.[107]

There are five possibilities for explaining the enumeration of the miracles: (1) The enumeration is a peculiarity of the "semeia source" that John used. But then we must ask why it stops with two. The suggestion that the readers themselves can count seven miracles is not a real answer to this

---

("Structure," 512ff.) spoke of a "semeia source," and in 1921 E. Meyer (*Urgeschichte des Christentums* I/1:332–40) postulated a Johannine "special source," to which most of the miracle stories were to be attributed. But it was only in 1922 that the existence of a pre-Johannine "semeia source" was given substantial foundation by Alexander Faure. In analyzing Old Testament citations in the Fourth Gospel, Faure was struck by the fact that John 12:37 would follow very well on 20:30-31 and that both texts could stand at the end of an independent written source, which he calls the "book of wonders" ("Die alttestamentlichen Zitate," 109). Faure evaluated the enumerations in John 2:11 and 4:54 as a further argument for the existence of a "book of wonders" (p. 110); the same can be said of the miracle stories' concept of faith, which deviates from that in the rest of the Gospel (pp. 111–12). According to Faure, the "book of wonders" would have contained the miracle traditions in John 2, 4, 5, 9, and 11, but not John 6 (p. 109 n. 1).

Among those who have accepted the thesis of a pre-Johannine "semeia source," initiated by Faure and successfully established by Bultmann, are Windisch, *Johannes und die Synoptiker,* 54–55; Käsemann, review of Bultmann, *Johannes,* 186; Conzelmann, *Grundriß,* 354; Bornkamm, "Interpretation," 115–16; Haenchen, "Johanneische Probleme," 28ff. (but now see his *John* 1:89: "It is inordinately risky to posit a semeia source."); Robinson, "The Johannine Trajectory," 235–38; H. W. Kuhn, *Sammlungen,* 210; Schnackenburg, *John* 1:64–68; Grundmann, *Zeugnis und Gestalt,* 14–15; Marxsen, *Einleitung,* 251; Schulz, *Johannes,* 7–8; Schottroff, *Der Glaubende,* 228–96; Lohse, *Entstehung des Neuen Testaments,* 108; Becker, *Johannes* 1:112–20; Fortna, *Gospel,* passim; Nicol, *Semeia,* passim; Martyn, *History and Theology,* 164–66; Smith, "Milieu," passim; Richter, "Semeia-Quelle," 281–87; Fuller, *Interpreting the Miracles,* 88–92; Vielhauer, *Geschichte,* 424; Koester, *Introduction* 2:184–85; Teeple, *Origin,* 143ff.; Schenke and Fischer, *Einleitung* 2:181; Gnilka, *Johannes,* 6; Tiede, *Miracle Worker,* 269ff.; Hoeferkamp, *Relationship,* 55–56; Lona, "Glaube und Sprache," 176ff.; Corsani, *I miracoli di Gesù,* passim; Kysar, *Maverick Gospel,* 15, 72; Weder, "Menschwerdung Gottes," 329.

Those who have taken a critical attitude to the thesis of a "semeia source" include Bauer, *Johannesevangelium,* 250; Dibelius, "Ein neuer Kommentar zum Johannes-Evangelium" (review of Bultmann, *Johannes*) 258–59; Jeremias, review of Bultmann, *Johannes,* 416–17; Michaelis, *Einleitung,* 107–9; Stauffer, review of Bultmann, *Johannes,* 347ff.; Noack, *Zur Johanneische Tradition,* 109ff.; Ruckstuhl, *Einheit,* 107–12, 212–16; Kümmel, *Introduction,* 212–14; Schneider, *Johannes,* 28–29; O. Betz, *EWNT* 3:573; Betz and Grimm, *Wunder Jesu,* 124.

[106] Thus, among others, Bultmann, *John,* 113; Haenchen, *John* 1:236; 2:71–72; Schulz, *Johannes,* 7–8; Schnider and Stenger, *Johannes und die Synoptiker,* 72 n. 19; E. Schweizer, "Heilung," 407 (the first two miracles are from a source); Schnackenburg, *John* 1:335 (the enumeration "may be due to the fact that he follows a σημεῖα-source"); Becker, *Johannes* 1:112ff.; Lindars, *John,* 132; Fortna, *Gospel,* passim; Nicol, *Semeia,* passim.

[107] See only Bultmann, *John,* 113.

question.[108] Moreover, our analysis of the first two miracle stories has shown that 2:11 and 4:54 are redactional. (2) John 4:46-54 is the second miracle that is *narrated;* there is thus no contradiction of 2:23 and 4:45.[109] But even this solution leaves unanswered the question why the enumeration ends at 4:54, since more miracles are still to be told. (3) John the evangelist introduced the enumeration of the miracles generally. Again we must ask why he counts only the first two. (4) Because both miracles are located in Cana, they are designated in the document John is using as the first and second miracles *in Cana.* The enumeration would then be traditional and would deliberately refer only to these first two miracles in Cana. Against this solution is the fact that, according to the analysis we have carried out above, 2:11 and 4:54 are redactional. (5) The enumeration was made by John the evangelist.[110] He counted the two miracles *in Cana* in order to highlight them as the beginning and end of Jesus' first public appearance. In addition, he apparently had a strong interest in Cana as a special place of Jesus' revelations.

In favor of this last explanation is, in the first place, the clearly redactional character of 2:11 and 4:54; second, there is no contradiction between these passages and the summary statements about miracles in 2:23 and 4:45 (events that did not take place in Cana but were deliberately located in hostile Jerusalem); third, the enumeration of the Cana miracles can be understood as a compositional technique of the evangelist (who places the two miracles at Cana at the beginning and end points of Jesus' first public appearance). Finally, 2:11 and 4:54 are in accord with the Johannine method of explication after the fact (cf. 2:17; 7:39; 11:13; 12:16, 33).

The enumeration of miracles in 2:11 and 4:54 is thus not an indication of a pre-Johannine "semeia source" or of a gospel of miracles; it is simply the evidence of Johannine composition.

3.3   John 5:1-9ab

3.3.1   *Context*

The second major section of the Gospel of John (5:1—12:50) also begins with a miracle story and culminates in a miracle: Jesus' raising of Lazarus brings on the Jewish leaders' final decision to put Jesus to death and thus is an important event in salvation history (cf. 11:47-53). Characteristic

---

[108] Against Becker, who thinks that this solves the problem (*Johannes* 1:114).

[109] Thus Conzelmann, *Grundriß,* 377; however, he regards the numbers as redactional.

[110] So Michaelis, *Einleitung,* 168; Ruckstuhl, *Einheit,* 109–10; Noack, *Zur Johanneische Tradition,* 114; Blank, *Johannes* 1:177; Wilkens, *Zeichen und Werke,* 35. Thyen ("Entwicklungen," 275 n. 42), Langbrandtner (*Weltferner Gott,* 71ff.), and Heekerens (*Zeichen-Quelle,* 51ff., 63ff.) see John 2:1-11 and 4:46-54 *not* as the beginning of a pre-Johannine "semeia source" but attribute both miracles to their "redactional level."

of this second section is the steadily increasing tension between Jesus and the Jews (see 5:16, 18; 7:1, 25, 40ff.; 8:44), but also the conflict with the disciples, leading to a division within the group of Jesus' followers (6:66-71).

In the narrower context, the sequence of chapters 5, 6, and 7 presents a problem. Rudolf Bultmann, following English exegetes,[111] attempted a reordering of John 4–7 that is still influential today and represents one of the principal difficulties in Johannine literary criticism. According to Bultmann, if John 6:1 says that Jesus crosses to the other side of the lake, then before that he must have been on this side. But in chapter 5 he is in Jerusalem! On the other hand, chapter 6 would follow conveniently after chapter 4, in which Jesus is already in Galilee. Similarly, chapter 5 fits well with chapter 7, since 7:1 presupposes Jesus' having been in Judea previously. "So the original order must have been chs. 4, 6, 5, 7."[112] But a simple rearrangement of chapters does not come close to solving the problems; in fact, Bultmann also undertakes a reordering within the rearranged chapters and arrives at the following sequence: 4:1-54; 6:1-26, 27a, 34, 35, 30-33, 47-51a, 41-46, 36-40, 59; 5:1-47; 7:15-24; 8:13-20; 7:1-14, 25-29. But how did this disorder in the Gospel come about? Bultmann suspects the principal reason was that before its publication the book was thrown into disorder by some outside disturbance.[113] He also presumes that some portions of text have been lost,[114] speaks of a disjointed text full of omissions,[115] and suggests that some leaves have been reversed or rearranged.[116]

These explanations are not persuasive, because, after the hypothesis of rearranged leaves had rightly been rejected by most present-day researchers,[117] there remained only the "catastrophe theory," which is more a conjecture than a real explanation. In addition, a correct methodology demands that rearrangements of text be proposed only as a last resort. Such reorderings could be made only if it is demonstrated that the order of the text as we have it is completely meaningless. But the traditional sequence of John 4–7 is not incomprehensible; all Bultmann has done is to propose an ordering that, in his opinion, gives a "better meaning."[118]

---

[111] On this point, see the exhaustive description of earlier suggestions for rearrangement in Howard, *Fourth Gospel*, 111–27. Newer theories are reviewed by Thyen, "Aus der Literatur," *ThR* 43, 329ff.

[112] Bultmann, *John*, 209.

[113] See Bultmann, *John*, 220.

[114] Ibid., 315.

[115] Ibid., 222 n. 2. Even earlier, Faure had suggested that "we have to do with an unfinished work, an incomplete draft" ("Zitate," 117).

[116] See Bultmann, "Hirschs Auslegung," 119.

[117] For a critique of this hypothesis of rearranged pages, see Haenchen, *John* 1:48–51; Schnackenburg, *John* 1:53–56; Brown, *John* 1:xxvi–xxviii; Thyen, "Aus der Literatur," *ThR* 39, 302ff.; Langbrandtner, *Weltferner Gott*, 80 n. 5.

[118] Particularly regarding chapter 6, Bultmann concedes that the original order cannot be

The transition from chapter 4 to chapter 5 presents no problems; in 5:1 the evangelist mentions the feast only in order to move Jesus to Jerusalem, where the miracle and the succeeding discourse take place. It is clear from 2:12, 13 that sudden transitions are not exceptional in the Gospel of John (see also 4:3, 43; 7:10; 10:10; 11:54ff.). Apparently it is possible for the evangelist to transfer Jesus from Galilee to Jerusalem in a single verse. Like many of the indefinite mentions of place, the Johannine journeys to feasts are "only literary devices, without historical or chronological value."[119] Consequently, they do not require a preparation in the context each time they occur.[120] This is evident from the very abrupt transition between chapters 5 and 6. This abruptness does not justify a reordering of the chapters, because 6:2 clearly presumes that the chapters follow their present sequence.[121] John 6:2b refers to 4:46-54; 5:1-9ab and is the work of the evangelist (cf. 2:23b; 4:45; 11:45), who arranged the chapters as they are. In addition, even a rearrangement so that chapter 6 follows chapter 4 would not produce a smooth order, since 6:1 presupposes that Jesus is on the western shore of Lake Gennesaret, more specifically in Capernaum, to which, according to 6:17, 24, he returns—but in 4:46 he is in Cana and in 4:54 he is simply in Galilee.

The evangelist is also responsible for 7:1-14.[122] With this Galilean episode, he not only connects chapters 6 and 7, but brings Jesus to Jerusalem once and for all, where, on a very high feast day, he again proclaims his mission to the Jews and meets with rejection. "The Jews in Jerusalem—the high priests and Pharisees, who are distinguished from the crowd, several times appear in their place—are the indocile representatives of this world. That they are intractable becomes evident, however, only when Jesus attempts, continually, to demonstrate his claim and his mission. He must therefore go to Jerusalem repeatedly as a pilgrim and the festivals provide the apparent occasion for those visits."[123] John has no interest in geographical or chrono-

---

reconstructed with certainty; still, he insists that an attempt at reordering must be made. See his *John*, 221.

[119] Haenchen, *John* 1:243. See also Bauer, *Johannesevangelium*, 251.

[120] Against Langbrandtner, who uses the unanticipated change of place as a foundation for positing the secondary placement of chapter 6 (*Weltferner Gott*, 79ff.). Langbrandtner regards the composition of chapters 5, 7, and 8, as well as the insertion of the Jewish festival calendar, as the work of his "redactor." It follows that 6:2; 7:1-14 come from the redactor; these presume the present chapter series. But it appears that Langbrandtner too is unable to give a satisfactory answer to the crucial question, Why did the redactor reverse chapters 5 and 6, thus creating the inconsistency that moves present exegetes to undertake a reordering?

[121] Bultmann sees v. 2 as probably an addition by the evangelist, but thinks that it refers only to 4:46-54 as an example of Jesus' miracles (*John*, 211 n. 4). In my opinion, the plural formulations in 6:2 imperatively presuppose 4:46-54 *and* 5:1-9ab.

[122] See Schnackenburg, *John* 2:136-44. It seems that, in connection with the raising of Lazarus, Jesus leaves Jerusalem once more (see 10:40-42; 11:54; 12:12), but that does not alter the function of the journey to the feast of Booths.

[123] Haenchen, *John* 2:3.

logical data. They are simply a vehicle for him in formulating his theological interests. The Jewish festivals in Jerusalem, in which Jesus never really takes part, are for the evangelist the place of Jesus' proclamation and the scene for his controversies with the Jews.

Thus, the sequence of chapters 4–7 is not to be regarded as an unsuccessful attempt to reconstruct a work that had fallen into disorder, nor is it a none-too-persuasive rearrangement by a redactor. It is the sequence planned by John the evangelist, whose purpose was to bring Jesus repeatedly to Jerusalem, where he carries on his confrontation with the unbelieving world and where he will fulfill his destiny.

3.3.2   Redaction and Tradition

The first verse should be assigned to the Johannine redaction: as in 2:13 and 6:13, the evangelist uses the indefinite statement of time, μετὰ ταῦτα [after this], to introduce a new section and shows Jesus going to a festival at Jerusalem.[124] We can no longer discover which feast is meant by ἑορτή without the article; it is not important to John.[125] The narrative available to the evangelist begins with v. 2; however, the present tense at the beginning of the verse does not mean that Jerusalem and the place where the subsequent action occurs were still existent at the time of the Johannine source document.[126] The simple τῇ προβατικῇ [(for the) sheep] must be supplemented with πύλη [gate],[127] and the original name of the place was Βηθζαθά [Bethzatha].[128] Verse 3a, which belongs to the tradition (κατακεῖσθαι [to lie (sick)] otherwise only at 5:6; πλῆθος [multitude] elsewhere only in 21:6; ξηρός [withered, i.e., paralyzed] only here), introduces the situation, whereas the action itself begins only in v. 5 with the description of the state of the sick person — a *topos* of miracle stories.[129] The notice of the length of the sickness is supposed to accent the magnitude of the miracle that follows (a typical motif in healing stories: cf. Mark 5:25-26; 9:11; Luke 13:11; Acts 3:2; 4:22;

---

[124] See Schnackenburg, *John* 2:93; Haenchen, *John* 1:243; Becker, *Johannes* 1:229; Bultmann, *John,* 240; Fortna, *Gospel,* 49.

[125] This is clear even from the aloof formulation "a festival of the Jews." See Bauer, *Johannesevangelium,* 79; Becker, *Johannes* 1:230. Bultmann argues that this is another Passover (*John,* 240); Schnackenburg (*John* 2:93) and Becker (*Johannes* 1:230) think it is Pentecost (=feast of Weeks); Bernard (*St. John* 1:226) and Strathmann (*Johannes,* 94) argue for the festival of Booths.

[126] See Bauer, *Johannesevangelium,* 79; Haenchen, *John* 1:243-44.

[127] See Bauer, *Johannesevangelium,* 79; Bultmann, *John,* 240; Haenchen, *John* 1:244; against Jeremias, who associates the adjective with κολυμβήθρα [pool] as a dative (*Bethesda,* 6).

[128] Thus Haenchen, *John* 1:244; Bauer, *Johannesevangelium,* 79; Metzger, *Textual Commentary,* 208; NA26 ad loc. For a discussion of the problem, see Barrett, *John,* 251–53. Leroy, in contrast, considers Βηθεσδά original (*EWNT* 1:512–13).

[129] The secondary character of vv. 3b-4 is not disputed; see Barrett, *John,* 253.

9:33; 14:8; John 9:1).[130] It could come from the evangelist, inasmuch as the New Testament incidence of ἔχειν with an expression of time in the accusative is limited to the Gospel of John (see 5:6; 8:57; 9:21, 23; 11:17)[131] and must therefore be regarded as a stylistic characteristic of the fourth evangelist. Jesus' mysterious knowledge in v. 6 of the length of the illness is also attributable to John[132] because it presupposes the thirty-eight years mentioned in v. 5 and also corresponds to Johannine theology (see 1:47-48; 2:25; etc.). In addition, we again find ἔχειν here with an accusative expression of time. It is noteworthy that Jesus himself addresses the sick person, and this action prepares for the great, miraculous deed that is to follow.

The description of the miracle in vv. 7-9ab is traditional. Jesus' great power to work wonders is emphasized by the sick man's indirect request that Jesus help him enter the water. Jesus is not dependent on the healing power of the pool; he can act on his own. The word of command in v. 8 corresponds in many ways to Mark 2:11, but this should not be thought to indicate direct literary dependence. Instead, it is a redactional use of an individual *logion* from the oral tradition contained in the Johannine source document.[133] The immediate (εὐθέως) demonstration of the healing is stylistically appropriate; it serves as the starting point for the succeeding Sabbath conflict.[134]

3.3.3   *John 5:1-9ab in Relationship to 5:9c-18*

John deliberately transforms the miracle story available to him into a conflict over the Sabbath, by means of the remark in v. 9c.[135] The traditional motif of Sabbath violation serves the evangelist primarily as a compositional tool; in contrast to the Synoptics, there is no extended discussion of the violation of the Sabbath (see only Mark 2:23-28; 3:1-6). John uses it to prepare for Jesus' great discourse in vv. 19-47; his intention is to provoke a conflict

---

[130] See G. Theissen, *Miracle Stories,* 51–52.

[131] With Barrett, *John,* 253; against Fortna, who attributes this stylistic feature to his "source" (*Gospel,* 50). It is certainly possible that the tradition contained a notice of the length of the illness, but the present formulation is the work of the evangelist.

[132] With Schnackenburg, *John* 2:95; Brown, *John* 1:207; Strathmann, *Johannes,* 97; against Fortna, *Gospel,* 50–51.

[133] See Dodd, *Tradition,* 176; Bultmann, *John,* 238. On the relationship between John 5:1-9ab and Matt. 9:1-8, see Schnackenburg, *John* 2:96–97.

[134] For the demonstration in v. 9b there is *only* a Hellenistic parallel: Lucian *Philopseudes* 11; see Nicol, *Semeia,* 52. Lucian writes about a slave named Midas who was bitten by a snake and made lame. He was brought forward on a portable chair and was healed by a Chaldean using a magical formula and a piece of the gravestone of a dead virgin. Midas arose, took up the chair on which he had been carried, set it on his shoulder and strode swiftly away. See also Philostratus *Vita Apol.* 4.45.

[135] Whereas Bultmann (*John,* 238) and Becker (*Johannes* 1:229–30) assign vv. 9c-16 essentially to their "semeia source," Fortna (*Gospel,* 52), Haenchen ("Johanneische Probleme," 107; *John* 1:246ff.), and Nicol (*Semeia,* 32) correctly argue for the evangelist's authorship.

with the Jews that, like those in chapters 9 and 11, has its beginning in a miraculous act of Jesus and results in persecution and the Jews' intention to kill him. The emphasis for John lies on Jesus' conflict with the Jews; this is evident from the stylized structure of vv. 10-18 and the peculiar attitude of the one who has been healed. The latter does not know who made him well[136] and makes no effort to find Jesus (v. 13). As in the healing story, so also here the initiative comes from Jesus. He brings about the second encounter (see 9:35-38) and warns the healed man about the consequences of his actions. The man, however, goes to the Jews and discloses who it was who healed him. He has spoken not a word to Jesus, but he talks with Jesus' opponents. He is not grateful for his healing; on the contrary, he accuses Jesus before the Jews on that account.[137] Verse 17 is preparatory to the discourse that follows and can be understood only on the basis of vv. 19-21.[138] Jesus claims the authority of God as a support for his actions, and in v. 18 this brings about a sharpening of the Jews' accusation and of their reaction.[139]

For John, the healed man is a means to an end and a supernumerary in the accelerating conflict between Jesus and the Jews. This conflict does not loose itself on Jesus without preliminary, since in the Johannine dramaturgy it is Jesus himself who, by his words and actions, deliberately seeks the confrontation.[140]

3.3.4 Interpretation

With the healing of the sick man at the pool, the conflict between Jesus and the Jews begins; already broad in scope, it will increase steadily in

---

[136] The word ὑγιής (sound, healthy), which occurs only here in John, is the linguistic and material connection between vv. 1-9ab and vv. 9c-18: see Haenchen, *John* 1:247. Rengstorf is right to suppose that there is a reference to the Asclepius cult behind the ὑγιὴ γίνεσθαι in vv. 5, 9a, because this expression is to be found in shrines to Asclepius (*Christusglaube und Asklepiosfrömmigkeit*, 16–17). In addition, the expression ὁ σωτὴρ τοῦ κόσμου [the savior of the world] in John 4:42; 1 John 4:14 could possibly be understood as a criticism of the Asclepius cult; see Schnackenburg, *Johannesbriefe*, 243.

[137] In my opinion, that is how the healed man's attitude must be interpreted. Haenchen speaks of the healed man's having denounced Jesus to the Jews (*John* 1:247).

[138] See Haenchen, *John* 1:248.

[139] Martyn finds in vv. 16 and 18 the two levels he has posited within the Gospel of John (*History and Theology*, 68–73). He says of v. 16: "We may note first that verse 16 is related to the drama on the 'einmalig' level" (p. 70). In contrast, v. 18 is supposed to reflect the persecution of the community by the Jewish leadership. These latter could have said, as a reason for their proceeding, 'We persecute Jesus as a second god!' (5:18b)" (p. 72). It seems to me that that kind of interpretation must be regarded as speculative.

[140] Windisch calls John 5:1-18 a "dramatic novella," and divides it into five scenes: (1) healing; (2) the healed man's negotiation with the Jews; (3) renewed encounter with Jesus; (4) communication to the Jews of the fact that Jesus was the miracle worker; (5) meeting of Jesus and the Jews ("Erzählungsstil," 189).

intensity. John the evangelist achieves this effect through a secondary transformation of the healing story into a Sabbath conflict in v. 9c. The miracle is the starting point and occasion for the confrontation over the Sabbath, which in turn leads to the christological discourse in 5:19-47. But this in no way relativizes the miracle; instead, Jesus demonstrates his majesty and *doxa* here, as in 2:1-11 and 4:46-54. He appears as a miracle worker who acts with sovereign power, who knows everything and requires no auxiliary means to accomplish the healing. The sick person is healed by his word alone. If the statement of the duration of the illness comes from the evangelist, this would only underscore the magnitude of the miracle and the power of the miracle worker. In addition, he effects a terminological connection between the healing and the succeeding conflict through the repetition of ὑγιής in v. 11 and v. 14. Finally, the word ἔγειρε [stand up] in v. 8 refers to 5:21 and thus to Jesus as one who raises the dead and gives life.[141] For the evangelist, the *doxa* of Jesus that is revealed in the miracle is not restrained even by the Sabbath,[142] since it is the expression of Jesus' unity with the Father and is not subject to any earthly limitation (vv. 17, 18). The deed of power makes visible what the christological discourse declares: Jesus' *doxa*, his power over present and future, over life and death, and his unity with the Father.

Like 2:1-11, this miracle story, which is not expressly called a σημεῖον, comes from a special Johannine tradition. In a completely undualistic terminology and thought pattern, Jesus is depicted as the great miracle worker who accomplishes deeds of power on his own initiative. There is no indication that this story was part of a Johannine source and certainly not that it was the seventh and final miracle in a "semeia source," as Fortna proposes.[143]

3.4   John 6:1-15

3.4.1   *Context*

The transition from chapter 5 to chapter 6 is sharp, but it does not justify a rearrangement of the text; it is quite possible for John to move Jesus within a single verse from Jerusalem to the far shore of the lake (cf. 2:12, 13; 4:54). Moreover, 6:2 presupposes the healings in 4:46-54 *and* 5:1-9ab (see section 3.1 above). After the conflicts in Jerusalem, Jesus performs two more signs in Galilee, and these give rise to the bread discourse and the eucharistic

---

[141] See Haenchen, *John* 1:246.

[142] See Wilkens, *Zeichen und Werke*, 41.

[143] Fortna, *Gospel*, 102–9. Fortna's suggestion that the seventh miracle (5:1-9) is introduced with the expression τοῦτο ἕκτον ἐποίησεν σημεῖον ὁ Ἰησοῦς [this sixth miracle Jesus did] and ends with τοῦτο ἕβδομον ἐποίησεν σημεῖον ὁ Ἰησοῦς [this seventh sign Jesus did] (p. 108) is completely hypothetical.

section (cf. σημεῖον in 6:26, 30), which in turn bring about a division within the group of disciples (6:60-66).

3.4.2   Redaction and Tradition

In v. 1, μετὰ ταῦτα must be regarded as a mark of Johannine structuring (cf. 2:12; 3:22; 5:1, 14; 7:1; etc.).[144] The rest of the verse is traditional. It is true that the double genitive qualification of θάλασσα [sea] is unusual, but it should nevertheless be seen as original.[145] Jesus' transfer to the other side of the lake does not seem necessary for the multiplication of the loaves, but it is required for the walking on the water, which follows. This is an indication that the two pericopes were connected even at a pre-Johannine stage.[146] The crowd following Jesus is necessary for the feeding miracle (cf. Mark 8:1) and belongs to tradition.[147] The crowd's motivation for following in v. 2b, however, can be attributed to the evangelist, because it presupposes the healings in 4:46-54; 5:1-9ab and is, like 4:48, to be seen as a way of averting a bald *demand* for a sign (cf. 6:26, 30).[148]

The whole of v. 3 must also be assigned to the redaction, since Jesus' ascent of the mountain is not a precondition for the feeding miracle (cf. the Synoptic parallels). Moreover, Jesus goes up the mountain again in 6:15, though nothing has been said in the meantime about his having left it. "Therefore the feeding is not to be located on the mountain, but below."[149] Verse 4, which according to J. Wellhausen is a "chronological milestone,"[150] is the work of the evangelist. This is supported both by the many notations of feasts in the Gospel of John (2:13, 23; 4:45; 5:1; 7:2; 13:1) and by the aloof τῶν Ἰουδαίων.[151]

With v. 5, which is part of the tradition, the miracle story proper begins. It is notable that the reason for buying bread is missing (in Mark 6:31 it is because of the hunger of the crowd, and in Mark 6:34 it is Jesus' pity on them). The motive for Jesus' action appears only in v. 6.[152] This verse

---

[144] See Haenchen, *John* 1:270.

[145] Against Schnackenburg, who, with a reference to 21:1, wants to ascribe τῆς Τιβεριάδος [of Tiberias] to a later redactor (*John* 2:13).

[146] See Schnider and Stenger, *Johannes und die Synoptiker,* 143.

[147] Ibid.

[148] See Bultmann, *John,* 211 n. 4; Schnider and Stenger, *Johannes und die Synoptiker,* 143–44. In contrast, Haenchen assigns the whole verse to a source document (*John* 1:270).

[149] Schnider and Stenger, *Johannes und die Synoptiker,* 144; see also Schnackenburg, *John* 2:14.

[150] Wellhausen, *Evangelium Johannis,* 28.

[151] See Wilkens, "Evangelist und Tradition," 83; Schnider and Stenger, *Johannes und die Synoptiker,* 144; against Becker, who assigns v. 4 to the "ecclesiastical redaction" (*Johannes* 1:191).

[152] See Becker, *Johannes* 1:191.

reveals characteristic marks of Johannine style (for τοῦτο δὲ ἔλεγεν [he said this], see 7:39; 11:51; 12:33; for αὐτὸς γάρ [for he himself], see 2:25; 4:44-45; 6:34; 13:11; 16:27),[153] and Jesus' advance knowledge also corresponds to Johannine theology (see 12:32-33; 18:4a),[154] so that v. 6, in spite of the unique πειράζειν [to test], should be assigned to the redaction.[155] John thus underscores the tendency in his tradition to represent Jesus as a sovereign wonder-worker who knows in advance how great his miracle will be and is not moved to perform it merely by the suffering of the crowd.[156]

Jesus' foreknowledge is spoken of also in Mark 2:8; Luke 6:8; 9:47; 11:17 par.; Matt. 17:27 (see also Mark 8:31 par.; 11:1ff.; 13:1ff.; 14:12ff.).[157] There are significant parallels to this miraculous foreknowledge on the part of the wonder-worker, especially in the stories about Apollonius of Tyana.[158] Apollonius was able to predict the course of a person's life (*Vita Apol.* 1.32, 34; 4.18; 5.7, 37) and to see catastrophes approaching (*Vita Apol.* 4.4, 10; 5.18). This extraordinary power was attributed to the gods (*Vita Apol.* 4.44; 5.7, 12, 37; 6.32; 7.10) or to the wise man's ascetic way of life (*Vita Apol.* 1.2; 2.36–37; 6.11, 13; 8.5, 7, 9).

At this point the evangelist is not only far removed from any kind of criticism of miracles; he even sharpens the features in the tradition that emphasize Jesus' powerful actions.

Verse 7 should be ascribed to the tradition. Here the magnitude of the miracle is increased, in contrast to the Markan version, for now two hundred denarii are not enough to satisfy the crowd (cf. Mark 6:37). A peculiarity of the Johannine source lies in the mentioning of the names of the disciples, although it is possible that the subsequent identification of the one disciple in v. 8b as 'Ανδρέας ὁ ἀδελφὸς Σίμωνος [Andrew, Simon's brother] could be due to John (cf. 1:40, 44; 12:22).[159] Verses 9-13 are part of the pre-Johannine tradition; in v. 11 εὐχαριστεῖν [give thanks][160] without an object is especially

---

[153] See Bultmann, *John,* 212 n. 4; Fortna, *Gospel,* 58.

[154] See Fortna, *Gospel,* 58.

[155] See Bultmann, *John,* 212 n. 4; Wilkens, "Evangelist und Tradition," 84; Fortna, *Gospel,* 58; Schnider and Stenger, *Johannes und die Synoptiker,* 145.

[156] See Schnider and Stenger, *Johannes und die Synoptiker,* 145. Against Haenchen, who thinks that "John, however, does not create this magnification of the miracle" ("Johanneische Probleme," 93).

[157] For the Old Testament, see especially 1 Sam. 9:19-20. Billerbeck offers a Jewish parallel (*Kommentar* 1:528).

[158] See Petzke, *Apollonius,* 172–73. For the Hellenistic field, see also the instances in Wetter, *Sohn Gottes,* 69–72; Bieler, Θεῖος ἀνήρ 1:89–94; Bultmann, *John,* 102 n. 1.

[159] Spitta (*Johannesevangelium,* 138) and Hirsch (*Studien,* 60) also argue for Johannine redaction.

[160] Ἐυχαριστεῖν, as a hellenistic translation of בָּרַךְ ("to bless"), is not a later substitution for εὐλογεῖν [to praise] but an equally valid variant translation; see Patsch, "Abendmahls-terminologie," 216–19; against Jeremias, who sees εὐχαριστεῖν as merely a substitute for εὐλογεῖν (*Abendmahlsworte,* 166–69). There is a parallel usage in 1 Cor. 14:16-17; Josephus *Ant.* 8.111; *Corp. Herm.* 1.26.6; 27.2.

important, because it indicates that the tradition of the Lord's Supper has affected 6:1-15.[161] In particular, the great similarity to 1 Cor. 11:23b-24 (John 6:11: ἔλαβεν . . . καὶ εὐχαριστήσας [he took . . . and when he had given thanks]; 1 Cor 11:23b-24: ἔλαβεν . . . καὶ εὐχαριστήσας)[162] shows how the Johannine tradition of the feeding story has been influenced, like its Synoptic parallels, by the terminology of the narrative of institution (cf. Mark 6:41; 8:6; Matt. 14:19; 15:31; Luke 9:16). The restriction of the absolute use of εὐχαριστεῖν in the four Gospels (and Paul) to the institution narratives (Mark 14:23; Matt. 26:27; Luke 22:17, 19; 1 Cor. 11:24) and the feeding stories (Mark 8:6; Matt. 15:36; John 6:11, 23) speaks in favor of the supposition that εὐχαριστεῖν had become a *terminus technicus* meaning "to pronounce the eucharistic prayer" (see later *Did.* 9.1; 10.1, 7).[163]

The expression ὅσον ἤθελον [as much as they wanted] at the end of v. 11 again underscores the greatness of the miracle, and vv. 12 and 13 are part of the process of verification, in accordance with the form. C. H. Dodd's suggestion that with ἵνα μή τι ἀπόληται [so that nothing may be lost (or: perish)] in v. 12d, in the sense of an "additional sign,"[164] John is pointing to βρῶσις ἀπολλυμένη [food that perishes] in v. 27, in order to forge a connection between the feeding miracle and the bread discourse, is worth consideration: the bread blessed by Jesus satisfies hunger and is not used up; it is βρῶσις μένουσα [food that endures].

Old Testament motifs in particular have affected the feeding stories in the New Testament tradition.[165] Besides the Moses tradition, according to which the people were miraculously fed in the wilderness (cf. Exod. 16:1-36; Num. 11:6-9; Deut. 8:3, 16; etc.), we should mention especially the feeding miracles from the Elijah and Elisha traditions (1 Kings 17:7-16; 2 Kings 4:42-44). There is a remarkable parallel between John 6:9 and 2 Kings 4:42, in the use of ἄρτους κριθίνους [barley loaves]. Moreover, in 2 Kings 4:38, 41, Elisha's servant is called παιδάριον [little boy] (cf. John 6:9, ἔστιν παιδάριον), and καὶ ἔφαγον καὶ κατέλιπον [and they ate and had some left] in 2 Kings 4:44 is close to καὶ ἔφαγον πάντες καὶ ἐχορτάσθησαν [and all ate and were filled] in Mark 6:42. But we may not conclude from these correspondences to a direct influence.[166]

---

[161] See Patsch, "Abendmahlsterminologie," 228–31; idem, *EWNT* 2:221; Barrett, *John*, 276. Langbrandtner simply ascribes εὐχαριστήσας in 6:11 to "the redaction," because the sacraments may not appear in the "basic document" as he reconstructs it (*Weltferner Gott*, 106).

[162] See Patsch, "Abendmahlsterminologie," 229.

[163] Ibid., 210ff.; Patsch, *EWNT* 2:221; Schlier, "Johannes 6," 109; against Bultmann, who understands εὐχαριστήσας to mean only the ordinary Jewish prayer of thanksgiving (*John* 213 n. 2).

[164] Dodd, *Tradition*, 207; see also Schnackenburg, *John* 2:17–18.

[165] For the Jewish and Hellenistic parallels, see Bultmann, *History of the Synoptic Tradition*, 229–30, 234, 236; van der Loos, *Miracles*, 624ff.; G. Theissen, *Miracle Stories*, 104, 105 n. 77.

[166] With H.-W. Kuhn, *Sammlungen*, 205; against Heising (*Brotvermehrung*, 18–19) and L. Schenke (*Wundererzählungen*, 228), who posit a direct influence of the Elijah-Elisha tradition. E. Schweizer speaks of an "itinerant legend" that has been applied to Jesus (*Markus*, 73).

Verses 14 and 15 reveal themselves both in their language and in their content as Johannine redaction.[167] Typically Johannine is οὖν at the beginning of both verses. Also, cf. ἰδόντες ὃ ἐποίησεν σημεῖον [after seeing the sign that he had done] in v. 14a with 2:23; 4:45; 6:2b; οὗτός ἐστιν ἀληθῶς ὁ προφήτης [this is indeed the prophet] in v. 14b has a direct parallel in 7:40; and cf. ὁ ἐρχόμενος εἰς τὸν κόσμον [who is to come into the world] with 1:9; 3:19; 9:39; 11:27; 12:46; 16:28; 18:37.[168] In v. 15a, Jesus' miraculous foreknowledge, expressed with γνοὺς [perceiving], corresponds to Johannine theology (see 2:24-25; 4:1; 8:59; 10:39), and the refusal of an earthly kingship, with its implicit reference to Jesus' true, nonearthly rule, has a parallel in 18:33-38.[169]

It is difficult to say whether John is referring to Deut. 18:15 when he employs the title ὁ προφήτης [the prophet]. In the first place, Taheb the Samaritan was seen, in a late stage of the development of Samaritan traditions, as the promised prophet like Moses.[170] The expectation of a prophet like Moses is recorded at Qumran as well (1QS 9:9-11; 4QTest 1-8), but this figure must be distinguished from the royal and priestly Messiah and may not be identified with the Teacher of Righteousness either.[171] In the New Testament, the interpretation of Deut. 18:15 as applying to Christ is found in Acts 3:22; 7:37. John, however, nowhere makes a direct reference to Deut. 18:15 (cf. 1:21, 25; 6:14; 7:40). He makes an emphatic distinction between the "prophet" and the Messiah (1:21, 25; 7:40), but in 6:14-15 there is a singular situation, in that here the figure of the prophet "combines [with] that of the (national) Messiah."[172] For John, Jesus is "the prophet" as miracle worker. The Jews in the New Testament period did not expect the Messiah to be a worker of miracles,[173] but there are a great number of notices about the arrival of "prophets" with miraculous powers. Josephus reports the appearance of "messianic" prophets accompanied by miracles;[174] they connected themselves with the time of the people's wandering in the wilderness and entry into

---

[167] With Bultmann, *John,* 210, 213–14; Schnackenburg, *John* 2:18–20; Schnider and Stenger, *Johannes und die Synoptiker,* 146; against Hahn, who regards the people's acclamation in v. 15 as traditional (*Hoheitstitel,* 391–92). Becker considers v. 14 traditional and v. 15 redactional (*Johannes* 1:193).

[168] See Fortna, *Gospel,* 60; Schnackenburg, *John* 2:18–19.

[169] See Fortna, *Gospel,* 60.

[170] See Kippenberg, *Garizim und Synagoge,* 306–10.

[171] See Schnackenburg, "Erwartung," 631ff.

[172] Ibid., 630. For the contemporary expectations of a Messiah associated with Moses, see Billerbeck, *Kommentar* 1:85–88; Jeremias, *TDNT* 4:848–73 (esp. p. 857: "Nowhere, however, in the older literature do we find the idea that the returning Moses will be the Messiah").

[173] See Billerbeck, *Kommentar* 1:593–96; Lohse, *RGG³* 6:1834; Nicol, *Semeia,* 79–80; Schweizer, *Jesus Christus,* 127; Martyn, *History and Theology,* 95–100. Martyn attempts to overcome this state of the sources, which is awkward for his interpretation. Following the work of Meeks, he finds strong affinities between Jewish expectations regarding Moses and Johannine christology (see *History and Theology,* 101–28). That solves the problem of the legitimation of the Messiah by miracles, because Moses performed miracles before the pharaoh. See also Klausner, *Messianic Idea,* 502–8; and Vielhauer, "Erwägungen," 203. For the discussion of different opinions, see Nicol, *Semeia,* 80 n. 1.

[174] The texts are discussed at length in Meyer, *Der Prophet aus Galiläa,* 82–88.

the holy land, but there is no evidence of an explicit reference to Deut. 18:15. In Hellenism also we find prophets as miracle workers. Apuleius mentions an Egyptian prophet who raised the dead (*Metamorphoses* 2.28-29), and Apollonius of Tyana is consistently portrayed as the perfect prophet.[175] Celsus's "prophets," as well, with their saying, ἐγὼ ὁ θεός εἰμι ἢ θεοῦ παῖς ἢ πνεῦμα θεῖον [I am God (or a son of God, or a divine Spirit)] (Origen *Contra Celsum* 7.9) belong in this category.[176] The religious-historical background of the Johannine concept of the prophet cannot be discerned with full clarity. There are four reasons to reject the idea so often voiced today that John understands Christ as an eschatological prophet like Moses:[177] (1) No Moses-Christ typology can be shown to exist in John, such that Jesus would be portrayed as the eschatological prophet like Moses. The evangelist does not place Moses and Christ in a typological relationship to each other; instead, he sets them as antitheses to each other (1:17; 6:32; 9:28).[178] (2) There is no place in the Gospel of John that refers unambiguously to Deut. 18:15, 18. (3) John deliberately presents the notion of the prophet only on the lips of the Jews: (1:21, 25, Jews from Jerusalem about John the Baptizer; 6:14, 15, the people about Jesus), and he does not give it a positive evaluation. The title "prophet" does *not* appear as a positive acclamation or a self-description in John. In the sense of a consciously developed christological conception, the expectation that Jesus would prove to be the eschatological prophet who would fulfill the promise of Deut. 18:15, 18 plays no part here. (4) Judaism furnishes no examples of the phrase ὁ προφήτης, which is characteristic for John.[179]

The Johannine interpretation of the feeding miracle does not refer to a particular historical event (Jesus' elevation by the crowd to the status of a political messiah);[180] instead, John uses the confession of the crowd here to reintroduce his connection between seeing the miracle and the resulting faith. The miracle is the occasion of the crowd's recognition and confession that Jesus is the prophet who has come into the world, something that presupposes faith on their part. Characteristic of John is the immediate securing in v. 15 of this positive affirmation against misunderstanding.[181] The title "prophet," bestowed on Jesus, is not to be understood in an earthly, political sense. Jesus is not a national liberator but rather the Son of God and the Bread of Life, who gives eternal life to those who believe in him. The revival of the concept of σημεῖον in v. 26 and v. 30 is to be understood in this sense: by this means John creates a connection between the feeding miracle and the

---

[175] See Fascher, Προφήτης, 199–203.

[176] See the further instances in Bauer, *Johannesevangelium,* 32ff. On the idea of the prophet in the Pseudo-Clementine documents, see Strecker, *Das Judenchristentum in den Pseudoklementinen,* 145–53.

[177] See only Hahn, *Hoheitstitel,* 391–92, 397.

[178] See Schnackenburg, "Erwartung," 639.

[179] See Bultmann, *John,* 89.

[180] With Schnackenburg, *John* 2:19; against Dodd, *Tradition,* 214.

[181] This does not mean that the evangelist evaluates the statement in v. 14 negatively; he merely protects it against false interpretation. Against Schnider and Stenger, *Johannes und die Synoptiker,* 146.

bread discourse. At the same time he averts a possible misunderstanding of the miracle by accenting the exclusively soteriological significance of the Son's mission and thus emphasizes that in the last analysis the true gift is the Son, and therefore the Giver in person (see 6:35).

3.4.3   John 6:1-15 in Relationship to Mark 6:32-44 and Parallels

The sixfold tradition of the miraculous multiplication of the loaves (Mark 6:32-44; 8:1-10; Matt. 14:13-21; 15:32-39; Luke 9:10-17; John 6:1-15) raises the question of the relationship of the Johannine tradition to the others. Since Matthew and Luke are secondary in relationship to Mark,[182] the comparison can be limited to Mark and John. Here the agreements give a first indication of connections within the tradition history of the texts:

Verbal Parallels

John	Mark
6:1 ἀπῆλθεν	6:32 ἀπῆλθον
6:2, 5 ὄχλος πολύς	6:34 πολὺν ὄχλον
6:5 ἀγοράσωμεν . . . φάγωσιν	6:36 ἀγοράσωσιν . . . φάγωσιν
6:7 αὐτῷ διακοσίων δηναρίων ἄρτοι	6:37 αὐτῷ δηναρίων διακοσίων ἄρτους
6:9 πέντε . . . καὶ δύο	6:38 πέντε καὶ δύο
6:10 ἀναπεσεῖν	8:6 ἀναπεσεῖν
	6:40 ἀνέπεσαν
χόρτος	χόρτῳ
ἄνδρες . . . πεντακισχίλιοι	6:44 πεντακισχίλιοι ἄνδρες
6:11 ἔλαβεν . . . τοὺς ἄρτους εὐχαριστήσας	6:41 λαβὼν τοὺς . . . ἄρτους
	8:6 εὐχαριστήσας
6:12 περισσεύσαντα κλάσματα	8:8 περισσεύματα κλασμάτων
6:13 δώδεκα κοφίνους κλασμάτων	6:43 κλασμάτων δώδεκα κοφίνων

Content Parallels[183]

1. Jesus goes to a retired place.   Mark 6:32, 8:3; John 6:1
2. The disciples have five loaves and two fish.   Mark 6:38; John 6:9
3. The people sit down.   Mark 6:39a; 8:6; John 6:10
4. There is much grass in the place.   Mark 6:39b; John 6:10

---

[182] See Haenchen, *Weg Jesu*, 246.
[183] See Schnackenburg, *John* 2:21.

5. Five thousand men are fed.   Mark 6:44; John 6:10
6. Twelve baskets are filled   Mark 6:43; John 6:13
   with fragments.

Structural Parallels[184]

1. Exposition   Mark 6:32-34; 8:1; John 6:1-4
2. Dialogue between Jesus and
   the disciples (preparatory to
   the miracle)   Mark 6:35-38; 8:2-5; John 6:5-9
3. The meal, with indirect
   description of the miracle   Mark 6:39-42; 8:6-8; John 6:10-11
4. Confirmation of the miracle   Mark 6:43-44; 8:9; John 6:12-13

Parallels in Arrangement of the Material[185]

Feeding   John 6:1-15; Mark 6:32-44
Walking on the sea   John 6:16-21; Mark 6:45-52
Crossing of the sea John 6:22-25; Mark 6:53-54; 8:10
Demand for a sign   John 6:26; Mark 8:11-13
Peter's confession   John 6:66-71; Mark 8:27-33

Differences

In contrast to these agreements are some important differences:[186]

1. In Mark 6:33 the people wait for Jesus and the disciples, but in John they follow Jesus (v. 2a).

2. It is only in John that Jesus goes up a mountain at the beginning of the narrative (v. 3).

3. In Mark 6:34, Jesus' pity on the crowd as "sheep without a shepherd" and in Mark 8:2 his compassion on their hunger, after they have been following him for three days, serve as motivation for the miracle that follows. In John, there is no motive given for the miracle.

4. There are notices of time in Mark 6:35a (evening) and 8:2 (three days), but John 6:4 contains nothing except a mention of the Passover.

5. In Mark 6:35 and 8:4, the disciples come to Jesus. In John 6:5, it is Jesus who questions Philip; then Andrew mentions a boy who has some provisions with him (vv. 8-9).

6. In Mark 6:37b, two hundred denarii are enough to buy bread, but in John 6:7 they are not sufficient.

---

[184] See Dodd, *Tradition,* 202–3.

[185] See Dodd, *Tradition,* 196; Becker, *Johannes* 1:217; Schnider and Stenger, *Johannes und die Synoptiker,* 119, who show that, in Mark, the two feedings are the starting points for parallel compositions.

[186] See Schnackenburg, *John* 2:21–22.

7.   In Mark 6:38 and John 6:9, the disciples have five loaves and two fish, but in Mark 8:5 they have seven loaves.

8.   In John (vv. 9, 13) it is expressly said that these are barley loaves; instead of ἰχθύς [fish], John writes ὀψάριον [small fish].

9.   In Mark 6:40 the men sit down in groups of fifty and one hundred; in John 6:9 we read only that they sit down.

10. John does not report that before the distribution of the bread Jesus looks up to heaven and breaks the bread (cf. Mark 6:41; 8:8).

11. Only in John 6:12b does Jesus order the disciples to gather up the fragments.

12. In Mark 6:43 and John 6:13 there are twelve baskets left over, but in Mark 8:8 there are only seven.

13. In Mark 6 and John 6, five thousand men are fed, but in Mark 8 only four thousand.

14. Only John mentions the crowd's reaction to the miracle (vv. 14-15). In Mark the miraculous character of the feeding apparently remains hidden from the crowd.

If Mark 6:32-44 and 8:1-10 are two independent, pre-Markan versions of a common basic narrative,[187] the Johannine account could also rest on this fundamental narrative. It would then have gone through an independent, pre-Johannine course of oral tradition. This would explain both the considerable similarities and the differences sketched above. In that case, John, or his tradition, would not have used the Gospel of Mark as a model.[188] Against this theory is the large number of verbal agreements, unusual for a narrative shared by John and the Synoptic tradition. In addition, the succession of the narratives (first the feeding of five thousand, then walking on the water) would speak in favor of John's use of the Gospel of Mark, if this arrangement is due to the redaction of Mark.[189] This question can be answered after a thorough analysis of the Johannine version of the walking on water and its Synoptic parallels; only then can the relationship between John 6:1-15 and the Markan feeding stories be clarified.

---

[187] In recent discussion, the thesis introduced by, among others, Dibelius (*From Tradition to Gospel,* 78 n. 1) that Mark himself created the second narrative in 8:1ff. has rightly been rejected by most scholars. On the relationship of the two feeding stories in Mark, see Gnilka, *Markus* 1:254ff., 300f.

[188] This position is represented, for example, by Bultmann, *John,* 210; Haenchen, *John* 1:276; Becker, *Johannes* 1:190.

[189] We should qualify the statement of Schnider and Stenger (*Johannes und die Synoptiker,* 142) that "if the combination of feeding and walking on water is due to Mark, we can suppose that the model document used by John knew the Synoptics, at least from oral recitation." What we ought to say is that, if the sequence of feeding of five thousand followed by walking on water is the work of Mark, then at least the Johannine tradition was acquainted with Mark's Gospel.

3.4.4 *Interpretation*

The feeding miracle also serves John as a demonstration of Jesus' majesty, revealed in his miraculous actions. The redactional σημεῖον in vv. 2 and 14 thus furnishes the parenthesis for the Johannine interpretation of the tradition: the crowd follows Jesus because they saw his great deeds among the sick, and it recognizes in him, through the sign, the messianic prophet who has come into the world. Therefore, here again the mighty sign evokes faith, and we find the Johannine conjunction between seeing the miracle and the faith that results.[190] In v. 15, John in no way devalues the crowd's confession; he merely shields it against the misconception that Jesus' messiahship is to be understood in an earthly, political sense. The Johannine view of Jesus' kingship is illustrated in 18:33-38; this also clarifies the redactional reference to the Passover in v. 4. At the same time, the evangelist strengthens the tendency already present in the tradition to present Jesus as a powerful worker of miracles. If the model document omitted any mention of the people's suffering, thus giving the miracle the character of a demonstration,[191] the evangelist underscores that tendency in v. 6: the masterful wonder-worker knows in advance how great his deed will be. Therefore, John 6:1-15 can be called a "gift miracle"[192] only in a very restricted sense, for the suffering of the crowd is no longer the focus of the narrative.

3.5 John 6:16-25

3.5.1 *Context*

As in Mark so also in John the walking on the sea directly follows after the feeding of the five thousand (cf. Mark 6:32-44, 45-52). It is difficult to judge the status of John 6:22-25, because the miracle itself ends with v. 21. Verses 22-25, however, witness to the reality of what has just been described, so that they function as a process of recognition and in that sense are part of the miracle story.[193] Also in favor of an original connection is the observation that in Mark 6:53-56; 8:10, as well, either the walking on water or the

---

[190] Against Schnackenburg, who says of v. 2 "that the crowd follows him only for the sake of these external advantages" (*John* 2:13–14). Neither the motive for discipleship in v. 2 nor the confession in v. 14 is judged negatively. On the contrary, they presuppose that the people have faith in Jesus' power and recognize his mission! This positive view is not retracted by v. 15; it is only protected against misunderstanding.

[191] See Schnider and Stenger, *Johannes und die Synoptiker,* 149.

[192] On this form-critical designation, see Theissen, *Miracle Stories,* 103–6.

[193] See Schnider and Stenger, *Johannes und die Synoptiker,* 148. See also Fortna (*Gospel,* 64ff.), who includes not only vv. 22-25 but also all of v. 15 in the walking on water pericope, whereas Heil (*Walking,* 75) sees the beginning of the pericope in v. 15b and calls vv. 22-25 the "transformation" (p. 144).

feeding of four thousand is followed by a voyage across the lake. Despite the differences in each case, this indicates a connection in the tradition history of the material.

3.5.2 Redaction and Tradition

Verses 16 and 17a should be assigned to the tradition: the disciples go to the lake and take ship on their own initiative (contrast Mark 6:45), in order to sail to Capernaum on the opposite shore. In contrast, v. 17b is from the evangelist,[194] since σκοτία [darkness] is a theologically charged concept for John, designating all that is far from God. Anyone who does not follow Jesus remains in darkness (see 1:5; 8:12; 12:35, 46).[195] Here John wishes to make clear, by the use of σκοτία, that the disciples are in the darkness without Jesus and therefore are in danger.[196] In addition, two pieces of information that are necessary for the miracle that is to follow are conveyed in v. 17b: Jesus is on land, whereas the disciples are in the middle of the lake.[197] No further Johannine redaction can be discerned in vv. 18-21. They differ considerably from Mark 6:48-52, for only v. 18 gives any reference to the quieting of the storm.[198] But the miracle itself is not reported: the center of the narrative is an epiphany of Jesus. As in Mark, Jesus encounters the men's fear with a majestic ἐγώ εἰμι, μὴ φοβεῖσθε [It is I (lit.: "I am"), do not be afraid], but in v. 21 the Johannine tradition again veers sharply away from Mark. Verse 21a creates the impression that Jesus passed by the disciples' boat (cf. Mark 6:48d)—that is, originally John 6:16-21a was a pure epiphany story, whose connection with the stilling of the storm could only be inferred indirectly from v. 18. In addition, v. 21b reports another miracle, since that is how the sudden transfer of the boat to the shore must be understood.

There are parallels for Jesus' walking on water both in the Old Testament and in Hellenism. God's powerful intervention for the people is seen also in Israel's passage through the Red Sea (Exod. 14:21-31) and in the crossing of the Jordan (Joshua 3; 4). God strides about on the waters (Ps. 77:20; Job 9:8; 38:16), and divine Wisdom also rules the sea (Sir. 24:5-6). In 2 Kings 2:7-8, 14-15, Elijah's and Elisha's crossing through the waters of the Jordan serves to legitimate the prophets in the eyes of their disciples, a motif that could have influenced the pericope of Jesus' walking on the water.[199] Lucian (*Philopseudes* 13) tells of a Hyperborean who in broad daylight

---

[194] See Schnider and Stenger, *Johannes und die Synoptiker*, 147.

[195] See Heil, *Walking*, 146.

[196] Ibid., 147.

[197] The word ἤρχοντο in v. 17 merely says that the disciples *began* to go their way, so that this supplementary information is necessary.

[198] Wellhausen thinks that v. 18 is a gloss added from Mark but can give no convincing reasons for his opinion (*Evangelium Johannis*, 29).

[199] See Kertelge, *Wunder*, 147.

elevated himself into the air, walked about on the water (ἐφ᾽ ὕδατος βαδίζοντα) and took a leisurely stroll through the fire.[200]

With the exception of τῇ ἐπαύριον [the next day], (cf. 1:29, 35, 44; 12:12), v. 22 should be assigned to tradition. Its function is to furnish "the objective 'proof' of the reality of the miracle."[201] The effect of the event is increased by the process of discovery. Verse 23 does not belong to tradition; this verse solves the problem of how the crowd had crossed the sea again from the place where the loaves were multiplied and makes it possible for them to encounter Jesus, as presupposed in v. 25. Because the disciples' boat is no longer on the shore (v. 22), a way must be found for the people to meet Jesus in Capernaum (v. 21) and thereby to confirm the miracle of the walking on water and to hear the discourse on bread that follows.

Although the function of the verse is clearly discernible, there are a great number of problems at the level of text criticism and as regards content. The omission of εὐχαριστήσαντος τοῦ κυρίου [after the Lord had given thanks] in D 091 it a, d, e syr c, s and others is significant. Most exegetes think that these words were absent from the original, seeing this eucharistic expression as a late gloss.[202] But the overwhelming external evidence[203] favors the expression's presence in the original, so that the textual tradition cannot be used to support a possible secondary character of the words. As regards content, the sudden appearance of the ships (which, according to Wellhausen, seem like "a *deus ex machina*")[204] always aroused the suspicion that this verse was an addition made after the evangelist had completed the Gospel, if not a still later gloss.[205] Further support for this supposition is found in the use of ὁ κύριος [the Lord] in a narrative, the singular ἄρτον φαγεῖν [to eat the bread], the eucharistic echoes, and the statement that the boats were "from Tiberias."[206] But these arguments are not persuasive: the unexpected appearance of the ships is required by the context, which demands an explanation for the encounter between Jesus and the crowd in Capernaum. Within narrative texts, ὁ κύριος is also found in 4:1; 11:2; 20:20, and thus is not unusual

---

[200] Bultmann (*History of the Synoptic Tradition*, 236–37; Bieler (Θεῖος ἀνήρ, 96) and Reitzenstein (*Wundererzählungen*, 125) offer further parallels. Also notable is Philostratus *Vita Apol.* 4.13, where he reports that all were convinced that Apollonius had power over storms, fire, and every other kind of disagreeable thing. On the motif of the miraculous landing, see Bultmann, *John*, 216 n. 4.

[201] Haenchen, *John* 1:280.

[202] See only Bultmann, *John*, 217 n. 3; J. Schneider, *Johannes*, 143 n. 1.

[203] See Metzger, *Textual Commentary*, 212.

[204] Wellhausen, *Evangelium Johannis*, 30.

[205] See Barrett, *John*, 285; Schnackenburg, *John* 2:33–35.

[206] Among those who regard this verse as secondary are Becker, *Johannes* 1:203 (ecclesiastical redaction); Haenchen, *John* 1:280–81 (added by a redactor); Strathmann, *Johannes*, 116 (secondary insertion); Fortna, *Gospel*, 68 (late gloss); Schnider and Stenger, *Johannes und die Synoptiker*, 148 (gloss by some later editor).

for John the evangelist.[207] Ἄρτον φαγεῖν in the singular is found also in 6:31 (cf., in contrast, the plural in 6:11, 13, 26) and is necessitated by the eucharistic expression εὐχαριστήσαντος τοῦ κυρίου. The analysis of v. 11 has shown that an absolute εὐχαριστεῖν in the sense of "pronouncing the eucharistic prayer" was technical terminology in the tradition of the Lord's Supper. The Johannine tradition (!) in v. 11 was already understood in that sense, and the evangelist's adoption of this understanding and its inclusion in v. 23 are thoroughly plausible. The reference ἐκ Τιβεριάδος is not unintelligible if we suppose that the feeding took place near Tiberias.[208]

Both v. 23 and v. 24 (which presupposes v. 23) are thus not to be regarded as late additions but are very probably the evangelist's redaction; they are used to explain the situation in v. 25, which was given in the tradition.[209]

3.5.3 John 6:16-21 in Relationship to Mark 6:45-52

Verbal Parallels

John	Mark
(6:15 εἰς τὸ ὄρος)	6:46 εἰς τὸ ὄρος
6:16 ὀψία ἐγένετο	6:47 ὀψίας γενομένης
6:17 πλοῖον . . . τῆς θαλάσσης	πλοῖον τῆς θαλάσσης
6:18 ἀνέμου (μεγάλου)	6:48 ὁ ἄνεμος
6:19 ἐληλακότεσ . . . περιπατοῦντα ἐπὶ τῆς θαλάσσης	6:48 ἐλαύνειν . . . περιπατῶν ἐπὶ τῆς θαλάσσης
6:20 λέγει αὐτοῖς· ἐγώ εἰμι μὴ φοβεῖσθε	6:50 λέγει αὐτοῖς . . . ἐγώ εἰμι μὴ φοβεῖσθε
6:21 εἰς τὸ πλοῖον	6:51 εἰς τὸ πλοῖον

Content Parallels

1. The disciples are on the lake without Jesus.	Mark 6:47b; John 6:17b
2. There is a great wind on the lake.	Mark 6:48b; John 6:18

---

[207] Against Schnackenburg, who ascribes the use of ὁ κύριος in reporting texts not to the evangelist but to a later redaction (*John* 1:422 n. 4; 2:33).

[208] This is favored by ἀκολουθεῖν [to follow] in v. 2.

[209] See Bultmann, who, however, considers εὐχαριστήσαντος τοῦ κυρίου secondary (*John*, 216–17). All attempts based on the sequence εἶδον (v. 22) . . . εἶδεν (v. 24) to reconstruct a "short text" excluding vv. 22b and 23 (see Schnackenburg, *John* 2:33) should be rejected, because there is no anacoluthon in 6:22-24; instead, τῇ ἐπαύριον ὁ ὄχλος εἶδον is taken up by ὅτι οὖν εἶδεν ὁ ὄχλος. See Blass-Debrunner-Rehkopf §467, 1.

3. The disciples in the boat see
   Jesus walking on the lake.   Mark 6:49a; John 6:19b
4. The disciples are terrified or
   afraid.   Mark 6:49b, 50a; John 6:19b
5. Jesus says: ἐγώ εἰμι· μὴ
   φοβεῖσθε.   Mark 6:50b; John 6:20.

Differences in Content

1. In Mark 6:45a, Jesus commands the disciples to get into the boat, whereas in John 6:16 the disciples enter the boat of their own accord.
2. In Mark, the disciples' goal is Bethsaida (v. 45b), but in John they are rowing toward Capernaum.
3. According to Mark 6:48, the disciples are in danger on the sea, and Jesus rescues them. In John, this motif is merely hinted at in v. 18.
4. Whereas in the Markan tradition Jesus gets into the boat with the disciples (6:51a), in John it is only said that the disciples wanted to take Jesus into the boat (v. 21a).
5. John does not report that the wind subsided after Jesus was in the boat (Mark 6:51).
6. The miraculous landing of the boat on the opposite shore in John 6:21b, a second miracle in addition to the walking on water, is not reported in Mark.

This listing of agreements and differences shows that the text of Mark in its present form can most probably not have served as a model for John in the direct literary sense, because the linguistic correspondences are balanced by strong divergence in the individual motifs that are part of the miracle. In Mark, the walking on water is combined with the motif of the disciples who are in danger on the lake and with the other motif of the stilling of the storm, so that the whole narrative has the characteristics of a rescue miracle; in John, however, we find a pure epiphany narrative. Its focus is the miraculous appearance of Jesus on the lake, where he does not get into the boat with the disciples but instead performs an additional miracle.

It has often been supposed that the Johannine tradition is older than the Markan text and that an epiphany on the water had acquired, even at the pre-Markan level, the secondary motifs of a rescue miracle.[210] In favor of this thesis is the expression καὶ ἤθελεν παρελθεῖν αὐτούς [and he intended to pass them by] in Mark 6:48d, omitted by Matthew as unintelligible. It seems still to point to the idea that originally Jesus passed by the boat. The tradition in Matt. 14:28-31 may also presume this,[211] because Peter's going to Jesus on

---

[210] See Bultmann, *History of the Synoptic Tradition*, 216; Lohmeyer, *Markus*, 131ff., 135; Theissen, *Miracle Stories*, 186–87; Schnackenburg, *John* 2:27–28.

[211] See Strecker, *Weg der Gerechtigkeit*, 199.

the water would be easier to understand if Jesus did not enter the boat. Moreover, the acclamation in Matt. 14:33, οἱ δὲ ἐν τῷ πλοίῳ προσεκύνησαν αὐτῷ [and those *in the boat* worshiped him], could indicate "that the person being worshipped here is not in the boat."[212] A pure epiphany narrative would then have been expanded by the addition of features of a rescue miracle, and John would preserve the older tradition, in contrast to Mark.[213]

It is also possible that Mark himself introduced the traits of the rescue miracle into the epiphany narrative before him. This proposal is favored both by the agreements between this story and that in Mark 4:37-41 and by Mark's thorough overall redaction of the walking on water episode. The pericopes of the stilling of the storm and the walking on water agree that the disciples are in peril because a strong wind has arisen (Mark 4:37; 6:48) and that Jesus' appearance (in different ways) causes the wind to die down (Mark 4:39; 6:51b: καὶ ἐκόπασεν ὁ ἄνεμος). There are further agreements beyond these: as in Mark 4:36, so also in Mark 6:51 Jesus enters the disciples' boat, creating the tension between the latter verse and 6:48d. In Mark 4:36, also, the crowd is dismissed (cf. the end of 6:45), and the subsequent voyage is toward the opposite shore (cf. Mark 4:35; 6:45).[214] These observations favor the proposal that Mark enriched the tradition he had received about the walking on water by adding motifs from the narrative of the stilling of the storm (especially vv. 48a and 51ab) and performed further redactional revisions as well. Thus v. 52[215] (and possibly v. 51c) should be credited to Mark, who interprets the disciples' distress as a failure to understand the feeding story. He thereby unites the bread miracle and the walking on water and introduces the characteristic Markan motif of the disciples' failure to understand (cf. Mark 4:10, 11, 13, 34, 40-41; 7:17-18; 8:14-21; 8:33; 9:10, 18, 19, 28, 31-32, 33-34, 38-39; 10:10; etc.).[216] The motif of the disciples' lack of understanding also reveals why Mark combines the feeding and walking on water: their emphasis on Jesus' miraculous power serves to illustrate human

---

[212] Theissen, *Miracle Stories,* 186.

[213] L. Schenke thinks it probable that the original story of the walking on water had a different sequence of scenes from that which we now find in the text ("Szenarium," 197ff.). In his version, the disciples would have gone to Capernaum after the feeding of the crowd and awaited Jesus there. But he did not come, although it had grown dark and a heavy storm had arisen on the lake. Although in this way the route to Capernaum by land and water was closed for Jesus, he came to the disciples quite unexpectedly across the lake. (For further details of Schenke's reconstruction, see "Szenarium," 199–200.) The transformation of this "original" scenario into the sequence as we have it would be the work of the "Johannine redaction" (=the author of John 21), with the purpose of adapting the version in the basic document to that of the Synoptics. Given the fact that this presupposition is highly doubtful in itself, Schenke's reconstruction as a whole must be regarded as purely hypothetical.

[214] See Schnider and Stenger, *Johannes und die Synoptiker,* 108.

[215] See Bultmann, *History of the Synoptic Tradition,* 216, and elsewhere.

[216] See Schnider and Stenger, *Johannes und die Synoptiker,* 115–24.

failure of understanding and thereby points to the true, hidden character of Jesus' revelation (cf. v. 52, but especially the redactional v. 37).[217]

Redactional interventions can also be found at the beginning of the pericope of the walking on water (vv. 45 and 46): Mark joins the feeding and walking on water by means of a shift in place, εἰς τὸ πέραν [to the other side] (cf. Mark 4:35; 5:1; 5:21; 8:13).[218] He also introduces, along with the motif of dismissing the people, which is derived from the feeding story (cf. Mark 6:36; 8:3, 9), a second reason for the separation of Jesus and the disciples, which is necessary for the subsequent walking on water.[219] Even the motif of Jesus' solitary prayer on the mountain (cf. Mark 1:35)[220] could be from Mark, its purpose being to take a doubtful motivation and develop out of it the necessary situation for v. 47. The supposition that the joining of the feeding story and the walking on water is artificial and is traceable to Mark[221] can be strengthened by further observations. In the first place, the dismissal of the people does not necessitate the disciples' setting out ahead of Jesus.[222] How should we imagine this scene, in which five thousand people are sent away in the evening from a lonely place? The statements of time in Mark 6:35, ἤδη ὥρας πολλῆς γενομένης [when it grew late] (before the feeding) and 6:47, καὶ ὀψίας γενομένης [when evening came], are unrelated to each other and can only be understood in the context of the individual narratives.[223] The redactional ἐν τῷ πλοίῳ in Mark 6:32[224] (cf. 4:1, 36-37; 5:1, 2, 18, 21; 6:45, 54) could be conditioned by the walking on water that follows; that is, Mark may not only have combined the two pericopes but also have fashioned pointers forward to the walking on water in v. 32 and backward to the feeding in v. 52.

In concluding this section, we can now give an answer to the question raised earlier, whether the Gospel of Mark served as a model for the feeding pericope and the walking on water in the Johannine tradition. Inasmuch as the union of the feeding with the walking on water is the work of the evangelist Mark and the Johannine tradition presupposes this combination (see John 6:1), it is probable that the Johannine tradition used the Gospel of

---

[217] See Kertelge, *Wunder*, 130–31.

[218] On this Markan motif, see Schreiber, *Theologie des Vertrauens*, 205–7.

[219] See Bultmann, *History of the Synoptic Tradition*, 216.

[220] See Schnider and Stenger, *Johannes und die Synoptiker*, 109 n. 6. On the ὄρος-motif see Schreiber, *Theologie des Vertrauens*, 164–67.

[221] So Bultmann, *History of the Synoptic Tradition*, 216; Schnider and Stenger, *Johannes und die Synoptiker*, 109. Kertelge (*Wunder*, 145) and Gnilka (*Markus* 1:266) argue for a pre-Markan connection.

[222] See Bultmann, *History of the Synoptic Tradition*, 216.

[223] See Haenchen, *Weg Jesu*, 252 n. 2; H.-W. Kuhn, *Sammlungen*, 207.

[224] There is a broad consensus among scholars that vv. 31-33 are the work of Mark; for details, see L. Schenke, *Wundererzählungen*, 217–19; Koch, *Wundererzählungen*, 99–111.

Mark.[225] Add to this the considerable agreements in language between Mark 6:32-44 (8:1-10) and John 6:1-15, which cannot be explained merely on the basis of a common oral tradition. Nevertheless, it cannot be shown in detail whether the Johannine tradition compared its model document with the Markan tradition or whether it created its narrative on the basis of the Gospel of Mark itself.

For the walking on water, the Johannine tradition may have received an epiphany narrative closely related to that in the Markan model, which it combined with the feeding pericope, in analogy with Mark. The Johannine tradition did not adopt the redactionally altered Markan version of the walking on water, because its intentions were not important for that tradition. The feeding and walking on water reveal that the Johannine tradition knew the Gospel of Mark, which means that this supposition is not unfounded in the case of the evangelist as well.[226]

3.6 John 9:1-41

3.6.1 Context

John 9:1-41 stands out from its immediate context as a relatively unified composition. Whereas widely differing traditions are woven together in John 8 and John 10,[227] the healing of the man born blind is circumscribed both in theme and structure in a manner that is unusual for the Gospel of John. The connection to the immediate context is established in v. 1; Jesus accomplishes the healing of the blind man immediately after leaving the Temple.[228] The theme that is demonstrated in the healing, "Jesus, the light of the world" (cf. 9:5, 39), is a development out of 8:12: ἐγώ εἰμι τὸ φῶς τοῦ κόσμου.[229] Beyond that, the key word φῶς creates a connection to 12:35-36, 46, and the theme of φῶς—κρίσις in 9:39-41 ties the story back to 3:19ff. Finally, the

---

[225] Among those who argue that John knew the Gospel of Mark at this point are Barrett, *John,* 217; Blinzler, *Johannes und die Synoptiker,* 57; and Kümmel, *Introduction,* 202–3. It is rejected by Brown, *John* 1:236ff.; Haenchen, *John* 1:281–83; idem, "Johanneische Probleme," 90–95; Dodd, *Tradition,* 196ff. (feeding and walking on water are based on independent traditions); Bultmann, *John,* 210; Lohse, "Miracles," 47; Becker, *Johannes* 1:190. The argument of Gnilka (*Markus* 1:266), Grundmann (*Markus,* 183), Haenchen (*Weg Jesu,* 253), and H.-W. Kuhn (*Sammlungen,* 206 n. 15) that the sequence of material in John also favors a pre-Markan combination of feeding and walking on water should be rejected. What cannot be proved in Mark cannot be established on the basis of John!

[226] In recent research there has been an increasing acknowledgment, as there should be, of John's knowledge of the Synoptics. See Neirynck, "John and the Synoptics," and also his *Jean et les synoptiques.*

[227] For the details, see Schnackenburg, *John* 2, ad loc.

[228] See Schnackenburg, *John* 2:238.

[229] Ibid.; Bornkamm, "Heilung des Blindgeborenen," 67; J. Schneider, *Johannes,* 186; Dodd, *Interpretation,* 357.

shepherd discourse in 10:1-18 contrasts with the dominant situation of perse-cution and oppression in John 9 (see vv. 22, 30-34).

The importance of John 9 is evident, however, only if we consider the position of this chapter in the structure of the Gospel as a whole. The repeated notation of Jewish festivals is the Johannine compositional principle in John 2–7 used to bring Jesus repeatedly to Jerusalem. But now that Jesus is continually in Jerusalem (see 7:10), the conflict with the Jews is portrayed especially in the two great thematically and compositionally closed units in John 9 and 11. The festival framework as a compositional device recedes dramatically[230] (being found again only in 10:22 and 11:55ff.), and the focus is on the two great miracle stories.

This formal principle of construction corresponds on the level of con-tent to a perceptible intensification of the conflict between Jesus and the Jews. In John 6:14, 26, 30; 7:31 the σημεῖον was still acknowledged as miracle and thus as an event that awakens and legitimates faith, but in 9:16, 24, 31 the miracle itself as such is called into question.[231] The Jews no longer acknowl-edge that Jesus can do miracles at all, and they eject the one who has come to believe as the result of a miracle (see vv. 30-34). The necessary conse-quence of this attitude is found in John 11, where both the wonder-worker (cf. 11:47ff.) and the resuscitated Lazarus are doomed to die (cf. 12:10).

3.6.2   Redaction and Tradition

With v. 1, the story of the healing of the blind man is nicely integrated with what went before; however, the imprecise statement of the situation, καὶ παράγων [as he passed by], could also have served as an introduction in a quite different context. Consequently, we may suppose that all of v. 1 belongs to the tradition.[232] Jesus again takes the initiative; the blind man does not ask to be healed. The fact that this is a τυφλὸν ἐκ γενετῆς [(person) blind from birth] only serves to magnify the miracle that follows. The disciples' question in v. 2 is unusual in a miracle story, inasmuch as the connection be-tween guilt and sickness that is introduced here raises additional difficulties in the case of someone blind from birth.[233] The function of the question

---

[230] See Schnackenburg, John 2:238.

[231] See Hofbeck, Semeion, 128.

[232] See Fortna, Gospel, 70; Bultmann, John, 230; Becker, Johannes 1:316.

[233] For the Jewish discussion of the relationship between sin and illness, see Billerbeck, Kom-mentar 2:527–29. We may regard as pagan parallel the frequently encountered motif of blinding as punishment; see Weinreich, Heilungswunder, 190ff. The idea of metempsychosis suggested by Bauer (Johannesevangelium, 133) could scarcely be the background of v. 2; for a critique of Bauer, see Bultmann, John, 330 n. 8. Bauer's other suggestion (previously offered by Spitta, Johannesevangelium, 201), that the model document contained γενηθῇ [became] rather than γεννηθῇ [was born], should also be rejected, since there is no basis for it in the text.

should therefore be sought not in theoretical speculation about the connection between action and consequence but in Jesus' rejection of it in v. 3a. The explanation of that rejection in vv. 3b-5 shows the hand of the evangelist both in its language (for the elliptical ἀλλ' ἵνα [but in order that], cf. 1:8, 31; 13:18; 14:31; 15:25; for φανεροῦν, cf. esp. 2:11; 3:21; for ἐργάζεσθαι [to work] and ἔργα [works], cf. only 5:17, 36; 6:28, 30) and in its content (in Jesus' actions, the works of God are revealed, 3:21; 5:17; 10:32; Jesus as light of the world, 3:19; 8:12; 11:9, 10; 12:46).[234] As far as the evangelist is concerned, the man born blind serves solely to demonstrate Jesus' power as a worker of miracles (cf. 11:4) and not as an occasion for discussing the relationship between sin and sickness. The miracle that follows is meant to be a striking demonstration of the fact that Jesus is the light of the world.

The description of the healing procedure in vv. 6-7 contains traditional features: in ancient times, saliva was an established medicine against eye diseases.[235] Here, saliva and earth are blended into a mud, which, together with washing at the pool of Siloam, produces a healing effect. The traditional character of v. 6 is supported also by the fact that πτύσμα [spittle] is a *hapax legomenon,* and that χαμαί [on the ground] is found only here and in 18:6. The only purpose of Jesus' word of command in v. 7 is to send the blind man to the pool of Siloam, from which he returns able to see. The (probably inaccurate)[236] explanation of the name "Siloam" is the work of the evangelist;[237] this is suggested both by the language (ἑρμηνεύειν [interpret, explain] in the New Testament only in 1:42; 9:7; Heb. 7:2; ἀποστέλλω [send] 28 times in the Gospel of John) and on theological grounds (Jesus as the one sent by the Father; see 3:17, 34; 5:38; 6:29; 10:36; 17:3, etc.). The evangelist thus makes clear that in the last analysis it is Jesus who, as the one sent by the Father, accomplishes the healing. This again underscores Jesus' miracle-working activity, which is so important for John.

Although there are also connections between the healing story itself and the cure of blind persons in Mark 8:22-26; 10:46-52 (Mark 8:23/John 9:6: saliva as medicine;

---

[234] See Schnackenburg, *John* 2:242; Fortna, *Gospel,* 72; Nicol, *Semeia,* 35; Becker, *Johannes* 1:316–17; Hartke, *Urchristliche Parteien,* 70 (3b-5); Martyn, *History and Theology,* 5 n. 13 (3b-5); Reim, "Joh 9," 246. Bultmann (*John,* 330), Wilkens (*Zeichen und Werke,* 42), and Haenchen (*John* 2:38) consider only vv. 4-5 redactional. Whether through this addition John has inserted another answer of Jesus into the tradition, as Bultmann, Fortna, and Becker think, can no longer be determined.

[235] See Pliny *Nat. Hist.* 28.7; Tacitus *Hist.* 4.81 (Suetonius *Caes.* 8.7.2–3); Billerbeck, *Kommentar* 2:15–17; Dio Cassius 66.8; Mark 8:22ff. (see also Mark 7:33). Extensive parallels from ancient religion showing the healing power of saliva can be found in Jacoby, "Heilung des Blinden," 185ff.

[236] For the details, which cannot be treated here, see Bauer, *Johannesevangelium,* 134–35; Schnackenburg, *John* 2:243.

[237] See Fortna, *Gospel,* 72; Schnackenburg, *John* 2:243; Becker, *Johannes* 1:316; Barrett, *John,* 358; Bultmann, *John,* 333 (in doubt whether it is the hand of the evangelist or of the redactor); Reim, "Joh 9," 247.

Mark 10:46/John 9:8: the blind person is called προσαίτης [beggar]; Mark 10:51/ John 9:2: Jesus is addressed as ῥαββί or ῥαββουνί),[238] no conclusions can be drawn that would point to a direct dependence of one tradition on the other, because the differences among the individual narratives are too great. (The places and personal names are different; John 9 speaks of one *born* blind; in John the initiative proceeds from Jesus; and there are differences in the individual procedures in healing.)

A comparison with a second-century inscription[239] to Asclepius is instructive. Here a blind soldier is told by the god to go (ἐλθεῖν; cf. John 9:7, ὕπαγε) and make a salve of blood and honey (cf. the mud made of dirt and saliva in John 9:6), which he is to rub on his eyes for three days (ἐπιχρεῖσαι ἐπὶ τοὺς ὀφθαλμούς; cf. John 9:6, ἐπέχρισεν . . . ἐπὶ τοὺς ὀφθαλμούς). Afterward, he could see again (ἀνέβλεψεν; cf. John 9:7, βλέπων). He then came (ἐλήλυθεν; cf. John 9:7, ἀπῆλθεν . . . ἦλθεν) and publicly thanked the god.

As early as v. 7, the sick man "by going to the pool of Siloam becomes an independent figure in the narrative, something that is presupposed by what follows; only at 9:35 does he meet Jesus again."[240] This observation speaks against all attempts to assign only vv. 1-7 to a pre-Johannine tradition, while considering everything that follows to be solely the work of the evangelist.[241] The description of the man born blind in v. 7 is already pointed toward the subsequent dialogue, which must be understood as the necessary reaction to the miracle and as a very skillfully constructed interpretation of the event. In addition, the compositional and theological unity of the pericope supports the supposition that the whole narrative of the one born blind, apart from some redactional additions, is pre-Johannine.[242]

First of all, the reaction of the neighbors is portrayed in vv. 8-12. We learn that the man born blind had formerly been a beggar (προσαίτης only here and in Mark 10:46) and that many people knew him. He has undergone

---

[238] See Schnackenburg, *John* 1:244, and the tables in Dodd, *Tradition,* 182.

[239] Text and commentary in Deissmann, *Light from the Ancient East,* 135–36; see also Barrett, *John,* 353.

[240] Haenchen, *John* 2:38.

[241] Thus, with minor differences, Fortna, *Gospel,* 70–74 (adding v. 8 also to the "model document" in order to retain the necessary reaction to the miracle, but v. 8 cannot be separated from vv. 9-12!); Schnackenburg, *John* 2:239; J. Schneider, *Johannes,* 187; Brown, *John* 1:378 (also assigning vv. 13-17 to tradition); Lindars, *John,* 339–40 (counting v. 1 and part of vv. 6-7 as tradition); Wilkens, *Zeichen und Werke,* 41–42; Martyn, *History and Theology,* 3ff.; Nicol, *Semeia,* 35.

[242] G. Bornkamm judges correctly: "The story of the healing of the one born blind is a skillfully constructed whole" ("Heilung des Blindegeborenen," 67). Haenchen considers only vv. 4-5 and 39-41 redactional (*John* 2:38, 40–41). Bultmann includes John 9 as a whole in his "semeia source," regarding vv. 4-5, 22-23, 29-34a, 39-41, in particular, as additions by the evangelist (*John,* 329). (The redaction is also supposed to have intervened in vv. 16-17, 35-38.) Spitta sees later additions in vv. 17-23, 35b-41 (*Johannesevangelium,* 199ff.); Hartke counts vv. 1-3a, 6-21, 24-29a, 30a, 33-34 as parts of the original version of John 9 (*Urchristliche Parteien,* 69–70). Becker associates himself closely with Bultmann (*Johannes* 1:315). Beyond the miracle story itself, he assigns vv. 8-12, 13-17, 18-23, 24-34 to his "semeia source."

a change, as the different reactions in v. 9 indicate. This confirms the reality of the miracle; the same function is performed by the ἐγώ εἰμι of the one born blind and by the repeated description of the process of healing in vv. 10-11.[243] Now the crowd wants to find Jesus (v. 12), but he has disappeared; as a result, the one who had been blind is again thrust into the center of the narrative. He is brought before the Pharisees, and the reader learns in v. 14, in a rather casual remark, that Jesus had done this healing on the Sabbath. Since making mud was work, and therefore forbidden on the Sabbath,[244] the conflict is exacerbated. Noteworthy here is the late introduction of the problem of the Sabbath, reminiscent of 5:9c. It was probably the evangelist who introduced this element, which emphasizes the drama of the event.[245] The man who had been blind is questioned by the Pharisees, and he describes the process of healing again, in a shorter form than that in v. 11. Thus, once again, the fact of the miracle is emphasized.

Verse 16, like v. 14, very probably stems from the evangelist, because the discussion that arises among the Pharisees presupposes a healing on the Sabbath. (In favor of this position is also the expression τοιαῦτα σημεῖα ποιεῖν [to perform such signs]: see 2:11, 23; 4:54; 6:14, 30; 7:31; 10:41; 11:47; 12:18, 37; 20:30).[246] John describes the possible reactions to Jesus' miracle working: on the one side, the rejection of the divine legitimation of Jesus by means of a remark on his nonobservance of the tradition: on the other side, the σημεῖα that evoke faith, permitting the witnesses to conclude to the divine origin of the miracle worker. Here again in modified form is that conjunction, so characteristic of the evangelist, of seeing the miracle and believing. The miracle provokes both rejection and trust, so that a disagreement now arises among the Pharisees, just as the neighbors had disagreed among themselves in v. 9. The Pharisees turn again to the man who had been blind and ask him his opinion about Jesus. He sees Jesus as a prophet, a clear advance beyond the ὁ ἄνθρωπος [the person] in v. 11.

The Jews[247] then question the identity of the formerly blind man with

---

[243] With Haenchen, *John* 2:38–39; against Martyn, who wishes to dissociate vv. 8-9 as a whole from the preceding description of the miracle (*History and Theology*, 5).

[244] See Billerbeck, *Kommentar* 2:530.

[245] So Schnackenburg, *John* 2:247; also Wellhausen, *Evangelium Johannis*, 46. Spitta (*Johannesevangelium*, 205) and Lindars (*John*, 345) consider the sabbath commandment a later addition.

[246] Becker (*Johannes* 1:319) assigns only v. 16b to the evangelist, and he counts v. 14 as part of the "semeia source."

[247] For Wellhausen (*Evangelium Johannis*, 46) and Spitta (*Johannesevangelium*, 202–3) the use of οἱ Ἰουδαῖοι [the Jews] in vv. 18 and 22 rather than Φαρισαῖοι [Pharisees] (vv. 13, 15, 16, 40) raised the suspicion that vv. 18-23 were secondary in this context. For a justified criticism of this view, see Bultmann, *John*, 329 n. 3. Bultmann regards the shift to οἱ Ἰουδαῖοι as the work of the evangelist, who wishes thereby to indicate the official character of the hearing before an official body (*John*, 335 n. 1).

the one who now can see, and they call in his parents to verify the identification. The parents merely confirm that this person who now has his sight is their son and that he formerly was blind. But they fearfully avoid making any statement about how their son received his sight and who brought this miracle about. As an explanation for this unusual attitude on the part of the parents, the readers are told that "the Jews" had decided to exclude from the synagogue anyone who confessed Christ.[248] It can no longer be determined whether vv. 22-23 are the work of the evangelist,[249] since only the introductory expressions ταῦτα εἶπαν [they said this] in v. 22 and διὰ τοῦτο [therefore] in v. 23 indicate redaction. This is too narrow a basis for a definite decision.

In contrast, it is clear that vv. 22-23 are an explanation of the preceding narrative, offering a motive for the parents' behavior and illustrating the full extent of the Jews' enmity. Beyond its purely literary function, 9:22 looks backward to the separation of Johannine Christians from the synagogue.[250] However, an *ongoing* conflict between the Johannine community and the synagogue is not reflected in this text.[251] It admits only the conclusion that "at the time of the narrator and in the circle of his acqaintances, there can no longer have been any Jewish Christians in a Jewish community."[252]

In the same way, 12:42 and 16:2 are not reflections of an *acute* conflict between the Johannine community and the synagogue. The faith of "many"[253] authorities in 12:42 and their anxiety about being excluded from the synagogues by the Pharisees[254] serve the evangelist merely as an elucidation of the preceding quotation from Isaiah: the obstinacy predicted in Scripture in no way obviates the necessity for a faith decision by individual persons, as is clear from the fact that "many" authorities believe.[255] Certainly, John immediately places restrictions on this positive statement in v. 43: the authorities did not confess their faith, because human glory was more important to them than the glory that comes from God (v. 43).

The prophecy in 16:2 is clearly marked by early Christian traditions of persecution,[256] as we find them in Matt. 5:10-11; 10:21ff.; Mark 13:12ff.; and Luke 6:22; 12:4, 21:12. Here the persecution, and even killing, of believers appears as a traditional motif (see Matt. 10:21, 28; 24:9; Mark 13:12; Luke 21:16). The expectation

---

[248] See Schrage, *TDNT* 7:848–52.

[249] So Bultmann, *John,* 335 n. 5; Reim, "Joh 9," 247. In contrast, Langbrandtner (*Weltferner Gott,* 75) and Bergmeier (*Glaube als Gabe,* 211) consider 9:22-23 a later addition.

[250] See Luz, *Gesetz,* 125.

[251] Against Martyn, *History and Theology,* 37ff.; Wengst, *Bedrängte Gemeinde,* 48–49.

[252] Haenchen, *John* 2:39.

[253] See only the Johannine portrayal in 7:48 and 11:47-48.

[254] For Wengst (*Bedrängte Gemeinde,* 57, 95), John 12:42 suggests that the Gospel of John was written even before (!) the formulation of the *birkat hammînîm,* since these passages presume that there are secret sympathizers with the Christian community, something that would have been impossible after Javneh. That kind of argument must be regarded as pure speculation.

[255] Perhaps the evangelist is thinking here of Nicodemus (3:1ff.; 19:39) and Joseph of Arimathea (19:38).

[256] See Barrett, *John,* 485; Becker, *Johannes* 2:493.

of the "hour" is also a current motif of persecution in Jewish apocalyptic (see Isa. 39:6; Jer. 7:32; 16:44; Zech. 14:1 LXX; 4 Ezra 5:1; 13:29; for the New Testament also Mark 2:20; Luke 17:22; 21:6; 23:29). These tradition-historical observations support the idea that John 16:2 does not refer to a concrete conflict but rather that traditional motifs have been worked into the situation of the farewell discourse.

The analyses in section 1.3 have shown that the introduction of the *birkat hammînîm* into the Eighteen Benedictions was primarily a movement within Judaism and that both the understanding of the law and the use of Ἰουδαῖος speak against a Jewish Christian interpretation of the Fourth Gospel. That conclusion is confirmed by the exegesis of 9:22; 12:42; 16:2: these verses can neither be interpreted as direct reaction to the formulation of the *birkat hammînîm,* nor can they support a Jewish Christian reading of the Gospel of John. If they are supposed to have a real historical background—something that should by no means be excluded—the evangelist is looking back to it, although no precise location in time (around the year 90, for example) is possible.[257]

Against that kind of late dating are both the persecutory actions of Paul, which can only be understood in terms of a jurisdictional commissioning (see Gal. 1:13; Phil. 3:6, and the persecution of the communities in Judea by Jews presupposed by 1 Thess. 2:14ff.), and also the single Synoptic parallel to our passages, in Luke 6:22 (see also Luke 11:49-51). The macarism for the persecuted[258] reflects conflicts between youthful Christianity and the Jewish synagogue. Here ἀφορίζειν "should be translated as 'excommunicate,' and is identical with ἀποσυνάγωγος γίνεσθαι; ἐκβάλλειν (τὸ ὄνομα) also has a Jewish-disciplinary significance, and therefore should not be translated as 'defame'; it is closer to 'exclude' or 'cast out.'"[259] Thus, ἀποσυνάγωγος describes a development that is already presupposed in the Synoptic tradition and in the Pauline writings.

In vv. 24-34 the healed man undergoes a second interrogation by the Jews,[260] centering on the question of divine legitimation both of the miracle worker and of the Jews. Although the Jews consider Jesus a sinner and thereby question the divine origin of the miracle worker and the reality of the miracle, the formerly blind man defends Jesus[261] and again emphasizes the reality of the miracle (v. 25). Thereupon a discussion of the course of the miracle's accomplishment develops once again, culminating in the healed man's ironic question: μὴ καὶ ὑμεῖς θέλετε αὐτοῦ μαθηταὶ γενέσθαι [do you also want to become his disciples]. The Jews resist that kind of suggestion

---

[257] Thus Schrage, *TDNT* 7:851–52.

[258] On the tradition-historical assessment of this macarism, see Horn, *Glaube und Handeln,* 122ff.

[259] Strecker, "Makarismen," 123–24.

[260] The expression δὸς δόξαν τῷ θεῷ [give glory to God] in v. 24 indicates that the Jews already regard the man born blind as a condemned person; see Billerbeck, *Kommentar* 2:535 ad loc.

[261] With Burchard; εἰ after an expression of knowledge requires that v. 25 be translated: "That he is a sinner is something unknown to me" ("Ei nach einem Ausdruck des Wissens," 81). See Becker, *Johannes* 1:320.

with a reference to themselves as disciples of Moses (v. 28).[262] This argument is expanded in v. 29, where the legitimation of Moses by God (cf. Exod. 33:11) is contrasted with the unknown origin of the miracle worker, Jesus. The expression τοῦτον δὲ οὐκ οἴδαμεν πόθεν ἐστίν [we do not know where he comes from] indicates Johannine redaction (cf. 7:27-28; 8:14; 3:8), so that probably the whole of v. 29 should be attributed to the evangelist.[263] The disciples of Moses betray themselves by not recognizing the one about whom Moses wrote (5:46). Thus the discussion arrives at its real goal: If the Jews assert that they are legitimated by Moses, whence is Jesus' legitimacy? The answer to this crucial question in vv. 30-33 comes largely from the evangelist, because v. 30 presumes the redactional v. 29. (Moreover, ἐν τούτῳ is a Johannine expression; see 4:37; 13:35; 15:8; 16:30.) Verse 33 too is certainly a Johannine composition (for οὗτος παρὰ θεοῦ [this one . . . from God], see 6:46; 7:29; 8:40; 17:5, 7, 8; for the expression "be able to do something," see 3:2; 5:19; 9:4, 16; 11:37; 15:5; for legitimation through miracles, see 3:2; 20:30-31).[264] The one who had been blind instructs the Pharisees with their own arguments. It is precisely the uniqueness of the miracle that witnesses to the divine origin of the miracle worker; therefore, he cannot be a sinner. God does not listen to sinners,[265] but only to those who are pious[266] and who do God's will (v. 30-31). In v. 32 the greatness and uniqueness of the miracle are again brought to the fore, in order that the only theologically appropriate conclusion can be drawn in v. 33: such a miracle cannot be done except by someone who is παρὰ θεοῦ (cf. the expression οὐκ ἔστιν οὗτος παρὰ θεοῦ [this man is not from God], also redactional, on the lips of the Pharisees in v. 16a). Here the interest of the evangelist is again clearly visible:[267] the magnitude of the miracle not only serves him as an argument in the conflict with the Jews but is a comprehensive legitimation of Jesus' divine origin. For John, the reality of the miracle, undeniable because of the existence of the man born blind, is proof of the divinity of the miracle worker. He is far

---

[262] See Billerbeck, Kommentar 2:535 ad loc. This expression probably refers to the Pharisees.

[263] See Bultmann, John, 336 n. 4; Reim, "Joh 9," 247.

[264] For Bultmann, v. 30 is surely from the evangelist, and he regards v. 33 as also a Johannine composition (John, 336 n. 4); but, in his opinion, nothing further can be determined with certainty. He indicates his agreement with Spitta (Johannesevangelium, 206–7), according to whom v. 34c was originally the continuation of v. 28. Reim considers vv. 28-30, 32 redactional ("Joh 9," 247–48). Becker assigns vv. 24-27a, 31-34 to his "semeia source" and thinks that vv. 27b-30 are from the evangelist (Johannes 1:320–21).

[265] See 1 John 3:21, 22; Isa. 1:15; Ps. 66:18; 108:7; Prov. 15:8, 29. Bauer offers further Hellenistic examples (Johannesevangelium, 136).

[266] In the New Testament, θεοσεβής [devout, religious] appears only here (which supports the traditional character of v. 32), but it was a common term in Hellenistic religious literature. See BAGD 358; Deissmann, Light from the Ancient East, 451–52.

[267] Against Becker, who simply assigns the massive theology of miracles to his "semeia source" (Johannes, 1:321), although this verse is clearly to be recognized as Johannine on the basis of its language.

removed from any dualistic conception of things: the miracle is a visible, this-worldly demonstration of Jesus' majesty.

The Jews react angrily to this lesson delivered by the man who had been blind; they attribute his blindness from birth to sinfulness and eject him from their company.[268] As in 5:14, the one who had been born blind is then "found" by Jesus (see also 1:41), and this is followed by the evangelist's description[269] of the healed man's acknowledgment and confession of faith. Whereas, before this, the man born blind had stubbornly defended Jesus before the people and the Jewish authorities, he now comes, through Jesus himself, to true sight and to faith. He recognizes in Jesus the "Son of man"[270] and worships him (cf. 4:20-24).[271] It is within the logic of the narrative that Jesus reveals himself here, because the healed man had not seen him before this. Thus he could not know who Jesus of Nazareth was, and it is only when, in v. 37, Jesus makes himself known by referring to the miracle (ἑώρακας αὐτόν [you have seen him]) that the healed man comes to believe.

Here again we find in the background the Johannine conjunction between seeing the miracle and the faith that arises from it; it is Jesus the miracle worker in whom the healed man believes and whose power he has experienced in his own body. In addition, ἑώρακας in v. 37 supports this interpretation: the perfect tense refers specifically to the miracle of the blind man's healing and emphasizes the ongoing effects of that event[272] (see 20:29; 14:7, 9). The miracle not only legitimates the miracle worker (v. 33) but also evokes faith (v. 38).[273]

The action as such concludes with the former blind man's confession of faith, but the evangelist adds vv. 39-41 as a further interpretation of the event.[274] Using one of his characteristic techniques, that of the ambiguous

---

[268] In the first instance, ἐκβάλλειν here refers to his being ejected from the room in which the interrogation has taken place. But beyond that it is probably to be understood in the sense of v. 22, as an exclusion from the synagogue. But see the usages in BAGD 237 s.v. 1, for "expel someone from a group."

[269] See J. Schneider, Johannes, 194; Becker, Johannes 1:321-23; Reim, "Joh 9," 248; Bultmann, John, 338 n. 1. Bultmann, however, does not think it is possible to distinguish precisely between redaction and tradition. In favor of Johannine redaction are, besides the parallel structure with John 5, especially v. 37 (for καί–καί see 4:36; 6:36; 7:28; 11:48; 12:28; 15:24, with a content parallel in 4:26). The formulation πιστεύειν εἰς is also Johannine.

[270] The concept of υἱὸς τοῦ ἀνθρώπου in v. 35 is probably conditioned by the forensic context in v. 39. There is a content parallel in 12:31-36. See Schnackenburg, John 2:252-54.

[271] For proskynēsis as an appropriate behavior toward miracle workers, see especially Philostratus Vita Apol. 7.21, where it is reported that the citizens of Ephesus worshiped Apollonius and regarded him as being like a god, after he had delivered their city from the plague.

[272] See Blass-Debrunner-Rehkopf §342.

[273] The omission of vv. 38 and 39a in 𝔭75 ℵ* W b (1) is secondary; for a discussion, see Metzger, Textual Commentary, 229; Becker, Johannes 1:322.

[274] See Haenchen, John 2:40-41; Reim, "Joh 9," 248. Bultmann includes v. 39 in his "revelatory discourse source" (John, 339). Favoring redaction in v. 39 is the expression εἰς τὸν κόσμον (cf. 8:23; 11:9; 12:25, 31; 13:1; 18:36); for ἐκ τῶν Φαρισαίων in v. 40, see 1:24; 3:1; 7:47-48; 9:16. For v. 41, see 15:22, 24.

expression,[275] John emphasizes that revelation is not only grace but can also become judgment, because one's attitude toward it determines who will see and who will remain blind. Only through a yes or no to God's revelation in Jesus of Nazareth is it apparent whether a person belongs to the realm of light or remains in darkness, having failed to grasp the opportunity to "see" in the real sense, and therefore becoming subject to judgment (see 8:12; 12:35-36; 12:46). The man born blind has come to sight in a double sense: he not only receives the sight of his eyes, but beyond that he recognizes that Jesus is παρὰ θεοῦ and believes in him.

In contrast, the Pharisees only think that they see, for they do not recognize Jesus as the revealer. Thus they are blind, even though they have the sight of their eyes. They have seen Jesus' great, miraculous deed; they have met the Revealer; and still they have not come to believe. Thus they remain in their sins — in their rejection of the Revealer (8:21; 15:22, 24; 16:9; 19:11). Therefore "seeing" means "believing," and "unbelief," on the contrary, means "being blind."

3.6.3 Interpretation

The extensive and compositionally unified tradition of the healing of a blind person serves John as an illustration and a demonstration of the christological statement ὅταν ἐν τῷ κόσμῳ ὦ, φῶς εἰμι τοῦ κόσμου [As long as I am in the world, I am the light of the world] (9:5; cf. 8:12; 12:46). The fact that Jesus is the light of the world is visibly evident in the unique healing of someone blind from birth. This extraordinary miracle legitimates Jesus' divine origin and reveals him as a miracle worker sent by God (see 9:7c, 16, 33). Thus, the miracle not only serves the interests of christology but is the *expression* of the evangelist's christological concept, apparent in his emphasis on the epiphanic character of the σημεῖα and thus on the this-worldly visibility of Jesus' activity and the reality of his incarnation.

The miracle evokes both faith and rejection (cf. vv. 9 and 16). While the Jews persist in their unbelief, interpreting Jesus' approach to tradition as sin (vv. 14 and 16a) and even denying the fact of the miracle, the man born blind arrives, by stages,[276] at a recognition of Jesus' divine origin that culminates in his πιστεύω in v. 38 (cf. v. 11: ἄνθρωπος; v. 17: προφήτης; v. 33: παρὰ θεοῦ; v. 35: υἱὸς τοῦ ἀνθρώπου). Thus, chapter 9 is further evidence of the Johannine conjunction between seeing the miracle and coming to believe (see especially vv. 16b and 33).

The man born blind had received the sight of his eyes through Jesus' action, but it is through faith that he truly becomes a seeing person. The

---

[275] For the transferred use of τυφλός [blind] in the Old Testament and in Judaism under Hellenistic influence, see Schrage, *TDNT* 8:284–85, 287–93.

[276] See Brown, *John* 1:377; J. Schneider, *Johannes*, 187.

Jews, however, succumb to the *krisis*, because they remain unbelieving (vv. 39-41). For the evangelist, the revelation of Jesus' *doxa* in miracle and that in judgment belong together, insofar as revelation is, on the one hand, a glimpse of the divine and, on the other hand, the offense that provokes unbelief. "This is the paradox of the revelation, that in order to bring grace it must also give offence, and so can turn to judgement."[277]

It is not historiographical concerns,[278] but a strong christological interest that directs John's redaction of the narrative of the one born blind. Jesus' existence as the one who comes from God is visible in the σημεῖον; the miracle reveals the *doxa* of the wonder-worker and at the same time legitimates him, evoking both faith and unbelief.

3.7   John 11:1-44

3.7.1   *Context*

The raising of Lazarus is the high point of Jesus' public activity. At the same time, it is the occasion of the Jews' final decision to put him to death (11:53). John quite deliberately placed the greatest miracle in the New Testament here, at the point where the conflict between belief and unbelief reaches its climax. After a heightened controversy with the Jews (10:22ff.) and the statement that John the Baptizer did not perform any signs but that many believed because of the signs that Jesus did (10:40-42), we find this extraordinary miracle worked by Jesus in Bethany—therefore in the immediate neighborhood of Jerusalem. This miracle in turn evokes faith (11:45) and at the same time calls forth unbelief (11:47-53). The revelation of Jesus as the giver of life, which is evident to all, is contrasted to the Jews' decision for death: out of the most powerful sign arises the greatest deed of unbelief.[279] Because Jesus raises someone from the dead, he himself must suffer death.

3.7.2   *Redaction and Tradition*

All of v. 1 should be seen as traditional, within the framework of the exposition.[280] For ἦν δέ τις ἀσθενῶν [a certain one was ill], see 5:5; the name

---

[277] Bultmann, *John,* 341–42.

[278] Against Martyn, who severely neglects the evangelist's christological interest (*History and Theology,* 24ff.).

[279] See Schnackenburg, *John* 2:316. The special place of chapter 11 in the total construction of the Gospel points to a deliberate composition by the evangelist John and speaks unequivocally against Brown's position (*John* 1:414): "We shall see in treating chs. XI–XII that they have peculiarities which suggest that they are an editorial addition to the original gospel outline."

[280] See Schnackenburg, *John* 2:321–23; Barrett, *John,* 389–90.

Λάζαρος[281] appears also in Luke 16:20, 23-25. "Bethany" refers to the town in Judea (cf. v. 18) and is to be distinguished from the place of the same name mentioned in 1:28; 10:40.[282] In v. 1b, along with Mary and Martha (cf. Luke 10:38-42), two other persons who are important for the following events are introduced, and with ἐκ τῆς κώμης [from the village] a connection with Lazarus (only geographical for the moment) is established.[283] Many exegetes think that v. 2 should be regarded as a post-Johannine gloss,[284] whose only function is to identify for the reader the Mary who has just been mentioned. An indication of this within the content of the passage is the anticipation of 12:3 (or perhaps the reminiscence of Luke 7:37-38); linguistically, the absolute ὁ κύριος is again noteworthy.[285] In contrast, the hung-on relative clause, ἧς ὁ ἀδελφὸς Λάζαρος ἠσθένει [whose brother Lazarus was ill], is a necessary preparation for αἱ ἀδελφαί [the sisters] in v. 3a, which would otherwise arrive without any explanation; in the same verse, αὐτόν refers to τὸν κύριον in v. 2. In addition, the placement of Mary before Martha (cf. vv. 1 and 2 in contrast to vv. 5, 20-27) should be seen as a mark of tradition. The evangelist deliberately changes the order; therefore, v. 2 should be considered traditional, perhaps as a pre-Johannine addition.[286]

The Lukan and Johannine traditions about Mary, Martha, and Lazarus agree in many respects.[287] Thus it is said of Martha in Luke 10:38-42 that she is constantly occupied with διακονεῖν [serving], and in John 12:2 we read καὶ ἡ Μάρθα διηκόνει [and Martha served].[288] There is also a parallel concerning Mary; in Luke 10:39 she sits at Jesus' feet and listens to his words, while in John 11:20b it is expressly said that Mary was sitting in the house, where in vv. 28-29 she receives a message from Jesus.

---

[281] For the form of the name Λάζαρος (=Hebrew לעזר, "God has helped"), see Barrett, John, 389.

[282] See G. Schneider, EWNT 1:511-12.

[283] There is no reason to consider the reference to the sisters here as secondary (thus Schwartz, "Aporien," III, 166; Wellhausen, Evangelium Johannis, 52-53), because v. 1 functions within the exposition to introduce the persons who will be important in the event that follows.

[284] See Wellhausen, Evangelium Johannis, 52; Schwartz, "Aporien," III, 166; Bultmann, John, 396 n. 1; Schnackenburg, John 2:322; Becker, Johannes 2:345; Wilkens, "Erweckung," 23.

[285] But see the analysis of 6:23, which has shown that an absolute ὁ κύριος is by no means a sure sign of a gloss: against Schnackenburg, John 2:322. In addition, the conspicuous parallel of τὸν κύριον in v. 2 and κύριε in v. 3 with Luke 10:39 (where Mary is sitting πρὸς τοὺς πόδας τοῦ κυρίου [at the Lord's feet) and Luke 10:40 (where Martha addresses Jesus as κύριε) supports tradition.

[286] See Fortna, who considers this a redactional remark by the author of the "gospel of signs" (Gospel, 77). Haenchen also considers v. 2 original (John 2:57). He points out that in the Gospel of John known persons are often presented in a similar fashion: see 7:50; 19:39 (Nicodemus); 11:49; 18:14 (Caiaphas); 6:71; 12:4; 13:2; 18:2, 3, 5 (Judas).

[287] See Haenchen, John 2:69-70; Schnackenburg, John 2:341-42.

[288] The insertion of Mary and Martha into the anointing story is, from the perspective of tradition history, secondary. Mark 14:3 speaks only of a woman, and in Luke 7:37 the woman is a sinner.

Luke knows nothing about Mary, Martha, and Lazarus as brother and sisters; there is also a suggestion of their nonrelationship in the awkward formulations in John 11:1, 2. The Lukan parable about the rich man and poor Lazarus (Luke 16:19-31)[289] closes with the statement that the Jews would not repent even if Lazarus were to rise from the dead and return to life. That is exactly what happens in John 11, and the Jews do not repent. Instead, they decide that both Jesus and Lazarus must die (11:45-53).

The agreements do not indicate literary dependence, but we may suspect some contacts in the oral tradition.[290]

Verses 3-4 and 5-6 are doublets in a twofold sense: v. 4a tells us that Jesus has received a message from the sisters about their brother's illness, but v. 6a gives the impression that Jesus is hearing of Lazarus's sickness for the first time. While v. 3 already tells us of the friendship between Jesus and Lazarus, v. 5 expressly states that Jesus loved Martha, her sister, and Lazarus. Moreover, in v. 3 φιλεῖν is used to describe these relationships, and in v. 5 ἀγαπᾶν is employed for the same purpose. There can be no doubt that v. 3 is traditional, since the mention of one or more messengers is a common motif in the healing of those who are mortally ill (4:47) or in the reviving of those who are dead (Mark 5:35; Acts 9:38).[291] Furthermore, it is only in this verse that Jesus first enters the action. In contrast, v. 4 should be considered Johannine redaction, except for the introductory ἀκούσας δὲ ὁ Ἰησοῦς εἶπεν [but when Jesus heard it];[292] it gives a preliminary interpretation of the event that is about to take place. This position is supported by linguistic observations (for οὐκ . . . ἀλλά . . . ἵνα, see John 1:7-8, 31; 9:3; 13:18; 14:30c-31; for πρὸς θάνατον, see 1 John 5:16; for δι' αὐτῆς, see John 1:7; 3:17)[293] as well as by the considerable similarity in content to 2:11; 9:3. Lazarus's illness is not to lead to death, since it is the occasion for the revelation of the δόξα θεοῦ through Jesus' miracle. For Jesus himself, on the contrary, it is paradoxically the very making visible of the δόξα θεοῦ in this event that will finally make inevitable his way to the cross, which John interprets as a mutual glorification of the Father and the Son. The evangelist thus underscores the connection with the passion that is already evident from the placement of the text: in the raising of Lazarus, Jesus' own death and resurrection are anticipated.[294]

Verse 5, like verse 4, is the work of the evangelist, who very deliberately

---

[289] For an analysis, see Horn, *Glaube und Handeln,* 81–85.

[290] See Schnackenburg, *John* 2:340–43.

[291] See Theissen, *Miracle Stories,* 49–50.

[292] In favor of this is the parallel expression in v. 6a; see Fortna, *Gospel,* 78. All of v. 4 is considered redactional by Bultmann, *John,* 397 n. 4; Schnackenburg, *John* 2:322–23; Becker, *Johannes* 2:355.

[293] See Bultmann, *John,* 377 n. 4.

[294] See Schnackenburg, *John* 2:322–23.

places Martha more in the foreground than her siblings (cf. vv. 20-27)²⁹⁵ and who describes Jesus' affection with the characteristic Johannine word ἀγαπᾶν (37 times in the Gospel of John: Jesus' love for his own is found especially in 13:1, 34; 14:21; 15:9, 10, 12; see also "the disciple whom Jesus loved" in 13:23; 19:26). Verse 6 is also redactional, since its beginning repeats v. 4a, and v. 6b clarifies the statement about the length of time in v. 17.²⁹⁶ In addition, John uses Jesus' unusual delay to increase the magnitude of the miracle: after a certain length of time, a mere healing of a sick person becomes a raising of the dead.²⁹⁷ Verse 7 begins a new section that extends initially as far as v. 10: Jesus turns to the disciples, who are suddenly present, and speaks of a journey to Judea, without mentioning Lazarus. Verse 8 refers to the conflict with the Jews in 10:31-39 and introduces the theme of the passion, which is further developed in vv. 9 and 10. Jesus works in the world during the time that is destined for him (cf. 9:4), until the hour when he goes to the Father (13:1). He is the light of the world (8:12); whoever does not follow him remains in darkness and thus fails to attain salvation (12:35). The shift in the address, the anticipation in v. 7 of the ἄγωμεν [let us go] of v. 15, the theme of the passion, which is firmly anchored in the context, the lack of any reference to Lazarus, and the repetition of μετὰ τοῦτο λέγει in vv. 7 and 11 make it probable that vv. 7-10 are to be attributed to the evangelist.²⁹⁸

It is difficult to separate redaction and tradition in vv. 11-16. Although the mention of Lazarus in vv. 11-15 favors tradition, there are numerous elements in the content that point to the hand of the evangelist: the ambiguous talk about "falling asleep" and "awakening" in v. 11; the disciples' misunderstanding in v. 12, which is commented on in v. 13; the motif of "speaking plainly" (for παρρησία, see 7:4; 10:24; 11:54; 16:25; 18:20); the conjunction between seeing the miracle and believing in v. 15; and the mention of Thomas (see 14:5; 20:24-29).²⁹⁹

The ambiguous expression in v. 11 emphasizes Jesus' miraculous prior knowledge and at the same time prepares for the disciples' misunderstanding in v. 12. The disciples interpret Jesus' words in a superficial, earthly sense and fail to recognize the divine dimension of the event that is about to happen.

²⁹⁵ See Stenger, "Auferweckung," 22–23.
²⁹⁶ See Wilkens, "Erweckung," 24.
²⁹⁷ See Haenchen, John 2:58.
²⁹⁸ See Stenger, "Auferweckung," 20; Fortna, Gospel, 78–79 (counting only λέγει τοῖς μαθηταῖς as part of the model document); Haenchen, John 2:59; Schnackenburg, John 2:319 (considering vv. 7-16 redactional); Wilkens, "Erweckung," 24; Brown, John 1:432 (regarding especially vv. 7-8 as an addition); Becker, Johannes 2:356. According to Bultmann, the two ἐάν-clauses in vv. 9-10 are from the "Discourse on Light in the revelation-discourses" (John, 399 n. 1); for a critique, see Schnackenburg, John 2:326.
²⁹⁹ See Schnackenburg, John 2:319; Fortna, Gospel, 79. Among those who consider this section (except for v. 16) redactional are Stenger, "Auferweckung," 21; Haenchen, John 2:59–60; Becker, Johannes 2:348; Wilkens, "Erweckung," 24–25. (Becker and Wilkens, however, do not consider these verses part of their oldest stratum of tradition.)

Their misunderstanding consists in the confusion of earthly and heavenly matters; this serves to underscore all the more clearly Jesus' marvelous knowledge.[300] John comments on the disciples' attitude for the readers and reveals what, for him, is really important in the subsequent event: the raising of someone from the dead. In v. 14 the disciples learn this also, as Jesus reveals the meaning of his words about "sleeping" and "waking" in v. 11 and, in v. 15, immediately announces to the disciples the soteriological dimension of the coming event. Through his powerful act of awakening someone from the dead, they will come to believe—in other words, here again the evangelist introduces his conjunction between the seeing of a miracle and the resulting faith. The words καὶ χαίρω δι' ὑμᾶς in the mouth of Jesus give additional force to the meaning of the miracle to follow. Jesus does not heal out of pity but in order to demonstrate his power. The expression ἀλλὰ ἄγωμεν πρὸς αὐτόν [but let us go to him] in v. 15c could be part of the tradition,[301] since the phrase overlaps with the redactional ἄγωμεν εἰς τὴν Ἰουδαίαν πάλιν [let us go to Judea again] in v. 7 and prepares, within the course of events in the tradition, for v. 17. The redactional v. 16 refers back to the passion theme: Thomas[302] calls on the other disciples to accompany Jesus even to death.

With v. 17 the action resumes. Jesus appears at the grave of Lazarus, who has already been dead four days. Since, according to Jewish ideas, the soul remains in the body for only three days,[303] this statement of the length of time increases the magnitude of the miracle that follows. Verse 17 should be seen as part of the tradition, but the reiterated mention of the place in v. 18 and the appearance of the Jews with Mary and Martha must be regarded as redactional,[304] because both the expression ἡ Βηθανία ἐγγὺς τῶν Ἱερο-σολύμων [Bethany (was) near Jerusalem] and the Jewish mourners who in vv. 45-46 spread the word that the dead man has been raised are part of the passion theme.

The dialogue between Jesus and Martha in vv. 20-27 also goes back to John: this is supported by the characteristic placing of Martha first, and the almost identical statements of the two sisters in vv. 21b and 32b.[305] Only

---

[300] Against Bultmann, who thinks that this is the usual Johannine misunderstanding (*John,* 399 n. 6). Leroy (*Rätsel,* 6-7) agrees with Bultmann, regarding this as a "false interpretation of what is said." For the motif of misunderstanding of a miracle, see also Philostratus *Vita Apol.* 4.45.

[301] So Fortna, *Gospel,* 79.

[302] On this name, see Bauer, *Johannesevangelium,* 150; on the Thomas tradition, see Schnackenburg, *John* 2:327-28.

[303] See Billerbeck, *Kommentar* 2:544-45.

[304] See Wilkens, "Erweckung," 24; Stenger, "Auferweckung," 21. In contrast, Fortna considers vv. 18-19 part of the tradition, except for ἐκ τῶν Ἰουδαίων (*Gospel,* 80).

[305] See Stenger, "Auferweckung," 23; Fortna, *Gospel,* 80-81 (Johannine redaction of a fundamental basis within the source); Wilkens, "Erweckung," 23; Nicol, *Semeia,* 38; Schnackenburg, *John* 2:319.

Martha hears that Jesus has come[306] and runs to meet him, while Mary remains in the house (cf. Luke 10:38-42). In v. 21, Martha expresses her trust in Jesus and asks him indirectly "that he might now nevertheless call Lazarus back to life."[307] Jesus' answer is given a deliberately ambiguous formulation, so that it will be misunderstood. Martha understands Jesus' words in the sense of Jewish belief in the resurrection: the expectation of a general raising of the dead in the eschatological future.[308] She thus provides the dark background against which Jesus' revelatory word in vv. 25-26 gleams all the more dazzlingly. His powerful self-description in v. 25a is clarified by the couplet in vv. 25b-26ab:[309] the resurrection, as an overcoming of death and a gift of life, takes place when one believes in Jesus. This presumes that God has given Jesus power over life and death, as the "I am" saying[310] clearly emphasizes. At this point, soteriology and christology are fully in accord: it is only in the context of faith in Jesus that the fullness of salvation is realized. Jesus not only reveals σωτηρία [salvation]; he is it. This unheard-of message demands faith, and therefore in v. 27 Martha pronounces a confession that, in full agreement with 20:31, emphasizes Jesus' messiahship and his status as Son of God.

Is the evangelist deliberately using vv. 25-26 to correct any kind of future eschatology, opposing it with his own concept of a salvation that is fully present in faith? Our text alone cannot answer this question, but it does provide an important indication: the contrast John presents in 11:23-26 is not one of principle; it is an acute issue in the context, because it is only the subsequent miracle that demands a strong emphasis on present eschatology. It is only the raising of Lazarus as an obvious demonstration of Jesus' present power over life and death that makes the terse stress on present eschatology necessary. To that extent, this text cannot be claimed as proof of a fundamental conflict between Johannine statements that emphasize the presence of salvation and those that take account of the future of believers.[311]

Verses 28-31 are the work of the evangelist; they prepare for the encounter between Jesus and Mary presupposed by v. 32 and also allow for the Jews who are in the house to come to the tomb, where they will be witnesses to the raising of Lazarus.[312] Under these conditions, Martha's communication to her sister in v. 28, made in private out of fear of the Jews, should be understood as a reference to the passion of Jesus. Moreover, the strange

---

[306] The evangelist is not interested in knowing who told her this news.

[307] Haenchen, John 2:61.

[308] See Volz, Eschatologie, 229–56.

[309] See Schnackenburg, John 2:331; Bultmann considers vv. 25-26 a text from the "revelation discourses" (John, 402).

[310] On the Johannine ἐγώ εἰμι sayings, see Schnackenburg, John 2:79–89.

[311] What is more evident here is John's characteristic collapsing of temporal levels: see Bühner, "Denkstrukturen," 224–25.

[312] See Schnackenburg, John 2:333–34; Stenger, "Auferweckung," 21–22.

remark in v. 30 that Jesus had not yet entered the village also gains meaning. Since Lazarus has been buried somewhere outside the village, Jesus does not go directly to the house of mourning, and he is able to bring Martha to a true understanding of the coming event in the absence of the mourners. He then meets Mary and finally encounters the Jews only at Lazarus's tomb.[313] Thus the introduction to v. 32 ('H . . . 'Ιησοῦς) is also redactional, because it presupposes the events preceding the encounter between Jesus and Mary in vv. 28-31. With these verses, John again establishes the connection with the tradition available to him and at the same time prepares for further redactional additions.

The prostration of sick persons (cf. Mark 1:40; 5:6) or their representatives (cf. Mark 5:22: ἰδὼν αὐτὸν πίπτει πρὸς τοὺς πόδας αὐτοῦ [when he saw him, he fell at his feet]; 7:25) before Jesus, in order to attract attention and demonstrate confidence in the power of the miracle worker, is a traditional motif in miracle stories. (For the pagan sphere, see Tacitus *Hist.* 4.81; Philostratus *Vita Apol.* 7.21.)[314] Mary also proclaims her trust in Jesus' power: here the identical, but redactional, formulation on the lips of Martha in v. 21b leads us to suspect that v. 32c is traditional.[315] Mary's and the mourners' weeping arouses Jesus' anger (cf. Mark 5:38-39; for ἐμβριμᾶσθαι [to be indignant, angry], cf. Mark 1:43; 14:5; Matt. 9:30; the expression καὶ ἐτάραξεν ἑαυτόν [he was troubled] is John's: cf. 12:27; 13:21; 14:1, 27) because it raises doubts about his miraculous power.[316] At this, he insists on going to Lazarus's tomb in order to accomplish the miracle.

Jesus' weeping in v. 35 contradicts the tradition in vv. 33-34. Before, he had been offended by the mourners' weeping, and now he himself sheds tears. We must therefore ascribe v. 35 and the interpretation of Jesus' behavior in v. 36 to the evangelist, who at this point places strong emphasis on Jesus' humanity. The reference to chapter 9 in v. 37 is also the work of John: here the Jews' doubt about Jesus' power to work miracles motivates his renewed anger in v. 38a ('Ιησοῦς . . . ἐν ἑαυτῷ).[317] Verse 38b would follow very neatly after the traditional v. 34, reprising ἔρχου καὶ ἴδε [come and see] with ἔρχεται [he came]; now Jesus has finally reached the place where the event is to occur. A stone covers Lazarus's tomb.[318] It is to be removed at Jesus'

---

[313] See Haenchen, *John* 2:65.

[314] See Theissen, *Miracle Stories,* 53.

[315] Against Fortna, who considers both v. 21b and v. 32c redactional (*Gospel,* 81–82). It must be objected that the traditional motif of falling down is regularly connected with confessions, expressions of trust, and acclamations, and that John emphasizes Martha but not Mary.

[316] In my opinion, v. 34 demands this interpretation, because Jesus' insistence on going to Lazarus's tomb serves to eliminate all doubt about his power to work miracles: against Brown, who sees here Jesus' rage at the power of death and thus of Satan (*John* 1:425–26).

[317] See Schnackenburg, *John* 2:335; Fortna, *Gospel,* 82–83. However, Fortna still assigns 'Ιησοῦς οὖν in v. 38 to his "source."

[318] See Billerbeck, *Kommentar* 1:1051.

command (v. 39a). But the order is obeyed only in v. 41a, a clear indication of the redactional character of the inserted dialogue between Martha and Jesus.[319] Also supporting redaction are the prominence of Martha and the reference in v. 40b (cf. 2:11) back to vv. 25-26. In addition, the stench of the corpse in v. 39c contradicts the embalming presumed by v. 44. The leading theological ideas that characterize the Johannine editing of received miracle traditions are prominently in evidence here: the heightening of the miraculous and the conjunction between seeing the miracle and the resulting faith. Martha's statement that Lazarus has already been dead four days and is emitting the odor of decay sharply underscores the magnitude of the miracle that follows.[320] Jesus' answer to Martha's advice again emphasizes the close connection between miracle and faith; the miracle overcomes doubt, strengthens already existing trust, and evokes new faith.

Verse 41a connects with Jesus' command in v. 39; its original continuation was probably the call to Lazarus to come forth from the grave (vv. 43-44).[321] The evangelist has inserted a prayer of Jesus into this traditional sequence.[322] Jesus' thanksgiving to God even before the miracle expresses the unique connection between Father and Son (cf. 1:51; 5:19; 10:30, etc.) but is also a reference to the miracle worker's knowledge that the miracle is about to occur. Verse 42 expresses the Johannine concept of miracles in a remarkably compact fashion. Jesus' pointed reference to the crowd around him shows that the purpose of the miracle is faith in the divine legitimation and mission of the miracle worker. It is the very magnitude of the miracle that points to the Son of God and thus also witnesses to the Father. By no means is it a mere appendix or a superfluous addition: it is a central means for describing the content of Johannine christology.

The depiction of the miracle itself follows in vv. 43-44.[323] At Jesus' majestic command, Λάζαρε, δεῦρο ἔξω [Lazarus, come out here] (cf. Mark 1:25-26; 5:8; Luke 4:41), Lazarus comes out of the grave, still with strips of linen on his hands and feet and a cloth around his head (cf. John 19:40; 20:6-7 for Jesus), thus realistically demonstrating the miracle (cf. Mark 1:31; 2:12; 5:42, 43; John 5:9). A second miracle is added to the raising of the dead man; although Lazarus's hands and feet are bound by the linen strips and a cloth covers his face, he is able to walk and to find the door of the tomb (cf. the walking on water and miraculous landing in John 6:21).[324]

---

[319] See Schnackenburg, *John* 2:338; Fortna, *Gospel,* 83. Against Becker, who assigns v. 39 to the "signs source," but attributes v. 40 to the evangelist (*Johannes* 2:354–55).

[320] See Haenchen, *John* 2:67.

[321] See Schnackenburg, *John* 2:339; Fortna, *Gospel,* 83; Bultmann, *John,* 407 n. 9.

[322] Stenger, "Auferweckung," 23.

[323] In favor of tradition is also the New Testament *hapax legomenon* περιδεῖσθαι [to be bound] in v. 44.

[324] See Haenchen, *John* 2:67; Bultmann, *John,* 409; Bauer, *Johannesevangelium,* 154; Stenger, "Auferweckung," 26.

The raising of Lazarus has a great number of connections to traditions within and outside the Synoptics. There are strong similarities to the raising of Jairus's daughter (Mark 5:22-24, 35-43).[325] In both narratives the mortally ill person has died before Jesus arrives (Mark 5:35/John 11:17). The death is metaphorically described as "sleep" (Mark 5:39b/John 11:11). Jesus opposes the mourners' wailing (Mark 5:38-39b/John 11:33). Jesus, with a word of command, calls the dead person back to life (Mark 5:41/John 11:43) and gives orders after the awakening (Mark 5:43b/John 11:44b). There is only a minor relationship in the motifs (cf. the word of command in Luke 7:14/John 11:43) between the Lazarus story and that of the youth of Nain (Luke 7:11-17), but this story from Luke's special source probably indicates that at a relatively early period there were reports of the raising of dead persons outside the stream of Markan tradition.

The similarities in language and content between John 11 and the raising of Tabitha by Peter in Acts 9:36-42 are noteworthy.[326] After the death of this disciple, a group is sent to tell Peter (Acts 9:38: ἀπέστειλαν . . . πρὸς αὐτόν; John 11:3: ἀπέστειλαν . . . πρὸς αὐτόν). Like Jesus in John 11, Peter also accomplishes the miracle through a word of command (Acts 9:40). Through the miracle, many come to believe (Acts 9:42: ἐπίστευσαν πολλοὶ ἐπὶ τὸν κύριον; John 11:45: πολλοί . . . ἐπίστευσαν εἰς αὐτόν). Notable examples of the raising of dead persons in the pagan sphere are

---

Bultmann (*John*, 395 n. 4), Wilkens ("Erweckung," 23ff.), and Becker, (*Johannes* 2:344ff.) not only distinguish between redaction and tradition in John 11 but posit in addition an original report that had already been edited before being included in the "*sēmeia* source" (see also Gnilka, *Johannes*, 90, who also supposes three layers). Bultmann declines to attempt a reconstruction of this original narrative and only proposes that the sisters were originally anonymous, but Wilkens ("Erweckung," 27) and Becker (*Johannes*, 2:345) try to reconstruct the earliest level of narrative, which they think was then redacted both at the pre-Johannine level and by the evangelist. In doing so, they seem to be following the classical axiom of form criticism according to which the postulated normal form of a genre is to be regarded as historically primary—that is, concretely, in this case, a brief miracle story like those in the Synoptics. It is true that they differ in their detailed analyses: whereas Becker regards the mention of the sisters as original, Wilkens thinks that Mary and Martha must be excluded from the traditional story. In contrast, Wilkens considers Jesus' anger at the weeping mourners in vv. 33-34 to be part of the oldest tradition, while according to Becker these verses are the work of "SQ" (semeia source). If we agree with Becker that the tradition was always connected to the two sisters (which is supported by v. 3a, in which one cannot simply eliminate αἱ ἀδελφαί), it is not at all clear why vv. 33-34 should not be part of the oldest layer. But if these verses are original, it seems to me that v. 32 must also be counted part of the earliest tradition. Finally, it is impossible to understand why the two authors do not count v. 4a (ἀκούσας δὲ ὁ Ἰησοῦς εἶπεν [but when Jesus heard it, he said]) and v. 15c (ἄγωμεν πρὸς αὐτόν [let us go to him]) as part of the first layer of tradition, because that is the only way in which a connection can be made between the report in v. 3 and Jesus' arrival at the tomb in v. 17.

The differing reconstructions of Wilkens and Becker, as well as the weak points in both their analyses as just described, show that definite decisions about this supposedly oldest traditional level are no longer possible. It is more natural, however, to assume that the evangelist was in possession of a tradition that had not already been subjected to editing.

[325] See especially Schnackenburg, *John* 2:341–42. A comparison with biblical and extra-biblical descriptions of the raising of dead persons can be found in Kremer, *Lazarus*, 39–45, 97–109.

[326] On the linguistic parallels, see Fortna, *Gospel*, 84 n. 2.

Philostratus *Vita Apol.* 4.45; Apuleius, *Flor.* 19. In these two stories, however, we should note that it is a matter of the raising of persons only apparently dead.

The parallels mentioned cannot establish any literary dependence, but they indicate what a variety of traditions and motifs have entered into the composition of John 11.

3.7.3   *Interpretation*

The Johannine depiction of Jesus' public activity is decisively shaped by the repeated revelation of the Son of God through miracles and the resulting enmity of the Jews. It is no accident that the wedding at Cana and the raising of Lazarus frame Jesus' public appearance. Rather, in John 2:11 and 11:4, 40 the evangelist reveals his understanding of Jesus' activity: in miracles, the one *doxa* of the Father and of the Son is revealed in order to evoke faith.[327] Whereas at the beginning it was only the disciples who were brought to faith by the miracle (2:11), now we find that even many of the Jews believe in Jesus (11:45).[328] Thus, if the miracle is the place in which the glory of the Father and the Son is revealed, in the eyes of John the evangelist it cannot be merely a pointer to the "real issue," a concession to human weakness or a traditional element that has been theologically surpassed long since; rather, it stands at the center of Johannine christology. The raising of Lazarus shows this clearly, for here the various lines that make up the Johannine image of Christ converge into a thrilling unity.

The revelation of the *doxa* in miracles not only evokes faith, but also provokes disbelief. Miracles in John are at the same time "faith's favorite child" and the first occasion of unbelief, so that the redactional references to the passion within the framework of the Lazarus story (see 11:4, 7-10, 18-19, 28, 46) sharply outline the essence of unbelief: deliberate failure to recognize the divinity of Jesus that is revealed in the miracle and is thereby visible in history. Jesus raises a dead person, and for this he himself must be put to death! The heightening of the miraculous, as well (redactional: vv. 6, 15; traditional: vv. 17, 43-44), serves to disclose unbelief, for it is precisely the reality of the miracle thus emphasized that makes unbelief so much more puzzling. Beyond this, the uniqueness of the miracle points to the greatness and the origin of the miracle worker; it is his legitimation. The redactional v. 42 makes this connection clear; at this point the miracle functions to

---

[327] See Stenger, "Auferweckung," 35; Kremer, *Lazarus,* 36–38. In John 11:4, δοξασθῆναι [to be glorified] is to be applied primarily to the revelation of Jesus in the miracle (δι' αὐτῆς [through it] undoubtedly refers to Lazarus's illness), which then leads to the cross. Against Thüsing, who interprets δοξασθῆναι in John 11:4 as well as elsewhere only in terms of Jesus' "hour" (*Erhöhung,* 230).

[328] Verses 45-46 are by the evangelist. Linguistic parallels are 2:11, 23; 6:14; 7:13; see Schnackenburg, *John* 2:347. Against Fortna, who considers οἱ ἐλθόντες . . . αὐτόν in v. 45 to be traditional (*Gospels,* 84).

confirm, in the eyes of the crowd, what is specifically mentioned at this point, Jesus' sending by the Father. In this way, the raising of Lazarus almost becomes a miracle done for purposes of demonstration. It is precisely in the eyes of the evangelist that the miracles are a legitimation of Jesus' divinity, to the extent that in them his unique *doxa* is revealed and faith is evoked. The conjunction between seeing the miracle and the faith that results is found in vv. 15, 40, and 42, and is constitutive for the Johannine interpretation of the Lazarus tradition. Thereby the evangelist, like his tradition, presumes the historical fact of the miracle; the seeing of the *doxa* (cf. v. 40: ὄψῃ) is connected with a visible and tangible event in space and time.

The power of Jesus over life and death that is present in the miracles occasions the evangelist's present-eschatological statements in vv. 20-27. They are worked compositionally into the tradition by means of the early introduction of Martha, and their importance lies in the translation into a general theological statement of an event that, in the miracle itself, occurs at a particular point in time. What happened to Lazarus is now, from the point of view of the evangelist, the lot of all believers: they enjoy complete participation in the saving significance of Jesus' activity. This pointed anticipation of the effects of God's saving action in Jesus Christ, which already includes the believers' present, is the real meaning of the present eschatology in John 11. It is not the often-proposed contrast to future eschatology that is determinative but rather the evocation of tendencies that are already latent in the miracle itself.[329]

3.8   Other Uses of the word σημεῖον

Before we can give a concluding description and evaluation of the christology that is developed in Johannine redaction of the miracle traditions and indicate the consequences for the thesis of a pre-Johannine "semeia source," we must examine the other uses of σημεῖον in the Fourth Gospel. Especially important in this connection is 20:30-31, which many exegetes regard as the conclusion of a "semeia source," the Thomas pericope connected with it, and the relationship between σημεῖον and ἔργα [works] in John.

3.8.1   John 20:30-31

The Gospel of John originally ended with 20:30-31; at this point there is a retrospective emphasis on the "selective" character[330] of what has been

---

[329] Against Bultmann, *John*, 403–4; Becker, "Wunder und Christologie," 146–47; Schottroff, *EWNT* 2:268. For a critique of Bultmann's notion of the correction of "traditional" eschatology in John 11, see Blank, *Krisis*, 155–56.

[330] Bultmann, *John*, 697.

told, and the purpose of the whole presentation is stated. In form-critical terms, John here employs the well-known ancient literary *topos* of "unutterability,"[331] used especially in concluding statements to express the inexhaustibility of the subject.[332] Such concluding sentences are not at all unusual in the Johannine school, as shown by the parallels in 2 John 12 and 3 John 13.[333] Finally, both the secondary addition of chapter 21 and the repetition and variation of 20:30 in 21:25 (ἄλλα πολλά, ἐποίησεν ὁ Ἰησοῦς, γράφειν, βιβλίον) are proof that 20:30-31 must be regarded as the original conclusion of the Gospel of John.

The proponents of a pre-Johannine "semeia source" see in 20:30-31 the end of their presumed model document, which is now used by the evangelist to form the conclusion to the Fourth Gospel as a whole.[334] The many peculiarly Johannine expressions are clear evidence against this notion:[335]

1. Πολύς [many] occurs 39 times in the Gospel of John, and ἄλλος [other] 29 times (outside chap. 21). For the expression πολλὰ . . . σημεῖα, see 11:47.
2. For constructions with μέν . . . δέ, see 10:41; 16:9-11; 16:22; 19:24-25; 19:32-33.
3. The Gospel of John (excluding chap. 21) contains οὖν 190 times.
4. For the expression σημεῖα ἐποίησεν ὁ Ἰησοῦς [Jesus did signs], see 4:54 (σημεῖον ἐποίησεν ὁ Ἰησοῦς); see also 2:11, 18, 23; 3:2; 6:2, 14, 30; 7:31; 9:16; 10:41; 12:18, 37.
5. Ἐνώπιον [in the presence of] is found only here in the Gospel of John, but it is also in 1 John 3:22 and 3 John 6 (as well as 35 times in Revelation), so that this preposition cannot be called "un-Johannine."

---

[331] See Thraede, "Untersuchungen," 120ff.

[332] See Dibelius, *From Tradition to Gospel*, 40; Bultmann, *John*, 697; Becker, *Johannes* 2:632. Examples include Sir. 43:27; 1 Macc. 9:22; Lucian *Dem.* 67; on this subject see Bultmann, *John*, 697 n. 2; Dibelius, *From Tradition to Gospel*, 40 n. 3; Bauer, *Johannesevangelium*, 234. Jewish parallels may be found in Billerbeck, *Kommentar* 2:587. On the motif of "miracles are more than a human can describe," in Hellenistic texts, see Weinreich, *Heilungswunder*, 199–201. There are numerous examples from post–New Testament times in Bauer, *Leben Jesu*, 364–65. It can be objected against the examples offered by Bultmann that Sir. 43:27 and 1 Macc. 9:22 are not at the end of any book, but Lucian *Dem.* 67 concludes the book!

[333] In my opinion, on the basis of the whole body of form-critical parallels, it is beyond question that John 20:30-31 forms the conclusion to the *whole* Gospel; against Reim, who sees in these verses only the conclusion of the miracle stories but not the end of the book ("Johannes 21," 336); and Minear, who regards vv. 30-31 as merely the conclusion to chap. 20 ("John 21," 87ff.).

[334] Thus Faure, "Zitate," 108–9; Schulz, *Johannes*, 248; Bultmann, *John*, 698; Haenchen, *John* 2:212–13; Becker, *Johannes* 2:632; Fortna, *Gospel*, 197–98; Nicol, *Semeia*, 29–30; Schnackenburg, *John* 3:336.

[335] Conzelmann also considers 20:30-31 redactional, but without giving any further reasons for this conclusion (*Grundriß*, 380). See also Barrett, who vigorously denies the thesis that 20:30-31 is the end of a pre-Johannine "semeia source" (*John*, 575). J. Schneider also criticizes Bultmann's thesis that 20:30-31 is the conclusion of a "semeia source" (*Johannes*, 325).

6. The Fourth Gospel has μαθητής [disciple] 68 times (excluding chap. 21). At this point we should read the plural τῶν μαθητῶν αὐτοῦ (A, B, K, et al). Μαθητής in the plural with a possessive pronoun following it can be found 34 times in the Gospel of John. In terms of content, the central position assigned to the disciples at this point does not correspond to their role in the traditional miracle stories, so that the mention of them here must be considered redactional.[336] There are close content parallels in 2:11 and 11:15.

7. Γράφειν [to write] occurs 18 times (excluding 21:24). For (οὐκ) ἐστιν γεγραμμένα [they are (not) written], see especially 10:34; also 2:17; 6:31, 45; 12:14.

8. In the Gospel of John, βιβλίον [book] appears only in 20:30 (and 21:25; there are 23 additional instances in Revelation). It only made sense for the evangelist to use this word at the end of his Gospel.

9. Typically Johannine is the construction in v. 31, with a double ἵνα-clause dependent on γέγραπται. (The Gospel has ἵνα 145 times, and it is found 26 times in the letters.) The first ἵνα-clause, whose verb governs the following ὅτι-clause, presents the object of faith, and the second describes the soteriological dimension of the faith event. Close parallels to 20:31 are 1 John 1:4; 2:1; 5:13, where in each case a ἵνα-clause depends on γράφειν.

   In addition, there are, both in the Gospel and in the Johannine letters, numerous comparable ἵνα-clauses depending on other verbs: (a) λέγειν (with Jesus as speaker): John 5:34; 13:19; 15:11; ἐντέλλεσθαι: John 15:17; (b) ὁρᾶν, ἀκούειν, ἀπαγγέλλειν: 1 John 1:3; (c) ἐρωτᾶν: 2 John 5; with substantives of teaching and instructing: ἐντολή: John 13:34; 15:12; 1 John 3:23; θέλημα: John 6:39, 40; ὑπόδειγμα: John 13:15; ἀγγελία: 1 John 3:11.[337]

10. For ἵνα πιστεύειν [in order to believe], see 1:7; 3:15, 16; 6:29, 30, 40; 11:42; 13:19; 17:21; 19:35.

11. Parallels to the conjunction between seeing the miracle and the resulting faith, also presumed by John 20:30-31, are 2:11, 23; 4:50, 53; 6:30; 7:31; 9:35, 36, 38; 10:42; 11:15, 45; 12:37.

12. The listing of christological titles, Ἰησοῦς ἐστιν ὁ Χριστὸς ὁ υἱὸς τοῦ θεοῦ [Jesus is the Christ, the Son of God], has its closest parallel in 11:27; see also 1:49; 6:69. A simple Ἰησοῦς (with or without article) is found 238 times in the Gospel of John, absolute Χριστός 16 times (excluding 20:31) and υἱὸς τοῦ θεοῦ 6 times.

13. For the expression ζωὴν (αἰώνιος) ἔχειν [to have (eternal) life], in the sense of a promise of salvation, see 3:15, 16, 36; 5:24, 39, 40; 6:40, 47, 54.

---

[336] Schnackenburg sees this difficulty and therefore considers "in the presence of his disciples" to be a redactional addition (*John* 3:336).

[337] See Riesenfeld, "Zu den johanneischen ἵνα-Sätzen," 217ff.

14.   In the Fourth Gospel we find ὄνομα 24 times (without 20:31). Close parallels to 20:31 are 1:12; 2:23; 3:18.

The linguistic analysis reveals that the original conclusion of the Gospel in 20:30-31 does not rest on a "semeia source," but is the work of John the evangelist himself.[338] This makes all the more crucial the question: What does John intend to say in this concluding remark?

First, in v. 30a the evangelist emphasizes the selective character of his account: he has not used all the miracle stories in the tradition available to him. But then why does he revive, at this very point, the concept of σημεῖον, which he had employed for the last time in 12:37, at the end of Jesus' public activity? Does John regard Jesus' whole life, including his passion and resurrection, as σημεῖον? This interpretation can appeal to the connection between σημεῖον and resurrection in 2:18-22,[339] but it expands the concept of σημεῖον too much and, moreover, cannot explain why it does not appear in the passion account.[340] Therefore it seems more promising to look in v. 31 for an explanation of the revival of the concept of σημεῖον.[341] It is here that John indicates his purpose in writing the Gospel: to awaken and renew faith in the Son of God. The concept of σημεῖον is employed by the evangelist at this point because it is particularly well suited to name, in the most emphatic way, the revelatory quality of the work of Jesus, the quality that evokes faith. What was emphasized in the miracle stories by means of the conjunction between seeing the miracle and the faith that results is now said of the whole Gospel: it is written to evoke faith in the Son of God and to preserve and strengthen that faith.[342] At the same time, the obvious emphasis on the identity between Ἰησοῦς and ὁ Χριστός is aimed at docetists within the Johannine school who deny that identity (cf. 1 John 2:22-23; 4:2-3; 5:1).[343]

If the use of σημεῖον in v. 30 is conditioned by the agreement between the function of the miracle stories in awakening faith, on the one hand, and the goal of the whole Gospel, on the other hand, we can discern here both

---

[338] We must also reject Langbrandtner's attempt (*Weltferner Gott,* 37) and that of Thyen, ("Aus der Literatur," *ThR* 42, 269) to assign 20:30-31 to a "redactor." (According to Thyen, this was the author of chap. 21, whom he regards as the "fourth evangelist." On this, see section 1.2 above.)

[339] See Nicol, *Semeia,* 115.

[340] See Schnackenburg, *John* 3:336–337.

[341] Those who see 20:30-31 as merely the end of a pre-Johannine "semeia source" must explain why the evangelist revives the σημεῖον concept at the very end of his account, when elsewhere it refers primarily to concrete miracle stories. This problem is usually ignored, for example, by Becker, who thinks that in 20:30-31 the evangelist is not at all concerned with the concept of sign and has only introduced it "under pressure from the [semeia source]" (*Johannes* 2:633). Is this to say that John wrote the conclusion of his work, as important as it is, without reflection?

[342] Along these lines, see Barrett, "Zweck des 4. Evangeliums," 272; Kümmel, *Introduction,* 228–29; Brown, *John* 1:lxxviii.

[343] See Neugebauer, *Entstehung,* 28ff.

a continuity and an expansion in the use of the concept of σημεῖον. John consciously alludes to his interpretation of the miracle traditions, but at the same time he uses σημεῖον as a tool for interpreting his whole description of the words and deeds of Jesus, in order to prepare for the statement of the purpose of his Gospel in v. 31. Σημεῖον at this point becomes the hermeneutical key to the Fourth Gospel.

With his reference to the disciples in v. 30, John looks back to his interpretation of the Cana miracle in 2:11 and at the same time creates a contrast to 12:37, where he spoke of the unbelief of the ὄχλος in the face of Jesus' many miracles. This sheds light also on the purpose of the Gospel's presentation: it is the disciples before whom Jesus has done many other signs. That is, the Gospel of John is not a missionary tract for Jews or Gentiles, but it has its *Sitz im Leben* within the Johannine community traditions and school, as indicated also by the ἵνα-clauses[344] and πιστεύητε in v. 31a, which should be translated "so that you may continue to believe."[345] Finally, the expression ἐνώπιον τῶν μαθητῶν [in the presence of the disciples] could also be occasioned by the preceding appearances of Jesus to his disciples (20:19-23, 24-29).

3.8.2   *John 20:24-29*

Among the appearance stories, the Thomas pericope has a special importance, because, by immediately following it with vv. 30-31, John interprets it as σημεῖον.[346] The miraculous features of the narrative and their emphasis on the reality of the events described, which is verifiable in space and time, are also closely associated with the intensified depiction of the miraculous in the other Johannine miracle stories. In addition, the theme of seeing and believing recalls the Johannine conjunction between seeing the miracle and the resulting faith. Finally, there are many hints, in language and content, that the evangelist himself constructed this story and placed it in this prominent spot. These serve to strengthen the interpretation of the Thomas pericope as a Johannine σημεῖον.

In v. 24, Thomas is described as "one of the Twelve." The readers

---

[344] See Riesenfeld, "Zu den johanneischen ἵνα-Sätzen," 220.

[345] The external witnesses (𝔭66vid ℵ* B Θ 0250, 892s) also support the present tense. See Neugebauer, *Entstehung*, 11–12; Schnackenburg, *John* 3:338. The authors who see 20:30-31 as the conclusion of a "semeia source," which is to be understood as a missionary tract, favor the aorist πιστεύσητε; see Fortna, *Gospel*, 197–99; Nicol, *Semeia*, 29.

[346] See Rengstorf, *TDNT* 7:254. Against Brown (*John* 2:1058), the concept of σημεῖον cannot be extended to all the appearance stories in chap. 20, since that kind of extension would flatten the Johannine notion of σημεῖον and make the absence of the concept in the passion account all the more puzzling. Only the use of σημεῖον immediately after the Thomas pericope and the overlap in content with the other miracle stories, as here described, justify the application of the concept of σημεῖον to 20:24-29.

already recognize him from the redactional sections in 11:16 and 14:5, where he appears as a faithful disciple. Thomas was willing to die with Jesus, something that apparently prevents him from believing in the resurrection of his Lord.[347] The redactional character of v. 24 is indicated by a number of linguistic observations: for εἷς ἐκ τῶν δώδεκα [one of the twelve], see 6:71; εἷς with partitive ἐκ is found also in 6:8; 11:49; 13:21, 23; 18:26.[348] The additional description of Thomas as ὁ λεγόμενος Δίδυμος [called the Twin] is also found in the redactional verse 11:16. For ὁ λεγόμενος, see also 4:5, 25; 5:2; 9:11; 11:54; 19:13, 17. There are fifteen instances of εἶναι μετά [to be with] with a genitive following it, and Ἰησοῦς without an article occurs some 74 times in the Fourth Gospel (excluding chap. 21).

No further reason is given for Thomas's absence during Jesus' previous appearances; like v. 25, the statement about his being absent serves merely to prepare us for his encounter with Jesus. The other disciples only tell Thomas that they have seen Jesus. (For ἑωράκαμεν τὸν κύριον, cf. Mary Magdalene's ἑώρακα τὸν κύριον in 20:18.) Thus Thomas demands proof of the identity of the Risen One with the earthly Jesus. Verse 25b is a deliberate reference to and variation on v. 20: the double negative particle οὐ μή appears 17 times in the Gospel of John, and ἐὰν μή is found 18 times. In form and content, the closest parallel for the use of οὐ μή to introduce a conditional clause is the redactional verse 4:48 (see also 8:51-52 and 16:7). Just as 4:48 does not contain a general rejection of the miracle, so also in 20:25b there is no negative judgment on the connection between the miraculous seeing of the Risen One and the faith that results.[349] On the contrary, Thomas's conditions are fulfilled in v. 27,[350] so that v. 25 cannot be claimed as proof of a Johannine critique of miracles.

The introductory "after eight days" takes up the time indication in v. 19, and Jesus' second appearance occurs on the following Sunday, the memorial day of the Lord's resurrection (cf. Ign. Magn. 9.1; Barn. 15.9; also Rev. 1:10; Acts 20:7; Did. 14.1).[351] Jesus' miraculous appearance is taken word for word from v. 19. Although in that verse it had appeared in a plausible context, it is here contructed solely for the purpose of the subsequent conversation between Jesus and Thomas.[352] Typically Johannine expressions are οἱ μαθηταί with possessive following, and the asyndetic coupling with ἔρχεται ὁ Ἰησοῦς.[353]

---

[347] See Schnackenburg, John 3:329.

[348] See Dauer, "Herkunft," 63.

[349] Against Schnackenburg, who suspects here, as in 4:48, a critique of miracles (John 3:330).

[350] Käsemann correctly makes a point of this (Jesu letzter Wille, 53–54).

[351] See Schnackenburg, John 3:331.

[352] See Hartmann, "Osterberichte," 212; Dauer, "Herkunft," 59.

[353] Cf. Blass-Debrunner-Rehkopf §462, 1. E. Schweizer finds asyndeton 39 times in John (Ego Eimi, 91).

In v. 27, Jesus satisfies Thomas's demands. The linguistic agreements show clearly that this is a variation on v. 25b.[354]

Verse 25b	Verse 27
δάκτυλόν μου	δάκτυλόν σου
ἴδω ἐν ταῖς χερσὶν αὐτοῦ	ἴδε τὰς χεῖράς μου
καὶ βάλω μου τὴν χεῖρα εἰς τὴν	καὶ φέρε τὴν χεῖρά σου καὶ βάλε
πλευρὰν αὐτοῦ	εἰς τὴν πλευράν μου
οὐ μὴ πιστεύσω	μὴ γίνου ἄπιστος ἀλλὰ πιστός

In miraculous fashion, Thomas is able to test the identity of the Risen One with the earthly Jesus within space and time,[355] and so comes to believe. With the command μὴ γίνου ἄπιστος ἀλλὰ πιστός [do not be unbelieving, but believing], Jesus expressly accepts the connection between miraculous seeing and the faith that results.

Really seeing the Risen One causes Thomas to believe and evokes the confession of faith in v. 28. The introductory formula ἀπεκρίθη . . . καὶ εἶπεν αὐτῷ [he answered . . . and said to him] is typically Johannine.[356] The combination of ὁ κύριος and ὁ θεός points to the Old Testament (Ps. 34:23 LXX: ὁ θεός μου καὶ ὁ κύριός μου)[357] and has a content parallel within the Gospel, in Nathanael's confession (1:49).[358] It may be occasioned here by the expression ἑώρακα τὸν κύριον in 20:18 and the deliberate reference to 1:1c (θεὸς ἦν ὁ λόγος [the word was God]) and 1:18 (μονογενὴς θεός [the unique (or only-begotten) God]).[359] Thomas confesses Jesus as his Lord and God and thereby expresses the faith of the Johannine community in the divine sonship of Jesus Christ.

The statement[360] ὅτι ἑώρακας με πεπίστευκας [because you have seen

---

[354] That is why there are few characteristic Johannine linguistic features in v. 27: for the rare εἶτα [then], see 13:5; 19:27; φέρειν [bring, put] is found 15 times in the Gospel of John; for the construction with μή +imperative+following ἀλλά, see 6:27; 7:24; 19:21.

[355] It is not expressly said in the text that Thomas really put his finger into Jesus' wounds and his hand into his side, but Jesus' command in v. 27 and the confession in v. 28 presume it: against Lindars (John, 614) and Schnackenburg (John 3:332), who think that Thomas declined to make the test.

[356] See Ruckstuhl, Einheit, 199.

[357] See also Pss. 29:3; 85:15; 87:2. Pagan instances may be found in Deissmann, Light from the Ancient East, 361–62 (see esp. Suetonius Domitian 13: "Dominus et Deus noster" [Our Lord and God]).

[358] See also the confessions in 4:42; 6:69; 9:37-38; 11:27; 16:30; 20:16.

[359] See Schnackenburg, John 3:332–33.

[360] Against NA²⁶ and others, this sentence is not to be taken as a question, even though this is suggested by the parallels in 1:50 and 16:31. The interrogative form would express a detachment that is not at all characteristic of John. In addition, the perfect of πιστεύειν (contrasting with the present in 1:50 and 16:31) indicates solid faith and is better designed to connect the beatitude that follows with a statement than with a question; see also Schnackenburg, John

me, have you believed] on the lips of Jesus emphasizes once more the connection between miraculous seeing and the faith that results. The beatitude that follows brings a shift in accent. It applies to the generations who can no longer come to faith by seeing the Risen One directly.[361] Thomas exemplifies something that was already true at the time the Gospel of John was written: faith without the miraculous direct seeing of the Risen One that was granted to Thomas, and dependence on the tradition of the eyewitnesses. The different temporal perspectives are crucial for the interpretation of the Thomas pericope. Whereas vv. 24-29a report an event that was possible only at the time of the epiphanies of the Risen One and the first generation of disciples, v. 29b turns our attention to the future, as is clear from the very form of the beatitude.[362] Thus v. 29b does not criticize or relativize Thomas's having seen the Risen One just before, but merely formulates something that was already true of the subsequent generations but had not been the case for the eyewitnesses.[363] Unmediated seeing is restricted to the generation of the eyewitnesses. But because that seeing is the foundation of the Johannine tradition, it has a present importance in the kerygma for the Johannine community. There is a remarkable continuity between the manifestations of the earthly Jesus in miracles and the miraculous appearance of the Risen One in 20:24-29a: here, as before, we find the conjunction between seeing and the resulting faith, and here also the tangible reality of Jesus' resurrection is emphasized, like the demonstrable reality of his works in the earlier scenes.

In addition to the numerous characteristic Johannine linguistic features demonstrated earlier, both the technique of composition and the employment of individual motifs from 20:19-23 indicate that the Thomas pericope is the work of John the evangelist.[364] Thus ἑωράκαμεν τὸν κύριον in v. 25a refers to ἰδόντες τὸν κύριον in v. 20b,

---

3:334. The use of language in v. 29 is typically Johannine: the introductory formula λέγει αὐτῷ ὁ Ἰησοῦς is often found: see only 2:7; 4:7, 17, 21, 26, 34, 50; 5:8; 7:6; etc. Perfect forms of πιστεύειν occur 6 times and forms of ὁρᾶν 20 times; there are 98 occurrences of πιστεύειν and 62 of ὁρᾶν in the Gospel of John. Μακάριος [blessed] is also redactional in 13:17; see Schnackenburg, *John* 3:334.

[361] See Schnackenburg, *John* 3:334–35; Kohler, *Kreuz und Menschwerdung,* 207ff.

[362] This future accent is very clear in 13:17, where the disciples are promised salvation if they realize Jesus' example in the future (= ἐάν; see Bultmann, *John,* 476 n. 5; Strecker, *EWNT* 2:931). The conspicuous aorist participles do not contradict this, since v. 29b refers to a situation that will always obtain for the Johannine Christians in the future but is thought of as already beginning. See Blass-Debrunner-Rehkopf §§333, 3a and 373, 7; Schnackenburg, *John* 3:334–35. Dodd (*Tradition,* 354) and Strecker (*EWNT* 2:931) see a tradition-critical connection between the macarism in 20:29 and the beatitude of the eyewitnesses in Luke 10:23 and Matt. 13:16.

[363] Against Wilckens, who understands v. 29 as a "highly critical saying" (*Auferstehung,* 53), and Haenchen, who thinks the story of Thomas is not "in harmony with the spirit of the evangelist" (*Weg Jesu,* 558). On the contrary, Käsemann sees the matter correctly (*Jesu letzter Wille,* 54), as do Cullmann, *Early Christian Worship,* 43; Lindars, *John,* 616; Barrett, *John,* 574; de Jonge, "Signs and Works," 109.

[364] See the comprehensive demonstration in Dauer, *Johannes und Lukas,* 251–59; see also

and Thomas's response in v. 25b is clearly modeled on v. 20a. The indication of time in v. 26a refers to v. 19a, and Jesus' miraculous coming in v. 26b corresponds to the description in v. 19b. Finally, the encounter between Jesus and Thomas in v. 27 is a variation of v. 25b.

The composition of the Thomas story also points to the hand of the evangelist: there are notable parallels to the Nathanael narrative (1:45-51).[365] Nathanael first reacts skeptically (1:46) to Philip's message (1:45). He then meets Jesus, and in the course of the encounter Jesus overcomes the disciple's disbelief (1:47, 48). Nathanael's confession of faith follows (1:49), and Jesus in turn comments on it and makes it the occasion of a general statement (1:50, 51).

Finally, the traditional narrative[366] in 20:19-23 also witnesses to the redactional character of the Thomas pericope, since it presumes that *all* the disciples are present when the Spirit and the power to forgive sins are bestowed.[367] Nowhere is it suggested that Thomas is to receive a special revelation.

The physical presence of the Risen One is also strongly emphasized in Luke 24:36-43, and the motif of the doubting disciple is found in Matt. 28:17 and Mark 16:11-14 as well. This indicates the strong interest of a late stage of tradition in the demonstrable reality of the resurrection body, but it is not proof of either literary or tradition-historical dependence.[368] There is an instructive pagan parallel in Philostratus *Vita Apol.* 7.41; 8.42.[369]

In the Thomas pericope, John the evangelist combines two current theological problems of his community: while fending off a docetic denial of the identity of the crucified Jesus with the risen Christ, he must also answer questions about the resurrection faith of those who were forced to rely on the testimony of the eyewitnesses. An antidocetic tendency is expressed in Thomas's desire to touch Jesus' wounds in order to confirm the bodiliness of the Risen One and his identity with the earthly Jesus.[370] Thomas is granted his wish, and thereby he as an eyewitness expressly confirms that the Risen

---

Fortna, *Gospel,* 142–43; Schnackenburg, *John* 3:328; Hirsch, *Auferstehungsgeschichten,* 10–11; Becker, *Johannes* 2:628; Kohler, *Kreuz und Menschwerdung,* 179–80.

[365] See Grundmann, *Zeugnis und Gestalt,* 92; Dauer, "Herkunft," 60–61.

[366] For an analysis, see Schnackenburg, *John* 3:321–28.

[367] Ibid., 327–28.

[368] Against Dodd, who supposes some tradition-historical connections (*Tradition,* 145–46).

[369] See Reitzenstein, *Wundererzählungen,* 48; Bauer, *Johannesevangelium,* 233; Bieler, Θεῖος ἀνήρ, 1:48–49. Billerbeck offers a Jewish parallel to the Thomas pericope (*Kommentar* 2:586).

[370] See Richter, who, however, considers the Thomas pericope a secondary insertion by his "antidocetic redactor" ("Fleischwerdung," 180ff.) Wellhausen (*Evangelium Johannis,* 93) and Schwartz ("Aporien" I, 348–49) saw the end of their Johannine "basic document" in 20:18 and therefore regarded the Thomas story as an addition; this thesis has recently been revived by Langbrandtner (*Weltferner Gott,* 35–38) and Thyen ("Aus der Literatur," ThR 42, 261–68). Both of them see 20:19-31 as the work of their "redactions." But neither literary-critical arguments nor observations about content substantiate this thesis; in addition, the analysis above has shown that the language of 20:24-29, 30-31 is clearly Johannine. For a critique of Langbrandtner and Thyen, see also Dauer, *Johannes und Lukas,* 289–95.

One exists in the same flesh in which he suffered and died.[371] The continuity thus asserted between the earthly body of Jesus and the resurrection body is directed against members of the Johannine community who deny Jesus' real coming in the flesh, and thus also his suffering and death and the reality of the resurrection body (cf. 1 John 2:22, 23; 4:2, 3, 5:1).[372] It is probable that the question of the resurrection faith of later generations was also provoked by these opponents within the community. If they denied Jesus' bodily resurrection, it must have caused other members of the community to question the character and reliability of the bases of their own faith. John responds with a reference to the eyewitnesses, who confirm Jesus' resurrection in the flesh and on whose trustworthiness the later community can and must rely. Thus, the Johannine community knows itself to be in continuity with the tradition that rests on the eyewitnesses' unrepeatable seeing, for Jesus has promised to this community: μακάριοι οἱ μὴ ἰδόντες καὶ πιστεύσαντες [blessed are those who have not seen and yet have come to believe].

3.8.3   Signs and Works

John's use of σημεῖον (σημεῖα) and his use of ἔργον (ἔργα) overlap, so that the individual concepts and their relationship to each other require investigation.

3.8.3.1   σημεῖον

The subject of all seventeen occurrences of σημεῖον in the Gospel of John is Jesus: this alone indicates the exclusively christological meaning of this concept.[373]

In 2:11; 4:54; 6:14; 9:16; 11:47; 12:18; and 20:30, σημεῖον (σημεῖα) serves as a designation and characterization of a miracle previously described. What the Synoptic tradition referred to as δύναμις [power, authority], John calls σημεῖον: Jesus' ability to do miracles and his actual doing of them. Only the healing of the lame man at the pool of Bethesda (5:1-9ab) is not called σημεῖον, but afterward it is apparently referred to as ἔργον (7:21). Σημεῖον (σημεῖα) serves as a summary description of miracle(s) in

---

[371] The fact that the disciple's wish is fulfilled by Jesus speaks decisively against Bultmann's opinion that Thomas's doubt is "representative of the common attitude of [those] who cannot believe without seeing miracles (4:48)" (*John,* 696; similarly Schulz, *Johannes,* 246–47; Dodd, *Interpretation,* 443). What we have here is not a critique of miracles; on the contrary, Thomas's miraculous seeing is a precondition for the later generations' belief without seeing. For criticism of Bultmann, see esp. Käsemann, *Jesu letzter Wille,* 53–54, 89–90; Kohler, *Kreuz und Menschwerdung,* 192–213.

[372] See the analysis of these texts in section 2.2.2.2 above. Against Schnackenburg (*John* 3:335) and Becker (*Johannes* 2:627), who dispute any antidocetic intention in the Thomas pericope and assign it merely a pastoral function.

[373] See Hofbeck, *Semeion,* 68.

2:23; 6:2; 7:31; 10:41; (11:47); 12:37; (20:30). In these passages it is primarily the people who, in light of Jesus' miracles, either come to believe or persist in unbelief.

As a demand for a sign, σημεῖον appears in 2:18; 6:30 on the lips of the Jews. This motif is common in the Synoptic tradition (cf. Mark 13:4 par., the disciples' request for a sign; Mark 8:11-12; Matt. 12:9-42; 16:1-2, 4; Luke 11:16, 29-32, the Jews' demand for a sign; see also 1 Cor. 1:22). But John adopts it in an altered form: Jesus does not, as in the Synoptics, reject the demand for a sign; instead, the σημεῖον is given a positive sign character. It points to Jesus, who is the real Temple (cf. 2:19-22) and the real food (cf. 6:31-35).[374] In 4:48, as well, Jesus only rejects the demand for signs and wonders in order subsequently to accomplish a miracle himself.[375] In 3:2 and 6:26, the σημεῖα are considered a legitimation of Jesus' divine mission.

The previous analyses have shown that the use of σημεῖον in 2:11; 4:48, 54; 6:2, 14; 9:16; 11:47; 20:30 can be traced to John the evangelist himself. It is difficult to decide whether 2:18 represents redaction or tradition. The immediate context favors the traditional character of this verse: v. 17 is clearly recognizable as a redactional insertion,[376] and v. 18 appears to be a continuation of the previous section, 2:14-16. In addition, Mark 11:27ff. and parallels indicate an original connection between the cleansing of the Temple and the question of authority. That is, from the point of view of tradition history, v. 18 must also be regarded as traditional. On the other hand, the language of the verse is Johannine;[377] the subject designation οἱ Ἰουδαῖοι is probably attributable to John;[378] and the transformation of the Synoptic question about authority into a *demand* for a sign could come from the intention of the evangelist to portray the Jews as a group as unbelieving, in contrast to the disciples.[379] John 2:18 could be traditional, but we must consider the possibility that the evangelist himself shaped the connection as given.

In contrast, John 2:23 is clearly redactional.[380] With the transitional verses 2:23-25, John connects the cleansing of the Temple with the Nicodemus dialogue (cf. 4:43-45; 10:19-21, 40-42; 11:55-57), and the reference to the σημεῖα in 2:23 is a precondition for 3:2.[381] The evangelist's linguistic

---

[374] On this, see Hofbeck, *Semeion*, 78–90.

[375] For an analysis of 4:48, see section 3.2.2 above.

[376] See Schnider and Stenger, *Johannes und die Synoptiker*, 38–39; Fortna, *Gospel*, 146.

[377] Thus, for example, the introductory expression ἀπεκρίθησαν [they answered] (ἀποκρίνομαι 77 times in the Gospel of John without chap. 21) οὖν in connection with a form of λέγειν is typically Johannine (1:26, 48; 3:3, 9, 10; 4:10, 13, etc.; overall, Johannine ἀπεκρίθη καὶ εἶπεν occurs 30 times in place of the Synoptic ἀποκριθεὶς εἶπεν); δείκνυμι occurs 9 times, ποιεῖν 110 times in the Fourth Gospel.

[378] See Schnider and Stenger, *Johannes und die Synoptiker*, 39.

[379] See Schnackenburg, *John* 1:348–49.

[380] See Bultmann, *John*, 130; Schnackenburg, *John* 1:357; Becker, *Johannes* 1:131.

[381] In addition, the mention of Jesus in 2:23-25 is precondition for 3:1ff., as shown by the simple ἦλθεν πρὸς αὐτόν [he came to him] in 3:2.

style[382] appears in the transitional ὡς δέ [now when] (cf. 7:10; ὡς οὖν in 4:1, 40; 18:6) and in the expressions πολλοὶ ἐπίστευσαν εἰς τὸ ὄνομα αὐτοῦ [many believed in his name] and σημεῖα ποιεῖν. The reference to the σημεῖα in 3:2 is also redactional, because the Nicodemus pericope is a didactic dialogue composed by the evangelist on the basis of the traditional words of the Lord in 3:3, 5.[383] In 6:26, Jesus does not respond at all to the crowd's question in v. 25; instead, with ζητεῖν [to seek], he continues the thought of the (redactional) v. 24.[384] Moreover, the key word σημεῖον refers back to 6:2, 14, and v. 27 also represents a renewed introduction both of the theme (beginning of the bread of life discourse) and the terminology (v. 26: ζητεῖν/ἄρτος; v. 27: ἐργάζεσθαι/βρῶσις). All these indicate the redactional character of 6:26.[385]

In contrast, the demand for a sign in the context of the bread of life discourse in 6:30 must be regarded as traditional. When the people, in v. 31, ask for a feeding miracle in the wilderness, as in the time of Moses, it appears that the feeding of five thousand, which took place immediately before this, has been completely forgotten. This contradiction must be due to the evangelist's combining of different traditions (v. 26!); that is, vv. 30ff. are a traditional element of the bread of life discourse. The use of σημεῖον in 7:31, however, is traceable to the evangelist. This is supported by the reference to the crowd's belief in miracles, which by this time is almost schematic (cf. 2:23; 6:14; 9:16; 10:42; 11:45, 47), as well as by the conception of the Messiah's miraculous works (in this form specifically Johannine), placed on the lips of the crowd in the debate over the Messiah in chapter 7. There are no convincing parallels for this concept in Jewish literature.[386]

The remark in 10:41 that, although John the Baptizer did no miracles, his witness to Jesus is nonetheless true should be understood against the background of the raising of Lazarus. This serves, on the one hand, to indicate that the accomplishment of miracles is an outstanding characteristic of Jesus' public activity and therefore a legitimation of his divine origin and, on the other hand, to reduce the Baptizer to a mere precursor who appears only in order to function as a witness (see 1:19-34; 3:28). The conscious emphasis on the distance between Jesus and John the Baptizer (see 1:8, 15, 19-27, 29-34; 3:26-30; 5:33-36) indicates the hand of the evangelist, as do the stereotypical reference to the faith of the crowd in v. 42 (see 2:23; 3:18; 7:31; 11:45) and the placement in this context of the transitional section (10:40-42)[387] (for typically Johannine transitional expressions, see 2:23-25;

---

[382] See Bultmann, *John*, 130 n. 3.

[383] For a thorough grounding of this statement, see section 4.1.3 below.

[384] See Haenchen, *John* 1:289.

[385] See Bultmann, *John*, 218.

[386] See the analysis of 6:1-15 in 3.4.2 above.

[387] Against Bultmann (*John*, 393 n. 2) and Becker (*Johannes* 1:340), who see 10:40-42 as part of their "semeia source." As support for this, Becker offers the statement of place in v. 40, but

4:43-45; 10:19-21; 11:55-57)—for John 11 is a powerful illustration of the validity of the statement in v. 41.[388] In addition, it can be shown that there are many features in this section that are characteristically Johannine in style.[389]

John connects Jesus' entry into Jerusalem with a renewed reference to the raising of Lazarus (12:12-19). Although vv. 12-15 should be assigned to the tradition,[390] vv. 16-19, and thus also τὸ σημεῖον in v. 18, can be traced to the evangelist; in the case of vv. 17-19 this is clear from the reference back to chapter 11.[391] John once again brings forward the crowd that was present at the raising of Lazarus[392] and that now appears in Jerusalem to witness to the greatness of this miracle. Because the crowd has heard about this great σημεῖον from the eyewitnesses,[393] it has come to meet Jesus (cf. v. 12). The Pharisees are worried over this development, because all the world seems to be going after Jesus. By combining an existing tradition about Jesus' entry into Jerusalem with the Lazarus pericope, the evangelist again emphasizes that Jesus' greatest miracle evokes both belief and unbelief, even to the point of deadly enmity.

The concluding remark in 12:37 about Jesus' public activity is also the work of the evangelist.[394] This is indicated, in the first place, by the numerous Johannine stylistic features: for the genitive absolute, see especially 8:30;[395]

---

this is not persuasive, because the evangelist is here deliberately referring (τὸ πρῶτον) to 1:28, probably because of the mention of "Bethany" (cf. 11:1, where, however, the reference is to a different Bethany).

[388] This observation alone speaks decisively against Brown's supposition that vv. 40-42 are the original conclusion of John 5-10, to which chaps. 11 and 12 were then secondarily appended (*John* 1:414).

[389] Verse 40: ἀπέρχομαι (21x), πάλιν (41x), τόπος (16x), ἐκεῖ (23x); v. 41: πολύς (39x), ἔρχομαι (151x), πρός (99x); for the expression ἦλθον πρὸς αὐτὸν καὶ ἔλεγον, see 3:2, 26; for σημεῖον ποιεῖν, see 2:11, 23; 4:54; 6:14, 30; 9:16; 20:30. For πολλοὶ ἐπίστευσαν in v. 42, see 2:23; 3:18; 4:39; 7:31; 8:30; 11:45; 12:11, 42.

[390] The motif of the disciples' remembering in v. 16 shows that it is redactional (see 2:22). On the traditional character of vv. 12-15, see Bultmann, *John*, 417; Schnackenburg, *John* 2:373.

[391] See Bultmann, *John*, 417; Schnackenburg, *John* 2:373; Becker, *Johannes* 2:376.

[392] The original reading ὅτι refers to 11:42.

[393] For the Johannine διὰ τοῦτο . . . ὅτι, see 5:18; 8:47; 10:17; 12:39.

[394] See Schnackenburg, *John* 2:412ff.; Fortna, *Gospel*, 199; Nicol, *Semeia*, 39. Against Faure ("Zitate," 108), Bultmann (*John*, 452), and Becker (*Johannes* 2:408–9), who see 12:37-38 as part of the "semeia source." The decisive argument for them is the difference between v. 38 and vv. 39-40, according to which vv. 39-40 are said to be a deterministic interpretation of. v. 38, from the pen of the evangelist. But this is not persuasive, because neither the introductory formula (cf. 15:25) nor the literal LXX citation of Isa. 53:1 (cf. the literal citations of LXX in 2:17; 10:34; 19:24) is evidence against the work of the evangelist. Thus, the dominant motif of human responsibility and guilt in vv. 37-38 is taken up again and extended in vv. 42-43; that is, the evangelist does *not* wish to have the quotation on unrepentance from Isa. 6:9-10, which he has freely reformulated (see the details in Schnackenburg, *John* 2:414–15), understood in a deterministic fashion. Instead, he emphasizes human (co)responsibility here as well as in vv. 37-38.

[395] See also 4:51; 5:13; 6:23; 7:14; 13:2; 20:19, 26.

for τοσοῦτος [so many], see 6:9; 14:9; and for ἔμπροσθεν [before], see 1:15, 30; 3:28; 10:4. Clearly Johannine is σημεῖα ποιεῖν (see 2:11, 23; 3:2; 4:54; 6:14, 30; 7:31; 9:16; 10:41; 11:47; 12:18; 20:30), and for (οὐκ) ἐπίστευον εἰς αὐτόν [they did not believe in him], see especially 2:11; 4:39; 3:16; 6:40; 7:31; 8:30; 9:36; 10:42; 11:45, 48; 12:42. In the immediate context, the key word πιστεύειν in this verse functions to prepare for the Old Testament quotation that follows. Consequently, the correspondence between 12:37 and 20:30-31 cannot be missed. The depiction of Jesus' public appearance closes with a negative judgment on the unbelief of the people in the face of Jesus' great miracles; the readers of the Gospel, in contrast, are to come to believe through the signs that are described. This contrast between unbelief in the face of the revelation of Jesus to the world and the faith demanded of the readers of the Gospel, precisely on the basis of Jesus' works, is to be attributed to the evangelist.

The use of σημεῖον in the Fourth Gospel is entirely redactional, except for 2:18 and 6:30; thus the concept of signs is a deliberate theological, that is, christological, tool for interpretation employed by the evangelist.[396] It is developed out of the traditional motif of the demand for a sign,[397] and serves John as a succinct term for Jesus' revelatory activity. The subject of σημεῖα ποιεῖν is exclusively Jesus, and no word of Jesus is ever called σημεῖον.[398]

The exclusive use of σημεῖον in the context of christology and of the theology of revelation, as we find it in the Fourth Gospel, is without analogy. It is to be seen as the unique theological achievement of John the evangelist.[399] In terms of the history of religion, the Septuagint may serve as the background, in the broad sense, for the Johannine concept of σημεῖον.[400] Here we may mention especially Num. 14:22, where God says to Moses: πάντες οἱ ἄνδρες οἱ δρῶντες τὴν δόξαν μου καὶ τὰ σημεῖα, ἃ ἐποίησα . . . [none of the men who have seen my glory and the signs that I did . . .]; see also Exod. 15:1ff.

---

[396] Against Becker ("Wunder und Christologie," 136), who ascribes all the "pejorative" uses of semeia to the evangelist (2:18, 23; 3:2; 4:48; 6:26, 30; 7:31; 9:16; 11:47; 12:18) and the "positive" uses to the "semeia source" (2:11; 4:54; 6:2, 14; 10:41; 12:37; 20:30-31). The correct interpretation, in contrast, is represented by Betz and Grimm, *Wunder Jesu,* 124: "The semeion concept is genuinely Johannine."

[397] It is probably no accident that only the demand for signs in 2:18 and 6:30 is traditional. The evangelist has independently developed this existing motif and made it a central component of his christology.

[398] See Rengstorf, *TDNT* 7:248–49. This fact alone speaks against Bultmann's conclusion (*Theology* 2:60) that "*the works of Jesus* (or, seen collectively as a whole, his work) *are his words.*"

[399] See Rengstorf, *TDNT* 7:251. Riga's suggestion that "the signs are invitations by Christ for men to interpret their deeper spiritual meaning" cannot be documented ("Signs of Glory," 423). A "deeper, spiritual" sense cannot be found in the texts themselves.

[400] See the comprehensive survey of the material in Rengstorf, *TDNT* 7:208–21; also Heiligenthal, *Werke als Zeichen,* 135ff. Pagan parallels are suggested in M. Whittaker, "'Signs and Wonders,'" 155ff.

3.8.3.2 ἔργον

Among the 27 occurrences of ἔργα in the Fourth Gospel, 4:34 and 17:4 stand out because of the singular ἔργον and because of their prominence as the first and last instances of the word. Here, as Jesus' individual ἔργα, or those of the Father, are summarized and the trajectory of interpretation is indicated, the whole event of incarnation is described as ἔργον.[401] In the first instance the "one work" of Jesus refers to the salvific work of the earthly Jesus, but this does not exclude a consideraton of the work of the exalted Lord. In 5:20 we read of the μείζονα ἔργα [greater works], which will surpass the miracle of healing the sick. In the context, this can only refer to the future (see the future tense, δείξει) work of the exalted Lord as judge and giver of life (5:21ff.; see also 14:12-14).[402]

Among the various types of works are, first, Jesus' miracles.[403] There is an unmistakable reference to the σημεῖα in 5:20, 36; 6:29, 30; 7:3, 21; 9:3, 4; 10:25, 32ff.; 14:10-11; 15:24. The miracles, as works of Jesus, have both the quality of revelation and the function of legitimation (cf. Matt. 11:2-6) and are the palpable expression of the unity of the Son with the Father. The works witness to the unity of Father and Son. This second major field of meaning for ἔργα in John's Gospel is evident in 4:34; 5:36; 6:28-29; 9:4; 10:25, 32, 37; 14:10; 17:4. The Son accomplishes the ἔργα τοῦ θεοῦ [works of God]; he does the will of the one who sent him, and for that precise reason the works witness to him.

The words of Jesus can also appear as ἔργα: see 5:36-38; 8:28; 14:10; 15:22-24. The interchangeability of words and works, however, does not in any way signify "the identity of work and word"[404] of Jesus in John. Although both of them are the vehicles of revelation, only the works constitute a demonstrable, obvious reality in space and time.[405] Moreover, 10:32-38 and 14:8-12 indicate that the evangelist is able to distinguish the two.[406] Jesus' works are continued by the disciples, to whom it is promised in 14:12 that they will do greater works than Jesus. Jesus' departure to the Father makes possible the μείζονα ἔργα, which are thus works of the exalted Lord performed through the disciples.[407] Jesus fulfills the requests made to him in his name and thus guarantees the μείζονα ἔργα (14:13-14). It is not only the disciples, Jesus, or God who accomplish ἔργα, but also people in general (3:19), the nation (6:28-29), or the cosmos (7:7) can perform works.

---

[401] See Bultmann, *John*, 222 n. 3; Thüsing, *Erhöhung*, 58, 62; Hofbeck, *Semeion*, 147.

[402] See Thüsing, *Erhöhung*, 58ff.

[403] The miraculous deeds of Apollonius can also be described as ἔργα καὶ λόγοι [works and words]; see Philostratus *Vita Apol.* 8.12; see also Sir. 48:14. For Philo's usage, see Delling, "Wunder," 80 n. 26.

[404] Bultmann, *Theology* 2:61.

[405] See Thüsing, *Erhöhung*, 59 n. 28.

[406] See de Jonge, *Signs and Works*, 124.

[407] See Thüsing, *Erhöhung*, 115.

In addition, John also speaks of the works of Abraham (8:39) and the works of the devil (8:41). The moral quality of these ἔργα is determined by whether they are accomplished by God (3:21) or come instead from the devil or from the world (3:19; 7:7; 8:41).

3.8.3.3   Signs and Works

Σημεῖα and ἔργα are parallel concepts only to the extent that both describe Jesus' miraculous activity. But only Jesus can do σημεῖα; ἔργα, on the other hand, can be done by the disciples, the nation, people in general, and even the devil. Whereas σημεῖον is always used absolutely, ἔργον is usually followed by a qualifying genitive (see 7:7; 9:4; 10:34).[408] The σημεῖον is exclusively a palpable work of revelation, but ἔργα can also be words of revelation. The σημεῖα are limited to Jesus' public activity, but there are also ἔργα of the exalted Lord.

For John, therefore, σημεῖον is a concept with an exclusively christological content. It designates, in particular, the palpable revelation of Jesus' *doxa* in miracles that evoke both faith and unbelief. In contrast, ἔργον is much more comprehensive than σημεῖον. It can refer to the whole salvific work of Jesus but functions primarily as a witness to Jesus' divine mission. The unity of the Father and the Son is apparent in the ἔργα, which in turn witness to that unity. While ἔργα appears here in a soteriological context, it also reveals an ecclesiological meaning in the works of the disciples and an ethical significance in human ἔργα πονηρά [evil works] or ἔργα ἀγαθά [good works].

The fourth evangelist thus deliberately distinguishes between σημεῖα and ἔργα. The exclusively christological meaning of σημεῖον as a precise designation of the revelatory work of the Incarnate One is in no way relativized by John's speaking of the ἔργα Χριστοῦ or θεοῦ; it is, instead, enhanced.[409]

3.9.   Objections to the Idea of a "Semeia Source"

Against the *opinio communis* in recent Johannine research that posits the existence of a pre-Johannine "semeia source" and is represented by, among others, R. Bultmann, R. Schnackenburg, E. Haenchen, G. Richter, R. Fortna, J. M. Robinson, J. L. Martyn, D. M. Smith, W. Nicol, and J. Becker, we must, on the basis of the preceding redaction-critical investigation, raise the following objections.

---

[408] See Wilkens, *Zeichen und Werke*, 85.

[409] Wilkens's suggestion (*Zeichen und Werke*, 86) that "the *erga* evidently have nothing to do with the *semeia*" cannot be documented.

3.9.1   *The Enumeration of the Miracles*

The enumeration in 2:11 and 4:54 is regarded as an essential indication of the existence of a "semeia source."[410] According to the theory, the source contained a numbering of the miracles, but this has been retained only in the case of the first two. But our exegesis of 2:11 and 4:54 showed that these verses, and thus the numbering as well, come from John the evangelist. He counted Jesus' two miracles in Cana in order to place emphasis on them as the beginning and end of Jesus' first public activity. There is no contradiction to the summary mention of miracles in 2:23 and 4:45, because those speak of miracles in *Jerusalem*. With this, the principal clue to the existence of a pre-Johannine "semeia source" drops out!

R. Fortna[411] and H. P. Heekerens,[412] in agreement with F. Spitta,[413] include 21:14 in their source, so that the miraculous catch of fish becomes the "third" numbered miracle. But the numbering in 21:14 is undoubtedly the work of the post-Gospel redaction, which at this point refers to the two previous appearances in 20:19-23, 24-29.

3.9.2   *The Conclusion of John's Gospel*

John 20:30-31 is frequently regarded as the end of a "semeia source" and is connected closely with the enumeration of miracles. Here again, the analysis has shown that these verses are to be attributed to the evangelist. He uses the concept of σημεῖον as a succinct expression of the revelatory quality of Jesus' actions, as depicted beforehand in the Gospel, with their power to evoke and strengthen faith.

3.9.3   *The Background in Tradition and the History of Religions of the Pre-Johannine Miracle Stories*

A tradition that is clearly unique to the Johannine school makes its appearance in 2:1-11. The imagery chosen by the narrator points to the world of Hellenistic thought; it is only in that context that we find the motif of changing water into wine (Philostratus *Vita Apol.* 6.10), and only there do we find instances of the title ἀρχιτρίκλινος [chief steward].[414]

---

[410] I refer here, by way of example, to the arguments offered by Bultmann (*John*, 113) and Becker (*Johannes* 1:114). Lindars remarks on this point: "Everyone knows that the main clue to the existence of the source is the numbering of the first two signs" (*Behind the Fourth Gospel*, 29).

[411] See Fortna, *Gospel*, 95ff.

[412] See Heekerens, *Zeichen-Quelle*, 45–47.

[413] See Spitta, *Johannesevangelium*, 3.

[414] Cf. Billerbeck, *Kommentar* 2:407ff.; Barrett, *John*, 193.

A special Johannine tradition of the Synoptic type is John 5:1-9ab. The structural similarities to the Synoptic miracle stories stand out (cf. Mark 2:1-12; 3:1-6; Luke 7:11-17; 13:10-17),[415] and there are even some literal correspondences (cf. John 5:8 with Mark 2:11). The motif of the healing power of water occurs both in Jewish[416] and in pagan contexts, and ὑγιὴς γίνεσθαι [to be healed] in vv. 6, 9a could be a reference to the cult of Asclepius.[417] There is a very close parallel to the demonstration of the healing (5:9ab) in Lucian *Philopseudes* 11 (see also Philostratus *Vita Apol.* 4.45).

The healing of the one born blind in John 9 is also a special tradition of the Johannine school. The miracle story proper, in vv. 1-7, has Synoptic (Mark 8:22-26; 10:46-52) and Hellenistic parallels.[418] The remark in v. 1 is to be regarded as a heightening of the miraculous: the beggar is said to have been blind from birth. The motif in v. 2 of blindness as the consequence of sin occurs especially in Jewish sources[419] but is also documented in Hellenistic miracle stories, in the altered form of blinding as punishment.[420] Finally, the healing power of saliva was generally recognized in ancient medicine.

A further Johannine special tradition that appears in a strongly redacted form is the raising of Lazarus in John 11. In its present state it seems heavily overburdened, but in its traditional, basic form it reveals, both in its characters (Luke 10:38-42; 16:19-31) and in its topic (Mark 5:22-24, 35-43), a significant closeness to Synoptic traditions, but more especially to Acts 9:36-42. Here also, a heightening of the miraculous is a characteristic touch: not only is Lazarus raised from the dead, but despite the linen bands on his hands and feet and the cloth over his face, he finds his way to the door of the tomb.

The healing of the son of a βασιλικός in John 4:46-54 rests on a tradition held in common with Matt. 8:5-13/Luke 7:1-10. Even though no literary dependence can be demonstrated, the common features in the tradition are unmistakable. From the point of view of the history of religions, John 4:46-54 has a close parallel in *b. Ber.* 34b, where it is reported of Rabbi Ḥanina ben Dosa that he healed a son of Gamaliel II through prayer.[421] Both are instances of healing at a distance, in which the motif of the "hour" plays a central role. Healings at a distance are found both in the Jewish and in the pagan sphere.[422] The motif of miraculous foreknowledge in v. 50 has

---

[415] See the table in Dodd, *Tradition,* 175.

[416] See Billerbeck, *Kommentar* 2:454; Nicol, *Semeia,* 56.

[417] Here we may think primarily of the Asclepius shrines. For the parallels, see Rengstorf, *Christusglaube und Asklepiosfrömmigkeit,* 16–17.

[418] See Deissmann, *Light from the Ancient East,* 135–36.

[419] See Billerbeck, *Kommentar* 2:527ff.

[420] See Weinreich, *Heilungswunder,* 189ff.

[421] See Billerbeck, *Kommentar* 2:441.

[422] See Reitzenstein, *Wundererzählungen,* 124; Clemen, *Religionsgeschichtliche Erklärung,* 153, 218.

impressive parallels in the stories about Apollonius of Tyana.[423]

The miraculous feeding of five thousand and Jesus' subsequent walking on water in John 6:1-25 are dependent, both literarily and in their tradition history, on Mark 6:32-52. Characteristic for the feeding story are the intensification of the miraculous in vv. 7 and 11(fin) and the eucharistic echoes in v. 11. The closest religious-historical parallel is 2 Kings 4:42-44.[424] Also characteristic for John 6:16-25 is an impressive description of the miracle; in this narrative, which originally was an epiphany, motifs of walking on the sea and stilling the storm are combined with another miracle — the sudden arrival of the boat at the shore in v. 21b. Religious-historical parallels to walking on the sea are found both in the Old Testament[425] and in Hellenism;[426] but it appears that in pre-Christian times the motif of a miraculously rapid landing of the boat existed only in Greek literature.[427]

John the evangelist apparently took miracle stories from the various strands of tradition that were available. Besides those that are clearly special traditions in the Johannine school, there are others of the Synoptic type, one narrative whose tradition history is very closely bound up with the Synoptic tradition, and finally two miracle stories taken from Mark's Gospel. The religious-historical findings are equally complex. Not only Old Testament and Jewish but also Hellenistic and pagan motifs and influences can be demonstrated.

This result speaks against all attempts to locate the pre-Johannine miracle tradition within the framework of a "semeia source" as part of a *closed* traditional and religious-historical background.

Thus, for example, R. Bultmann thought that the "semeia source" was part of the propaganda for Christian faith developed by former disciples of the Baptizer.[428] It was to show "Jesus as the θεῖος ἄνθρωπος, whose miraculous knowledge overwhelms those who meet him."[429] More recent studies tend to locate the "semeia source" in the Jewish sphere. R. Fortna sees the *Sitz im Leben* of the source in the early Christian mission to the Jews.[430] It was "a textbook for potential Jewish converts," and its purpose was simply "to prove one thing, and one thing only: that Jesus was the Messiah in whom

---

[423] See section 3.4.2 above.

[424] For pagan parallels, see Bultmann, *History of the Synoptic Tradition,* 236.

[425] See Nicol, *Semeia,* 58–59.

[426] See Bieler, Θεῖος ἀνήρ 1:96–97; Bultmann, *History of the Synoptic Tradition,* 236–37.

[427] See Bultmann, *John,* 216 n. 4.

[428] See Bultmann, *John,* 108 n. 6. Smith makes a similar suggestion, that the "semeia source" has its *Sitz im Leben* in the mission of the Baptizer's disciples ("Milieu," 175ff.).

[429] Bultmann, *John,* 106. See also in this sense Dibelius, *From Tradition to Gospel,* 94; Haenchen, *John* 1:192–93, etc.; Koester, *Introduction* 2:184; H. D. Betz, *RAC* 12:304; Schottroff, *Der Glaubende,* 257ff.; Becker, "Wunder und Christologie," 137ff.; Fortna, *Gospel,* 230–31 (very cautiously); Martyn, "Source Criticism," 254 (also with reservations).

[430] See Fortna, *Gospel,* 223–25. Here Fortna also posits a connection between the "gospel of signs" and Paul's opponents in 2 Corinthians 10–13.

men should believe."[431] The source is said to have originated in Syria before 70 C.E.[432] W. Nicol also emphasizes the Jewish background[433] and missionary purpose[434] of the Johannine miracle stories. H. P. Heekerens interprets his "signs source" against the background of controversy with the Baptizer movement in Samaria;[435] its religious-historical starting point would have been the Old Testament Elijah traditions.[436] Heekerens thinks that the purpose of the "signs source" must have been "strengthening the faith of the (Samaritan) followers of Jesus against attacks by the Baptizer movement."[437] H. M. Teeple locates the "semeia source" in the controversy between Christianity and Judaism after Javneh.[438] It would have been written after 75 C.E. by a Gentile Christian as an apologetic document.[439]

3.9.4   Stylistic Criticism and the "Semeia Source"

Stylistic peculiarities have been used in different ways to indicate the presence of a "semeia source." H. M. Teeple makes them the single criterion for his reconstruction of sources;[440] R. Fortna places great value on them;[441] and W. Nicol[442] recognizes the assessment of characteristic features of style as one among several methodological approaches. But J. Becker does without them completely,[443] and E. Haenchen expressly rejects them.[444] This spectrum alone makes clear how necessary it is to give some consideration to this methodological problem.

Language, as the expression of authorial and theological individuality, in principle permits us to draw conclusions about the author of a text. Literary unity points to a single author, just as linguistic and stylistic variations can indicate the work of several hands. If an author is distinguished from other comparable writers by a particular style, then we have found a criterion for the attribution of texts to that author.[445] E. Schweizer and E. Ruckstuhl, in particular, have attempted to establish this criterion for John; they postulate, respectively, thirty-three or fifty characteristic features of

---

[431] Fortna, *Gospel,* 234.
[432] Ibid., 225.
[433] See Nicol, *Semeia,* 53–68.
[434] Ibid., 77–79.
[435] See Heekerens, "Zeichen-Quelle," 133ff.
[436] Ibid., 132.
[437] Ibid., 139.
[438] See Teeple, *Origin,* 145.
[439] Ibid., 143–47.
[440] Ibid., 142ff.
[441] See Fortna, *Gospel,* 203ff.
[442] See Nicol, *Semeia,* 16ff.
[443] See Becker, *Johannes* 1:113ff.
[444] See Haenchen, *John* 1:55–66.
[445] See Schweizer, *Ego Eimi,* 87–88.

Johannine style.[446] A word or construction is regarded as Johannine if it is found frequently in John but seldom or never in the rest of the New Testament. If these characteristic features of Johannine style do not appear in particular parts of the Gospel, then we may conclude that reworked traditions are present. If, however, the characteristic features are distributed throughout the whole Gospel, its unity would appear to be established.

To these basic principles of methodology, we add the following critical reflections:

1. An author's style cannot be established simply by contrast with other authors. Words, expressions, and constructions that are frequently found in the rest of the New Testament can also be "Johannine."

2. A comparison limited to the New Testament is not sufficient, because a number of Johannine stylistic features are found also in the nonliterary *koine*.[447] An expansion of the material used for comparison results in a reduction in Johannine linguistic individuality.[448]

3. We should not look merely for an "idiolect" of the evangelist or the traditions he edits, but for a Johannine "sociolect." Within the Johannine school there evidently developed a kind of group language that makes it difficult to draw conclusions about a particular author on the basis of stylistic features.[449]

4. Johannine stylistic criticism is always in danger of circular reasoning, because it is used at one point to reconstruct literary layers and then, later, to verify them. Thus it is at the same time an analytic and a synthetic method.

5. The power of stylistic analysis to offer proof essentially depends on the texts that an exegete assigns to a postulated literary layer. The larger the posited literary basis, the more conclusive the stylistic analysis. For example, for R. Fortna, John 21:1-14 plays an important part in proving a unified style in the "semeia source." But if one denies that this miracle story was part of the original Gospel of John, for the reasons given in section 1.2. above, his stylistic analysis loses a great deal of its persuasive force.

---

[446] See Schweizer, *Ego Eimi*, 88ff.; Ruckstuhl, *Einheit*, 203ff. Jeremias ("Johanneische Literarkritik," 35, 37, 40–41) and Menoud (*L'Évangile de Jean d'après les recherches récentes*, 16) extend Schweizer's list by four characteristics each. Nicol even extended the list to eighty-two characteristics (*Semeia*, 23–24).

[447] Colwell has conclusively demonstrated that the nonliterary *koine* is the linguistic home of the fourth evangelist (*The Greek of the Fourth Gospel*). Epictetus, in particular, must be considered parallel.

[448] This is forcefully stated by Haenchen, *John* 1:55ff.

[449] See Thyen, "Aus der Literatur," *ThR* 39, 299; idem, "Aus der Literatur," *ThR* 42, 214; Heekerens, *Zeichen-Quelle*, 27–32.

6. Extensive literary-critical or tradition-historical theories based on stylistic criticism cannot rest simply on words that occur once, twice, or three times in the whole of the Gospel.

7. If texts are significantly different from the style of John the evangelist, this for the moment indicates only the possibility that the texts are traditional. Something that proves to be pre-Johannine tradition is not a priori part of a "source." We can speak of a connected or unitary "source" only if, on the one hand, the texts do not reveal features of Johannine style and, on the other hand, we can show that they *consistently* evince stylistic features of their own.

Rudolf Bultmann was the first to make extensive use of stylistic analysis as a method for Johannine literary criticism. In 1927 he demanded a methodology that would collect "stylistic characteristics in a careful manner, . . . whereby criteria for the distinction of tradition and redaction, sources and author could be established."[450] In his commentary on John he responded to his own demand, by employing numerous stylistic characteristics in reconstructing the "semeia source" and "revelatory discourse source." Characteristic of the "semeia source," according to Bultmann, is a slightly semitizing Greek:[451] the verb is consistently placed at the beginning of the sentence; there are frequent occurrences of asyndetic sentences in series, connected by καί, δέ, οὖν; superfluous αὐτοῦ and ἡμεῖς are almost completely missing; and Semitic expressions can be pointed out. "The source was therefore probably written in Greek by a Greek-speaking Semite."[452] Bultmann's stylistic analysis has been energetically contradicted by E. Schweizer, but more especially by E. Ruckstuhl. Both see the linguistic unity of the Fourth Gospel, which they affirm, as a decisive argument against source hypotheses. "The Fourth Gospel is a thoroughly unified work; the author has laid down a clear plan for it and incorporated in it a single spirit."[453]

In more recent research, stylistic analysis is not used as evidence against, but rather as a support for, the reconstruction of sources. Thus R. Fortna regards the absence from his "source" of thirty-two of the fifty stylistic characteristics established by Ruckstuhl as a clear proof of the source's existence. "Thirty-two (or 64%) of the characteristics are never found in the source."[454] Although in the first instance this result only supports the traditional character of individual pericopes, Fortna attempts beyond this to demonstrate a particular style within the "source." This style, in turn, serves

---

[450] Bultmann, "Johannesevangelium in der neuesten Forschung," 503.
[451] See Bultmann, *John* 98–99 n. 6; 180 n. 2; 238 n. 1; 329 n. 2; 395 nn. 2, 4.
[452] Ibid., 98–99 n. 6.
[453] Ruckstuhl, *Einheit*, 218.
[454] Fortna, *Gospel*, 205.

as the principal support for the thesis of a combination of miracle and passion traditions in his "gospel of signs."[455]

Fortna finds that, with one exception (1:19-34), each individual pericope contains a stylistic characteristic of the whole "source." His argumentation is not persuasive in detail.[456] Of nine words that appear frequently in the New Testament but only in the "source" in John's Gospel,[457] five occur only once in the Gospel of John (ἕτερος, ἐνώπιον, ἄρχεσθαι, ὑπὸ with the accusative, ἰσχύειν), so that they cannot demonstrate a connection between the miracle and passion traditions. Moreover, ἐνώπιον is redactional in 20:30, and ἰσχύειν appears in the additional chapter in 21:6, so that it scarcely bears authority as a proof. Four words appear three times each in the Gospel of John, three of them at least once each in the miracle and in the passion traditions (ἕκαστος, εὐθέως, and adverbial πρῶτον).[458] Of eight words that are rare in the New Testament and appear in the Gospel of John only in the "source," κραυγάζειν alone is found both in the passion story and in the miracle tradition. It occurs elsewhere in the New Testament only three times (Matt. 12:19; Luke 4:41; Acts 22:23).

Five stylistic features that Ruckstuhl attributes to the evangelist are regarded by Fortna as characteristic of the "source."[459] Ἱεροσόλυμα with the article appears in 2:23; 5:2; 11:18. John 5:2 contains traditional material, but 2:23 and 11:18 are clearly redactional.[460] With regard to the typically Johannine ἑλκύειν [to draw, drag] (8 instances in the New Testament, 5 of them in John), Fortna distinguishes between a metaphorical use (6:44; 12:32) and a literal use (18:10; 21:6, 11).[461] The metaphorical use is said to be typical of the evangelist, but the literal use is characteristic of the "source." We must object that metaphorical ἑλκύειν cannot appear in the "source" at all, because it only fits the Johannine discourses, which are not part of the "source."[462] Moreover, 21:6, 11 cannot be regarded as serious proof.

Fortna ascribes the plural ὀψάρια [fish] (6:9, 11; 21:10) to the "source," as one of its stylistic characteristics; he thinks that, in contrast, the evangelist used the collective singular ὀψάριον (21:9, 13).[463] In the first place, it is highly doubtful that ὀψάριον in 21:9, 13 can be the work of the evangelist; beyond that, the different uses of the word are founded in the material, not in its belonging or not belonging to a source. The collective singular ὀψάριον always refers to fish as food, which does not need to be counted. In contrast, ὀψάρια is used when the fish are counted.[464] The typically Johannine πιάζειν (12 times in the New Testament, 8 times in John) is,

---

[455] Ibid., 214–17.

[456] See the critique of Fortna by Robinson, "The Johannine Trajectory," 236–52; Ruckstuhl, "Johannine Language and Style," 125–47.

[457] See Fortna, Gospel, 214–15.

[458] Contrary to what Fortna says (Gospel, 215), σύν (John 12:2; 18:1; 21:3) cannot be counted among these, because it does not appear in a miracle tradition.

[459] Fortna, Gospel, 216.

[460] Even Fortna (Gospel, 213) cannot deny this with regard to 2:23; he therefore supposes that here the evangelist was imitating the style of the source.

[461] Ibid., 208–9.

[462] See Nicol, Semeia, 13 n. 3.

[463] See Fortna, Gospel, 209.

[464] See Nicol, Semeia, 13 n. 3.

according to Fortna, a stylistic characteristic of the "source" in 21:3, 10. He gives as foundation for this the fact that here πιάζειν means "to catch" (fish), but elsewhere it means "to arrest."[465] Here again we must object that this slight shift in meaning is grounded in the matter at issue, for 7:30, 32, 44; 8:20; 10:39; 11:57 speak of Jesus, not of fish. Only one characteristic (substantive + ἐκ = made of) occurs both in the miracle and passion traditions (2:15; 9:6; 19:2).[466] But here again, the construction is demanded by the material (making a whip of cords, a paste of earth and saliva, a crown of thorns), and it may not be regarded as an unchanging element of style.

Fortna includes eleven further features that are said to be unique to the "source."[467] They appear elsewhere in the New Testament but are seldom found in the work of John the evangelist. Introductory or reintroductory ἦν (δέ) can scarcely be called a stylistic criterion, since Fortna deliberately omits the comparable usages, καὶ ἦν or ἦν with the participle, which are frequent in the Synoptics.[468] Nor can an interpolative or explanatory ἦν (see 11:2, 18; 18:10, 13, 28, 40; 19:14, 19, 23) serve to prove the Johannine unity of miracle and passion traditions, since John the evangelist uses exactly the same construction with reference to Jewish festivals (see 5:9; 6:4; 7:2; 9:14; 11:55).[469] In addition, ὡς with a number can be regarded as a stylistic characteristic only in a restricted sense, for the eight Johannine occurrences (1:39; 4:6; 6:10, 19; 11:18; 19:14[39]; 21:8) must be compared to ten other New Testament instances (Mark 5:13; 8:9; Luke 1:56; 8:42; Acts 4:4; 5:7, 36; 13:18, 20; Rev. 8:1).[470]

When Fortna mentions, as an additional feature, the use of a singular verb with a double subject (1:35, 45; 2:2, 12 [cf. Acts 11:14; 16:31]; 4:53; 18:1b, 15; etc.) we should consider that with a double subject a preceding predicate in the singular corresponds to normal Greek style and is often found in the New Testament.[471] The fact that John the evangelist also used this construction is shown by the redactional ἔρχεται Ἀνδρέας καὶ Φίλιππος καὶ λέγουσιν [Andrew and Philip went and told] in 12:22.

Fortna also considers οὖν after a command (1:39; 6:10; 9:7; 11:41; 21:6) as a further stylistic feature of the "source."[472] But with a total of 202 occurrences of οὖν in the Fourth Gospel, it is methodologically very doubtful to regard this particular usage as a stylistic characteristic.

Similarly, a number with ἐκ cannot be regarded as a characteristic feature; it is so frequent in the Synoptics that E. Schweizer did not include it in his list of Johannine stylistic features.[473] Furthermore, it is attested also for the evangelist in 7:50; 20:24.[474]

---

[465] See Fortna, *Gospel,* 211 n. 3.

[466] Ibid., 211.

[467] Ibid., 216.

[468] Ibid., 216 n. 4.

[469] Fortna does mention this in a footnote (*Gospel,* 216 n. 5) but deliberately does not evaluate its significance.

[470] See *BAGD,* 899.

[471] See Blass-Debrunner-Rehkopf §135.

[472] See Fortna, *Gospel,* 216.

[473] See E. Schweizer, *Ego Eimi,* 92.

[474] See Robinson, "The Johannine Trajectory," 248.

Partitive ἐκ with a substantive is, for Fortna, a further feature of the "source" (3:1; 4:7; 6:13; 18:3). Here again we must raise doubt, since ἐκ in place of the partitive genitive is a characteristic of Johannine style,[475] and it is highly questionable whether 3:1 and 4:7 can be considered part of a source.

Fortna regards ῥαββί(-ουνί) as a title of address for Jesus as a further indication of the connection between the miracle and passion traditions.[476] The facts are clearly contrary to this thesis. Although ῥαββουνί appears in 20:16, elsewhere in the Gospel the address is always ῥαββί (1:38, 49; 3:2, 26; 4:31; 6:25; 9:2; 11:8)! Ἔχειν with an indication of time is found both in traditional (9:21, 23; 11:17) and redactional (5:5, 6; 8:57) sections of the Gospel and can therefore not be seen as a stylistic feature of the "source."

In addition, Fortna's posited unity between the miracle and passion traditions cannot be established by ὄνομα αὐτῷ [his name] (1:6; 3:1; 18:10) or ἔρχου καὶ ἴδε [come and see] (1:39, 46; 4:29; 11:34); the first of these expressions does not appear in miracle stories, and the second is not found in the passion traditions.

Fortna's analyses can demonstrate neither a characteristic style of the "source" nor a unity between the miracle and passion traditions at a pre-Johannine stage.[477]

For W. Nicol, stylistic criticism is one of four methods for demonstrating the existence of a "semeia source." (The other three are form, aporiae, and ideological tensions.) In contrast to Schweizer and Ruckstuhl, he is interested not in the presence but in the absence of characteristic features of Johannine style in individual texts.[478] Nicol extends Ruckstuhl's list by thirty-two features and then inquires about the distribution of these (now eighty-two) stylistic characteristics within the Gospel.[479] He thus finds that five miracle stories (2:1-12; 4:46-47, 50-54; 5:1-9; 6:16-21; 9:1-2, 6-7) have remarkably few of these stylistic features, and he concludes from this: "I contend that this cannot be ascribed to chance and must mean that in these five miracle stories there is evidence of the influence of a style different from that of John: he must have taken them from tradition."[480] With this conclusion we entirely agree. It tells us that John took miracle stories from available tradition but not that these narratives stem from a unified "source"!

Stylistic criticism is useful, as one among a number of methods in Johannine exegesis, for demonstrating the traditional character of *individual* pericopes.[481] But it cannot prove the existence of a unified "semeia source,"

---

[475] See E. Schweizer, *Ego Eimi,* 92; Ruckstuhl, *Einheit,* 195.

[476] See Fortna, *Gospel,* 217.

[477] See also Schnackenburg, *John* 2:522 n. 3: "The combination of σημεῖα stories with a passion narrative to form a 'Gospel of Signs' is perhaps the main weakness of R. T. Fortna's view."

[478] See Nicol, *Semeia,* 22.

[479] Ibid., 22–27. For a critique of Nicol, see Ruckstuhl, "Johannine Language and Style," 145–47.

[480] Nicol, *Semeia,* 26.

[481] Demke remarks accurately ("Logos-Hymnus," 48): "The results of so-called stylistic criticism are, as concerns literary-critical questions . . . at most a forum for testing, but not for decision."

because there is no "style" that, on the one hand, diverges from that of the evangelist and, on the other hand, can be demonstrated in a series of pericopes stemming from the "semeia source."

3.9.5   The Form of the "Semeia Source"

A further objection to the existence of a "semeia source" is that it is not subject to form-critical classification. Although R. Bultmann included material other than miracle stories within his "semeia source" (e.g., parts of 1:35-51; 4:1-42; 7:1-13),[482] he deliberately excluded passion traditions. In contrast, E. Haenchen and R. Fortna speak of a "gospel of miracles." Haenchen sees in the "signs source" a miracle gospel of a non-Synoptic type, but he does not postulate its precise limits.[483] Fortna, in contrast, considers his "gospel of signs" to be a gospel of the Synoptic type,[484] containing extensive passion traditions and susceptible of detailed reconstruction. What Bultmann traces to two independent strains of tradition (signs source and source for passion and resurrection stories) is combined by Fortna into a single "gospel."[485] He takes his methodological starting point from the observation that both the miracle stories and the description of the passion contain material related to that in the Synoptics and thus could be derived from a "source."[486] Here we can see a fundamental weakness in Fortna's work: anything that proves to be pre-Johannine tradition he regards immediately as belonging to his "source." In the preceding section we have shown that Fortna's stylistic analyses cannot establish the unity of the miracle and passion traditions. Now we must add some further arguments against his thesis.

The present position of the cleansing of the Temple (2:14-22) is due to the evangelist.[487] Because the raising of Lazarus in chapter 11 is the final event in the structure of his Gospel, leading to the decision to put Jesus to death, John has placed the cleansing of the Temple in this prominent spot. He himself combined the passion and miracle traditions! Nothing supports Fortna's arbitrary supposition that the cleansing of the Temple originally followed 5:1-9, as Jesus' last miracle in the "source."[488] In addition, the many references to festivals (see 2:13; 2:23; 5:1; 6:4; 7:1-2) and to the passion in the individual miracle stories (see 2:4c; 6:4; 11:4ff.) show that the evangelist

---

[482] See the precise reconstruction in Smith, *Composition and Order,* 38ff.

[483] See Haenchen, "Johanneische Probleme," 113; idem, "Aus der Literatur des Johannesevangeliums," 303; idem, *John* 2:71 ("gospel of miracles" as a gospel writing created by a great poet). Becker ("Wunder und Christologie," 142 n. 1) agrees with Haenchen.

[484] See Fortna, *Gospel,* 221 n. 2.

[485] This thesis was anticipated by Wilkens, whose "basic gospel" ends with the passion and the Easter story (*Entstehungsgeschichte,* 77ff.).

[486] See Fortna, *Gospel,* 113.

[487] With the redactional v. 13, the evangelist joins Jesus' first miracle to the cleansing of the Temple, which he then interprets in vv. 17, 20-22. See section 3.10.5 below.

[488] See Fortna, *Gospel,* 240–41, where he reconstructs the Greek text of his "gospel of signs."

brought miracle and passion traditions together. Finally, 20:30-31 speaks clearly against Fortna's reconstruction.[489] He himself regards these verses as the conclusion of the "gospel of signs,"[490] but he silently ignores the absence of the key concept of σημεῖον in the passion tradition. This conclusion can, under Fortna's own presuppositions, only relate to miracle traditions and not to Passion traditions.

W. Nicol considers the form-critical similarity between some of the Johannine miracle stories and those in the Synoptic tradition to be evidence of the existence of a "semeia source."[491] But his accurate observation that there are form-critical parallels between the Johannine and Synoptic miracle traditions indicates only that John took *some* miracle stories from the available traditions. There are no form-critical parallels for a "source" of miracle stories, which Nicol calls the "mission gospel."[492] Moreover, no common *Sitz im Leben* for this "source" can be demonstrated, because obvious mission terminology is found only in 4:53.

The "semeia source" is often called an aretalogy.[493] It is questionable, in the first place, to propose the miracle stories of Mark's Gospel as form-critical parallels,[494] and it is still more problematic to apply the term "aretal-ogy," as used by R. Reitzenstein. In classical philology "aretalogy" refers not to the form "but to the content and purpose of some very different literary genres."[495] Aretalogical motifs are found in hymns, letters, dedicatory in-scriptions, and novels;[496] "but one can never speak of a fixed literary genre."[497] Therefore we ought to abandon the concept of "aretalogy" in the sense of a fixed form-critical genre.

There is no form-critical parallel for the "semeia source." In contrast, the *individual* Johannine miracle stories reveal a multitude of form-critical agreements with Synoptic and non-Synoptic traditions. This conclusion also speaks against the existence of a connected, pre-Johannine "semeia source."

3.9.6 *The Number of Miracles*

The number of miracles included by John in the Gospel is not acci-dental. In the whole ancient world, seven was regarded as the number of

---

[489] See Lindars, *Behind the Fourth Gospel,* 30ff.

[490] See Fortna, *Gospel,* 197–98.

[491] See Nicol, *Semeia,* 15–16.

[492] Ibid., 6. Nicol concludes directly from his accurate form-critical observations on *in-dividual* pericopes to the existence of a genre called "mission gospel."

[493] See only Koester, "One Jesus and Four Primitive Gospels," 187–93; Robinson, "The Johan-nine Trajectory," 251–52; Fortna calls his "gospel of signs" an "aretalogy with sequel" ("Christology and the Fourth Gospel," 501).

[494] Thus Koester, *Introduction* 2:184.

[495] Vielhauer, *Geschichte,* 310, referring to Esser, "Studien," 98ff.

[496] On this, see Reitzenstein, *Wundererzählungen,* 1–99; Esser, *Studien,* 98–102, which also offers a critique of Reitzenstein's broad interpretation of the concept of aretalogy.

[497] Esser, *Studien,* 101.

completeness and fulfillment.[498] The Johannine apocalypse shows that the number seven was important in circles surrounding the Johannine school (see Rev. 1:4, 12; 5:1; 8:2; 10:3; 12:3). Apparently the number seven is a device in Johannine composition used to emphasize the completeness of the revelations of Jesus in the miracles.[499] The individual miracles are distributed throughout Jesus' public activity according to plan and embedded in the constantly increasing conflict with the Jews that reaches its high point in John 11.

R. Fortna raises the question whether there had not been ten miracles in the "source," parallel to the miracles of Moses in Exodus.[500] In that case, the evangelist would have omitted two or three miracles. In the end Fortna decides for the number seven. But since he sees 21:1-14 as the third miracle in the source, he has eight miracles. Therefore, the feeding and walking on water in John 6 are summarily declared to be a single miracle, in order to retain the number seven.[501] Fortna can also give the original order of the eight (or seven) miracles. Since the "source" is based on a geographical scheme leading from Galilee to Jerusalem, the following order is necessary according to Fortna: chapters 2, 4, 21, 6, 11, 9, 5.[502]

Methodologically, this procedure must be said to be arbitrary. Fortna analyzes eight miracle stories but then presumes that the "source" contained only seven. He postulates an "original" order of the miracles, even though he is unable to demonstrate the existence of a geographical scheme in the narratives themselves at the pre-Johannine level.

Both the place of Jesus' miracles in the structure of the Gospel and the use of the number seven as a compositional tool indicate that John the evangelist deliberately chose individual miracle traditions known to the Johannine school and integrated them into his Gospel according to plan.

3.9.7 Σημεῖον and the "Semeia Source"

If there had been a pre-Johannine "semeia source," we would expect that the concept of σημεῖον would have played a central role in it. But of the seventeen occurrences of σημεῖον (σημεῖα), fifteen are attributable to John the evangelist, as our analysis has shown.[503] Only in 2:18 and 6:30 does σημεῖον appear in traditional sections, as a Johannine variation on the Synoptic demand for a sign. Σημεῖον as a succinct description of Jesus' earthly work of revelation is a central concept in the christology of the fourth evangelist. This conclusion also speaks against the presence of a pre-Johannine "semeia source."

---

[498] See Rengstorf, TDNT 2:627–35.

[499] See H. J. Holtzmann, Theologie 2:459; E. Lohmeyer, "Aufbau," 12; Dodd, Interpretation, 297ff.; Grundmann, Zeugnis und Gestalt, 13; Windisch, "Erzählungsstil," 178ff.

[500] See Fortna, Gospel, 101. In contrast, Clark sees the Exodus tradition in Wisdom 11–19 as the background for the Johannine miracle stories ("Signs in Wisdom and John," 202ff.).

[501] Fortna, Gospel, 101.

[502] Ibid., 102–9.

[503] See section 3.8.3.1.

3.9.8 On the Theology of the "Semeia Source"

Quite often the supposed tensions, contradictions, and oppositions between the theology of the fourth evangelist and that of the "semeia source" are offered as proof of the latter's existence.[504] Thus, literary-critical analyses are given an additional foundation in theology.

First we must ask, in the face of this procedure, why the evangelist took over the "semeia source" if its christology was counter to his own.[505] Moreover, tensions can also be created by individual pericopes, so that it is necessary to demonstrate the existence of a unified theology or christology of the "semeia source" that is not compatible with the evangelist's christology.

But there is no unified theology in the pre-Johannine miracle traditions! If the key concept of σημεῖον, except in 2:18 and 6:30, is due to the evangelist, then it cannot be regarded as a theologoumenon of the "source."[506] It is improbable that the "source" intended to demonstrate Jesus' messiahship in order to win Jews for the Christian faith, because the idea of the Messiah as a miracle worker, which is presumed by this demonstration, cannot be persuasively shown to have existed in Judaism.[507] Moreover, as far as the individual miracle stories are concerned, a missionary intention can be discerned only in 4:53. In no way were the pre-Johannine miracle traditions shaped throughout by an expectation that Jesus would be a prophet like Moses, and not even in the redactional section 6:14-15 is this motif really demonstrable. Nor is the expansive depiction of the miracles characteristic of all the traditions; rather, it is to a great extent the work of John the evangelist.[508] Finally, one may not conclude from the absence of individual theological *topoi* in the miracle stories (dualism, eschatology, christology of mission) to the existence of a hypothetically reconstructed "source" with a discernible theological conception. The absence of these motifs is grounded in the genre of the miracle traditions and their pre-Johannine character.[509]

Instead, the following description of the theological motifs that guided John in his revision of the received miracle traditions will show that the

---

[504] Even for Bultmann this was a substantive criterion for his reconstruction of sources. See Smith, *Composition and Order*, 11–12; also Fortna, *Gospel*, 16–17; Nicol, *Semeia*, 27–30; Becker, *Johannes* 1:113–14.

[505] One may search the literature in vain for answers to this obvious question. Typical is the remark of Becker ("Wunder und Christologie," 142–43): "It may be conceded from the start that the evangelist's decision to allow this christology [sc. that of the "semeia source"] to reside under his roof bordered on audacity."

[506] Against Nicol, who calls σημεῖον a "key word" of the "semeia source" (*Semeia*, 89).

[507] See n. 173 above.

[508] See section 3.10.1 below.

[509] Against Becker, who presents this as proof of the existence of the "semeia source" (*Johannes* 1:114).

evangelist very deliberately interpreted the *individual* miracle stories and connected them in more than one way with the other parts of his Gospel.

3.10   The Johannine Interpretation of Jesus' Miracles

3.10.1   *Miracles and the Revelation of the Doxa*

For John, Jesus' miracles have the character of revelation.[510] The *doxa* of the Son, bestowed by the Father before the foundation of the world (17:5bc, 24cd; 12:41), visible in the incarnation of the Preexistent One (1:14ab), is manifested in the miracles (2:11; 11:4, 40) and perfected on the cross, in order to return to the one *doxa* with the Father (17:1b, 5, 10b, 22, 24c). Jesus' *doxa* is revealed early, in the wine miracle at Cana (2:11), and the last and greatest miracle serves the single purpose of glorifying the Son (11:4) and revealing the *doxa* of the Father (11:40). It is scarcely an accident that the evangelist interprets the first and last miracles with the concept of *doxa;* this permits Jesus' whole miracle-working activity to appear as a repeated revelation of his *doxa*. The miracles are manifestations of the *doxa* of Jesus; it is only in this context that John uses δόξα, with the sense that it has in the theology of revelation, in connection with Jesus' public activity.[511] John uses δόξα both as a tool for theological interpretation of the received miracle traditions and as a connector with which he embeds the miracle stories in his total theological conception.

John 7:39 and 12:16 in no way relativize the revelation of the δοξα of Jesus in the miracles; in those passages δοξάζειν refers exclusively to the soteriological meaning for the disciples of Jesus' exaltation (gift of the Spirit and delayed understanding of the Christ event). To call the activity of the fleshly Jesus in the miracles "not yet the real thing"[512] is not possible in view of 2:11; 11:4, 40.

If it is true that Jesus' whole revelatory activity serves the glorification of the Father through the Son and the Son through the Father (see 8:54; 12:28; 13:31, 32; 14:13), and if the departing Christ says to God, ἐγώ σε ἐδόξασα ἐπὶ τῆς γῆς τὸ ἔργον τελειώσας ὃ δέδωκάς μοι ἵνα ποιήσω [I glorified you on earth by finishing the work that you gave me to do] (17:4), then the miracle is the special place where this occurs. It is not only an indication of the *doxa,* but an expression of the *doxa* itself. Certainly, Jesus' *doxa* is more than his miracle working, but at the same time, the *doxa* is fully present in each miracle.

The magnitude of the miracle shows *Jesus' divinity.* John the evangelist

---

510 See Wilkens, *Zeichen und Werke,* 50–51.

511 See Nicol, *Semeia,* 119: ". . . but after the prologue doxa (δόξα) occurs only thrice in connection with the life of Jesus — and in all three cases it is said to be revealed in a miracle. . . ."

512 Thüsing, *Erhöhung,* 94. Thüsing consistently seeks to relativize the activity of the earthly Jesus by referring to 7:39. For criticism of this approach, see Hofbeck, *Semeion,* 100.

elevates the synoptists' comparative to a superlative.[513] Jesus not only changes water into wine but fills six gigantic jars with a quantity approaching seven hundred liters.[514] The healing at a distance of the son of a royal official in Capernaum no longer takes place there, but while Jesus is in Cana. The lame man at the pool of Bethesda has been ill for thirty-eight years. At the miraculous feeding of five thousand, all the people can take as much as they want, yet twelve baskets of bread remain. Jesus not only walks on the lake and helps the disciples in their distress but accomplishes a further miracle by bringing the boat to the shore at which they are aiming. Jesus gives sight to one who was born blind. Lazarus has been dead four days and is already beginning to decay when Jesus raises him from the dead. Although he was bound hand and foot and his face was covered with a cloth, Lazarus came out from the grave.

The evangelist found this characteristic expansion of the miraculous already present in 2:1-11; 6:1-15, 16-25; 9:1-41, but in 4:46-54; 5:1-9ab; 11:1-44 he himself introduced or intensified it. In the healing of the son of a βασιλικός, he introduced v. 46a to increase the distance and thereby the magnitude of the miracle. His is the statement of the length of the illness in 5:5, and through Jesus' question in v. 6, θέλεις ὑγιὴς γενέσθαι [do you want to be healed] (also redactional), the healing at the pool is given something of the quality of a demonstration miracle, showing Jesus' divine power. John uses dramatic elements to expand and interpret the raising of Lazarus. What at first seems only a harmless sickness (11:4, 6), allowing Jesus to remain two more days in the same place (11:6), and is then called Lazarus's "sleeping" (11:11), ends with his being awakened from the dead. John makes the raising of Lazarus the greatest miracle in the New Testament; it is John who inserts the remark in v. 39bc that Lazarus must already be stinking, because he has been dead four days.

In addition, Jesus' miraculous foreknowledge and insight are signs of his divinity. This ability on Jesus' part is traditional in 4:50, but the motif was introduced by the evangelist in 5:6; 6:6, 15a; 11:11. Jesus knows that the lame man at the pool has been ill for thirty-eight years, and he takes the initiative in curing him. According to 6:6, Jesus knows exactly what should be done for the hungry crowd in the lonely place. It is only to test the disciples that he asks Philip where bread can be bought (6:5). Thus the evangelist gives heavy emphasis to the picture of the powerful miracle worker who knows the greatness of his deed in advance, is not driven by the crowd's suffering, and can even put his disciples to the test. In 6:15a, Jesus recognizes the crowd's intention to make of him an earthly king, and he flees. Jesus knows, in 11:11, that he will awaken Lazarus from the dead (see 11:4); it is only for that reason

---

[513] See H. J. Holtzmann, *Theologie* 2:459.
[514] See Billerbeck, *Kommentar* 2:407.

that he can say: Λάζαρος ὁ φίλος ἡμῶν κεκοίμηται [our friend Lazarus has fallen asleep].

Jesus' miraculous foreknowledge is often mentioned outside the miracle stories as well. Jesus knows his destiny (see 2:19, 21; 3:14; 4:35; 6:64, 70; 8:21, 40; 13:1, 19, 38; 18:4, 32; 19:28); he discerns the disciples' thoughts (16:19); he knows human beings and sees into their hearts (2:24, 25; 5:42; 6:64); he is acquainted with the Scriptures, though he has never been taught (7:15). He knows Nathanael (1:47-48) and is informed about the Samaritan woman's previous life (4:16-18, 29). Finally, in 16:30, the disciples confess: νῦν οἴδαμεν ὅτι οἶδας πάντα καὶ οὐ χρείαν ἔχεις ἵνα τίς σε ἐρωτᾷ · ἐν τούτῳ πιστεύομεν ὅτι ἀπὸ θεοῦ ἐξῆλθες [Now we know that you know all things, and do not need to have anyone question you; by this we believe that you came from God] (cf. 21:17). Jesus' miraculous foreknowledge as a sign of his divinity is thus a motif deliberately employed by the evangelist to tie the miracle traditions to the other parts of the Gospel. This serves to intensify Jesus' miraculous powers, but at the same time it organically embeds his miracle working as evidence of his divinity in the totality of the Gospel.

The magnitude of the miracle underscores Jesus' divinity, but at the same time the miracles with their materiality, which is bound up with the earthly and subject to verification in space and time, point to Jesus' *humanity*. Their conspicuous character confirms that the one who does such deeds has really entered into fleshly existence. They take place in the world and are performed for concrete human persons.

Both the huge quantity of the wine Jesus produces from water (2:6-7) and its testing by the "neutral" ἀρχιτρίκλινος, who vehemently praises the quality of the wine (2:9-10), witness to the reality of the miracle. The servants of the βασιλικός confirm (4:51ff.) that his son was healed at the very hour when Jesus said to him: ὁ υἱός σου ζῇ [your son will live]. The man at the pool, who had been ill for thirty-eight years, stands up at Jesus' command, in the sight of all, takes his bed and goes away (5:8-9). The five thousand in a lonely place can take as much bread and fish as they desire; all are filled, and still twelve baskets of bread remain (6:13). Jesus' miraculous walking on water is emphatically confirmed by the people, who sought him in vain on the other shore and then were surprised to find him in Capernaum, even though he did not leave the other shore in the boat with the disciples (6:22-25). The identity of the one who was blind from birth with the one who now can see is expressly and repeatedly emphasized (9:9, 20, 25, 30), and thereby the fact of the miracle is also stressed. Lazarus was really dead; he had lain in the grave four days and there was already a stench (11:39). He emerges from the tomb before the very eyes of the Jews who are present (11:44).

The evangelist's interest in miracles as expressions of Jesus' humanity is revealed also in his redaction of the Lazarus pericope. The pre-Johannine tradition of the raising of Lazarus already said that Jesus loved his friend

Lazarus (11:3). John strongly expands this motif of Jesus' humanity. Jesus not only loves Lazarus, but his sisters Martha and Mary as well (11:5). In 11:35, Jesus weeps, out of his own sorrow and anguish, over the death of Lazarus. This is a peculiar remark on the part of the evangelist and stands in sharp contradiction to the tradition he is redacting, according to which Jesus is incensed at the crowd's mourning (11:33, 34). In v. 36, which is also redactional, Jesus' weeping is regarded by the Jews as an expression of his friendship and love for Lazarus.

Other texts in the Gospel expressly emphasize Jesus' human reactions and feelings. It is out of extreme human passion that Jesus cleanses the Temple (2:14-22), and the evangelist comments on the scene with the words of Ps. 69:10: "Zeal for your house will consume me." Jesus is exhausted and thirsty after a long journey (4:6-7). He is troubled or agitated (ταράσσω) in the face of the fate that is about to befall him (12:27; see also 13:21). On the cross he asks for a drink (19:28). Jesus is continually referred to in the Fourth Gospel as (ὁ) ἄνθρωπος (5:12; 8:40; 9:11; 11:50; 18:27, 29; 19:5).

The miracles are the expression both of the divinity and the humanity of Jesus. The evangelist emphasizes both, and for that very reason he can unite miracle and *doxa*, because the incarnation is not the loss but the making visible of the *doxa* of Jesus (1:14).

3.10.2   Miracles and the Unity
of Father and Son

The miracles testify to the unity of the Son with the Father. The Son only does the works of the one who sent him, and the miracles are nothing other than ἔργα τοῦ θεοῦ (see 5:20, 36; 6:29, 30; 7:3, 21; 9:3b-5; 10:25, 32ff., 38; 14:10-11; 15:24). Particularly in 9:3b-5, the evangelist connects Jesus' miracle-working activity with the whole saving event that in 4:34 and 17:4 is called ἔργον. It is precisely as an expression of the inner union of Father and Son that the miracles legitimate Jesus. The one who does such things can only come from God (see 9:16, 30, 33; 11:42). God must be with him (3:2). They point to Jesus' origins (see πόθεν [whence] in 9:30) and confirm that he is sent by the Father. Because the Father and Son are one (10:30: ἐγὼ καὶ ὁ πατὴρ ἕν ἐσμεν; see in addition only 8:28; 12:45; 14:9), the Father has given the Son power over life (10:28-30; 17:2). Jesus uses this power when he heals the dying son of a royal person (see esp. 4:47c, 49) and raises Lazarus from the dead (see esp. 11:20-27).

Through the motif of the unity of Father and Son, the evangelist unites the miracle stories with the center of his christology: the definitive and unsurpassable revelation of the Father, which appears in the Son.

3.10.3   Miracles and Faith

The revelation of Jesus' *doxa* through miracles evokes faith.[515] As early as the wedding at Cana, the evangelist uses the disciples as examples of his understanding of miracles and faith (2:11): it is not faith that sees the miracle; instead, faith comes about through the revelation of the *doxa* in the miracle. Because the miracle has revelatory character and is a powerful testimony to the unity of the Son with the Father, it is able to awaken faith. After the disciples, it is the crowd that believes in Jesus because of miracles (2:23). Anyone who does such deeds can only be the true prophet come into the world, or the Christ (6:14; 7:31; see also 6:2; 9:16; 12:18). The one who was born blind comes, through a miracle, to believe in the one who opened his eyes (9:35-38). John 10:40-42 shows how direct was the evangelist's connection between miracles and faith. Jesus and the Baptizer are essentially different because Jesus alone does miracles (v. 41), so that the "many" can only believe in Jesus (v. 42). Similarly, 11:15 makes it clear that faith comes about through miracles. Jesus rejoices that the disciples were not present at the death of Lazarus. Now he can raise his friend from the dead so that the disciples may come to believe (ἵνα πιστεύσητε). Here the miracle is not an accidental occasion of faith; instead, it is deliberately done in order to evoke faith. Verses 40 and 45 also shed light on the connection between miracle and faith in the Lazarus pericope. Trusting in Jesus' power, Martha will see the δόξα τοῦ θεοῦ, and after the miracle many Jews also believe in Jesus (11:45, 48; 12:11).

The Johannine connection between seeing and believing also plays an important part in the resurrection and appearance stories. In the redactional verse 20:8 it is said of the Beloved Disciple that he entered the tomb καὶ εἶδεν καὶ ἐπίστευσεν [and he saw and believed]. Without any hidden cosmological dualism, faith in the miracle of the resurrection is proclaimed. Thomas makes seeing the wounds of his Lord the condition of his faith (20:25). Jesus does not refuse this demand but fulfills it (v. 28)! In v. 29a the connection between seeing and believing is again emphasized (ὅτι ἑώρακας με πεπίστευ-κας [because you have seen me have you believed]), before the macarism in v. 29b formulates what applies to the *subsequent* generations: having faith without directly seeing the risen Son of God. Immediate seeing is reserved for the eyewitnesses. But it gives rise to a tradition, and to that extent it applies to the community that, in the kerygma, fully participates in the eyewitnesses' seeing. In this sense the connection between seeing and believing is in no way restricted to the *vita Jesu* but has a present meaning in the community's proclamation.

---

[515] For the linguistic background of πιστεύειν in John, see especially Dodd, *Interpretation*, 179–83.

In 2:24-25; 4:48; 6:30 there is no fundamental critique of miracles; what Jesus rejects is the mere *demand* for miracles (4:48; 6:30) or a doubting faith on the part of the crowd (2:24-25). When Jesus says in 10:38; 14:11 that if people do not believe him they should at least believe his works, the works (and thus also the miracles) are not devalued.[516] On the contrary, they are so impressive and important that they witness to the unity of Father and Son and justify faith in and of themselves.

For John the evangelist, the miracle produces faith: the seeing of the σημεῖον is followed by a πιστεύειν εἰς 'Ιησοῦν Χριστόν [believing in Jesus Christ]. This quite undualistic connection between seeing and believing is explicitly stated in 2:11, 23; 4:53; 6:14; 7:31; 9:35-38; 10:40-42; 11:15, 40, 45; 12:11; 20:8, 25, 27, 29a, and it is presupposed in 4:39; 6:2; 9:16; 12:18, so that it clearly has a central importance for the fourth evangelist's concept of faith. Faith in Jesus Christ as the Son of God is not only the goal of John's Gospel writing; it is the whole purpose of the incarnation (1:7, 12) and thus of the whole event of salvation. Whoever believes has eternal life (3:15, 16, 36; 5:24; 6:35, 40, 47, 69; 7:38), but unbelief is subject to the judgment (3:18). If Jesus Christ's identity as Son of God is the content of faith and its consequence eternal life, then faith is bound up with Jesus' word (2:22), his speech (5:46-47), and especially his σημεῖα. Here faith is the result of the preceding miracle, and not the condition that makes the miracle possible.

What does this mean for the Johannine concept of faith? Does John see faith in miracles as merely a preliminary stage of faith?[517] Does Jesus reveal nothing more in the miracles than "that he is the Revealer"?[518]

Against a relativizing and purely literal understanding of the Johannine concept of faith, it must be emphasized that for John the miracles are ἀρεταὶ θεοῦ [great (works) of God], because the revelation of the *doxa* in the miracle evokes faith. This is not merely a tentative, second-rate, or incomplete faith, but faith in the fullest sense of the word: recognition and acknowledgment of Jesus Christ as Son of God. When faith begins in an encounter with Jesus, who reveals his *doxa* in miracles, it encompasses both Jesus' fleshly and heavenly existence. Thus its content is not only the "that" of revelation; instead, the miracles describe, with a virtually unsurpassable palpability and reality, the activity of the Revealer within history. Seeing the miracle is not a spiritual vision reserved only for the predestined; it is a seeing with the senses. To the extent that the revelation of the *doxa* of the Incarnate One makes possible a θεᾶσθαι, a clear, vivid, bodily seeing (1:14), and to the

---

[516] Against Schnackenburg, who here sees faith as a higher motive in contrast to works (*John* 1:562).

[517] So Lührmann, *RAC* 11:74; see also Hahn, "Glaubensverständnis," 54–55.

[518] Bultmann, "Bedeutung," 57. For a critique of Bultmann's description of the relationship between "seeing" and "believing," see especially Wenz, "Sehen und Glauben," 22; Lammers, *Hören, Sehen und Glauben,* 51ff.

extent that the miracles of the fleshly Jesus are the places where his *doxa* is repeatedly made visible, seeing the miracle can be the basis for faith.[519]

Undoubtedly, faith cannot be separated from Jesus' proclamation (see only 5:46; 17:8, 20; 6:68-69), but the frequently underestimated importance of miracles in the Johannine concept of faith makes clear that for the evangelist both were important: the words and the works of Jesus, the revelation of his divine Sonship in the ῥήματα and in the σημεῖα.

3.10.4   *Miracles and Unbelief*

Jesus' miracles evoke both faith and unbelief. This situation is formulated by the evangelist in programmatic fashion in 12:37: τοσαῦτα δὲ αὐτοῦ σημεῖα πεποιηκότος ἔμπροσθεν αὐτῶν οὐκ ἐπίστευον εἰς αὐτόν [Although he had performed so many signs in their presence, they did not believe in him]. Even Jesus' brothers do not believe in him (7:5), although they have seen his works (7:3). The healing of the one born blind results in both belief and unbelief among the Jews (9:16). Jesus takes the once-blind man's confession, πιστεύω κύριε [Lord, I believe], in 9:38 as an occasion to emphasize the character of his mission as judgment. Like faith or unbelief as such (see 3:18), one's attitude toward Jesus' miracle working is decisive for judgment (9:39). The raising of Lazarus brings many Jews to faith (11:45), but at the same time some go to the Jewish leaders to betray Jesus (11:46).

John uses the miracles to demonstrate the nature of unbelief, for in light of the σημεῖα, unbelief is the denial of an undeniable reality: Jesus Christ is the Son of God. The marks of unbelief are not lack of knowledge or inability to believe; rather, unbelief is the deliberate denial of an unmistakable and publicly visible fact.

The connection between miracles and unbelief also shows that for the evangelist the miracles do not work magically. Despite their revelatory character, their materiality and reality, they demand a decision on the part of human witnesses. To the extent that Jesus' miracles can be the occasion both of faith and of unbelief, they are a central element in Jesus' whole activity, the result of which is both believing and disbelieving (see only 5:47; 6:36, 64; 8:45, 46; 10:25, 26; 16:9).

3.10.5   *Miracles and the Passion*

The Jewish leaders' unbelief leads to Jesus' passion. Their final decision to put Jesus to death follows his most powerful deed, the raising of Lazarus (11:53). Here the compositional independence of the fourth evangelist is evident: he has placed the cleansing of the Temple, which for the Synoptics was the ultimate reason for the decision to kill Jesus (cf. Mark 11:17; Luke 19:47),

---

[519] See Hahn, "Sehen und Glauben," 129.

at the beginning of his Gospel (John 2:14-22), thereby lending a central importance to the *theologia crucis* and to the miracle stories as stages on the way to the cross. The close connection between miracles and the passion, evident both compositionally and materially in John 11 (esp. vv. 8-10, 16), occasions and also clarifies the references to the passion in the other miracle stories.

From the beginning, the title ὁ ἀμνὸς τοῦ θεοῦ [the lamb of God] on the lips of the Baptizer (1:29, 36)[520] points toward the passion, and this connection becomes quite evident in 2:1-11. With the redactional τῇ ἡμέρᾳ τῇ τρίτῃ [on the third day] in v. 1, John refers to the morning of the resurrection, and οὔπω ἡ ὥρα μου [not yet my hour] in v. 4c, also the work of the evangelist, points to the hour of the passion. Already in this first miracle there is a hint of what will happen in the last: Jesus' miracle working will give rise to the passion. At the very place where the Son of God reveals his *doxa*, unbelief is kindled.

With 2:13, the evangelist connects the first part of the double tradition available to him (2:1-10, 12; 4:46b, 47, 50-53) with the cleansing of the Temple, which, through its prominent placement at the beginning of the Gospel, sets Jesus' activity from the very beginning within the shadow of the cross.[521]

Within 2:14-22, vv. 20-22 stand out because of their different perspective. In the Jews' reflection on Jesus' words, the post-Easter situation comes into view.[522] Supporting redaction are, in addition, the typically Johannine motif of misunderstanding (3:3-4; 4:10ff.; 6:32ff.; 7:34ff.; etc.) and the Johannine expression ἐκεῖνος δὲ ἔλεγεν περί [but he was speaking about] (7:39; 11:13; 12:33).[523] Verse 17 is also the work of the evangelist;[524] in its present context it can be understood only in light of vv. 20-22, and it fits the Johannine technique of giving short commentaries from a post-Easter perspective (see 7:39; 11:13; 12:16, 33). The Johannine "remembering" in vv. 17 and 22 is made possible by the sending of the Paraclete, who reminds the community of Jesus (14:26).

The model document used by John had two special features: (1) the quotation from Isa. 56:7; Jer. 7:11 (cf. Mark 11:17 par.) is missing. (2) Nothing is said of Jesus' teaching in the Temple (cf. Mark 11:17; Luke 19:47). The omission of the quotation is explained by v. 17, in which the evangelist himself creates the connection with the passion. John has placed the motif of Jesus' teaching in the Temple nearer the end of his public activity (see 17:14). Thus there is nothing against the idea that John knew a Synoptic account (Mark) of the cleansing of the Temple.[525]

---

[520] On ἀμνὸς τοῦ θεοῦ, see Schnackenburg, *John* 1:297–301.

[521] Against J. Schneider, according to whom the cleansing of the Temple only says "that the Messiah has the authority to found a new cult" (*Johannes,* 85).

[522] See Schnider and Stenger, *Johannes und die Synoptiker,* 37–38.

[523] See Bultmann, *John* 126 n. 2.

[524] See Schnider and Stenger, *Johannes und die Synoptiker,* 39.

[525] See Barrett, *John,* 195; J. Schneider, *Johannes,* 85. For the close connections between the Markan and Johannine traditions, see also Schnider and Stenger, *Johannes und die Synoptiker,*

John 2:17, 20-22 gives an indication of the evangelist's post-Easter perspective; he interprets the story of Jesus on the basis of the cross and resurrection. Jesus' activity and Scripture as well disclose their meaning only through the cross and resurrection, because it is in the surrender of his own body that Jesus completes his saving work.

The journeys to festivals, which the evangelist repeatedly describes, and other references to the feasts (2:23; 5:1; 6:4; 7:2, 10; 11:18, 55ff.) also have the sole purpose of bringing Jesus again and again to Jerusalem or connecting his activity with Jerusalem, where his destiny will be fulfilled. Many Jews come to believe in Jesus when he performs miracles during the Passover in Jerusalem. The healing at the pool takes place during a feast in Jerusalem. The feeding of five thousand and the walking on the lake occur—by no accident, from the evangelist's point of view—in immediate connection with the Passover and in the presence of a large crowd of people. Jesus' brothers urge him to go to the festival of Booths in order to do miracles in the sight of the crowds there. But Jesus goes to the festival in secret, because he knows that the Jews want to kill him. John deliberately expands the healing of the lame man at the pool and the cure of the one born blind into Sabbath conflicts (5:9c; 9:14). By this means he sharpens the conflict between Jesus and the Jews, and the miracles become a cause for the persecution of Jesus and his followers (5:16; 9:4, 16, 22, 34).

For John, the miracles are both compositionally and in their content the matter and the expression of his *theologia crucis.*

Following E. Käsemann,[526] U. B. Müller believes that it is not possible to speak of a theology of the cross in John. Müller sees the characteristically Johannine concept in the passages that speak of Jesus' going to God (ὑπάγειν [to withdraw], see only 7:33; 8:14; 13:4; 14:28) and of his ascending and descending (see ἀναβαίνειν/καταβαίνειν in 3:13; also 1:51; 6:62; 20:17). Here, according to Müller, the idea of returning to God, not the cross, is the focus.[527] In the specifically Johannine ὑψωθῆναι [to be lifted up] (3:14; 8:28; 12:32, 34), also, the cross "does not yet have a content that is constitutive of salvation."[528] Finally, Müller wishes to detach the Johannine concept of *doxa* from any kind of theology of the cross. "The death of Jesus indeed appears as a necessary event on the way to life, but only as something that lies within the shadow of the glorification that the Father bestows on the Son both in his earthly activity and in and through his death."[529] Thus, according to Müller, the cross has

---

40ff. Among those who reject a Synoptic model for John are Haenchen, *Weg Jesu,* 389; Becker, *Johannes* 1:122.

[526] See Käsemann, *Jesu letzter Wille,* 111: "The real difference from Paul is indicated by the absence of the *theologia crucis.*" For the importance of the theology of the cross, see now, in contrast, Kohler (*Kreuz und Menschwerdung,* passim), who shows that in the Gospel of John the cross is not obscured but is given a more comprehensive value, inasmuch as it is thought of as the place of the perfected union of Father and Son; see also Klaiber, "Aufgabe," 311–12.

[527] See Müller, "Bedeutung," 53–56.

[528] Ibid., 57.

[529] Ibid., 63.

no further saving significance for John; instead, it touches only the this-worldly sphere, from which the evangelist and his community, as pneumatics, consider themselves removed.[530]

Müller comes to this conclusion because, from the outset, he excludes from his analysis the placement of the cleansing of the Temple and the numerous references to the passion throughout the Gospel.[531] Methodologically speaking, this is a very dubious procedure, for in such an instance the desired result prejudices the exegesis. In addition, the designation of Jesus as ἀμνὸς τοῦ θεοῦ (1:29, 36) and the statements about Jesus' atoning death (10:11, 15, 17; 15:13) are simply said to be "specifically Johannine"[532] in order to secure Müller's own proposal. In contrast, it should be emphasized that the Johannine understanding of Jesus' death is adequately grasped only when *all* the statements about Jesus' suffering and death are taken into account. The numerous redactional references to the passion in the miracle stories; Jesus' repeated journeys to feasts in Jerusalem, the place of his suffering and death; the statements about his atoning death; and the placement of the cleansing of the Temple (as well as the anointing story in 12:1-11) — all these, taken together, show that we must speak of a Johannine *theologia crucis*. Moreover, according to 19:30, the revelation of Jesus reaches its fulfillment on the cross (τετέλεσται [it is finished]!). The particular accentuation, contrasting with that of Paul and Mark, is undeniable, but it does not permit us to dispute the existence of a *theologia crucis* in John.

3.11   The Meaning of Miracles in Johannine Christology

As early as 1841, Alexander Schweizer remarked, concerning the Johannine miracle stories: "It is true that John places value on σημεῖα, but this is only a secondary value, so that on this basis reference may be made to the 'greater works' that Christ accomplishes in the life of the soul."[533] While the σημεῖα may arouse attention and give rise to a preliminary faith, they are on the periphery, not at the center, of Johannine theology. This evaluation, or rather devaluation, of miracles in John has dominated research up to the present. Thus K. L. Schmidt wrote in 1921: "Only the one who understands its symbolic meaning has really understood the σημεῖον."[534] For R. Bultmann, the miracles are merely concessions to human weakness,[535] pure symbols,[536] of whose historicity the evangelist is not at all convinced.[537]

---

[530] Ibid., 64ff.
[531] Ibid., 53.
[532] Ibid., 63.
[533] A. Schweizer, *Johannes,* 66–67.
[534] Schmidt, "Der johanneische Charakter," 40.
[535] Bultmann, *John,* 233.
[536] Bultmann, *Theology* 2:44.
[537] Bultmann, *John,* 119 n. 2.

Although a purely symbolic interpretation of the miracles is only occasionally proposed,[538] there is a general notion that the miracles have a merely indicative function in John; they only aroused a preliminary kind of faith and had a purely subordinate value for the evangelist's christology. E. Haenchen sees in the miracles "pointers to something totally different";[539] L. Schottroff considers them purely this-worldly events;[540] and J. Becker even thinks that miracles "have no further independent meaning for the evangelist"[541] and are "meaningless events as far as faith is concerned."[542]

In contrast to the devaluation of the Johannine miracle stories that is current among scholars, we must emphasize on the basis of the preceding analyses that, because the revelation of the one *doxa* of Jesus occurs not behind but *in* the miracles, they are of fundamental importance for the christology of the fourth evangelist.[543] The miracles are not merely a concession to human weakness; instead, they are demonstrations of the δόξα θεοῦ.

The Johannine concept of miracles is nondualistic. The presentation is not shaped by two independent and contradictory principles; rather, for the evangelist, faith follows immediately on the seeing of the miracle (2:11, 23; 4:53; 6:14; 7:31; 9:35, 38; 10:40-42; 11:15, 40, 45). For John there are not "two measures of 'seeing,' two levels of miracle."[544] The comprehensive integration of the Johannine miracle stories within an imposed, all-determining, and dualistic system of relationships, as proposed by L. Schottroff on the basis of a questionable interpretation of 4:48, cannot be sustained by the miracle stories themselves. John nowhere distinguishes between a "false," this-worldly faith in miracles and a "true" miracle faith that is directed to the heavenly Revealer. On the contrary, for him the this-worldly reality and magnitude of the miracle and the *doxa* of the Revealer that emerges in it are inextricably united. In the miracle the *sarx* [flesh] and *doxa* of the Revealer

---

[538] See Brown, who speaks of a "spiritual symbolism" (*John* 1:529). For a critique of Bultmann's symbolic interpretation of the Johannine miracles, see Haenchen, "'Der Vater, der mich gesandt hat,'" 68–69; Käsemann, *Jesu letzter Wille,* 51–52; Wilkens, *Zeichen und Werke,* 32; Appold, *Oneness,* 100. The eschatological dimension of the Johannine miracles is emphasized especially by Léon-Dufour, "Sēmeion Johannique," 373ff.

[539] Haenchen, "Wandel," 10. The position of Grundmann ("Bewegung des Glaubens," 142) should also be rejected. He sees in John a development in stages from belief in signs to belief in the word.

[540] See Schottroff, *Der Glaubende,* 155; see also Haenchen, *John* 2:60: "the greatest miracles are also events within the mundane world."

[541] Becker, "Wunder und Christologie," 146.

[542] Ibid., 147. Lona ("Glaube und Sprache," 176ff.) makes a more nuanced judgment than Becker. He also supposes a concept of faith on the part of the evangelist that is critical of the "semeia source," but he posits a much narrower discrepancy between the evangelist and his source than does Becker.

[543] See Wilkens, *Zeichen und Werke,* 32.

[544] Schottroff, *Der Glaubende,* 254.

are equally epiphanies. A fundamental Johannine criticism of miracles does not exist![545]

As powerful deeds of the λόγος ἔνσαρκος [enfleshed Logos], the miracles in the Gospel of John have an antidocetic function.[546] With their mass and their reality, they show that Jesus Christ has really entered space and time. The simultaneous emphasis on Jesus' humanity also serves the purpose of indicating the fleshly existence of the miracle worker. If faith follows a vivid seeing of the miracle, this means that John insists on the importance for faith of Jesus' appearing in the flesh and that he opposes any docetic erasure of it. Since the miracles are visible, this-worldly demonstrations of Jesus' majesty, and at the same time are part of the Johannine *theologia crucis,* because in them the *doxa* of the Incarnate One is visible and evokes faith, they emphatically secure the identity of the Preexistent One with the fleshly, suffering, and exalted Jesus Christ. Consequently, from the point of view of the evangelist, they are to be understood as antidocetic.

---

[545] Against Schottroff, *Der Glaubende,* 256, and frequently elsewhere. She speaks throughout of a Johannine criticism of miracles.

[546] See Wilkens, "Evangelist und Tradition," 89. Against Käsemann, who although he emphasizes the reality of Jesus' miracles in the Gospel of John, does not acknowledge their antidocetic function (*Jesu letzter Wille,* 51ff.).

4

The Present Christ: Sacraments and Johannine Christology

The importance of the sacraments in Johannine christology has been widely undervalued, even to the present time. This is the consequence of Rudolf Bultmann's interpretation.[1] Radicalizing some initiatives of the Reformers,[2] Bultmann denied that the sacraments had any influence on Johannine thought. "The truth is that the sacraments are superfluous for him [sc. John]: the disciples are 'clean' through the word (15.3), just as they are 'holy' through the word, according to the prayer that takes the place of the Lord's Supper (17.17)."[3] It is true that, even for Bultmann, John presumes the church's use of baptism and the Lord's Supper,[4] but his understanding of them is "that in them the word is made present in a special way."[5] The word takes the place of the sacraments and assumes their functions. Bultmann concludes, in summary, "that though in John there is no direct polemic against the sacraments, his attitude toward them is nevertheless critical or at least reserved."[6]

In contrast to Bultmann's nonsacramental interpretation of John, O. Cullmann sees the Fourth Gospel as wholly and completely imbued with a cultic-sacramental interest.[7] "[T]here can be traced in the Gospel of John a

---

[1] Among those who follow Bultmann, though using different argumentation, are E. Lohse, G. Bornkamm, H. Koester, E. Schweizer, and J. Becker. See the review of research in Klos, *Sakramente,* 11–21.

[2] Lindars traces the different evaluations of Johannine presentation of the sacraments in German and British exegesis to the different course taken by the Reformation in Germany and England ("Word and Sacrament," 52).

[3] Bultmann, *John,* 472.

[4] See Bultmann, *Theology* 2:54, 58–59.

[5] Bultmann, *John,* 472.

[6] Bultmann, *Theology* 2:59.

[7] There is an anticipation of Cullman's position in Schweitzer, *Mystik,* 340ff. Authors who accept Cullmann's argumentation are reviewed in Klos, *Sakramente,* 24–32.

176

distinct line of thought connecting with the service of worship,"[8] and the evangelist is at pains "to set forth the connexion between the contemporary Christian worship and the historical life of Jesus."[9] Cullmann sees in the ambiguity and multiple meanings of Johannine concepts a methodological justification for a deliberately symbolic interpretation of Johannine discourses and narratives.[10] Hence, he interprets a great number of Johannine texts sacramentally, even though they are not otherwise related to baptism or the Lord's Supper (e.g., 1:6-8, 15, 19-34; 2:1-11, 12-22; 3:22-36; 4:1-30; 5:1-19; 6:1-13; 9:1-39). Cullmann makes "enquiry into the deeper unexpressed sense . . . a principle of interpretation,"[11] and he comes close to an allegorical interpretation of John.

Both Bultmann and Cullmann represent extreme positions, neither of which can be maintained in light of the Johannine text. Bultmann's nonsacramental interpretation is forced, since at least in the case of 3:5 there are no literary-critical indications of the secondary character of ὕδατος καί [water and]. On the other hand, Cullmann's sacramentalist interpretation collapses in the face of the demand, indispensable for historical-critical exegesis, that only the words and content of the text as it stands, and not a supposed "deeper meaning," can be the object of investigation. Therefore in what follows we will examine only those texts whose reference to baptism and the Lord's Supper is unquestioned: 3:5, 22, 26; 4:1; 6:51c-58; 19:34-35.

4.1   Baptism in John's Gospel

4.1.1   *Position and Construction of John 3*

In the third chapter of the Gospel, the Johannine Christ gives the first comprehensive presentation of his teaching.[12] Whereas before this it was Jesus' deeds that were the focus of the narrative (miracle at Cana and cleansing of the Temple), now a discussion with a Jew takes up the question of the things that are necessary for salvation. Hence, the Nicodemus discourse leads us into the center of Johannine theology.

In the structure of John 3, it is primarily vv. 31-36 that present a problem. Formally, they are the continuation of the Baptizer's speech in vv. 27ff., but their content shows that they are not the words of the Baptizer

---

[8]   Cullmann, *Early Christian Worship*, 37.

[9]   Ibid.

[10]   Ibid., 50ff.; see also his "Der johanneische Gebrauch."

[11]   Cullmann, *Early Christian Worship*, 57. The attempts of Mussner, ("'Kultische' Aspekte im johanneischen Christusbild") and Bühner ("Denkstrukturen") to detect a basic "cultic" layer in Johannine christology should be sharply distinguished from Cullmann's approach.

[12]   See Becker, *Johannes* 1:129.

(especially vv. 35 and 36).[13] This has led to many attempts at rearrangement:[14] R. Bultmann places vv. 31-36 after v. 21 and arrives at the following divisions: 3:1-8, 9-21, 31-36, 22-30.[15] For R. Schnackenburg, the Nicodemus discourse ends with 3:12, and there follow the "free-floating," "kerygmatic" sections of discourse in 3:31-36 and 3:13-21, and 3:22-30 is understood as a pericope concerning the Baptizer.[16] These kinds of reconstructional hypotheses are not convincing, since any attempt at rearrangement in this particular text is highly questionable.[17] Moreover, it is only the place and function of vv. 31-36 that present difficulties, and these cannot be solved by shifting the problems to vv. 1-30. Instead, vv. 31-36 can be seen as a concluding commentary by the evangelist on the Nicodemus pericope and the witness of the Baptizer.[18]

Under these conditions, Y. Ibuki's suggestion for dividing this section, following C. H. Dodd,[19] is plausible. This author sees two parallel complexes edited together in John 3:[20]

	First Section	Second Section
Exposition	2:23-25	3:22-24
Dialogue	3:1-12	3:25-30
Monologue	3:13-21	3:31-36

The transitional character of 2:23-25 and 3:22-24 cannot be disputed,[21] and the shift from dialogue to monologue at the end of a unit of thought is typically Johannine (see chapters 6, 8, 14).[22] Thus chapter 3 must be regarded as a studied composition by the evangelist.

4.1.2 The Meaning of Jesus' Baptizing (John 3:22, 26; 4:1)

The Nicodemus pericope is the *locus classicus* for discerning the Johannine view of baptism. In addition, there are a number of texts to which little

---

[13] See Bultmann, *John,* 131; Schnackenburg, *John* 1:360–61; Becker, *Johannes* 1:130; against Bauer (*Johannesevangelium,* 63ff.) and Barrett (*John,* 219), who regard vv. 31-36 as the words of the Baptizer.

[14] See the overviews in Blank, *Krisis,* 53–56; Porsch, *Pneuma,* 83–89.

[15] See Bultmann, *John,* 131–33.

[16] See Schnackenburg, *John* 1:360–63.

[17] See Haenchen, *John* 1:45–51, 209–10 (on John 3:22ff.).

[18] Lagrange correctly calls vv. 31-36 "a reflection by the evangelist" (*Jean*). Against Thyen ("Aus der Literatur," *ThR* 44, 112) and Becker (*Johannes* 1:130), who consider vv. 31-36 the work of the post-evangelist redaction. On the Johannine style of the discourse, see the analysis by Schnackenburg, *John* 1:380–92.

[19] See Dodd, *Interpretation,* 303ff.; idem, *Tradition,* 279. Among those who argue for the unity of John 3 are Hoskyns, *Fourth Gospel,* 221ff.; Cullmann, *Early Christian Worship,* 78–80; Barrett, *John,* 219; Lightfoot, *John,* 115–20; Brown, *John* 1:160.

[20] See Ibuki, "Gedankenaufbau und Hintergrund," 11.

[21] See Schnackenburg, *John* vol. 1, ad loc.

[22] See Becker, *Johannes* 1:130.

attention has been paid by scholars,[23] but which witness to the fourth evangelist's knowledge of baptism. They speak of Jesus' baptizing, an activity unknown to the Synoptics.

John 3:22 mentions Jesus' baptizing while he was in Judea. The imperfect form ἐβάπτιζεν gives the impression of a fairly long period of activity on Jesus' part.[24] The redactional character of v. 22 is indicated by the Johannine transitional formula μετὰ ταῦτα (see 5:1, 14; 6:1; 7:1; 19:38), the continuation of the itinerary from 2:23; 3:1, and the imprecise indication of place, in contrast to v. 23.[25] On the other hand, the note about John the Baptizer in 3:23 may be traditional,[26] as seems to be indicated by the precise geographical information.[27] By means of v. 24, the evangelist[28] clarifies the simultaneous baptizing by Jesus and John the Baptizer.

John 3:25-29 is a traditional section indicating that there was a conflict between the Johannine community and the followers of the Baptizer over correct baptismal practice. Tradition is suggested by καθαρισμός [purification] in v. 25, unmotivated in this context.[29] It refers to the relationship between Jesus' baptism and John's baptism, which means that the occasion for the conflict must have been Jesus' baptizing. This is apparent also from v. 26, whose content seems to demand a conjectural change in v. 25 from μετὰ Ἰουδαίου [with a Jew], which seems to have no function in the progress of the narrative,[30] to μετὰ τῶν Ἰησοῦ [with Jesus']³¹ or μετὰ (τοῦ) Ἰησοῦ.[32] In v. 26, the conflict situation between the Johannine community and the Baptizer group is clearly expressed in the polemic πάντες [all]. The Johannine community projects its successful advance in numbers, in contrast to the Baptizer group, back into the life of Jesus and reduces John the Baptizer to a mere witness. Except for the syntactically difficult relative clause, ᾧ σὺ μεμαρτύρηκας [to whom you bore witness] (cf. 1:19-34), the verse could well

---

²³ See only Bultmann, *John,* 472: "But 3.22 and 4.1 are far from being stressed, and the sacraments play no part in Jesus' proclamation."

²⁴ See Bauer, *Johannesevangelium,* 62; Bultmann, *John,* 170 n. 5.

²⁵ See Becker, *Johannes* 1:153; Schnackenburg, *John* 1:410–11.

²⁶ See Becker, who, however, wishes to include v. 23 in his "semeia source" (*Johannes* 1:153), although there is no basis for such an inclusion. Either this note comes from the Johannine school or the evangelist took it from a Baptizer tradition available to him (so Bultmann, *John,* 170 n. 9).

²⁷ See Brown, *John* 1:151; Bauer, *Johannesevangelium,* 62; Schnackenburg, *John* 1:412–13.

²⁸ See Schnackenburg, *John* 1:413; against Becker (*Johannes* 1:153), who also assigns v. 24 to his "semeia source." But v. 24 presupposes v. 22, which even Becker regards as redactional! Bultmann sees v. 24 as a gloss by the "ecclesiastical editor" (*John,* 171 n. 2), although there is no evidence for this.

²⁹ See Bultmann, *John,* 169.

³⁰ 𝔓⁶⁶ ℵ* and others change this striking singular to plural.

³¹ See O. Holtzmann, *Johannesevangelium,* 210.

³² See Loisy, *Le quatrième évangile,* 171; Becker, *Johannes* 1:153.

be traditional,[33] especially since John borrowed his statement about Jesus' baptizing (v. 22) from this verse. Verse 27 can be read as a saying of the Baptizer,[34] in which the latter originally referred to the authority given him by God.[35] But in the present context it confirms Jesus' claims. With vv. 28-29 the Johannine community calls the members of the competing group to witness to the Baptizer's role as forerunner. While vv. 28-29 belong to the traditional polemic against the Baptizer, v. 30 reveals a redactional interest on the part of the evangelist:[36] after 3:30, John the Baptizer no longer appears as an active presence,[37] so that the image of increasing and decreasing is given both a compositional and an ecclesiological function.

In *John 4:1* Jesus' "increasing" is presented in the sense of a successful mission and thus is ecclesiologically interpreted. "The Baptizer community must decrease, but the Jesus community must grow."[38] The polemic accent of 4:1 is quite evident in the comparative formula πλείονας . . . ἤ [more . . . than]. As Jesus had more success than John, so the Johannine community triumphs over the followers of the Baptizer.[39] Entrance into discipleship and thus into the Johannine community was connected with baptism, as the connection between μαθητὰς ποιεῖν [to make disciples] and βαπτίζειν indicates. It is true that nothing is said about the manner of baptizing,[40] but in 4:1 it is regarded as the normal rite of initiation.[41]

A period of baptizing by the historical Jesus cannot be established on the basis of

---

[33] See Becker, *Johannes* 1:154; against Bultmann, *John,* 171 n. 7.

[34] See Bultmann, *John,* 172; Haenchen (*John* 1:210) differs with Bultmann.

[35] The expression ἐκ τοῦ οὐρανοῦ [from heaven] is another way of saying "from God." See Schlatter, *Johannes,* ad loc.

[36] See Bultmann, *John,* 174–75; against Becker, who considers v. 30 part of his "semeia source" (*Johannes* 1:155). Redaction is suggested also by the necessity of the divine saving event expressed in δεῖ; cf. 3:14; 12:34; 20:9.

[37] See 5:33, 36; 10:40-41.

[38] Schulz, *Johannes,* 65.

[39] Although John 4:1, in the framework of the itinerary (4:1, 3, 4) is seen to be the work of the evangelist (see Bultmann, *John,* 175; Becker, *Johannes* 1:166), 4:2 is probably a secondary gloss, whose purpose was to reconcile the startling baptismal praxis of Jesus with the image of Jesus in the Synoptics (thus also Bultmann, *John,* 176 n. 2; Dodd, *Interpretation,* 311 n. 3; Schnackenburg, *John* 1:422, etc.). Besides, the continuity of thought in vv. 1 and 3 is interrupted, and 4:2 is linguistically remarkable as well: καίτοιγε [although] is a *hapax legomenon* in the New Testament, and Ἰησοῦς without the article is also unusual.

[40] Among those who argue for a "baptism of the Spirit" are Cullmann, *Early Christian Worship,* 78–80; Dodd, *Interpretation,* 310; Porsch, *Pneuma,* 126–27. Against this interpretation are Aland, "Vorgeschichte," 195; Haenchen, *John* 1:210; W. Michaelis, *Sakramente,* 14; Schnackenburg, *John* 1:411. According to 7:39 (cf. 20:19-23), the Spirit is only given after Jesus' glorification; we ought, therefore, to avoid the concept of "baptism of the Spirit" in an exclusive sense. Water baptism was probably the usual thing, even in the Johannine school. But it was at the same time the moment of the bestowal of the Spirit, since in the time of the community Jesus was already exalted.

[41] See Lindars, "Word and Sacrament," 53.

3:23-26; 4:1.[42] Against it are the silence of the Synoptics[43] and the discernible theological interest of the evangelist in depicting Jesus as baptizing. We may, of course, suspect that the Synoptics, in their tendentious portrayal of the Baptizer, would have suppressed any information that would have made Jesus a disciple of John. On the other hand, they report Jesus' baptism by John (Mark 1:9-11 par.), while the fourth evangelist speaks of it only indirectly (John 1:29-34).

As in other early Christian groups (see Paul, and Matt. 28:18-20), so also in the Johannine school, baptism was the normative rite of initiation. But this is the only point at which this practice is anchored in the life of the historical Jesus, which shows that both the evangelist and the Johannine tradition accorded it great importance. The Johannine school carried on the work of the historical Jesus in its own area and thus demonstrated that it was his legitimate successor. It is possible that the initial situation of competition with the Baptizer's followers also gave rise to a strengthened reflection on their own baptismal practice and its historical and theological foundations. The evangelist does not merely presume the practice of baptism in passing; 3:23, 25-30; and 4:1 document a strong theological interest. For John, baptism is a legitimate continuation of Jesus' work, and, as the constitutive rite of acceptance into the community, it is the *conditio sine qua non* of Christian existence. Therefore, it is logical that the fourth evangelist also makes statements about the nature of baptism.

4.1.3   Redaction and Tradition in John 3:1-21

The discourse with Nicodemus is prepared for and introduced by the redactional transition in 2:23-25.[44] This passage describes the situation that forms the background of the encounter. The mention of the σημεῖα in 2:23 is a preparation for Nicodemus's statement in 3:2b, and Jesus' reaction to the faith of the crowd in 2:24-25 anticipates Nicodemus's misunderstanding in 3:4, 9.

The Nicodemus pericope begins with an "ideal scene"[45] (3:1-2a) introducing the persons and time of the action to follow. Though vv. 1 and 2 were constructed by the evangelist,[46] v. 3 represents a tradition of the Johannine

---

[42] Among those who argue that the historical Jesus baptized are K. Aland, "Vorgeschichte," 194–95; Becker, *Johannes* 1:152–53; idem, *Johannes der Täufer,* 13–14; Dodd, *Tradition,* 286; Jeremias, *Theology* 1:45–46; Schnackenburg, *John* 1:411; J. Schneider, *Johannes,* 109; those taking the opposite position include Barth, *Taufe,* 42–43; Dinkler, "Taufaussagen," 66.

[43] See Barth, *Taufe,* 42.

[44] See the remarks in section 3.8.3.1 above.

[45] Becker, *Johannes* 1:131.

[46] It is true that John may have found the figure of Nicodemus in the tradition, but the shaping and exposition of the instructional dialogue are the work of the evangelist. This is clear from v. 2, where ἦλθεν πρὸς αὐτόν [he came to him] presupposes the redactional passage 2:23-25 and therefore must also be regarded as redactional. In addition, v. 2 reveals a multitude of Johannine expressions (οἴδαμεν, ἔρχομαι, δύνασθαι, ταῦτα, σημεῖα ποιεῖν, ἐὰν μή).

school. This is evident from the expression βασιλεία τοῦ θεοῦ [reign of God], which occurs only in 3:3, 5; this is not a common term for eschatological fulfillment in the Fourth Gospel in contrast to the Synoptics. The preposition ἄνωθεν, important for understanding v. 3, has a double meaning:[47] either "again" or "from above." The other uses of ἄνωθεν in the Gospel of John (3:31; 19:11, 23) make the translation "from above" more likely.[48] In particular, the christological reference of ἄνωθεν in 3:31 and 8:23 (Christ says: ἐγὼ ἐκ τῶν ἄνω εἰμί) demands this interpretation, inasmuch as Christ and his own are essentially related in the place of their origin. To be sure, a measure of ambiguity in ἄνωθεν is not excluded,[49] because the Johannine notion of being "begotten by God" (cf. 1 John 2:29; 3:9; 4:7; 5:1, 4, 18; John 1:13) is related to this γεννηθῆναι ἄνωθεν and undoubtedly contains within itself the aspect of rebirth as well (cf. Titus 3:5; 1 Pet. 1:3, 23; Justin Apol. 1.61.3, 10; 66.1; Justin Dial. 138.2; Acts of Thomas 132).[50] The tradition emphasizes that it is not within the power of human beings to see the reign of God. God alone creates the basis for that possibility.[51]

The Synoptics also know the idea of "seeing" the reign of God (cf. Mark 9:1/Luke 9:27) or "entering" it (cf. Matt. 5:20; 7:21; 18:3; 19:23-24; 23:14; Mark 9:47; 10:15, 23ff.; Luke 18:17, 25). There are some possible variant traditions related to John 3:3, 5 in Mark 10:15; Matt. 18:3; Hermas Sim. 9.16.2 and Justin Apol. 1.61.4.[52] A tradition-historical dependence of John 3:3, 5 on Mark 10:15 cannot be excluded,[53] because both sayings reveal structural similarities (same introductory formula, negative conditional clause, comparable posterior clauses).[54] Nevertheless, the differences in content cannot be overlooked; Mark 10:15 is aimed at human conversion, while John 3:3, 5 speaks in real terms of a new creation or new birth as a pure act of God.[55]

---

[47] For the possible meanings of ἄνωθεν, see especially Bauer, Johannesevangelium, 50–51; Schnackenburg, John 1:367–68.

[48] Thus, among others, Schnackenburg, John 1:367–68; Becker, Johannes 1:134; Porsch, Pneuma, 97; Klos, Sakramente, 70; Lindars, "John and the Synoptic Gospels," 291; Haenchen, John 1:200; Pesch, "'Ihr müßt von oben geboren werden,'" 208; Blank, Krisis, 57; Leroy, Rätsel, 132. Bultmann differs: he strongly emphasizes that ἄνωθεν here can only mean "again" (John 135 n. 1). Thus also Strathmann, Johannes, 68; Schulz, Johannes, 55; Barth, Taufe, 108.

[49] See Dodd, Interpretation, 303 n. 2; Barrett, John, 205–6.

[50] On the Johannine idea of being "begotten of God," see Schnackenburg, Johannesbriefe, Excursus, 175–83; Bauer, Johannesevangelium, Excursus, 51–53; Windisch, Johannesbriefe, Excursus, 121–23; Dodd, Interpretation, 303–5. In terms of the history of religions, the notion of rebirth connected with being "begotten of God" may stem from the mystery religions; see only Apuleius Metamorphoses 11.21.

[51] See Bultmann, John, 137–38.

[52] Worth noting is also Wis. 10:10, where it is said of σοφία: ἔδειξεν αὐτῷ (sc. Jacob in Bethel) βασιλείαν θεοῦ [she showed him the kingdom of God].

[53] Among those who argue in favor of this are Jeremias, Infant Baptism, 51–52; de la Potterie, "'Naître,'" 438.

[54] See the list in Jeremias, Infant Baptism, 51.

[55] This is emphasized by Schnackenburg, John 1:367. Richter's proposal ("Joh 3,5," 328–29) that 3:3 originally spoke, as does Justin Apol. 1.61.4, of being born again (ἀναγεννηθῆναι) and

In v. 2, the evangelist presents Nicodemus as a spokesman for liberal Judaism (see 7:50; 19:39),[56] while in v. 3 the tradition describes what, from the Johannine point of view, is necessary for salvation: a totally new creation, which is the work of God alone. Thus Nicodemus does not appear simply as the "representative . . . of an inadequate faith in miracles"[57] or as the spokesman of the epiphany christology of a supposed "semeia source."[58] Instead, in the evangelist's composition he serves primarily as a mere conversation partner, who does not engage in dialogue but is simply present to utter certain key words and otherwise to listen to a monologue by the Johannine Christ. Nicodemus's misunderstanding in v. 4 should be viewed against this background: he supposes that Jesus' words γεννηθῆναι ἄνωθεν refer to the rebirth of someone who is already old. The function of this verse, created by the evangelist, is to give greater effectiveness to Jesus' answer in v. 5.

The motif of misunderstanding is a literary form employed by the evangelist and rests on the ambiguity of Johannine concepts.[59] According to R. Bultmann the ambiguity "does not consist in one word having two meanings, so that the misunderstanding comes as a result of choosing the wrong one; it is rather that there are concepts and statements, which at first sight refer to earthly matters, but properly refer to divine matters. The misunderstanding comes when someone sees the right meaning of the word but mistakenly imagines that its meaning is exhausted by the reference to earthly matters. . . ."[60] The misunderstanding is the sign of a judgment κατ' ὄψιν [by appearance] (7:24) or κατὰ τὴν σάρκα [according to the flesh] (8:15) and therefore belongs to a dualistic conception. It is no accident that it is always the Jews, in their role as representatives of the unbelieving world, who misunderstand Jesus (see 2:19-22; 3:4, 9; 4:10-11, 31ff.; 6:41-42, 51-52; 7:33-36; 8:21-22, 31-33, 51-53, 56-58).[61]

A true understanding of the Revealer's words takes place only in the believing community (see 3:11), which knows that it is in possession of the Spirit of truth. The unbelieving world cannot receive this Spirit (14:17), but the Spirit teaches the community and reminds it of everything Jesus had said (14:26; see also 16:12-15). The community understands and speaks the language of the Revealer, so that the evangelist can presume that the hearers and readers of the Gospel will understand his words. "One who knows speaks to those who know; the evangelist speaks to a

---

that it was the evangelist who, with polemic intent, changed rebirth to birth from above (see pp. 334ff.) must be rejected. The text offers no support for positing such a procedure on the part of the evangelist. For a critique of Richter's position, see Thyen, "Aus der Literatur," ThR 44, 112ff.

[56] See Leroy, Rätsel, 135–36.

[57] Thus Pesch, "'Ihr müßt von oben geboren werden,'" 209.

[58] Against Becker, Johannes 1:132.

[59] On the history of research on the motif of misundersanding in John, see Carson, "Understanding Misunderstanding," 60–67.

[60] Bultmann, John, 135 n. 1.

[61] The disciples' lack of understanding (see 13:13ff.; 14:4-5, 8, 22; 16:17-18) must be distinguished from the motif of misunderstanding. The former merely expresses a failure of comprehension that can be alleviated; see Becker, Johannes 1:136.

believing community."[62] On the sociological level, this theological circle of those who know corresponds to the "special language" of the Johannine school.[63] This circle knows that it is distinguished from the world around it by its attitude to the Revealer,[64] and one way in which it expresses this primary theological judgment is by use of the stylistic theme of misunderstanding.

In its structure, the tradition in 3:5 parallels 3:3; its content represents a step forward in the argumentation. While the introductory formula, conditional clause, and statement of the object correspond, the ἄνωθεν in v. 3 is clarified in v. 5 with ἐξ ὕδατος καὶ πνεύματος [of water and spirit], and the ἰδεῖν [to see] of v. 3 is elaborated with εἰσελθεῖν εἰς [enter into] in v. 5. The begetting/birth from above is accomplished in the begetting/birth in water and Spirit. There is a clear theological advance between v. 3 and v. 5, characteristic of the Johannine tradition and adopted by the evangelist. Both verses would have been available to John as traditional formulae of the Johannine school; he cites them with variations in vv. 7 and 8c.[65]

The interpretation of v. 5 is determined by how one understands ὕδατος καί. Following H. H. Wendt,[66] R. Bultmann stated his opinion that ὕδατος καί was "an insertion of the ecclesiastical redaction,"[67] but there is no basis, either text-critical or literary-critical, for such a judgment. As regards the text, the apparent[68] omission of ὕδατος καί in the Vulgate codex Harleianus 1023 and in part of the textual tradition of the works of Origen is not sufficient to demonstrate the secondary nature of these words. Moreover, the insertion of ὕδατος καί by ℵ, 01 and other manuscripts in v. 8 presupposes that ὕδατος καί was originally present in v. 5.

In terms of literary criticism as well, nothing speaks against the originality of these two words; they do not bring about any break in the thought that would indicate a secondary insertion. R. Bultmann's argument about the supposed lack of relationship to the context[69] is prejudiced by his general opinion on the sacraments in John, according to which "the Evangelist consciously rejects the sacramentalism of ecclesiastical piety."[70] This argument

---

[62] Leroy, "Das johanneische Mißverständnis," 205.

[63] See Leroy, Rätsel, 157ff.

[64] I find it questionable whether we can also deduce from this situation that the Johannine community felt itself "misunderstood, cut off and isolated from the world around it" (Becker, Johannes 1:136).

[65] Berger thinks that v. 5 is traditional but that v. 3 is a variant composed by the evangelist (Amen-Worte, 103). On the contrary, Bultmann holds v. 3 to be traditional and v. 5 to be interpretation (John 135 n. 4). Becker considers vv. 3 and 5 to be two already-existing variants of the same tradition (Johannes 1:130, 134).

[66] See Wendt, Johannesevangelium, 112; see also Wellhausen, Evangelium Johannis, 17–18.

[67] Bultmann, John, 138 n. 3; Richter even assigns ὕδατος καί to a tertiary redactor ("Joh 3,5," 335 n. 39).

[68] See de la Potterie, "'Naître,'" 424 n. 33.

[69] See Bultmann, John, 138 n. 3.

[70] Ibid. Schottroff and Becker make an attempt to undergird Bultmann's theological position

is entirely at the level of theological interpretation, not that of literary-critical analysis! In addition, the accounts of Jesus' baptizing have shown that the evangelist presumes baptism as the normal rite of initiation into his community, so that statements about the nature of baptism are to be expected. Both for the tradition and for the evangelist, begetting/birth from water and Spirit, and therefore baptism, are the conditions for participation in eschatological, salvation. The generalizing τις and the formula ἐὰν μή . . . οὐ, which suggests exclusivity, indicate the fundamental importance of this statement. There is no other access to the reign of God except baptism. Baptism alone confers the eschatological saving gift of the Spirit. As in the letters of Paul (see 1 Cor. 6:11; 10:1ff.; 12:13; 2 Cor. 1:21-22; Gal. 5:24, 25; Rom. 5:5)[71] and in the Acts of the Apostles (see 1:5; 2:38; 8:17; 11:16; 19:1-6), in John 3:5 the bestowal of the Spirit is connected with baptism. Thus baptism and the conferral of the Spirit are, for the Johannine school as well, the primary data of Christian existence (in addition to John 3:5-6 and 6:63a, see esp. 1 John 2:27; 3:24; 4:13; 5:6-8). In John 3:5 the standpoint of the post-Easter community is articulated: they regard baptism as the "condition of admittance" into the reign of God and thus as an initiatory rite that is necessary for salvation. John adopts the tradition of his school in its full extent; there are not even the slightest hints of a criticism or a shift in accent. This does not mean that the fourth evangelist advocates "sacramentalism" in a modern sense, but simply that he shares an idea of sacraments that was current throughout early Christianity.

In v. 6, John interprets his tradition by use of the σάρξ–πνεῦμα dualism that was already closely bound up with baptism in Hellenistic Jewish Christianity (see Gal. 5:13ff.; Rom. 1:3, 4; 8:5-8).[72] For John, the origin determines the essence, so that the statement of origins, with ἐκ (see 3:31; 8:23, 44, 47; 15:19; 17:14, 16) is at the same time a statement of essence. "This is the application of a general 'principle,' according to which the essence of a being is determined by its origin, and like can only bring forth like."[73] If

---

on 3:5 without declaring ὕδατος καί secondary. Schottroff thinks that "the fact that John's understanding of salvation is unsacramental becomes clear at the point when we acknowledge that ἐξ ὕδατος καί in Joh III.5 is an original part of the text" ("Entweltlichung," 300). Becker thinks that John is here polemicizing "not against baptism as such," but on the other hand it is not the subject of the discourse (Johannes 1:137). "Not the sacrament, as understood in vv. 3 and 5, but rather the relationship between word and faith is the Archimedean point for salvation, and the understanding of baptism is to be subordinated to that" (p. 138). Against these attempts to maintain Bultmann's position by introducing dualistic or personal categories in 3:5, we must object that in 3:5 baptism is the sole condition for salvation, and this position is accepted by the evangelist without any discernible criticism.

[71] See Schnelle, Gerechtigkeit und Christusgegenwart, 124ff.

[72] Ibid., 126ff. Bultmann considers the σάρξ–πνεῦμα dualism to be gnostic (John, 141 n. 2); against this position, see E. Schweizer, TDNT 6:415–24, 433–42; Brandenburger, Fleisch und Geist, passim.

[73] Porsch, Pneuma, 99.

what is begotten from flesh belongs essentially to the sphere of σάρξ, it is thereby fundamentally removed from the sphere of *pneuma*. In John the *pneuma* appears as a principle of life—it gives life—and the flesh, by contrast, is useless (6:63). This is different from Paul's approach: the flesh is not disqualified because of sin. Instead, the antithesis between flesh and spirit reveals the nothingness of the σάρξ.[74] The fleshly person has no access to the reign of God. It is only through receiving a new origin from God that a human being can obtain access to the sphere of divine rule. Thus, πνεῦμα does not primarily describe a gift but must be understood in a more comprehensive sense as a principle of divine agency or as the divine creative power. As for Paul the καινὴ κτίσις [new creation] is ultimately identical with being ἐν Χριστῷ [in Christ] or ἐν πνεύματι [in the spirit] (2 Cor. 3:17; 5:17), so in John the new birth ἐξ ὕδατος καὶ πνεύματος describes an all-embracing new creation that is accomplished in baptism with water and leads to a life filled and determined by the Spirit.[75] If the Spirit creates the qualitative, essential difference from the fleshly person, baptism is "factual salvation,"[76] insofar as it is the place where the transition from the sphere of flesh and death to the divine sphere takes place.

Two elements mark the evangelist's dualistic revision of the school tradition in 3:3, 5: on the one hand, the necessity of birth from above is emphasized (v. 7), and, on the other hand, v. 8 clearly shows that being begotten by the Spirit is not something that lies at human disposal. In particular, v. 8a with its wisdom overtones (cf. Prov. 30:4; Eccl. 11:5; Sir. 16:21)[77] brings out the uncontrollable nature of this new birth: it is not a human possibility, but exclusively at God's disposal. Just as the human being cannot influence the wind, so also God's action is sovereign and beyond human control. John thus preserves the *extra nos* [apart from us] of the event of salvation and at the same time indicates the place where a human person can receive a share in salvation: in the baptism of the Johannine community. The evangelist's dualistic conception is not metaphysically exalted, and it would be difficult to call it an ontological dualism, in which human beings by their very nature participate in salvation or are excluded from it. Instead, the transition from the realm of no salvation to that of salvation is accomplished in baptism. Therefore it is a historical event, so that Johannine dualism should be designated a "dualism of decision." There is no natural access to salvation for human beings; instead, each human person must make a decision of faith in favor of the humanly inaccessible divine gift of salvation.

In the third and final movement of the discourse (vv. 9-12), John again documents Nicodemus's lack of understanding, by means of the question in

---

[74] See Schnackenburg, *John* 1:371.
[75] See Porsch, *Pneuma,* 129.
[76] Ratschow, *Die eine christliche Taufe,* 233.
[77] Against Bultmann, who traces 3:8 to gnostic traditions (*John,* 143 n. 1).

v. 9 and the expression οὐ γινώσκεις [you do not understand] in v. 10. As one learned in the law, Nicodemus ought to understand Jesus' words about being begotten of water and Spirit, as well as the uncontrollable activity of the Spirit. Here it is again clear that for the fourth evangelist the Scripture can be comprehended only through God's revelation in Jesus Christ; its meaning is hidden from the scribe Nicodemus.[78] In v. 11 the point of view of the post-Easter community emerges (see the *pluralis ecclesiasticus*),[79] as the situation of Nicodemus and those like him is contrasted with the immediate knowing and seeing available to the Johannine community. If Nicodemus and the group he represents cannot understand even the beginning of Jesus' saving revelation, they will not be able to understand the "heavenly things" that have not yet been told. In τὰ ἐπίγεια [earthly things], John summarizes his teaching on the new birth of the earthly human being from water and Spirit. For John, baptism is the key step toward salvation. If the "earthly things" have to do with the entrance of the *human being* into the sphere of salvation, the "heavenly things" concern the work of the *Revealer*, as depicted in vv. 13-21.[80]

Verse 12 marks the first division in the Nicodemus discourse. Up to this verse, Jesus addresses his interlocutor in the second person plural,[81] and the nearest form-critical parallel, 2 Esdras 4:1-11 (12-21), also gives good reason to see a caesura occurring at this point. In the dialogue between Ezra and the angel, Ezra, like Nicodemus, serves exclusively as a passive learner who, by a threefold awkward reply and question, gives the teacher the opportunity to pronounce a lecture ending with the words "How can one who is already worn out by the corrupt world understand incorruption?" (2 Esd. 4:11b).[82] Typical of a teaching discourse is, in addition to the role of the knowledgeable teacher and that of the ignorant student, a reference to heavenly revelations that are by their nature closed to the student, who is but an earthly human person. The contrast between "earthly" and "heavenly" also reveals an escalation:[83] from here on the subject is the "heavenly." In and of itself, this can only occur in a monologue by the Revealer, who alone knows about the heavenly things.

---

[78] In 5:39, 46-47 also, the Johannine Jesus refers to Scripture, or to Moses, without mentioning particular passages. The reference must be to passages that speak of the eschatological activity of the Spirit; see Schnackenburg, *John* 1:370–71, 375.

[79] See Schnackenburg, *John* 1:376. Against Bühner (*Der Gesandte*, 378ff.), who follows Berger in thinking that the sentence beginning with ἀμήν points to knowledge received through a vision, and that 3:11 is to be understood against an "anabaptist-apocalyptic background."

[80] Schnackenburg is imprecise (*John* 1:379). On the basis of his literary-critical criteria, he is forced to deny a relationship between v. 12 and vv. 13-21, and understand τὰ ἐπουράνια in general terms as "the whole way which Christ opened to the heavenly world."

[81] See Schnackenburg, *John* 1:361. We should, however, emphasize, against Schnackenburg, that v. 12 is not yet the end of the Nicodemus pericope. The monologue in vv. 13-21 is, from John's point of view, a continuation of the preceding dialogue.

[82] *RSV* translation.

[83] There is no real parallel to the escalation from "earthly" to "heavenly"; the often-cited parallels, Wis. 9:16, 2 Esd. 4:8, 21, *Odes of Solomon* 34:4-5, regard the two as opposites. See Schnackenburg, *John* 1:378–79. Verse 12 may well be a composition of the evangelist.

In v. 13, the evangelist takes up a tradition of the Johannine school that reveals wisdom traits (cf. Deut. 30:11, 12; Prov. 30:4; Wis. 9:16; *Bar.* 3:29; Rom. 10:6; Eph. 4:10).[84] From the point of view of the community, this tradition emphasizes the identity between the One who has ascended into heaven and abides there (perfect tense: ἀναβέβηκεν) and the Incarnate One (aorist: ὁ καταβάς).[85]

J.-A. Bühner sees in 3:13 (and 3:31-32) a "call vision": "the anabatic one is transformed by his 'call vision' into a heavenly being, and it is as such that he returns to earth. Apparently, the heavenly transformation of the anabatic one was christologically formulated in the Johannine tradition from the beginning, although it should be recognized that the Son of Man context has a tradition-historical priority."[86] According to Bühner, the Johannine Jesus apparently accomplishes a twofold "going up": an apocalyptic-visionary one (3:13, 31-32) "and a return to the heavenly world after his sojourn on earth (6:62; 20:17). But it is difficult to interpret the historically concrete καταβάς (3:13) in such a way that the anabatic one returns to earth after being taken up into heaven (cf. 3:31-32); instead, it should be referred to the sending of the Son of God into the world, to which the Gospel of John testifies throughout; this is evident in 6:33, 38, 41-42, 50-51, 58."[87]

In John's eyes, the Son of man, as the one who descends from heaven and returns there (1:51; 3:13; 6:62), already fulfills in the present time his functions as judge (5:27), giver of life (6:27, 53, 62), and Messiah (8:28; 9:35; 12:23, 34; 13:31-32).[88] The Johannine Son-of-man sayings are shaped both by their incorporation into the christology of preexistence and incarnation, and by their interpretation in the context of the theology of the cross (ὑψωθῆναι [being lifted up]) and resurrection (δοξασθῆναι [being glorified]).[89] The *anabasis* of the Son of man is interpreted in v. 14, in a specifically Johannine fashion, as "being lifted up." As in 8:28 and 12:32, ὑψοῦν also refers here to Jesus' crucifixion.[90] The typological interpretation of Num. 21:8-9 is evident in v. 14b, because it is from there that John takes his characteristic ὑψοῦν, which is found neither in the Hebrew text nor in the LXX. Like the lifting up of the serpent in the desert, the exaltation of Jesus functions to save others.[91] In v. 14b, the evangelist is citing a kerygmatic tradition[92] that, like Mark 8:31,

---

[84] See Schulz, *Menschensohn-Christologie*, 104ff. Verse 13 gives the impression of being an independent logion; it reveals no special Johannine stylistic features.

[85] See Schnackenburg, *John* 1:393–94.

[86] Bühner, *Der Gesandte*, 382.

[87] Schnackenburg, "Paulinische und johanneische Christologie," 106.

[88] For the Johannine understanding of the Son of man, see Schnackenburg, *John* 1:529–42.

[89] See Hahn, *EWNT* 3:932ff.

[90] See Thüsing, *Erhöhung*, 3–4.

[91] In my opinion, every interpretation of the Old Testament text that goes beyond this is in error. See Thüsing, *Erhöhung*, 4ff.; Schnackenburg, *John* 1:395–96.

[92] Since the evangelist interprets the Old Testament text with the aid of the ὑψοῦν in v. 14b, we may suspect tradition behind this part of the verse.

offers a succinct expression of the δεῖ [it is necessary] of the divine will. The lifting up of Jesus on the cross is the precondition for the salvation of believers, something that is stated with emphasis in v. 15 as well as in 12:32, 34. The Johannine interpretation of Jesus' crucifixion as "lifting up" and also "glorification" (cf. 12:23; 13:31) testifies to an advanced stage in the development of early Christian theology.[93] Cross and exaltation are not two separate actions within the event of salvation (cf. Phil. 2:8-11); instead, the cross, as the place of exaltation and glorification, is the saving event. Here there is evidence of a christological "concentration" that can be observed also in the "intercalation" of times in the Gospel of John (see 5:25). The saving event is not primarily described in its factual or temporal stages; instead, although the individual aspects are preserved,[94] it is regarded as a present eschatological unity.

In vv. 16-17, John takes up traditions of his school, as indicated in particular by form-critical observations. Verse 16 agrees with Rom. 8:32 in the sense that God is the active subject of both verses and that both speak of the giving (John 3:16: ἔδωκεν) or giving up (Rom. 8:32: παρέδωκεν) of the Son and describe the salvific significance of that event.[95] The general agreement of v. 17 with Gal. 4:4-5; Rom. 8:3; and 1 John 4:9, 10, 14 lies in the saying about mission in the first part of the sentence and the description of the saving meaning of the mission in the second part.[96] All these texts presume the preexistence of the Son as their basis; their real object is the statement of the soteriological purpose of the saving event. It is also characteristic of the Johannine texts that the love of God is cited as the motive force for God's action and that the cosmos, as the object of that love, is given a positive evaluation. The agreements in form and content between the Pauline and Johannine texts point to a common traditional and religious-historical background.

There are some remarkable parallels to our texts in Hellenistic Jewish wisdom literature. In a prayer of Solomon in Wis. 9:9, Sophia is first presented as God's preexistent companion and witness to creation. Then Solomon asks of God: ἐξαπόστειλον αὐτὴν (sc. σοφία) ἐξ ἁγίων οὐρανῶν καὶ ἀπὸ θρόνου δόξης σου πέμψον αὐτήν, ἵνα συμπαροῦσά μοι κοπιάσῃ καὶ γνῶ τί εὐάρεστόν ἐστιν παρὰ σοι [send her (Wisdom) forth from the holy heavens, and from the throne of your glory send her, that she may labor at my side, and that I may learn what is pleasing to you] (v. 10). In v. 17 we read: βουλὴν δέ σου τίς ἔγνω, εἰ μὴ σὺ ἔδωκας σοφίαν καὶ ἔπεμψας τὸ ἅγιόν σου πνεῦμα

---

[93] For the details, which cannot be discussed here, see Schnackenburg, *John* 1:396–98. It is possible that behind the Johannine exaltation-and-glorification christology is Isa. 52:13 LXX, where it is said of the Servant of God: ἰδοὺ συνήσει ὁ παῖς καὶ ὑψωθήσεται καὶ δοξασθήσεται σφόδρα [see, my child (or: servant) shall understand, and be exalted, and glorified exceedingly].

[94] Against Becker, who thinks that the cross, as a symbol of suffering, plays no further role in 3:14 (*Johannes* 1:144). Accurately in opposition is Thüsing, *Erhöhung*, 7–8.

[95] See Kramer, *Christos Kyrios*, 112–13.

[96] Ibid., 110.

ἀπὸ ὑψίστων [Who has learned your counsel, unless you have given wisdom and sent your holy spirit from on high]. Here there are agreements with Paul and John in the combination of preexistence, sending, and gift of the Spirit (cf. esp. Gal. 4:4-6), as well as the statement of the soteriological purpose of the sending in a ἵνα-clause (Wis. 9:10). Moreover, Philo also uses the title of Son in the immediate context of statements about the Logos and mission (*Agric.* 51; see also *Her.* 205; *Conf.* 63; *Fug.* 12).[97]

The texts testify to the separation of God "from the divine powers at work on earth."[98] In cosmogony, in particular, there developed a notion of a δύναμις [power, authority] sent by God, a λόγος or σοφία, that either gives order to chaotic matter or is itself (himself/herself) immediately involved in creation. "Thus the motif of the mediator sent from heaven, who is at the same time the preexistent divine organ for the creation and preservation of the world, lay ready to hand. The title 'Son of God' was already connected with this figure, at least in Philo's work, even if it was not reserved exclusively for that."[99] The statements about preexistence and mission in Paul and John have their immediate ancestors in the Sophia and Logos speculations of Hellenistic Judaism and Jewish Christianity.[100]

This position, represented by E. Schweizer, among others, has recently been criticized by J.-A. Bühner, whose purpose is to derive Johannine christology of mission entirely from Old Testament and ancient Jewish ideas concerning prophets and messengers. Bühner's interpretation of Wis. 9:10, 17 is not persuasive,[101] and he is unable to give a satisfactory explanation of three fundamental characteristics of Johannine christology of mission: (1) the preexistence of the one sent; (2) the divinity of the one sent, who is not simply a messenger or prophet, but the Son of God; (3) the fact that, in John, the messenger does not bring a message but is *himself*, as preexistent Logos, the message. The idea of revelation, which for John is constitutive, cannot be explained with the notion of the messenger. Moreover, the alternative between "christology of mission" and "idea of revelation," which is presupposed throughout his presentation,[102] is inadequate to the Johannine texts. The broad spectrum of material introduced by Bühner as a solution to this problem[103] is by no means

---

[97] Further parallels in Philo are suggested by E. Schweizer, "'Sendungsformel,'" 88–90, 92.

[98] Ibid., 92.

[99] Ibid., 93.

[100] Miranda (*Der Vater, der mich gesandt hat,* 147–304) undertakes a comprehensive analysis of the religious-historical backgrounds of the Johannine mission formulae and, like E. Schweizer, finds that early Christian Sophia theology was their immediate starting point; however, the same author takes a different position in his *Die Sendung Jesu im vierten Evangelium,* where he states that the Johannine concept of mission is modeled on the prophets and that its background lies in the Semitic and late Jewish legal regulations for ambassadors and official messengers (p. 90).

[101] Bühner dismisses this text simply by noting that here Solomon is uttering a prayer and that this genre sharply reduces the scope of statements contained in it (*Der Gesandte,* 94ff.). Therefore Wis. 9:10, 17 cannot be related to the historical-theological statements in Gal. 4:4ff.; Rom. 8:3; John 3:16; 1 John 4:19. In the first place, it is not at all clear why a prayer text should not be the starting point for the development of a tradition; besides this, Bühner overlooks the fact that Wisdom 10–19, formally speaking, constitutes a continuation of the prayer in chap. 9.

[102] See Bühner, *Der Gesandte,* 180, and frequently elsewhere.

[103] Bühner introduces, without any apparent differentiation regarding the history of traditions, material from the Old Testament, from Samaritan traditions, from Jewish apocalyptic and esoteric writings, and from rabbinic materials.

adequate to the succinct fullness of the Johannine statements, and the central thesis of his proposal, that the anabatic one is transformed through a "call vision,"[104] cannot begin to be verified from the Johannine texts.

God's love for the world culminated in a unique historical act: the giving[105] of the Son. Because here the world is the object of God's love, and not merely the place where it becomes visible, κόσμος must be understood in a positive sense. But what is that sense? In the first place, we must reject the position of L. Schottroff, according to whom "the purpose of the statement about the divine concern for the world [is] only to represent the rejection of the world as sharply as possible; it had had an opportunity to believe."[106] In that case, 3:16 would be merely an unrealized possibility, the originally positive indication of a de facto exclusively negative evaluation of the world in John's Gospel. This conception does not do justice to the text; the gift of eternal life as the soteriological purpose of God's saving activity appears in v. 16b as a present possibility to be grasped in faith. Thus, in 3:16-17 κόσμος is first of all an anthropological concept referring to the world of human beings in need of salvation as the object for God's action; in faith, that world is able to grasp the possibility of salvation opened up by the sending of the Son.

The concept of faith is the key to the Johannine understanding of the cosmos, for in the mind of the fourth evangelist the world is the product of the creative work of the Logos (1:3) and thus a priori is not a second-rate thing. Instead, it is only faith in the Revealer that decides whether a human person belongs to the world, which is inimical to God, or to the Johannine community. Only unbelief qualifies the cosmos as a negative field, so that John can speak of the world positively, as the object of God's love; neutrally, as the place of divine action; and negatively, as the realm of unbelief.[107] The many positive statements do not allow us to posit an inferiority of the cosmos throughout the Gospel of John: it was out of love that God sent the Son into the world (John 3:16; cf. 10:36; 1 John 4:9, 14); Jesus appears as σωτὴρ τοῦ κόσμου (John 4:42; cf. 1 John 2:2, 4:14); he is the prophet who has come into the world, or the Son of God (6:14; 11:27; cf. 18:37); as the bread that comes down from heaven, he gives life to the cosmos (6:33; cf. 6:51); he is the light of the world (9:5); he has come to save the cosmos (3:17; 12:47); Jesus sends his disciples into the world (17:18; cf. 17:15); and finally, the cosmos is promised the ability of γινώσκειν and πιστεύειν in Jesus' mission (17:21, 23; cf. 14:31). In a neutral sense, the cosmos appears in the work of

---

[104] See Bühner, *Der Gesandte,* 374ff.

[105] Against Cullmann (*Christology,* 300), ἔδωκεν is not to be understood simply in the same sense as παρέδωκεν. Kohler interprets the mission of the Son correctly as an explication of his death on the cross (*Kreuz und Menschwerdung,* 290ff.).

[106] Schottroff, *Der Glaubende,* 288.

[107] There are overviews of the Johannine use of κόσμος in Brown, *John* 1:508–10; and Cassem, "Use of κόσμος," 88.

the fourth evangelist as a space in which Jesus works (1:10; 9:5a; 14:19; 16:28; 17:5). The cosmos is judged negatively because it does not accept Jesus (1:10; cf. 17:25); hates him and the disciples (7:7; 15:18, 19; 17:14); appears as the realm of what is opposed to God (8:23; 12:25; 14:17, 22, 27, 30; 15:19; 16:8, 20, 33; 17:6, 9, 11, 13-14, 16; 18:36); and therefore Jesus brings judgment upon it (9:39; 12:31; 16:11).

John has neither a purely negative nor a double view of the cosmos.[108] Instead, it is only unbelief that makes of the cosmos a world opposed to God (see 16:9). Because the world is conceived of as God's creation, and therefore not a thing that is essentially inferior, both the traditions of the Johannine school (1 John 4:9; John 3:16-17)[109] and the fourth evangelist himself give a positive evaluation of the saving event of the Son's mission and the cosmos as the object of God's love. The cosmos is evaluated negatively only to the extent that it can become the place of unbelief and of judgment. Therefore, the Johannine conception aims not at a rejection of the world but at an over-coming, within the world (17:15!), of the cosmos as the place of unbelief.[110] The negative statements must be understood trans-cosmically (cf. 1 John 5:4-5; John 16:33) and not anti-cosmically.

The fundamental importance of the concept of faith for the Johannine understanding of the cosmos is evident also in v. 18, where John interprets the statements of his tradition: only faith, as the form in which the saving event is appropriated, decides whether God's care for the world will be accomplished for individuals as salvation or as judgment. Verse 18 does not retract the universal soteriological affirmations of the tradition in vv. 16-17. Instead, they are transformed at the anthropological level at which, from the Johannine point of view, the transition to salvation or obstinate resistance takes place. Even vv. 19-21, which are marked by a deterministic ethical dualism, must be interpreted in the context of Johannine anthropology, because in this section the evangelist is attempting to explain the phenomena of belief and unbelief. According to this interpretation, the sending of the Son as light reveals the works of human persons, and thus a "determinism that is always being carried through, even in the process of change . . . is lifted from latency to visibility."[111] The one who does evil hates the light and remains in darkness; but the one who does the truth comes to the light—that is, in the Johannine sense, to salvation—and that person's works will be revealed as having been done in God. Here we may see the beginnings of a

---

[108] See Bultmann, *John,* 55.

[109] Schottroff incorrectly supposes that there is a difference between John 3:16 and 1 John 4:9 (*Der Glaubende,* 287), because 1 John 4:14 makes it clear that even in 1 John 4:9 the cosmos is the object of God's love. On the one hand, Schottroff must admit that there cannot be a gnostic parallel to John 3:16 (see *Der Glaubende,* 187), but, on the other hand, she thinks "that even in 3:16, John has not departed from the Gnostic basis" (p. 288).

[110] See Balz, *EWNT* 2:772.

[111] Becker, *Johannes* 1:146.

predestinarian determinism, in which humanity is divided into two groups and judged according to works. The sending of the Son uncovers a situation that was really present beforehand. This concept, which deviates from the evangelist's thought, may point to the presence of a tradition in vv. 19-21; this is suggested also by the arrangement of this section, in three three-part parallelisms.[112] John can make use of this tradition without the concept of faith that for him is constitutive, because he understands it as an explication of the fundamental statements in v. 18: belief and unbelief correspond to ethical attitudes on the part of human beings. They are not foreordained but result from the person's moral actions. The cooperation of God and the human person in bringing faith into existence is not explained by this, but ethical behavior appears as a demand and result of faith, just as evil deeds correspond to unbelief.

4.1.4 Interpretation

For the Johannine school, baptism was the constitutive rite of initiation. This conclusion can be drawn from the use of the expression μαθητὰς ποιεῖν in combination with βαπτίζειν in 4:1, together with the further reports of Jesus' baptizing in 3:22, 25-29. In contrast to the Synoptics, and in initial agreement with the Baptizer group, the Johannine school roots baptism in the life of Jesus and thus gives its own baptismal practice a special dignity. This community is continuing Jesus' baptizing activity in its own sphere and is thereby showing itself to be the legitimate heir of Jesus' activity in this point also. An eminently theological interest in baptism is evident already at this stage, as confirmed by the statements about the nature of baptism in the Nicodemus pericope.

In this "teaching discourse," John incorporates some traditions of his school describing both the soteriological importance of baptism as the condition of entry into the reign of God (vv. 3, 5) and the way in which the sending of the Son has made salvation possible (vv. 13, 14b, 16-17). Verses 1-12 deal with the necessity and opportunity for being begotten of water and Spirit; vv. 13-21 tell of the fundamental events that made this possible. But the theme of the first section of the text by no means disappears from view in vv. 13-21, since the evangelist thinks of the person begotten of water and Spirit as a believer (cf. vv. 18, 19-21). "Birth from above is being born into faith as well as the birth of faith."[113] It is as an action set in motion by God that baptism preserves the character of the saving event as something beyond human control. At the same time, it is the place where the human person, as a believer, enters into salvation. Therefore, it is also true of the Gospel of

---

[112] See Becker, *Johannes* 1:146; idem, "Schuldiskussion," 92.

[113] Pesch, "'Ihr müßt von oben geboren werden,'" 215.

John that baptism cannot be understood as a purely symbolic action that only visually documents what has been accomplished in faith long before.[114]

4.2 The Discourse on the Bread of Life and the Eucharistic Section (John 6:30-58)

4.2.1 *Context*

The discourse on the bread of life and the eucharistic section come to a clear conclusion in 6:59 (ταῦτα εἶπεν [this he said]). The statement of place refers back to the redactional v. 24 (see also v. 17),[115] and the verb διδάσκειν designates the preceding discourse expressly as "teaching." The typically Johannine shape of the discourse, the comparable redactional transition verses 2:12 and 4:46, and the reference back to 6:24 point to the evangelist as the author of this verse. With vv. 60-71 a new sense unit within John 6 begins: on the one hand, it looks back to the bread of life discourse and the eucharistic section (cf. vv. 60, 61, 63, 65, 68), but, on the other hand, it has its own theme. Jesus' dialogue partners are now the disciples for whom his speech is a *skandalon*. In v. 62, Jesus succeeds only in exacerbating this offense,[116] for ἀναβαίνειν is an antithetical reference to the καταβαίνειν of the preceding discourse (cf. 6:33, 41, 42, 50, 51, 58). If Jesus as the bread that has come down from heaven is an offense to the faith of many disciples, Jesus' *anabasis* is set before them as a still greater offense.

This retrospective concentration on the christological statements in the bread discourse and the eucharistic section leads to a schism among the disciples. Only the Twelve,[117] through Peter, affirm their allegiance to Jesus (v. 68b: ῥήματα ζωῆς αἰωνίου ἔχεις [you have the words of eternal life]). Peter's statement, with the key word ζωή [life], refers back to v. 63b. The interpretation of v. 63a emerges from Peter's confession *of faith* in combination with Jesus' designation of his own words as πνεῦμα . . . καὶ ζωή. The σάρξ– πνεῦμα dualism in this verse is to be understood anthropologically, not christologically.[118] "Σάρξ and πνεῦμα refer to real conditions of belief and

---

[114] Against Thyen, who seems to vote for the originality of ὕδατος καί in 3:5, but in contrast says that "this scarcely makes it right to represent birth 'from above' as instrumentally accomplished through water baptism. . . . Perhaps one should speak more cautiously and say that, in baptism, 'birth from above' is ratified and accepted by the believer in the purifying symbol of water" ("Aus der Literatur," *ThR* 44, 101). This kind of distinction may well correspond to Barthian baptismal theology, but not to John 3:5!

[115] See section 3.5.2 above.

[116] See Bornkamm, "Eucharistische Rede," 64; Wilckens, "Der eucharistische Abschnitt," 244; Becker, *Johannes* 1:215.

[117] Only in 6:67, 70-71 does τοῖς δώδεκα [the twelve] appear.

[118] Thus also Wilckens, "Der eucharistische Abschnitt," 245; Becker, *Johannes* 1:216, against Schürmann, "Schlüssel," 165; Thyen, "Aus der Literatur," *ThR* 44, 108; Schnackenburg, *John* 2:72; J. Schneider, *Johannes,* 156; Bornkamm, "Eucharistische Rede," 65.

unbelief."[119] Thus 6:63a is shown to be parallel to 3:6. At the same time it is clear that σάρξ in 6:63a does not follow 6:51c, for whereas here the flesh, as designation for what is earthly and mortal, is useless, in 6:51 the eating of the flesh has salvific value, and σάρξ must be understood christologically.

With vv. 26-29 as transition and introduction, the evangelist ties together the double tradition of the miraculous feeding and the walking on water with the bread of life discourse.[120] In v. 26, Jesus does not respond at all to the crowd's question in v. 25; instead, with ζητεῖν, he takes up the (redactional) v. 24. This confirms the redactional character of v. 26.[121] Verse 27 prepares for the theme of the bread of life discourse and the eucharistic section, as is clear from the numerous common features between this verse and the text that follows. The key concepts of βρῶσις [food], ζωὴ αἰώνιος [eternal life], and υἱὸς τοῦ ἀνθρώπου [son of man] look forward to vv. 53, 54, and 55. In content, the expression ἡ βρῶσις ἡ μένουσα εἰς ζωὴν αἰώνιον [the food that endures for eternal life] anticipates the bread of life theme in vv. 32-33, 48-51. In addition, the future δώσει [he will give] in v. 27 already points to δώσω in v. 51c.[122] The imperative ἐργάζεσθε [work] is not only taken up in the Jews' question in v. 28; instead, vv. 53-58 show how the reception of salvation and thereby the ἐργάζεσθαι are to take place. Verses 27 and 58 constitute an inclusion,[123] for v. 58 gives the definitive answer to the challenge in v. 27: the imperishable food that gives eternal life is the Son of man himself, who has come down from heaven. The many connections, both in language and content, between 6:27 and 6:30-58, the structuring function of the verse in the whole composition of chapter 6, and the grammatical construction of v. 27 (μή + imperative + ἀλλά; cf. the redactional verse 20:27) make it probable that we should regard the evangelist as its author.[124] Moreover, v. 27 reveals two characteristic features of Johannine style (a reason given with γάρ, and substantive with article as an attribute).[125]

---

[119] Wilckens, "Der eucharistische Abschnitt," 245.

[120] On the redactional character of vv. 26-29, see also Schnackenburg, *John* 2:35.

[121] See Bultmann, *John,* 218. According to Ruckstuhl's listing, marks of Johannine style in v. 26 are οὐχ' ὅτι . . . ἀλλ' ὅτι (no. 14), ἀπεκρίθη καὶ εἶπεν (no. 16), and ἀμὴν ἀμὴν (no. 40).

[122] See L. Schenke, "Struktur," 38.

[123] See Meeks, "Funktion," 264. There are the following terminological connections between the two verses:

verse 58	verse 27
ἄρτος	βρῶσις
ὁ ἐξ οὐρανοῦ καταβάς	υἱὸς τοῦ ἀνθρώπου
ζήσει εἰς τὸν αἰῶνα	ζωὴ αἰώνιος

[124] Against J. Becker, who without any real reason assigns v. 27 to the "ecclesiastical redaction" (*Johannes* 1:201). Bultmann thinks that v. 27a is from the source of "revelation-discourses" (*John,* 222 n. 5) but that v. 27b was added by the "ecclesiastical redaction" (p. 221 n. 2); so also Richter, "Formgeschichte," 105 n. 56.

[125] The latter is stylistic characteristic no. 9 in Ruckstuhl's list.

The content of v. 28 presumes v. 27, and this verse takes up the fundamental key words ἐργάζεσθαι and θεός.[126] In v. 29, John goes beyond the Jews' diversionary question to state a further demand on the part of Jesus that is central to the bread discourse. The work that is required[127] is belief in Jesus as the one sent by God. The demand for faith unites v. 29 with 6:35b, 47, a further indication of redactional composition.

4.2.2   Redaction and Tradition in John 6:30-58

The Johannine discourse on the bread of life begins with vv. 30-31; the crowd, in demanding a miracle of feeding in the wilderness like that in the time of Moses, seems to have forgotten the feeding of the five thousand that occurred just previously. This contradiction can have resulted only from the evangelist's combining of several traditions (cf. the parallels, Mark 8:1-10/ 8:11-13).[128] With a free combination of material from the Old Testament (cf. LXX Exod. 16:4, 15; Pss. 77:24; 104:40; Neh. 9:15a [=2 Ezra 19:15]; Wis. 16:20)[129] the Jews demand a manna miracle, like the one that preserved the lives of their ancestors in the desert.[130] The interpretation of the quotation in v. 32 is antithetical in style: it was not Moses who gave (δέδωκεν) bread from heaven; instead, the Father of Jesus gives (δίδωσιν) the true and genuine bread. In this way, the Jewish nation's hope of salvation is both circumscribed and universalized. "The Johannine typology is thus structured antithetically,

---

[126] The evident redactional connection between v. 27 and vv. 28-29 speaks against Bultmann's supposition (*John,* 221–22) that vv. 28-29 were a separated fragment placed after v. 27 by the "ecclesiastical redaction."

[127] Τοῦ θεοῦ is objective genitive.

[128] Against Borgen, who has the bread of life discourse begin with the quotation in v. 31 (*Bread from Heaven,* 45–46), because the "homiletic schema" that he posits as a basis for 6:31-58 always begins with a quotation from the Old Testament that is then explained in the homily. For another critique of this division, see Thyen, "Aus der Literatur," *ThR* 43, 347; also Richter, "Formgeschichte," 114. For a more general critique of Borgen's position, see Richter, "Formgeschichte," 88–119, and Thyen, "Aus der Literatur," *ThR* 43, 338–51 (with discussion of other essays that, like Borgen's work, are inspired by Odeberg, *Fourth Gospel*). In my opinion, both these authors demonstrate persuasively that Borgen's postulated "homiletic pattern" did not exist in that form in contemporary Jewish literature and is not an appropriate explanatory model for John 6.

[129] The quotation does not exist in this form in the Old Testament! I believe that, at this point, the Johannine tradition is citing Ps. 77:24b (LXX: [καὶ] ἄρτον οὐρανοῦ ἔδωκεν αὐτοῖς), but because of v. 33 it writes ἐκ τοῦ οὐρανοῦ and adds φαγεῖν from Ps. 77:24a. Against Borgen (*Bread from Heaven,* 40ff.), who supposes that the Exodus texts form the basis of the quotation (without being able to explain the omission of ὑμῖν in Exod. 16:15), in order to demonstrate that John uses a schema found in contemporary Jewish literature (first a text from the Pentateuch, then one from the Prophets). Richter is also unpersuasive; he regards the quotation as part of a Jewish haggadah on the manna ("Die alttestamentlichen Zitate," 211ff.).

[130] See also Billerbeck, *Kommentar* 2:481.

and there follows a moment in which, in principle, the old is overtrumped."[131] In no way does Jesus appear here as a "new Moses"; he is not the miracle worker but rather is simultaneously, in his own person, both giver and gift. It is true that in v. 33 Jesus has not yet identified himself with the bread, but καταβαίνων [coming down] (cf. 3:13, 31) and the expression καὶ ζωὴν διδοὺς τῷ κόσμῳ [and gives life to the world] (cf. esp. 6:51c) already point toward the equation in v. 35. In addition, the Jews' request for this bread in v. 34 serves merely to prepare for the climax of the first section of the bread of life discourse. The ἐγώ εἰμι [I am] saying in v. 35 discloses the meaning of what has been said thus far: the bread of life is not a miraculous material gift, but Jesus himself. He himself, in his own person, takes the place of the traditional hope for salvation: he is both the giver of salvation and the saving gift. He alone mediates eternal life, and the image of "bread" emphasizes the character of this event as gift: in the gift of the bread of life, Jesus gives his very self.

The only parallels to the expression ὁ ἄρτος τῆς ζωῆς [the bread of life] are found in the wisdom-influenced[132] Jewish work called *Joseph and Aseneth*.[133] In five places we read of ἄρτος ζωῆς and ποτήριον ἀθανασίας [cup of immortality] (*Jos. Asen.* 8:5, 9; 15:5; 16:16; 19:5), and *Jos. Asen.* 21:21 (=Aseneth's psalm, vv. 3 and 11) speaks of ἄρτος ζωῆς and ποτήριον σοφίας.[134] In addition, there are three places where a χρῖσμα ἀφθαρσίας [ointment of incorruptibility] (*Jos. Asen.* 8:5; 15:5; 16:16) is mentioned. Whether these meal formulae are only a way of describing Jewish in contrast to pagan food,[135] or whether they are influenced by mystery religions[136] is a matter of dispute.

For an understanding of ἄρτος τῆς ζωῆς, *Jos. Asen.* 15:5 is very helpful. At this point the angel Michael announces to Aseneth that from this day forward she will "eat the [blessed] bread of life and drink the [blessed] cup of immortality. . . ."[137] What Aseneth is actually given to eat is a heavenly honeycomb: the description of the food in *Jos. Asen.* 16:8 makes it clear that this is manna.[138] This manna is identified in *Jos. Asen.* 16:16 with the ἄρτος ζωῆς, ποτήριον ἀθανασίας, and χρῖσμα ἀφθαρσίας. The effect of eating this bread of life is that Aseneth is given new life (*Jos.*

---

[131] Blank, "Die johanneische Brotrede," 203; see also his *Johannes* 1:358–59. See also Saito, *Mosevorstellungen,* 110: "Christ is not a second Moses, but rather the bread of life."

[132] See Sänger, *Judentum und die Mysterien,* 72–74, 191ff.

[133] For other attempts at derivation, see Schnackenburg, "Brot des Lebens," 119–25.

[134] Statistics from Burchard, *Joseph und Aseneth,* JSHRZ 2/4.

[135] Thus especially Jeremias, *Eucharistic Words,* 32–33; Burchard, *Untersuchungen,* 121–33; Sänger, *Judentum und die Mysterien,* 167–74.

[136] Thus again Klauck, *Herrenmahl,* 196.

[137] *Joseph and Aseneth,* translated by D. Cook, in H. F. D. Sparks, *The Apocryphal Old Testament,* 465–503. [Translator's note: The text in Sparks is based on the Greek text edited by M. Philonenko (Leiden, 1968) and differs substantially from Burchard's. The author's citations correspond to Burchard's text.]

[138] See Sänger, *Judentum und die Mysterien,* 192; Burchard, *Joseph und Aseneth,* JSHRZ 2/4, 679.

Asen. 15:4, 5), because whoever eats of it will not die forever (*Jos. Asen.* 16:14). Like wisdom (Wis. 3:4; 6:18-19; 8:13, 17), the bread of life also bestows ἀθανασία [immortality] (see *Jos. Asen.* 8:5; 15:5; 16:16). "Manna as the bread of life thus produces what it is in itself, namely life."[139] Aseneth is already eating the heavenly manna, like the angel and the just (*Jos. Asen.* 16:14).

At the basis of these assertions is the idea that eating a substance brings about a transfer of its essential qualities.[140] This idea is found especially in Philo, who compares the reception of wisdom with eating and drinking (see *Fug.* 176–77, 195, 202; *Virt.* 79). The just person thirsts for wisdom and is given to drink from the fountain of wisdom (see *Post.* 122, 125, 151–53; *Fug.* 138, 202). The θεῖος λόγος [divine Logos] gives τὴν οὐράνιον τροφὴν [celestial nourishment] — σοφία δέ ἐστιν [which is wisdom] — τῆς ψυχῆς, ἣν καλεῖ μάννα [to the soul, which (Scripture) calls manna], πᾶσι τοῖς χρησομένοις . . . ἐξ ἴσου [(equally) among all who make use of it . . . with care] (*Her.* 191). *Ethiopic Enoch* 32:3; 48:1 also furnishes a metaphorical description of the reception of wisdom as eating and drinking (see also *Eth. Enoch* 49:1; *Sir.* 15:3; 24:21).

The agreements between *Joseph and Aseneth* and Philo (eating and drinking as an image of the incorporation of divine food or wisdom) cause D. Sänger to conclude that the living bread/manna in *Joseph and Aseneth* also refers to divine wisdom.[141] He refers to *Jos. Asen.* 16:14, where the honeycomb is called πνεῦμα ζωῆς [spirit of life]. "The closest analogy to Sophia as a pneumatic being that is incorporated in human beings as heavenly nourishment is found in Philo."[142] *Joseph and Aseneth*, Philo, and probably the Johannine bread of life discourse all belong to the tradition of a wisdom-influenced manna allegory that in turn is conditioned by the Stoic idea that everything exists in some kind of matter and can therefore only be conceived as having substance.[143]

The Revealer's self-presentation in v. 35a is followed, in v. 35b, by a challenge and a soteriological promise.[144] The double image of hunger and thirst has parallels in the exegesis of Exodus,[145] but more particularly in wisdom literature (see Prov. 9:5; Sir. 15:3; 24:21; 51:24).[146] It promises that human subjection to death will be and already is overcome in faith.

A new section of the bread of life discourse begins with vv. 36-40,[147] taking up only the key word πιστεύειν from v. 35 and referring, in its content, to the feeding miracle.[148] While ὁρᾶν in v. 36 refers to the feeding of the five

---

139 Sänger, *Judentum und die Mysterien,* 193.
140 Ibid., 193ff.
141 Ibid., 195ff.
142 Ibid., 195 (with textual references).
143 Ibid., 196–97.
144 See Norden, *Agnostos Theos,* 177ff.
145 See Billerbeck, *Kommentar* 3:407.
146 See Brown, *John* 1:273; Schnackenburg, "Brot des Lebens," 124.
147 See Schnackenburg, *John* 2:45–46; Becker, *Johannes* 1:200. Against L. Schenke, who sees the division after v. 36 ("Struktur," 27). With v. 35, the first section has undoubtedly reached its climax, and there is no continuation in v. 36.
148 See Ruckstuhl, "Wesen und Kraft der Eucharistie," 50.

thousand, οὐ πιστεύειν anticipates the defection of the disciples in 6:64. The witnesses to the miraculous feeding were the ὄχλος [crowd] (cf. vv. 2, 5, 22, 24), whereas in v. 36 the "Jews" (cf. v. 41: οἱ Ἰουδαῖοι) are addressed concerning a miracle they did not see! Jesus' "I am" saying in v. 35 is taken up only at v. 41. In addition, the theme of the section (the one sent by God does the will of the Father by not allowing believers to be lost) is only loosely related to its context,[149] inasmuch as the key theological term, τὸ θέλημα (τοῦ θεοῦ) [the will (of God)] appears, within 6:30-58, only in this text (vv. 38, 39, 40).[150]

All these observations taken together permit the conclusion that vv. 36-40 constitute a redactional insertion by the evangelist in the traditional bread of life discourse.[151] In this way he bound the tradition available to him even more tightly into the immediate context and emphasized what for him was the central idea: that human beings' opportunity for salvation is founded on the unity of the Father and the Son.

Verse 41 follows immediately from Jesus' revelatory saying in v. 35. The complaining Jews[152] repeat Jesus' words and then deny Jesus' heavenly origin by referring to his earthly parents (v. 41). Unbelief recognizes in Jesus only the son of Joseph and Mary; it rejects Jesus' claim to be the bread that has come down from heaven. Jesus' reply has two parts: in the first (vv. 44-46),[153] Jesus' origin with the *heavenly* Father is established, and only the second part (vv. 48-51) deals with Jesus' description of himself as *bread* and emphasizes his eschatological meaning for salvation. Verse 47 connects the argumentation in the two parts.[154]

This compositional structure makes it impossible to infer a literary division at v. 48 (or v. 47) that would indicate a secondary reinterpretation of the bread of life discourse.[155] Only in vv. 48-51 is the expression ἐγώ εἰμι ὁ ἄρτος [I am the bread] from v. 41 explicated; moreover, these verses are an extended commentary on v. 35, to which v. 41 is immediately connected.[156]

---

[149] Terminologically, only καταβέβηκα ἀπὸ τοῦ οὐρανοῦ [I have come down from heaven] in v. 38 refers back to ὁ καταβαίνων ἐκ τοῦ οὐρανοῦ in v. 33; the content of vv. 44-46 is partly anticipated.

[150] Θέλημα is found 11 times in the Gospel of John, 4 of those instances in 6:38-40!

[151] Wellhausen correctly supposes "that 6:36-40 did not originally belong to the previous discourse" (*Evangelium Johannis*, 31). See also J. Schneider, "Komposition," 137: "Verses 37-40 probably did not originally stand in this context." This was observed earlier by Spitta, *Johannes-evangelium*, 151. S. Temple also considers these verses redactional ("Key," 228).

[152] This motif represents a deliberate play on the attitude of the wilderness generation; see Exod. 16:2, 7, 8, 9, 12 LXX.

[153] Verse 43 is to be regarded as transitional.

[154] Correctly noted by L. Schenke, "Struktur," 28 n. 23: "Verse 47 constitutes a rhetorical climax."

[155] Against Bornkamm, "Tradition," 59ff.; Thyen, "Aus der Literatur," *ThR* 44, 97.

[156] The clear reference in v. 48 to vv. 41 and 35 makes it obvious that we have here a *new*

The explication of the "I am" saying in vv. 48-51ab is a necessary part of the bread of life discourse, and the further development of the thought that is perceptible in this section cannot be used as a literary-critical argument.[157]

Verse 44 develops an idea comparable to that in v. 37: no one can come to Jesus unless drawn by the Father.[158] Recognition of the one sent by God is possible only through the prior grace of God. Verse 45 emphasizes the presence of God's gracious action, making use of a scriptural citation (cf. Isa. 54:13 LXX). Now the "universality of being taught by God"[159] has become reality. Whoever listens to and learns from the Father comes to Jesus. But this should not be understood in the sense of a mystical union with the Father, and this is emphasized in v. 46.[160] The believers do not have the same immediate access to the Father that the Son has.[161] Only in the Son is the Father made known (cf. 12:45; 14:9), so that "no one can come to the Son, without having received the teaching from the Father; no one can hear and learn from the Father except through the Son."[162] An immediate vision of the Father is possible only for the one who was with God: the preexistent Christ. Thus v. 46 again stresses Jesus' having come from the *heavenly Father*.

The bread of life discourse reaches its climax in vv. 48-51ab. Verse 48 repeats Jesus' witness to himself as found in v. 35 (ἐγώ εἰμι ὁ ἄρτος τῆς ζωῆς) and thereby explains, at the same time, the first part of the bread saying in v. 41 (ἐγώ εἰμι ὁ ἄρτος). The thesis in v. 48 is developed through a contrast with the manna of the generation in the desert. Eating manna in the desert did not preserve the ancestors from death: this revives Jesus' objection in v. 32 that it was not Moses who gave the bread from heaven. God alone can send the true bread from heaven, whose characteristic mark is life (see v. 33). The death of the wilderness generation proves "that the idea of the true bread of God is fulfilled in Jesus."[163] Whoever eats the true bread from heaven does not die (v. 50; cf. *Jos. Asen.* 16:14). The soteriological point of the bread of life discourse is stated in v. 51ab: Jesus is the living bread that came down from heaven, and whoever eats of this bread will live forever. With the promise, ζήσει εἰς τὸν αἰῶνα [she or he will live forever], the bread of life discourse reaches its high point and conclusion. The death of the ancestors in the desert is contrasted to the unsurpassable saving gift of the ζωὴ αἰώνιος [everlasting life]. Jesus is life, because he gives life. The concept of ζωή is the key

beginning, and in no event the conclusion of the first part of the bread of life discourse, as Borgen supposes (*Bread from Heaven,* 80).

[157] Against Bornkamm, "Tradition," 59.

[158] On ἑλκύειν, see Oepke, *TDNT* 2:503–4. In 12:32 the Exalted One draws all to himself.

[159] Becker, *Johannes* 1:213.

[160] It can no longer be determined whether the intention of v. 46 is to polemicize against a mystical piety (so Meeks, *Prophet-King,* 299).

[161] See Thüsing, *Erhöhung,* 27.

[162] Odeberg, *Fourth Gospel,* 257–58.

[163] Schürmann, "Schlüssel," 158.

to understanding the bread of life discourse. It is equally decisive as terminology (vv. 33, 35, 40, 47, 48, 51) and as content: it is only in the gift of ζωή that Jesus proves himself to be the bread that has come down from heaven, for in this way he surpasses Moses and the manna of the wilderness generation.[164]

The pre-Johannine character of 6:30-35, 41-51ab cannot be established on a linguistic basis. But Johannine language as such is not a sure sign that the evangelist is the author of a text, especially because at this point there are many indications that we have before us a text composed within the written tradition of the Johannine school: (1) Verse 30 clearly marks a new beginning, at which point the miraculous feeding and the walking on water have been forgotten; that is, v. 30 does not presume its present context. With the promise in v. 51ab, the bread of life discourse reaches an appropriate conclusion, both formally and in content. But v. 51c opens a new level of argumentation. (2) The witness to the feeding and walking on water is "the crowd" (vv. 2, 5, 22, 24), but Jesus' conversation partners in the bread of life discourse are "the Jews" (v. 41). (3) Verses 36-40 refer back to the feeding miracle, give evidence of only a loose relationship to the context (v. 41 makes the first connection back to v. 35), and treat an independent theme (τὸ θέλημα τοῦ θεοῦ), so that they may be regarded as an insertion by the evangelist in the preexisting bread of life discourse. (4) In religious-historical terms, 6:30-35, 41-51ab represent a unit, since the term ἄρτος τῆς ζωῆς and the idea of "not hungering or thirsting," together with the gift of eternal life, reveal a wisdom background. (5) A central structural element in the bread of life discourse is represented by the hearers' objections in vv. 30, 34, 41, each of which serves to prepare for the introduction of a new idea. The center of the text is at v. 35 and is taken up again at v. 41; this verse, in turn, is interpreted in vv. 44-46 and vv. 48-51ab. In terms of form criticism, 6:30-35, 41-51ab should be called a "dialogue" influenced by wisdom traditions. The dialogue is governed throughout by a single theme: Jesus is the true bread of life that has come down from heaven. The literary techniques employed to develop the theme include repetition, variation, and reinforcement. Eucharistic overtones are undeniably present in the text, inasmuch as the idea of manna was a common motif in early Christian eucharistic traditions (see 1 Cor. 10:3-4; Rev. 2:14, 17). But the dialogue on the bread of life does not contain any definite sacramental pronouncements.

A new level of argumentation begins with v. 51c. There are five major shifts in the content of this passage, in comparison with 6:30-51ab:[165] (1) In the bread of life discourse it is Jesus himself who is the living bread come down from heaven, but in this eucharistic section it is Jesus' flesh and blood that are the bread from heaven. (2) The heavenly bread is given (δίδωσιν) by the Father in 6:32, but in 6:51c it is the Son who will give (δώσω) the bread. (3) Eating the bread (φαγεῖν) can only be taken symbolically in the bread of

---

[164] See Mussner, ZΩH, 132.

[165] See only Bultmann, *John*, 218–20; Richter, "Formgeschichte," 105ff.; Lohse, "Wort und Sakrament," 200–201; Thyen, "Aus der Literatur," *ThR* 43, 353–54; L. Schenke, "Vorgeschichte," 73–74.

life discourse. In contrast, in the eucharistic section φαγεῖν and τρώγειν [to chew] are to be taken literally. (4) While in the bread of life discourse the theme was the demonstration of Jesus' heavenly origin, in the eucharistic section it is Jesus' corporeality and humanity that are the focus. (5) In contrast to the bread of life discourse, the eucharistic section accords special meaning to human action (vv. 54, 56).

These important changes at the level of content compel us to posit a new literary layer in 6:51c-58.[166] It appears that these verses are a conscious interpretation and continuation of the bread of life discourse. If they come from the existing written tradition of the Johannine school, detailed exegesis must determine whether the eucharistic section is essentially the work of the evangelist or stems from a post-Gospel redaction. The latter possibility can be considered likely only if 6:51c-58 is not to be explained at the level of the evangelist.

Verse 51c explains what has gone before, to the extent that it takes up the theme of the earlier verses. At the same time, a new section begins with καί . . . δέ (see 8:16, 17; 15:27; 1 John 1:3),[167] and it is distinct in its content from the previous passage.[168] The key word σάρξ marks a new topic, not motivated by the context, and extending through vv. 51c-58. Since σάρξ introduces a new and independent theme, v. 51c cannot be regarded as the end of the bread of life discourse, which instead has its organic conclusion in v. 51ab.

Besides the sequence of particles καί . . . δέ, the correspondence between the redactional v. 27 and the expression ὁ ἄρτος δὲ ὃν ἐγὼ δώσω [the bread that I will give] betrays the hand of the evangelist. The promise given in v. 27 is reiterated and clarified: the enduring food that I will give is my flesh.[169] The future tense, δώσω, points forward to the founding of the

---

[166] The terminological differences between the bread of life discourse and the eucharistic section (absence of πιστεύειν in 6:51c-58; μάχομαι [to dispute] in v. 52 instead of γογγύζω [to complain]; ἔχετε ζωὴν ἐν ἑαυτοῖς only in v. 53; the immanence formula in v. 56) are not sufficient to lead us to conclude to the presence of different levels. It is equally impossible, however, to avoid this problem by pointing to the parallel structure of the bread of life discourse and the eucharistic section; see, e.g., Schlier, "Johannes 6," 106ff.; Léon-Dufour, *Abendmahl und Abschiedsrede*, 331; Schnackenburg, *John* 2:53–54; Wilckens, "Der eucharistische Abschnitt," 225; L. Schenke, "Struktur," 33, 41.

[167] Bultmann sees in καί . . . δέ a characteristic feature of Johannine style, but one that is easily imitated (*John*, 234 n. 4). On καί . . . δέ, see *BAGD*, 171; Blass-Debrunner-Rehkopf §447.

[168] Against Schürmann, who understands v. 51c exclusively as the conclusion of the bread of life discourse and sees a caesura only at v. 52 ("Schlüssel," 157ff.). Schürmann does not observe the shift in content between v. 51ab and v. 51c and incorrectly posits the beginning of the bread of life discourse as early as v. 26 in order to use the correspondence between v. 27 and v. 51c as an argument for his thesis (see p. 160).

[169] It is possible that behind the expression ἡ σάρξ μού ἐστιν ὑπέρ . . . lies an explanatory saying or word of institution proper to the Johannine school and differing from that in the Synoptics and Paul. See Jeremias, "Joh 6,51c-58," 256–57: in his opinion, the evangelist used a pre-Johannine eucharistic homily beginning with v. 51c. See also his *Abendmahlsworte*, 101–2;

Eucharist in Jesus' death on the cross (19:34b). The new concept of σάρξ introduced by John must be understood as a clear reference to 1:14 and therefore as initially incarnational in meaning. In saying that Jesus gave his flesh for the life of the world, the evangelist points to his death. If Jesus' death, in turn, instituted the Eucharist, then ἡ σάρξ μού ἐστιν means nothing other than the salvific partaking of his flesh (and blood) in the eucharistic, celebration.[170] The incarnational and sacramental understandings of σάρξ are not in any way contradictory at this point, because the real incarnation is the indispensable precondition for the soteriological dimension of the Eucharist.

Like John, Ignatius uses σάρξ instead of σῶμα to describe an element in the eucharistic meal (see Ign. *Smyrn.* 7.1; Ign. *Rom.* 7.3; *Phld.* 4; *Trall.* 8.1; as well as Justin *Apol.* 1.66.2), in order to defend both the reality of Jesus' death and the salvific importance of the Eucharist against the Docetists, for whom, as a consequence of their denial of Jesus' incarnation, the Eucharist was emptied of all significance. We also suppose that the fourth evangelist had an antidocetic purpose[171] in deliberately reminding the readers of John 1:14 by using the word σάρξ, thereby emphasizing both the incarnation and the death of Jesus as fundamental preconditions for the Eucharist and highlighting the soteriological importance of the Eucharist through the use of remarkably realistic terminology.

John stresses the saving universality of incarnation and cross, present in the Eucharist, by using the expression ὑπὲρ τῆς τοῦ κόσμου ζωῆς [for the life of the world] (cf. 6:33; 8:12; also 10:11, 15; 11:4; 13:37; 15:13).[172] The Christ-event cannot be limited; in its intention, it extends to all humanity.

In v. 52 the Jews reappear as the paradigmatic representatives of un-belief (cf. vv. 30, 34, 41) who understand Jesus' revelatory word in a material sense. The Johannine *hapax legomenon* μάχεσθαι [to dispute] does not indicate the hand of a late "redaction." It is the evangelist's[173] deliberate play on the wilderness generation's "disputing" with Moses (Exod. 17:2; Num. 20:3)

Wilkens, "Abendmahlszeugnis," 355ff.; Schnackenburg, *John* 2:55–56. If the evangelist replaced the original word σῶμα with σάρξ, the antidocetic tendency of the section would be still clearer than it already is.

[170] Against Borgen, who does not wish to refer "flesh" in vv. 51c-58 to the Eucharist (*Bread from Heaven,* 181, 184, 185), but infers here an Old Testament understanding (of the total human person as a historical being). We must also reject the position of Dunn that the elements are symbols of Jesus but not of the Eucharist ("Joh VI," 333).

[171] Against Wilckens, who disputes the antidocetic intention of vv. 51c-58 ("Der eucha-ristische Abschnitt," 224, etc.). Correctly, in contrast: Wilkens, "Abendmahlszeugnis," 356; J. Schneider, *Johannes,* 153; Brooks, "The Johannine Eucharist," 293ff.; Schnackenburg, *John* 2:62; Dunn, "Joh VI," 335. See also Richter, "Formgeschichte," 113, etc.; Bornkamm, "Tradi-tion," 62; Weder, "Menschwerdung Gottes," 348–49; L. Schenke, "Vorgeschichte," 88 (anti-docetism of a later "redaction").

[172] On the Johannine character of this expression, see Ruckstuhl, *Einheit,* 250.

[173] Typically Johannine in v. 52 is historical οὖν.

and with God (Num. 20:13), which was preceded by the people's "murmuring."[174] The sole function of v. 52 is to prepare for the answer, in vv. 53–55, to the question raised in v. 51c: namely, why eating Jesus' flesh guarantees the gift of eternal life.

In a negative conditional clause, v. 53 formulates the conditions for receiving eternal life: eating the flesh and drinking the blood of the Son of man. The surprising sharpness of the statement and the emphasis on the Eucharist as the indispensable condition for salvation give the impression that the evangelist is deliberately placing an antidocetic accent on his words at this point.[175] It is only the Eucharist, so devalued by the Docetists, that mediates the saving gift of eternal life. The saying about having life ἐν ἑαυτοῖς [in oneself], so unusual for Johannine anthropology, does not mean that flesh and blood, as substances, are the vehicles of life. As is made clear in v. 57, the evangelist thinks not in material but in personal categories. It is only the identity of the Incarnate and Crucified One with the heavenly Son of man that explains why reception of the eucharistic gifts can give ζωὴ αἰώνιος. The Son of man title underscores the humanity of the Incarnate, insofar as the heavenly Son of man is none other than the Crucified and Risen One.[176]

In its present form, v. 53 is the work of the evangelist, as indicated especially by the Johannine stylistic features: (1) historical οὖν; (2) introduction with ἀμὴν ἀμήν; (3) ἐὰν μὴ . . . οὐ.[177]

Verse 54 is a revelatory saying composed in the third person singular with participial substantives.[178] This form-critical classification, the lack of Johannine stylistic features, and the literal repetition in v. 56 indicate that this is a eucharistic tradition of the Johannine school that has been incorporated by the evangelist at this point.[179] The drastic τρώγειν must be understood in the sense of "gnaw,"[180] and it clearly has an antidocetic accent: it is not a symbolic "eating" of the bread of heaven or a spirit-filled "eating" of the Son of man that gives eternal life, but only the real eating and drinking of the flesh

---

[174] See Schnackenburg, *John* 2:60.

[175] See Schnackenburg, *John* 2:61; differing: Wilckens, "Der eucharistische Abschnitt," 238–39.

[176] Bultmann (*John*, 235) and Colpe (*TDNT* 8:465–66) understand υἱὸς τοῦ ἀνθρώπου here in the sense of "I" or "my."

[177] Ruckstuhl, nos. 2, 40, 44. It is primarily Wilckens who posits a tradition behind v. 53 ("Der eucharistische Abschnitt," 240). In terms of language, there are no un-Johannine expressions to be found in v. 53: so Ruckstuhl, *Einheit,* 264; E. Schweizer, "Zeugnis," 385; against Jeremias, "Literarkritik," 44.

[178] See Schnackenburg, *John* 2:61.

[179] Wilckens considers all of v. 54 traditional ("Der eucharistische Abschnitt," 204–5).

[180] See Bultmann, *John,* 236 n. 3; Haenchen, *John* 1:295; Bauer, *Johannesevangelium,* 98. Τρώγειν here can scarcely be a mere vulgar synonym for ἐσθίειν, as some exegetes think (referring to John 13:18: replacement of ὁ ἐσθίων in Ps. 40:10 LXX with τρώγειν). The strong word τρώγειν cannot be explained as a mere substitution for another word.

and blood of Jesus Christ in the Eucharist. Thus τρώγειν "offset[s] any Docetic tendencies to 'spiritualize' the concept,"[181] in that it unmistakably emphasizes the reality of incarnation and crucifixion that are present in the Eucharist. The expression κἀγὼ ἀναστήσω αὐτὸν τῇ ἐσχάτῃ ἡμέρᾳ [and I will raise him/her up on the last day] in v. 54b is like a refrain (cf. vv. 39, 40, 44): it is the work of the evangelist.[182] Here also we may suspect an anti-docetic tendency: John, with a view to the raising of the dead at the last day, protects the inaccessibility of salvation to human control from the Docetists, who believed exclusively in the fullness of salvation in the present (see also v. 57: ζήσει; v. 58: ζήσει εἰς τὸν αἰῶνα). In doing so, the evangelist in no way restricts the soteriological meaning of the benefits of salvation that are already the possession of believers, but these can only endure if, "beyond this earthly life . . . there is a resurrection of the dead; i.e., present eschatology needs to be supplemented by future eschatology."[183]

In v. 55, an initial interpretation is added to the school tradition: in the Eucharist, Jesus' flesh is real, genuine, true food, and Jesus' blood is real, genuine, true drink. The adjective ἀληθής [real, true] includes both the reliability and the exclusivity and reality of the elements of the Lord's Supper.[184] The eucharistic gifts really guarantee eternal life, and they alone are divine food and drink. An alternative between the emphasis on the realistic act of eating and drinking and the stress on the trustworthiness of the saving gift of the Eucharist does not exist, for the realistic world of imagery in v. 55 cannot be eliminated as the proposed foundation (γάρ!) for v. 54.[185]

Verse 56 must also be understood as an interpretation of the school tradition in v. 54a. This is clear from the literal correspondences between the two verses. The reception of the eucharistic gifts creates a very intimate union between the communicants and Jesus. They abide in Jesus and he in them. Through this union with the divine giver of life, the one who receives the Eucharist receives the saving gift of everlasting life.[186] The Johannine formulae

---

[181] *BAGD*, 829.

[182] Τῇ ἐσχάτῃ ἡμέρᾳ is stylistic feature no. 32 in Ruckstuhl's enumeration. Bultmann (*John*, 219–20) and others, following Spitta (*Johannesevangelium*, 151ff.) eliminate the idea of resurrection throughout chap. 6. Among those who argue for the originality of the expression are E. Schweizer, "Zeugnis," 386–87; Wilckens, "Der eucharistische Abschnitt," 242; J. Schneider, "Komposition," 133; Schürmann, "Eucharistie," 181 n. 79. Also in vv. 39, 40, and 44 τῇ ἐσχάτῃ ἡμέρᾳ may well be by the evangelist.

[183] J. Schneider, "Komposition," 133.

[184] Since John can make a promiscuous use of ἀληθής and ἀληθινός (cf. esp. 7:28; 8:26), it seems to me that an alternative interpretation is inadmissible and overburdens the text. As regards the content, what is intended is best expressed by ἀληθῶς (D 𝔭66 Θ, etc.); see Bultmann, *John*, 236 n. 4. Ruckstuhl's suggestion that at this point ἀληθής means "a quite ordinary food, a quite ordinary drink" does not fit the context (*Einheit*, 240).

[185] Against Schnackenburg, *John* 2:62–63; E. Schweizer, "Zeugnis," 393–94.

[186] See Schnackenburg, *John* 2:63–64.

of immanence (see 1 John 3:24; 4:13, 16b; John 10:38; 14:10-11; 15:4-7; 17:21-23), like the Pauline notion of ἐν Χριστῷ, describe the unique mutual "existence-in" of Revealer and believers, without surrender of each one's personal identity. These formulae originate in Johannine christology and are introduced from there into the eucharistic sayings.[187]

In v. 57, we find a succinct summary of the Johannine conception of the Eucharist.[188] As the Son lives because of the Father, so believers will live because of Jesus (cf. vv. 33, 35, 48, 51a). The Father, as the epitome of life, sends the Son (cf. vv. 29, 38-39, 44) to save the world that is marked for death, and believers, by participating in the Eucharist, share in that salvation. Here the connection between incarnation and Eucharist is obvious! From the intimate union of communicants with Jesus in the sacramental action (ὁ τρώγων με [the one who chews me]) the evangelist derives a statement about the future life of believers (ζήσει). The gifts of the Eucharist in no way guarantee a salvation that refers only to present fulfillment (cf. vv. 54b, 58c). Instead, they are the foundation of a communion with Christ that extends beyond death.

Verse 58 summarizes all that has been said in the preceding discourse: Jesus Christ, who is present in the Eucharist, is the bread of life that has come down from heaven (cf. vv. 33, 50). Again the overcoming of death and life everlasting are said to be the saving gifts of the bread from heaven. The antithesis to the ancestors in the desert connects this verse back to v. 49, and the promise of eternal life refers to v. 51b. In this way, at the end of the eucharistic section the evangelist recapitulates the central statements of the bread of life discourse and again effectively juxtaposes the death-giving manna of the generation of Moses with the life-giving food of the Eucharist.

4.2.3   Interpretation

The evangelist has coupled the double tradition of the feeding miracle and the walking on water with a preexisting dialogue from written traditions of the Johannine school about Jesus as the true bread of life. The occasion for this was the parallelism of motifs between the miraculous feeding in the wilderness and the sayings about manna and the bread of life. In vv. 26-29, John created a transition that at the same time serves as an introduction to the text that follows. In particular, v. 27 anticipates both in content and terminology the bread of life discourse as well as the eucharistic section.

The dialogue about the bread of life is marked by wisdom traditions and is antithetically presented: Jesus alone, as the bread of life that has come down from heaven, is able to give the saving gift of ζωὴ αἰώνιος. With the insertion of vv. 36-40, the evangelist joined the preformulated bread of life

---

[187]   Ibid.

[188]   Καθὼς καί is Ruckstuhl's stylistic feature no. 12.

discourse more closely to the context, since ὁρᾶν in v. 36 looks backward to the feeding miracle, while οὐ πιστεύειν points to the schism between the disciples that is about to occur.

To the traditional bread of life discourse, John added a eucharistic interpretation (vv. 51c-58). Apparently, Docetists within the Johannine school denied the soteriological importance of the Lord's Supper, with the result that the evangelist felt it necessary to present his own understanding of the Eucharist.[189] The end of the bread of life discourse presented an apt opportunity for these reflections, since the image of the manna was closely connected with the Eucharist in early Christianity. The antidocetic intention of the text is evident in the use of σάρξ in v. 51c, in the exclusive conditional clause in v. 53, and in the use of the realistic τρώγειν and the eschatological perspective in vv. 54b and 58b. In v. 54a, and possibly also in v. 51c (ἡ σάρξ μού ἐστιν ὑπέρ . . .) the evangelist used eucharistic traditions of the Johannine school that were in accord with his antidocetic purpose. John was not interested in a substantive teaching about the Eucharist. In his controversy with the Docetists he was guided exclusively by a christological interest: in the Lord's Supper the identity of the exalted Son of man with the Incarnate and Crucified One is made visible. In its eucharistic practice, the community confirms this identity, but it is denied by those who absent themselves from the Lord's Supper.

We can now give a reasonable explanation for the positioning of 6:60-71 as well. The schism among the disciples reflects the division within the Johannine school that was kindled by disagreements over the soteriological importance of Jesus' earthly existence. The Eucharist apparently played an important role in this dispute. Thus the evangelist projects a problem in his own time back into the life of Jesus, and legitimates his own position through Jesus himself.

John 6 is not a unit in the history of tradition, but it does seem to have compositional unity. The whole chapter can be regarded as a well-considered composition by John the evangelist and can be so interpreted. This makes the positing of a post-Gospel layer superfluous.

The absence of the concept of faith in vv. 51c-58 is not an indication of the secondary character of this section. Instead, the evangelist presumes as a matter of course that participants in the Eucharist are those who believe in Jesus.[190] Moreover, John wishes to have the eucharistic section understood against the background of its present context—the bread of life discourse—in which πιστεύειν is a central idea.

The redactional mention of the Passover in v. 4 already anticipates the eucharistic section. Another clear reference to the Lord's Supper is the

---

[189] An antidocetic accent in vv. 51c-58 is unmistakable, but this is not the case in vv. 31-51ab, as Borgen thinks (*Bread from Heaven,* 179–87).

[190] See Wilckens, "Der eucharistische Abschnitt," 231.

evangelist's use of εὐχαριστεῖν in v. 23 (cf. v. 11), since εὐχαριστεῖν without an object meant "to recite the eucharistic prayer." The redactional verses 26-29 prepare for the theme of 6:30-51ab and 6:51c-58 and at the same time join together the two principal parts (6:1-25, 30-58) of the chapter as a whole. The bread of life discourse and the eucharistic section are again joined by a web of forward and backward references. Finally, with v. 59 John anticipates the schism among the disciples, which then appears as a reaction to Jesus' eucharistic teaching. In John 6, the evangelist has taken up some traditions of his school that are independent of one another, but have a related theme and set of motifs, and has shaped them into a compositional unit. The center and goal of the chapter are the eucharistic section in vv. 51c-58: the evangelist's redactional efforts are all aimed toward it, and in its antidocetic purpose it serves as the occasion for John 6 in the form in which it now exists.

4.3 John 19:34-35

In 19:31-37 the evangelist incorporates a special tradition[191] telling about the *crucifragium* [breaking the legs of those crucified] inflicted on those crucified with Jesus and the lance thrust into Jesus' side. The traditional character of this section is evident, first, from the tension between the statement of time in v. 31 and the rest of the Johannine chronology of the passion.[192] Moreover, v. 31 seems overburdened, since the parenthesis ἦν γὰρ μεγάλη ἡ ἡμέρα ἐκείνου τοῦ σαββάτου [because that sabbath was a great day] sounds like an afterthought. It may be an addition by the evangelist,[193] who intended in this way to effect a harmonization with the chronology of the passion tradition (cf. 7:37). Specifically Johannine ideas are found only in vv. 34b and 35, whereas the scriptural reference betrays an interest of the community tradition.[194] Finally, an un-Johannine feature is εἷς τῶν στρατιωτῶν [one of the soldiers] in v. 34a, since John regularly replaces the partitive genitive after εἷς with ἐκ.[195]

Verse 35 refers exclusively to the *effect* of the lance thrust in v. 34b, while vv. 36 and 37, with ταῦτα and the Old Testament quotation, have reference to the *crucifragium* as well as the thrust of the lance. Thus vv. 34b

---

[191] Among those who argue for tradition are Bultmann, *John,* 667; Schulz, *Johannes,* 239; Brown, *John* 2:944–45; Haenchen, *John* 2:194; and Becker, *Johannes* 2:596.

[192] See Bultmann, *John,* 676 n. 6; Schnackenburg, *John* 3:287–88.

[193] See Schnackenburg, *John* 3:286; Mohr, *Johannespassion,* 359.

[194] See Bultmann, *John,* 666–67; E. Schweizer, "Zeugnis," 380. On the traditional character of the Old Testament citations, see Dodd, *Tradition,* 42–49, 131–36.

[195] See Schnackenburg, *John* 3:286–87. The only characteristically Johannine stylistic feature in vv. 32-34a is the historical οὖν.

and 35 are an insertion by the evangelist[196] or by a post-Johannine redaction.[197] The language of this part reveals the hand of John the evangelist: μαρτυρεῖν, μαρτυρία, ἀληθινός, πιστεύειν, ἀληθής, and ὕδωρ are favorite Johannine words.[198] Moreover, the theme of the text, especially its antidocetic tendency, leads one to think of the evangelist:

1. The mention of blood and water in v. 34b is evidently intended to emphasize the reality of Jesus' death.[199] The outflow of blood and water, which constitute the human being,[200] furnishes proof of Jesus' real human body. At the end of the passion, John stresses once more the corporeality of the Redeemer: this is especially evident from the prominent placement of the word αἷμα [blood].

2. Because Jesus' death is the precondition for the saving effects of the sacraments, αἷμα and ὕδωρ refer to Eucharist and baptism.[201] The evangelist uses αἷμα almost exclusively in a eucharistic sense (6:53-56),[202] and 3:5 establishes a sacramental understanding of ὕδωρ.[203] It is true that 19:34b, 35 admits of no immediate or exclusive sacramental interpretation, but John sees the fact of Jesus' death and its present meaning for salvation in the community as one and the same. In addition, the witness motif in v. 35 makes this connection very evident; the μαρτυρία of the eyewitness ultimately serves to undergird the community's sacramental praxis.

3. The unnamed witness in v. 35 can only be the Beloved Disciple (cf. 19:25-27),[204] because no other disciples of Jesus have been mentioned before this, and ἐκεῖνος in v. 35c refers to the preceding αὐτοῦ.[205] The Beloved Disciple again appears as the truthful witness to the Christ-event and the most prominent agent of tradition. This disciple is the guarantor of the

---

[196] Thus, e.g., Barrett, *John*, 554–55; Mohr, *Johannespassion*, 360; E. Schweizer, "Zeugnis," 381–82; Dauer, *Johannes und Lukas*, 228ff.

[197] See Bultmann, *John*, 677–78; Schnackenburg, *John* 3:287 (v. 35 an addition by a later redactor); Becker, *Johannes* 2:597; S. Schulz, *Johannes*, 239–40; Richter, "Blut und Wasser," 134ff.; Thyen, "Aus der Literatur," *ThR* 42, 250–51.

[198] Μαρτυρεῖν in John 33x (Matthew 1x, Mark 0x, Luke 1x); μαρτυρία in John 14x (Matthew 0x, Mark 3x, Luke 1x); ἀληθής in John 14x (Matthew 1x, Mark 1x, Luke 0x); πιστεύειν in John 98x (Matthew 11x, Mark 14x, Luke 9x); ὕδωρ in John 21x (Matthew 7x, Mark 5x, Luke 6x).

[199] See Richter, "Blut und Wasser," 135.

[200] See the citations in E. Schweizer, "Zeugnis," 382.

[201] See Thüsing, *Erhöhung*, 171–72; Roloff, "'Lieblingsjünger,'" 138; Klos, *Sakramente*, 74ff.

[202] The only exception is 1:13.

[203] Klos's attempt to interpret ὕδωρ in v. 34b on the basis of 7:37-39 must be rejected (*Sakramente*, 76–77). Before any such effort can be made, 19:34b, 35 must be interpreted in its own terms and within the immediate context.

[204] See Lorenzen, *Lieblingsjünger*, 53–59 (including the extensive discussion and critique of Bultmann's position); Dauer, *Passionsgeschichte*, 332–33; Bauer, *Johannesevangelium*, 226.

[205] See Barrett, *John*, 557–58.

Johannine witness to Christ against all falsifications brought about by false docetic teachers.

In 21:24 it is precisely *not* the witness himself who proclaims the truth of the Johannine tradition on the basis of his eyewitness. The editors of the Gospel simply document their knowledge of the testimony of the Beloved Disciple, so that the two texts differ significantly in their content, but also in their language.[206]

With ἵνα καὶ ὑμεῖς πιστεύητε [so that you also may believe] in v. 35d, as in 20:31, John speaks of the faith of his community,[207] which is to be strengthened and protected from false teachers by the truthful witness of the Beloved Disciple. Typically Johannine, finally, is the connection, presupposed by v. 35 (cf. 1:34; 3:11, 32; 4:39, 42; 5:31-34), between seeing, testifying, and knowing the truth of what is witnessed: this expresses the reliability and exclusivity of the Johannine witness to Christ and serves to render the community secure in its belief.

To conclude the passion story, John the evangelist formulated in 19:34b, 35 his own antidocetic understanding of Jesus' death. He claims the witness of the Beloved Disciple as recognized guarantor of the Johannine tradition and thus secures the basis for the sacramental praxis of his community.

---

[206] On this, see Schnackenburg, *John* 3:290–91. On the linguistic structure of 19:35, see also Ruckstuhl, *Einheit,* 225–27.

[207] Richter wishes to use 20:31 to establish the secondary character of vv. 34b and 35, since they do not speak of faith in Jesus as Messiah ("Blut und Wasser," 141). This argument is not persuasive, because in 19:34b, 35 also the issue is the correct understanding of Jesus' status as Son of God.

5

Christ Incarnate: The Prologue and Johannine Christology

5.1 Prologue and Gospel

Understanding and interpretation of the prologue to John's Gospel are inextricably bound up with the question of the relationship between the prologue and the Gospel. Does the Gospel begin where the prologue ends? Does the prologue contain within itself the quintessence of the Gospel, so that the two are inseparable?[1] Is the prologue intended to prepare Hellenistic readers for the Gospel, as Adolf von Harnack thought?[2] Or is W. Heitmüller's conclusion valid? He wrote that "the Prologue is like an overture to the Gospel that follows. The principal themes are sounded here, and will be more fully developed in the Gospel itself."[3] Finally, is it possible that the prologue, with its statement about the incarnation, is not at all the center of Johannine theology,[4] so that our question is inappropriate? Is there a discontinuity between the prologue and the Gospel?[5]

These alternatives and variants on the question by no means touch what are only marginal problems in Johannine exegesis. As a rule, the question of the place and interpretation of the prologue is decisive for one's understanding of the whole Gospel.

In the first place, the prologue is a beginning[6] — the opening of a work of literature and of an action. This statement, which sounds so banal at the outset, acquires meaning in face of L. Schottroff's thesis that "for John, the temporal statement, 'in the beginning,' is not at all a matter of time, but a

---

[1] Thus Hoskyns, *Fourth Gospel*, 137.

[2] See Harnack, "Über das Verhältnis des Prologs," 230; see also Dodd, *Interpretation*, 296.

[3] Heitmüller, *Johannes*, 37.

[4] Thus Käsemann, *Jesu letzter Wille*, 27; Becker, "Ich bin die Auferstehung und das Leben," 139–40.

[5] Thus especially Bühner, *Der Gesandte*, 4.

[6] See Hirsch, *Das vierte Evangelium*, 101; Haenchen, "Probleme des johanneischen 'Prologs,'" 117.

statement about nature: the Logos is the heavenly Revealer."[7] Against this opinion there remains the fact of the obvious reference to Gen. 1:1 LXX (ἐν ἀρχῇ [in the beginning]), as well as the simple truth that John 1:1 is de facto a beginning. It is true that the prologue makes no quantitative statement about time, but the phenomenon of the "beginning" implies, *eo ipso,* a temporal notion.

Like the Synoptic Gospels, John also determines a beginning point for the event of salvation.[8] For Mark, the ἀρχὴ τοῦ εὐαγγελίου [beginning of the gospel] is the appearance of John the Baptizer; Luke places a literary proemium (Luke 1:1-4) and an infancy narrative at the beginning of his Gospel, and Matthew opens his work with a genealogy of Jesus. There was an evident tendency in gospel writing to expand salvation history "backward," and in this John surpassed his predecessors. He reaches back to the beginning of all things in Gen. 1:1, thereby establishing a beginning that cannot be surpassed.[9]

If the prologue represents the opening of the Gospel both in time and in content, it has an introductory function. It leads us into the theme of the Gospel by treating central features of the content of what is to come, and thus it prepares us to understand the Gospel and gives a substantial direction to that understanding. This is clear from the terminological and material agreements between the prologue and the rest of the Gospel.

In the prologue, ζωή [life] appears twice (v. 4), and in the other parts of the Gospel it is found 34 times (see, e.g., 3:15; 5:24; 6:40; 11:25). In the prologue, φῶς [light] appears 6 times (vv. 4, 5, 7, 8, 9), and it is found 17 times in the rest of the Gospel (see, e.g., 3:19; 8:12; 9:5; 12:46). Direct parallels to the expression ἐρχόμενον εἰς τὸν κόσμον [coming into the world] (1:9) are found in 6:14; 9:39; 11:27; 12:46; 16:28. In addition, the prologue already contains statements about the world (vv. 9, 10) that are highly important for the Johannine view of cosmic reality. The meaning of central concepts in Johannine christology, such as δόξα (18 times) and ἀλήθεια (75 times),[10] is predetermined for the reader by 1:14(17). It is true that only 1:1 speaks of the work of the preexistent λόγος, but Jesus' preexistence is presumed in 6:46, 62; 16:27-28; 17:5. Beyond the prologue, the Gospel also speaks of the divinity of the Logos, Jesus Christ, in 5:18; 10:33; 20:28. The dualism of light and darkness appears in 1:5 and also in 3:19; 8:12; 12:35, 46. The μαρτυρία [testimony] of the Baptizer (1:6-8, 15) is taken up again in 1:19-34 and constitutes a vital connector between the prologue and the rest of the Gospel. Finally, v. 18 leads us to exactly the point at which the revelatory activity of the incarnate Logos begins.[11] (For "seeing God," see 5:37; 6:46;

---

[7] Schottroff, *Der Glaubende,* 232.

[8] See Wikenhauser, *Johannes,* 40; Barrett, *John,* 149; Haenchen, *John* 1:109; Schnackenburg, *John* 1:222.

[9] See Haenchen, *John* 1:109.

[10] See also ἀληθινός (once in the prologue, 8 times in the rest of the Gospel).

[11] See Schnackenburg, *John* 1:224; Klaiber, "Aufgabe," 307–10.

14:9.) In what follows, Jesus Christ appears as the one authentic interpretation of God.

5.2 Redaction and Tradition in John 1:1-18

Verse 1 reveals itself, both formally and in its content, as tradition.[12] The three subsections, v. 1a-c, are united by the common subject, ὁ λόγος, the predicate ἦν, and the paratactic καί.[13] Verse 1 is built on the pattern a-b, b-c, c-b, with two words setting the tone of each part of the verse, and the second in each pair appearing as the first in the subsequent pair (ἀρχή—λόγος; λόγος—ὁ θεός; θεός—λόγος).[14] In addition to this discernible shaping, the absolute ὁ λόγος, which appears only in vv. 1 and 14a, supports tradition in this verse.[15]

With ἐν ἀρχῇ, John 1:1 makes a connection to Gen. 1:1 LXX, but at the same time it reaches beyond it. What is in view here is not the beginning of creation but the absolute beginning.[16] In any case, ἐν ἀρχῇ ἦν is not predicated of the Logos in the same way as was θεός in v. 1c; the precision ὁ λόγος ἦν πρὸς τὸν θεόν in v. 1b demands God as the functional subject of ἐν ἀρχῇ.[17] Ultimately, in thi̊ case as in all others, the beginning cannot be conceived of without God.

The intimate personal communion of the Logos with God is emphasized in v. 1b. In the koine, πρός with the accusative frequently stands for ἐν or παρά τινι to mean "with."[18] Any statement about the Logos proceeding from God is deliberately avoided.[19] The Logos abides with God from the beginning; both are equally original; and God cannot be thought of without the divine Word.[20]

Statements about the existence of Wisdom with God from the very beginning should be regarded as the religious-historical background of 1:1ab (Prov. 8:22-23, 27, 30;

---

[12] In contrast, the thoroughly redactional (or unitary) character of the prologue is defended by Pohlenz, "Paulus und die Stoa," 557–60; Ruckstuhl, Einheit, 63–97 (but see his own contrary position in "Johannesprolog," 447ff.); Eltester, "Der Logos und sein Prophet"; Ridderbos, "Structure and Scope," 190ff.; Borgen, "Der Logos," 116; Barrett, The Prologue of St. John's Gospel, 27; Culpepper, "The Pivot of John's Prologue," 1ff.; Berger, Exegese des NT, 27–28; Dodd, Interpretation, 268ff.

[13] See Haenchen, John 1:110; Theobald, Im Anfang, 18.

[14] See Bultmann, John, 15; Haenchen, John 1:110; Becker, Johannes 1:68.

[15] Against Zimmermann ("Christushymnus," 253ff.) and Theobald (Im Anfang, 76ff.), who attribute vv. 1 and 14a, and therefore the predication of "Logos," to the evangelist.

[16] Against Becker, who thinks that "there is no interest . . . beyond the time of creation" (Johannes 1:72).

[17] See Demke, "Logos-Hymnus," 51.

[18] See Blass-Debrunner-Rehkopf §239.

[19] See Bultmann, John, 32–33.

[20] See Theobald, Im Anfang, 42.

Wis. 8:3; 9:4, 9; Sir. 1:1; 24:3-4; Job 28:12-27; *1 Enoch* 42:1-3; *Bar.* 3:29. See also *NHL* 13, 1, 35:4-6: "[I] am . . . [the first]-born among those who [came to be, . . .]").[21]

In v. 1c the Logos is given the predicate θεός. The Logos is neither God,[22] nor is there a second God beside the most high God. Rather, the Logos is of the nature of God.[23] Philo gives a clear glimpse of a differentiated use of ὁ θεός and θεός, in which the predicate ὁ θεός belongs to the one God alone (*Som.* 1.229–30). Verse 1c deliberately uses the predicate noun θεός, in order to express both the divine nature of the Logos and its distinction from the most high God. Verse 1c contains the ultimate statement about the being and nature of the Logos,[24] who is unsurpassable in dignity and importance.

The religious-historical origins of the Johannine concept of λόγος cannot be given a monocausal explanation. A first possible point of contact is found in the Old Testament statements about the action of God's Word in creation and in history (see Isa. 55:11; Hab. 3:5-6 LXX; Gen. 1:3; Deut. 8:3; Pss. 33:6; 46:6; Exod. 20:1; also 2 Esd. 6:38ff.)[25] Like the Word of God, Wisdom is involved in God's deeds (Ps. 104:24) and in creation (Jer. 10:12; Sir. 1:4; 24:3ff.; Wis. 7:22, 25, 27; Isa. 10:13; Prov. 3:19).

Also highly important is the Logos philosophy of Heraclitus of Ephesus. There are agreements between his concept of Logos and the prologue on the following points:[26] (1) the Logos is eternal and preexistent (*Fg.* 1: τοῦ δὲ λόγου τοῦδε ἐόντος ἀεί [though this is the Logos]); (2) the Logos is the mediator of creation (*Fg. 1*: γινομένων γὰρ πάντων κατὰ τὸν λόγον τόνδε [for although everything takes place in accordance with this Logos]); (3) rejection and acceptance of the Logos (*Fg.* 1: τοῦ δὲ λόγου τοῦδε . . . ἀεί ἀξύνετοι γίνονται ἄνθρωποι καὶ πρόσθεν ἢ ἀκοῦσαι καὶ ἀκούσαντες τὸ πρῶτον [though this, the Logos, (is), human beings prove themselves continually without understanding for it, both before and after having heard it]; *Fg.* 50: οὐκ ἐμοῦ, ἀλλὰ τοῦ λόγου ἀκούσαντας ὁμολογεῖν σοφόν ἐστιν ἓν πάντα εἶναι [inasmuch as they do not hear one, but rather the Logos, it is wise to say the same: all is one]); (4) although Heraclitus never calls the Logos god or divine, this attribute can be deduced especially from *Fg.* 67 and *Fg.* 30.[27]

In the monistic system of the Stoa, the Logos is the power that pervades all bodies. In its notion of the λόγοι σπερματικοί [lit. spermatic ("seedlike") words], the Stoa developed the basic idea of the ubiquitous presence of the divine in the world. A tradition of Zeno says that God has "penetrated through" matter "like honey through the comb" (*SVF* 1:155). According to Stoic ideas, nothing was, is, or will be

---

[21] The quotations from the *Trimorphic Protennoia* are given in the translation by John D. Turner, in *The Nag Hammadi Library in English,* ed. James M. Robinson, 3rd ed., 511–22.

[22] Against Bultmann, *John,* 34: "The Logos is therefore given the same status as God."

[23] See Haenchen, *John* 1:110–11; Theobald, *Im Anfang,* 42ff.

[24] See Schnackenburg, *John* 1:234; Haenchen, *John* 1:109.

[25] See Freed, "Theological Prelude," 258–59. Dodd sees the Old Testament as background for the Johannine idea of λόγος (*Interpretation,* 272).

[26] See Jendorff, *Der Logosbegriff,* 75ff.; Kelber, *Die Logoslehre,* 22ff.

[27] See Jendorff, *Der Logosbegriff,* 63ff., 82ff.

in the world without the Logos. It is the principle that reigns in the world, down to the lowest level of relationships. Despite some important agreements,[28] it would remain unimaginable for the Stoa that the divine Logos would take shape exclusively in a historical person. Nor did the Stoa develop a real concept of redemption, because the dualism that is constitutive for such a notion was foreign to it.

Fundamental to the Johannine concept of Logos is the equation of λόγος and σοφία in Hellenistic Judaism. In Wis. 9:1, 2 it is said of God, ὁ ποιήσας τὰ πάντα ἐν λόγῳ σου καὶ τῇ σοφίᾳ σου κατασκευάσας ἄνθρωπον . . . [who has made all things by your word, and by your wisdom have formed humankind].[29] In Wisdom of Solomon, after chapter 18 it is no longer Sophia but the Logos who is the central figure.[30] God defeats enemies through God's word, which springs from heaven midway through the night and goes about like a sword (Wis. 18:15: ὁ παντοδύναμός σου λόγος ἀπ᾽ οὐρανῶν ἐκ θρόνων βασιλείων . . . [your all-powerful word (leaped) from heaven, from the royal throne]).

In Philo, the Logos frequently replaces Wisdom.[31] As Wisdom is the "firstborn" (πρωτίστη, Ebr. 31) and ἀρχή (Op. 54), so also the Logos can be called "the firstborn of God" (πρωτόγονος, Conf. 146) and ἀρχή (Conf. 146). The Logos is older than all created things (Migr. 6), appears as light (Som. 1.75), is son and icon of God (Conf. 146–47; Fug. 109), is divine (θεός) but not ὁ θεός (Som. 1.229–30). The Logos comes down among humans (Som. 1.75, 85–86) and is their governor. It dwells with humanity (Post. 122) and saves those who are associated with virtue, while destroying their enemies (Som. 1.85). The Logos is friend (φίλος, Fug. 6), counselor (Fug. 6) and teacher (διδάσκαλος, Ebr. 157; Som. 1.129, 191).

Οὗτος in v. 2, with its backward reference, connects with v. 1c and refines the statement about the divine Logos. The adoption of ἐν ἀρχῇ and πρὸς τὸν θεόν from v. 1a and 1b makes it clear that there also the text was speaking of the divine Logos.[32] Therefore, v. 2 is not a mere repetition; it is a studied interpretation that rounds off the statement, and it belongs to the tradition.[33] While v. 2 looks backward, describing the relationship of the Logos to God, v. 3 introduces the idea of the Logos's activity in creation. The change of subject signals a new theme: the relationship of the Logos to creation (πάντα) will be treated in six paired clauses in vv. 3-5.[34] The early placement of πάντα emphasizes the universal mediating role of the Logos and

---

[28] The Logos, as πῦρ τεχνικόν [artistic fire] is also creator, is identified with the highest divinity (Zeus), and is the revealer (see Cornutus, Theol. Graec. 16).

[29] See also Prov. 4:5, where "word of my mouth" and "wisdom" are parallel. A comprehensive demonstration of the wisdom background of the prologue is offered in Grundmann, Der Zeuge der Wahrheit, 16–29; and Ashton, "The Transformation of Wisdom," 162ff.

[30] See Mack, Logos und Sophia, 96.

[31] For a full treatment, see Mack, Logos und Sophia, 133ff. Mack suggests that the equation of Logos and Sophia in Philo was facilitated by the use of Egyptian motifs. For the agreements between Philo and the statements in the prologue, see also Dodd, Interpretation, 276.

[32] See Haenchen, John 1:112; Theobald, Im Anfang, 47–48.

[33] Against Käsemann ("Aufbau und Anliegen," 167), Schnackenburg (John 1:236), Demke ("Logos-Hymnus," 52–53), and Blank (Johannes 1:70), who do not assign v. 2 to tradition.

[34] See Haenchen, John 1:112–13; Theobald, Im Anfang, 18–19.

refers not only to the world of human beings[35] but to creation as a whole.[36] The recapitulating and strengthening v. 3b admits only the conclusion that πάντα refers to the totality of creation.

The religious-historical background of the idea of the Logos as mediator of creation is found in Prov. 3:19; 8:22-30; Wis. 7:12, 8:6; 9:1, 9; Job 28:27, which speak of Wisdom's participation in creation (see also NHL 13, 1, 38:12-13: "and it is through me that the All took shape"). For early Christian tradition, see also 1 Cor. 8:6; Rom. 11:36; Col. 1:16; Heb. 1:2.

The disputed question whether a caesura between οὐδὲ ἕν and ὃ γέγο-νεν, or between ὃ γέγονεν and ἐν αὐτῷ marks the end of v. 3 and the beginning of v. 4 must be decided, in text-critical terms, in favor of the first variant.[37] Syntactically and semantically, on the other hand, this arrangement creates problems.[38] If ὃ γέγονεν is included in v. 4a, the subject can only be contained in ἦν (sc. ὁ λόγος). Ζωή without the article is a predicate noun, and ὃ γέγονεν cannot be the subject, because ζωή is a characteristic of the Logos.[39] But the personal pronoun in v. 3 refers to the Logos, so that here also ἐν αὐτῷ would have to be interpreted in reference to the Logos. Semantically, the difficulty of the first reading is created by the lack of relationship to the Logos, since the "connection of ὃ γέγονεν with v. 4 does not allow the sentence to speak of the Logos."[40] Moreover, in that case ζωή, strictly speaking, cannot refer only to humanity but must apply to the whole of creation, and v. 4b speaks against that.[41] Therefore, in terms of content, preference must be given to the second variant.[42] As it is in the Father (6:57), so also in the Logos, and thus in the Son, is the life that is the light of all people. The Logos has in itself the ζωή that will in turn be the φῶς τῶν ἀνθρώπων [light of all people]. In no way are πάντα in v. 3a and ἄνθρωπος in v. 4b identical.[43] That is to say, the statement of v. 4 is primarily soteriological and not about the theology of creation.[44]

---

[35] Thus Bultmann, John, 36–38.

[36] Correctly Haenchen, John 1:112.

[37] Thus Bauer, Johannesevangelium, 11ff.; Bultmann, John, 39–40; K. Aland, "Über die Bedeutung eines Punktes," 390–91. But see the weighty objections of Haenchen, "Probleme des johanneischen 'Prologs,'" 127ff.; idem, John 1:113–14; Schnackenburg, John 1:239–40.

[38] See Theobald, Im Anfang, 19.

[39] See Gese, "Johannesprolog," 163.

[40] Haenchen, "Probleme des johanneischen 'Prologs,'" 128 n. 61.

[41] See Schnackenburg, John 1:240.

[42] Thus, besides Haenchen, also Schnackenburg, John 1:240; and Demke, "Logos-Hymnus," 54.

[43] See Demke, "Logos-Hymnus," 55.

[44] For the religious-historical background of the predication of "light," see especially Wis. 6:12; 7:10, 29 (Wisdom as light), and Philo Som.1.75, where φῶς and λόγος are identified. See also, for v. 5, NHL 13, 1, 36:6 ("I shone [down upon the] darkness"), and for v. 9 NHL 13, 1, 47:28-29 ("[I] am the Light that illumines the All").

Verse 5a is linked, in chain fashion, with v. 4b by the repetition of the absolute τὸ φῶς and the introductory καί.[45] The present tense of φαίνει [shine] seems to speak already of the work of the Logos made flesh and in that sense to anticipate v. 14a.[46] But three observations tell against this kind of interpretation of v. 5:[47] (1) It remains unclear at what point the human world becomes darkness as a result of its rejection of the light. In fact, the striking shift from the present (φαίνει [it shines]) to the aorist (κατέλαβεν [it has (not) overcome]) leaves open the question of the precise event to which this refers and in what way it is evident that the human world has made itself to be darkness. (2) Nothing is said about why the Logos became human. The soteriological dimension of the event remains unstated, in contrast to v. 14 (ἐθεασάμεθα τὴν δόξαν αὐτοῦ [we have seen its glory]). (3) If v. 5a already referred to the incarnation of the preexistent Logos, this statement, so essential for the Christian community, has been very imprecisely formulated in a piece of Christian tradition and is subject to grave misinterpretation. That is why v. 5 speaks, as did the model document, of a fruitless working of the λόγος ἄσαρκος [unfleshed word] in history. The light's shining is something that happens within history (cf. Wis. 7:29) and is fulfilled in the acceptance or rejection of the Logos present in creation.[48] Jewish wisdom traditions as well speak of the sad fate of Wisdom, who found no dwelling on earth (1 Enoch 42:1-2; Sir. 24:2-22; see also 1 Cor. 1:21), and such texts make this interpretation probable. The evangelist may have differed from his model in already referring φαίνει to the Logos's becoming flesh, for that is the only sensible explanation for the insertion of the redactional passage about the Baptizer (vv. 6-8) at this point. The statement in v. 14 is not at all weakened; instead, the evangelist, in interpreting v. 5 on the basis of v. 14, has achieved a christological concentration: even the Logos's illumination, from the beginning of creation forward, can ultimately be understood only on the basis of the incarnation and the revelation in Christ.[49] Here already we see that for John, even more than for his model, v. 14 constitutes the high point and key to interpretation of the prologue.

For an understanding of the antithesis "light–darkness," which appears first in v. 5, the priority of creation is of the greatest importance. Creation precedes darkness and thus is not, as in gnostic systems, a work of darkness. Light and darkness are constituted in view of revelation, so that Johannine dualism, in contrast to gnostic writings, has no protological meaning.

---

[45] Bultmann, John, 15: "chain-locking of the sentences."

[46] Thus especially Käsemann, "Aufbau und Anliegen," 161ff.; Ridderbos, "Structure and Scope," 191; see also Demke, "Logos-Hymnus," 58; Theobald, Im Anfang, 50–51. Schnackenburg considers v. 5 "a digression of the evangelist" ("Logos-Hymnus," 103–5; John 1:245). He is joined in this opinion by Onuki, Gemeinde und Welt, 103.

[47] See Haenchen, "Probleme des johanneischen 'Prologs,'" 130ff.; idem, John 1:114–16.

[48] See Becker, Johannes 1:75.

[49] See Schmithals, "Prolog," 39.

Instead, it must be understood as a function of christology.[50] What we find in the Fourth Gospel is not an anticosmic dualism that is prior in time or in content to the event of revelation; rather, revelation brings about a split between the world that stubbornly remains in unbelief and the believing community. As light is a sign of revelation, so darkness reveals its absence.[51]

The structure, unique expressions (ἐν ἀρχῇ, ὁ λόγος, πρὸς τὸν θεόν),[52] and religious-historical parallels we have cited all show that John 1:1-5 is traditional material. But vv. 6-8 lead us into a very different world. First, the Old Testament style of the language is striking (cf. 1 Sam. 1:1-2 LXX: ἄνθρωπος ἦν . . . καὶ ὄνομα αὐτῷ . . . [there was a person . . . whose name was]). This is clear in the close connection of the three finite principal clauses, each with a subordinate clause, to form a single extended sentence.[53] Each of the pronouns with backward reference, οὗτος and ἐκεῖνος, takes up the preceding phrase, and the final clause περὶ τοῦ φωτός [about the light], from v. 7a, is repeated in v. 8b. The governing style in vv. 1-5 was hymnic, but that in vv. 6-8 is narrative!

This shift in language corresponds to a new level of narration; the text now speaks no longer of the heavenly prologue but of events in history.[54] The transition from vv. 1-5 to vv. 6-8 seems abrupt, both in content and in language, while the theme and narrative style of vv. 6-8 are continued in vv. 15, 19ff. These observations lead us to the conclusion that vv. 6-8 are a redactional insertion by the evangelist.[55] On the one hand, in this fashion he connects the prologue with the continuing narrative that begins in vv. 19ff., and he makes clear that the prologue is the beginning of the whole Gospel. On the other hand, the prologue appears to be the origin of the depiction that follows, for that story develops things that were already explicitly contained or suggested, in concentrated language and ideas, in the prologue.[56] Beyond this, the evangelist is guided by a christological interest; through

---

[50] See Onuki, *Gemeinde und Welt,* 41ff. Against Becker, "Ich bin die Auferstehung und das Leben," 143; Schottroff, *Der Glaubende,* 228ff.; and others who accord Johannine dualism priority over the idea of revelation.

[51] See Rissi, "Logoslieder," 327–28.

[52] Πρὸς τὸν θεόν occurs elsewhere only in 13:3.

[53] See Theobald, *Im Anfang,* 21.

[54] See Bauer, *Johannesevangelium,* 15.

[55] This is the conclusion also of, e.g., Wellhausen, *Evangelium Johannis,* 7–8; Bauer, *Johannesevangelium,* 14–15; Bultmann, *John,* 15–16; Schnackenburg, *John* 1:249–50; Becker, *Johannes* 1:67–68; Schmithals, "Prolog," 22; Demke, "Logos-Hymnus," 65–66; Blank, *Johannes* 1:70; Rissi, "Logoslieder," 323; Painter, "Prologue," 462; Ruckstuhl, "Johannesprolog," 448. Haenchen's proposal that the author of John 21 inserted vv. 6-8 and 15 is not persuasive (*John* 1:116–17). In addition, Hofrichter proposes to assign the section on the Baptizer, except for vv. 6ab and 8b, to a post-Gospel redaction ("'Egeneto anthropos,'" 217, 223–24). He thinks that the words ἐγένετο ἄνθρωπος ἀπεσταλμένος παρὰ θεοῦ [there was one sent from God] were in the original hymn and referred to Jesus.

[56] See Demke, "Logos-Hymnus," 65–66.

the appearance of the Baptizer, v. 5 is made to point to v. 14. For John, the activity of the Logos in creation was aimed toward the *Christus incarnatus:* his protology is bound up with his christology and soteriology.[57]

Verse 5 had already referred to the darkness's rejection of the light. Verse 9 now makes a general reference to the light's saving illumination, while v. 10 advances the thought of v. 5—the rejection of the light, or the Logos, by the world and by its own. Linguistic observations also indicate that v. 9 is a redactional transition;[58] the subject of v. 9a is disputed (φῶς or λόγος),[59] and the syntactic status of the expression ἐρχόμενον εἰς τὸν κόσμον is unclear.[60] Following the inserted section on the Baptizer, the evangelist recapitulates vv. 4-5 in order to return to the point at which he had departed from his model.[61]

Verses 10 and 11 are two asyndetic sets of clauses arranged in a series.[62] They follow up the statements of vv. 3-5 and render them more precise. In comparison to v. 5a, v. 10a adds a further idea: the existence of the Logos within the world was not so succinctly expressed in the earlier verse. Verse 10b takes up two expressions that are familiar from vv. 3a and 5b, but in combination they acquire an altered meaning.[63] A new element, in contrast to vv. 3-5, is the preeminent placement of the incarnational expression, ἐν τῷ κόσμῳ ἦν [(it) was in the world], which now interprets the Logos's mediating role in creation.[64] The coming of the Logos into the world had its origin in creation itself. In the incarnation of the Logos, creation reaches its goal, so that the rejection of the Logos by the world is still more incomprehensible. Thus v. 10c is not a repetition of v. 5b but an intensification of it.[65]

The expressions τὰ ἴδια [(what was) his/her/its own] and οἱ ἴδιοι [his/ her/its own (people)] in v. 11 do not correspond to any of the terminology in vv. 3-5. The development from πάντα in v. 3a to τὰ ἴδια and the reference to human beings as οἱ ἴδιοι (cf. 4b) emphasize once again that all being has

---

[57] Verses 6-8 also retain a polemical accent: see Painter, "Prologue," 468–69.

[58] Thus also Käsemann, "Aufbau und Anliegen," 167; Demke, "Logos-Hymnus," 58; Schulz, *Johannes,* 23–24; Rissi, "Logoslieder," 323–24; Brown, *John* 1:9–10; Becker, *Johannes* 1:71; Müller, *Geschichte der Christologie,* 14; Theobald, *Im Anfang,* 23; Schmithals, "Prolog," 25; Painter, "Prologue," 462. Among those who assign v. 9 to the model document are Bultmann, *John,* 52–53; Schnackenburg, *John* 1:255 (without v. 9c); and Haenchen, *John* 117–18.

[59] For a discussion of the possibilities, see Theobald, *Im Anfang,* 22.

[60] See Theobald, *Im Anfang,* 22–23.

[61] See Demke, "Logos-Hymnus," 58.

[62] Ibid., 57.

[63] See Theobald, *Im Anfang,* 51.

[64] This is not recognized by Schnackenburg (*John* 1:256), Becker (*Johannes* 1:69), and Müller (*Geschichte der Christologie,* 14), all of whom regard v. 10b or all of v. 10 as redactional.

[65] These observations speak decisively against Eltester ("Der Logos und sein Prophet," 129) and Schmithals ("Prolog," 25-26), who regard vv. (9) 10-11 as a mere repetition of vv. 3-5 and do not consider the verses traditional.

its origin and its life in the Logos, and still it is true that αὐτὸν οὐ παρέλαβον [they did not accept (or: receive) him].[66]

Verse 12 is coupled with v. 11 by means of an adversative δέ, and ἔλαβον αὐτόν [they received him] in v. 12a takes up the αὐτὸν οὐ παρέλαβον in v. 11b. The dative object of the principal clause (αὐτοῖς) is explained in two relative clauses (vv. 12a and 13) and an added participial construction in v. 12c.[67] There were only a few[68] who accepted the Logos (cf. Prov. 1:20-33; Bar. 3:9-37; Sir. 6:20-22; Wis. 7:27; NHL 13, 1, 50:15-16) and received the gift of becoming children of God. The emphasis in v. 12ab lies on this soteriological statement,[69] which, like v. 5a, speaks of the saving activity of the λόγος ἄσαρκος.

Whereas v. 12ab is usually assigned to tradition,[70] there is broad consensus on the redactional character of vv. 12c and 13.[71] The reasons for this are as follows: (1) πιστεύειν εἰς τὸ ὄνομα αὐτοῦ [to believe in his name] is, in contrast to τέκνα θεοῦ γενέσθαι [to become children of God], a typically Johannine expression.[72] (2) Verse 12c constitutes a "meta-reflection" on v. 12ab: it gives more precise content to the αὐτοῖς in v. 12b and, at the same time and differently from the model document, it speaks of faith in the λόγος ἔνσαρκος [enfleshed word].[73] (3) Verse 13 is written in prose. (4) The expansion of a Jewish idea of restricted salvation to embrace the concept of universal salvation of all who believe is to be attributed to John the evangelist (cf. 4:1-42; 8:41ff.).

In v. 14a, the initial καί first draws attention to itself.[74] The two verse segments 14ab are united by their common subject, ὁ λόγος, while the new

---

[66] See Demke, "Logos-Hymnus," 59.

[67] See Theobald, Im Anfang, 24.

[68] See Bauer, Johannesevangelium, 21.

[69] Thus correctly Theobald, Im Anfang, 24.

[70] See Bultmann, John, 57 n. 5 (with the exception of ἐξουσία); Käsemann, "Aufbau und Anliegen," 167–68 (v. 12 as a whole constituted the conclusion of the model document); Müller, Geschichte der Christologie, 18 (v. 12ab was the conclusion of the model document); Demke, "Logos-Hymnus," 59–60; Schulz, Johannes, 16 (v. 12ab was the conclusion of the model document); H. M. Schenke, "Christologie," 100; Theobald, Im Anfang, 88–89; Schmithals, "Prolog," 31. Schnackenburg thinks differently, assigning v. 12 to the evangelist (John 1:261). Haenchen attributes vv. 12-13 to someone after the evangelist who expanded the Gospel ("Probleme des johanneischen 'Prologs,'" 138).

[71] See Bultmann, John, 59–60; Schnackenburg, John 1:263–64; Schulz, Johannes, 16; Becker, Johannes 1:71; Müller, Geschichte der Christologie, 13; Brown, John 1:10ff.; Rissi, "Logoslieder," 329ff.; Painter, "Prologue," 461.

[72] See Zimmermann, "Christushymnus," 257.

[73] See Schmithals, "Prolog," 30. But Hofrichter differs (Nicht aus Blut, 33ff.). He considers v. 13 part of the original text but without the introductory pronoun, and singular rather than plural (οὐκ ἐξ αἱμάτων . . . ἐγεννήθη). In that case, the logical subject of v. 13 would be the earthly revealer.

[74] See Theobald, Im Anfang, 25.

subject of v. 14c takes up the ἡμῖν in v. 14b. The object of v. 14c, τὴν δόξαν αὐτοῦ [his glory], is explained in v. 14de.

The basic components of v. 14 belong to the Johannine tradition: (1) Verse 14 takes up the absolute ὁ λόγος in v. 1. (2) The incarnation introduces a new theme. (3) In v. 14 there are several *hapax legomena*: σκηνοῦν, χάρις (also in vv. 16 and 17), and πλήρης. In addition, θεᾶσθαι appears in combination with δόξα only in v. 14c.[75] (4) Verse 15 is a literary insertion between v. 14 and v. 16, connected in its content and form with vv. 6-8. (5) Verse 14 reveals a confessional style. (6) The motif parallel in the Wisdom myth of Sir. 24:8 (in which σοφία pitches her tent in Israel) indicates that the concept of the incarnation is a natural part of the text. (7) For the first time in v. 14, the fate of the Logos is described and, in the expression ἐθεασάμεθα τὴν δόξαν αὐτοῦ, the soteriological goal of the whole event is indicated. Thus v. 14 reveals itself to be an integral part of the tradition,[76] which cannot be attributed to a preredactional accretion,[77] or to the evangelist,[78] or to a redactor working after the evangelist.[79]

With its subject, ὁ λόγος, v. 14a deliberately echoes v. 1 and emphasizes that the following statements apply to the Logos, who was with God in the beginning. The verb, γίνομαι, in combinaton with a predicate noun, expresses a change in a person or thing. It applies to "pers[ons] and things which change their nature, to indicate their entering a new condition: *become something.*"[80] Moreover, in John's Gospel σάρξ describes created human beings of flesh (see 1:13; 3:6; 6:51, 52, 53, 54, 55, 56, 63; 8:15; 17:2) and blood, "sheer humanity,"[81] so that σάρξ ἐγένετο in v. 14a cannot be understood

---

[75] See Zimmermann, "Christushymnus," 257; Ibuki, "Lobhymnus," 150 n. 5.

[76] Among those who consider v. 14 traditional (usually positing redactional intervention at the end of the verse) are Bultmann, *John,* 15–17 (though in 1923 Bultmann still saw v. 14 as a creation of the evangelist: see his "Der religionsgeschichtliche Hintergrund," 33–34); Schnackenburg, *John* 1:226–27; J. Schneider, *Johannes,* 60ff.; Schmithals, "Prolog," 21–22. Zimmermann ("Christushymnus," 254) and Theobald (*Im Anfang,* 89–90) consider v. 14a redactional and v. 14b-e traditional, although they can produce no persuasive arguments for this position.

[77] See Müller, *Geschichte der Christologie,* 20; Becker, *Johannes* 1:71.

[78] See Käsemann, "Aufbau und Anliegen," 168ff.; Schulz, *Johannes,* 16; H. M. Schenke, "Christologie," 227. Thyen ("Aus der Literatur," *ThR* 39, 241ff., esp. 248) assigns vv. 14-18 to his "evangelist" (=the author of John 21). Demke considers vv. 14 and 16 to be a piece of tradition edited by the evangelist but not originally part of the Logos hymn ("Logos-Hymnus," 61ff.). Painter's position is similar ("Prologue," 466ff.): he sees in vv. 14e, 16-17 a "Hellenistic" addition, at a pre-Johannine stage, to a Sophia hymn embracing vv. 1-5, 10-12b, 14a-c. Hofrichter discerns in vv. 14e-17 a "Deuteropauline-Asia Minor" expansion ("'Egeneto anthropos,'" 215ff.). Rissi distinguishes two independent Logos hymns in 1:1-18: first hymn, vv. 1-5, 10ac, 11, 12b; second hymn, vv. 14, 16, 17 ("Logoslieder," 323ff.). But against all these attempts we must insist on the obvious original correspondence between v. 1 and v. 14, and the trajectory of vv. 1-13 toward the climax in v. 14.

[79] See Richter, "Fleischwerdung des Logos," 169, etc. (antidocetic redaction).

[80] *BAGD,* 159, s.v. γίνομαι, 4; see also Liddell-Scott (s.v. γίνομαι, II, 1).

[81] See Bultmann, *John,* 63.

merely as "contact with what is earthly,"[82] as an "irreducible minimum of personal equipment,"[83] or as a mere means of communication between heaven and earth. Instead, it describes a change in the Logos: it now is what it previously was not, namely, a real, genuine human being. The incarnation of the preexistent Logos contains both a statement of identity and a statement of essence, since the identity of subjects in v. 14a and v. 1 produces an affirmation about the essence and the true humanity of Jesus. The human being, Jesus, is the divine Revealer who brings himself as message. If καὶ ὁ λόγος σὰρξ ἐγένετο emphasizes the real incarnation of the Son of God and also represents a succinct statement of the fundamental change in the nature of the Logos, while preserving the Logos's divine identity, v. 14a cannot be the expression of a "naïve docetism" but instead must be understood as decidedly antidocetic.[84] The complete incarnation of the Revealer is unacceptable to Docetists, and therefore v. 14a should be interpreted, at the level both of tradition and of the evangelist, as conscious polemic against Docetists.

Verse 14b intensifies v. 14a with a parallelism that advances the thought,[85] by emphasizing the bodily presence of the preexistent Logos in the human community. The Logos not only became human, but lived as a human being "among us," something that is confirmed by the group of original witnesses from Andrew to Thomas. The verb σκηνοῦν [to tent, dwell] is not so much a reflection of the tent as God's dwelling place (see Exod. 33:9-11); its closest parallel is Sophia's "tenting" in the world (see Sir. 24:4, 8; 1 Enoch 42:2; Ps. 19:4; Bar. 3:38; see also NHL 13, 1, 47:14-15).[86] Here σκηνοῦν refers to the mortal human body[87] (cf. Wis. 9:15; 2 Cor. 5:1, 4; 2 Pet. 1:13, 14), so that v. 14b represents an intensification of the statement about the incarnation in v. 14a.[88]

---

[82] See Käsemann, Jesu letzter Wille, 28.

[83] Ibid.

[84] See Bultmann, John, 60–70; Schnackenburg, John 1:170–71, 267–68; Bousset, Kyrios Christos, 262; Bauer, Johannesevangelium, 23; Bornkamm, "Interpretation," 117; Brown, John 1:31–32; Cullmann, The Johannine Circle, 61; Richter, "Fleischwerdung des Logos," 155; Thyen, "Aus der Literatur," ThR 39, 227–28. (Richter and Thyen, however, see an antidocetic tendency only in their post-Gospel "redaction.") Among those who differ are Becker, Johannes 1:77; Rissi, "Logoslieder," 332 n. 55; Theobald, Im Anfang, 55; Schottroff, Der Glaubende, 276–77; Hofrichter, Nicht aus Blut, 136 n. 1. (Hofrichter thinks that v. 14a-d represents "a still unchallenged 'kenotic' christology.") The ways in which the concept of incarnation was interpreted in later gnostic circles are described in Fischer, "Der johanneische Christus," 262–64; and Pokorný, "Der irdische Jesus," 220–21.

[85] See Jeremias, Prolog, 9–10; Wilkens, Zeichen und Werke, 131; Richter, "Fleischwerdung des Logos," 156–57; Thyen, "Aus der Literatur," ThR 39, 230.

[86] For an analysis of these texts, see Robinson, "Sethians and Johannine Thought," 659–60.

[87] See Bauer, Johannesevangelium, 24.

[88] Against Käsemann, who understands v. 14b simply as an "epiphany of the creator on earth" ("Aufbau und Anliegen," 174).

The believers' seeing[89] the δόξα of the incarnate Logos in v. 14c forms a high point of the prologue. It is precisely in becoming flesh that the pre-existent Logos reveals its glory. If the "seeing" of the *doxa* applies to the σὰρξ γενόμενος, then at this point Johannine Christianity formulates its fundamental confession of faith: in Jesus of Nazareth, God became human; the Logos entered into flesh. To those who recognize this and join in the confession of the community, the *doxa* of the Preexistent One is revealed, and they receive a share in the saving work of the Son of God.

Δόξα as a designation for the divine epiphany may reflect Old Testament theophany traditions (cf. Exod. 16:10; 24:16-17; 33:18-19; 40:34-35, etc.). But Wis. 7:25 is much more revealing: here it is said of Sophia: καὶ ἀπόρροια τῆς τοῦ παντοκράτορος δόξης εἰλικρινής [(she is) a pure emanation of the glory of the Almighty]. Wisdom 9:11 also speaks of the *doxa* of Sophia: καὶ φυλάξει (sc. σοφία) με ἐν τῇ δόξῃ αὐτῆς [and (she will) guard me with her glory].

The object in v. 14c, τὴν δόξαν αὐτοῦ, is clarified in v. 14de. The first apposition is widely regarded as an addition by the evangelist,[90] a conclusion that is supported by the overloaded construction (with the unclear reference of πλήρης [full]),[91] the Johannine μονογενής [only, unique, only-begotten] (John 1:18; 3:16, 18; 1 John 4:9), and the unusual phrase παρὰ πατρός [from (the) father]. Μονογενής[92] (cf. Wis. 7:22) is a qualitative circumscription of the *doxa* of the preexistent Logos. It is the *doxa* of the only-begotten Son. In this single word, both the special relationship between Father and Son and the uniqueness and extraordinary quality of this *doxa* are emphasized. The expression χάρις καὶ ἀλήθεια [grace and truth] in v. 14e is probably a reflection of the Old Testament חסד ואמת [*ḥesed wĕ'emet*] (cf. esp. Exod. 34:6).[93] Whereas δόξα describes the essence of divinity, χάρις and ἀλήθεια, as designations of the richness of grace and the true recognition of the divine, indicate the divinity of the incarnate Logos.

Verse 15, like vv. 6-8, is almost unanimously regarded as a redactional addition by the evangelist.[94] This verse separates itself from its immediate context through both a shift in subject (vv. 14 and 16: "we"; v. 15: John) and a change in tense (vv. 14 and 16: aorist; v. 15: present). Verse 15 is couched in narrative prose that interrupts the thought and continues the polemic

---

[89] Bultmann correctly rejects a restriction of the "we" at this point to the eyewitnesses (*John*, 69–70).

[90] See Schnackenburg, *John* 1:270–71; Müller, *Geschichte der Christologie*, 16–17; Becker, *Johannes* 1:70; Theobald, *Im Anfang*, 92.

[91] According to Bauer, it belongs with αὐτοῦ (*Johannesevangelium*, 26).

[92] On μονογενής, see Bauer, *Johannesevangelium*, 25–26.

[93] This is the opinion of nearly all exegetes; but see the powerful counterarguments presented by Bauer, *Johannesevangelium*, 26–27.

[94] See only Bultmann, *John*, 15–16; Schnackenburg, *John* 1:273.

against the Baptizer that was hinted at as early as v. 8: the Incarnate One is superior to the Baptizer, because he really existed before him.[95]

Verse 16, which begins with a recitative ὅτι, takes up the thread of v. 14 through the connection of key words: πληρώματα / πλήρης [fullness/full].[96] With great emphasis, the believers' experience of the epiphanic Logos and the saving dimension of the incarnation (χάριν ἀντὶ χάριτος) are stressed. The subject of v. 14 is both expanded and made more precise in the phrase ἡμεῖς πάντες [all of us]: it is not merely the "eyewitnesses" who can testify to the salvation event but the believing community as well. Therefore v. 16 cannot be regarded as a mere redactional repetition of v. 14,[97] since v. 16 both varies and defines: it connects with v. 14, but its subject carries us beyond the content of that verse.[98] In addition, the placement of v. 15 could scarcely be explained if v. 16 were also to be attributed to the evangelist.[99]

Verse 17, with its antithetical construction,[100] is connected to v. 16b through a causative ὅτι and gives a clarification of the key word χάρις. This verse announces the absolute claim of God's revelation in Jesus Christ and relativizes the function of Moses as mediator of salvation, which is here limited to that of a mere transmitter of the law. Although both the transmission of the law and the "grace and truth" now announced rest on an action of God, there is a strict contrast between Moses the "mediator" and Jesus. The accent of the verse is located in 17b, with the paired words ἡ χάρις καὶ ἀλήθεια from v. 14e. While Moses only received the law, through Christ grace and truth have become reality in the believing community. Only in the incarnation of the Logos is the reality of divine grace revealed; thus the Moses-event is degraded to a mere act of transmission.[101] The theme of v. 17, so surprising in this context, indicates the authorship of the evangelist, who is always interested in the exclusive character and absolute claim of the Christ-event.[102]

Verse 1 had stressed that the Logos, with regard to its existence before the beginning of the world, was as much "in the beginning" as God. Verse 18 now emphasizes the uniqueness of the revelation of God in Jesus Christ,

---

[95] See Schnackenburg, John 1:273–75.

[96] See Demke, "Logos-Hymnus," 61–62.

[97] Against Schmithals, who ascribes all of v. 16 to the evangelist ("Prolog," 27). Zimmermann ("Christushymnus," 257) and Theobald (Im Anfang, 93–94), without adequate reason, consider only ἡμεῖς πάντες redactional.

[98] See Müller, Geschichte der Christologie, 18.

[99] In that case, the evangelist would have to have written v. 15 artificially in the style of an inserted parenthesis in order to resume the train of thought from v. 14 in v. 16!

[100] For an interpretation of v. 17, see section 1.3 above.

[101] See Theobald, Im Anfang, 61–62.

[102] Among those who consider v. 17 redactional are Bultmann, John, 78–79; Schnackenburg, John 1:276; Demke, "Logos-Hymnus," 63; Theobald, Im Anfang, 94–95. Those who argue for tradition include Haenchen, "Probleme des johanneischen 'Prologs,'" 132–33; Zimmermann, "Christushymnus," 20; and Schmithals, "Prolog," 27–28.

a revelation presently to be unfolded in the Gospel. Thus v. 18 shows itself to be a transitional verse applying the statements of the prologue to the forthcoming depiction of the history of Jesus Christ: what was accomplished in the deeds, words, and suffering of Jesus Christ corresponded from the very beginning to the will of God. The exclusiveness of the Christ-event is thus doubly secured; Jesus Christ alone was able to give information about God, and his revelation is derived from the existence of the Logos with God from all eternity.[103] The transitional function, the typically Johannine theme of the exclusive revelation of God in Jesus Christ (cf. 5:37; 6:46; 16:28), and the linguistic character of the verses (μονογενής, ἐκεῖνος) reveal that v. 18 was constructed by the evangelist.[104]

In form-critical terms, the reconstructed pre-Johannine tradition can be described as a hymn, to the extent that a hymn is characterized as a form that "lists, with praise and exaltation, the deeds or characteristics of a divinity."[105] The many correspondences, both in content and in terminology, with other hymnic texts in the New Testament also suggest this classification (cf. Col. 1:11; Heb. 1:3; 1 Pet. 1:25; Eph. 1:6, 12; Rev. 1:6: note also δόξα in Col. 1:19; πλήρωμα in Eph. 1:10; χάρις in Eph. 1:6, 7).[106] The hymn consists of couplets and triplets in a loose series; no dominant metric form can be demonstrated.[107] It is characterized by its usage of ὁ λόγος at the beginning of the two unequally long strophes and by the transition from third person singular to first person plural (for this, see Eph. 1:3ff.; 2:14-16; Col. 1:13ff.; 2:13-15; Rev. 1:5-6; 5:9-10; 7:10, 12; 11:15, 17-18; 19:1, 5). The first strophe describes the existence of the Logos with God, its role as mediator of creation, and its activity in the world as λόγος ἄσαρκος, while the second strophe articulates the Christian communities' confession of the *doxa* of the Incarnate One. The believers' confession corresponds to the direct, immediate description of the event of salvation (cf. Phil. 2:6-9, 10-11).

5.3   Interpretation

The tradition John has adopted in the prologue is determined not by the christological "schema of the way" (see 16:28, and frequently elsewhere;

---

[103] See Theobald, *Im Anfang*, 48–49. The correspondence between v. 1 and v. 18 is emphasized especially by de la Potterie, "Prologue," 375.

[104] Among those who assign v. 18 to the evangelist are Bultmann, *John*, 79 n. 3; Schnackenburg, *John* 1:278; Haenchen, *John* 1:121; Demke, "Logos-Hymnus," 61, 67; Becker, *Johannes* 1:70; Müller, *Geschichte der Christologie*, 13, 15; Wengst, *Christologische Formeln*, 204; Rissi, "Logoslieder," 331; Theobald, *Im Anfang*, 95; Schmithals, "Prolog," 30. Verse 18 is counted as part of the model document by Gese ("Johannesprolog," 170–71) and by Hofrichter ("'Egeneto anthropos,'" 222, 231–32).

[105] Deichgräber, *Gotteshymnus*, 22. Wengst classifies the prologue as a "song" (*Christologische Formeln*, 205); Jeremias calls it a psalm (*Prolog*, 8); Hofrichter refers to it as a "confessional text" (*Johannesprolog*, 41).

[106] Against Jeremias, *Prolog*, 9–10, for whom the prologue is composed in "parallel steps."

[107] See Ibuki, "Lobhymnus," 154 n. 45; Deichgräber, *Gotteshymnus*, 45–46; Jörns, *Das hymnische Evangelium*, 17–19.

also Phil. 2:6-11)[108] but rather by the idea of preexistence. Jesus Christ, as the one Logos of God, is revealed in his equality with God from all eternity and in his activity in creation. The Logos is implicitly identified with divine Wisdom: it is light, and it contains within itself the fullness of life. In it the original creative will of God is revealed, and turning toward the Logos is the only thing that makes possible a life as children of God in accordance with creation. In the second strophe of the hymn, the community confesses the revelation of glory, grace, and truth in the incarnate Logos, Jesus Christ. It knows that it is guided and supported by the Logos's fullness of life that has been bestowed on it.

For the evangelist, the prologue functions as a programmatic introductory text.[109] Both its placement and the meta-reflection worked into it by the evangelist suggest this classification. Standing at the beginning of the Gospel, the prologue serves as a guide for the readers by offering a succinct formulation of the interpretation of what follows as envisioned by the evangelist. With the meta-reflections in vv. 12c, 13, 17, and 18, John expands his model's spectrum of expression. For him, the Christ-event has universal features; it escapes any kind of particularism of salvation and must be understood as the unique interpretation of God. The inserted sections on the Baptizer also cause the prologue to appear to be a historical account, and the Gospel as a whole is nothing other than the narrative of the history of the Logos, who was in the beginning with God.[110] In addition, the inserted sections on the Baptizer lead to a christological concentration, because they cause φαίνει in v. 5 to refer directly to the incarnation of the Logos and thus prepare for the thematic statement of the incarnation in v. 14. The evangelist's christological interpretation is evident in vv. 17 and 18 as well. Only in v. 17 does the name of Jesus Christ appear within the prologue, and v. 18 underscores that Jesus alone can truly make God known.

The high point of the prologue, for the evangelist as also for his tradition, is the statement about the incarnation in v. 14.[111] The new beginning

---

108 See Becker, *Johannes* 1:77.

109 See Dunn, "Let John be John," 334: "The Fourth Evangelist really did intend his Gospel to be read through the window of the Prologue." Hofrichter reverses the relationship of prologue and Gospel and sees the Gospel as nothing but a cumulative commentary on the prologue (*Johannesprolog*, 15ff.). Hofrichter's thesis that the Logos confession, as he reconstructs it (see pp. 76–77), was used by the Synoptics, Acts, Paul, and the Deutero-Paulines (see pp. 239ff.) and that a large part of New Testament theology was based on "the interpretative explication of the Logos-confession" (p. 305) is fully hypothetical and should be rejected. The proofs Hofrichter introduces in support of this thesis are, of their very nature, minimal and are necessarily given a tendentious interpretation.

110 See Ibuki, "Offene Fragen," 111ff. Von der Osten-Sacken sees the Baptizer sections as the real center of the prologue, because they testify to the identity of the preexistent Logos with the man Jesus ("Der erste Christ," 163ff.).

111 Against Haacker, who sees the high point of the prologue in v. 17 (*Stiftung*, 35).

marked by the initial καί and the reintroduction of ὁ λόγος, the "we" of the confessing community, and the central soteriological concepts of δόξα, χάρις, and ἀλήθεια, which appear here for the first time, testify to the central importance of this verse. In the incarnation of the preexistent Son of God and in the vision of salvation that thus becomes available to the believing community, both the original existence of the Logos with God and the creation as a whole reach their goal. Verse 14a gives a clear semantic indication of a change in the Logos: here σάρξ cannot be understood as merely an irrelevant factor or a necessary medium.[112] On the contrary, the Logos, Jesus Christ, equal to God and existing with the Father from the beginning, was a real human being, who really entered into flesh, so that "flesh" means what is "this-worldly-human, visible and tangible, limited and substantial, frail and susceptible."[113] The expression ἐθεασάμεθα τὴν δόξαν αὐτοῦ in no way erases this antidocetic affirmation, because what is seen is the *doxa* of the Incarnate One! Verse 14 constitutes a theological unity, in which the individual statements do not exist in a relationship of tension or in competition with one another; rather, they describe a movement from the incarnation, as the basis for salvation, to a vision of the *doxa* as the presence of grace and truth.

---

[112] Against Schottroff, *Der Glaubende,* 274.

[113] Schlier, "Im Anfang," 281.

6

The Position of the Gospel in the Johannine School

The antidocetic tendency in central features of Johannine christology, which has been demonstrated in the preceding exegetical investigation, causes the Fourth Gospel to appear to be, in some essential ways, a reaction to docetic christology.[1] The Johannine letters restrict themselves to polemic and a defense of correct beliefs, while the Gospel undertakes a comprehensive theological combat with Docetism.[2] Because this conflict with docetic opponents is the only methodologically secure point from which to proceed in determining the time sequence of 1 John and the Gospel,[3] 1 John is seen to have temporal priority, in that the Gospel evidently presupposes the acute conflict reflected in the letter and deals with it in theological terms. The fundamental and broadly conceived argumentation of the evangelist against a docetic christology reveals a distance in time and subject matter from 1 John, which is still engaged in acute controversy. The letter names the problem, but a theological answer is found only later, in the Gospel.

The necessity for a theologically founded rejection of Docetism is evident from the consequences of such a christology. The Docetists, by dissolving the historical Jesus of Nazareth into a δόκησις [appearance] and denying his οὐσία [substance], were able to maintain the reality of cross and resurrection in a superficial sense but without accepting the soteriological significance of that event. Docetism was suited to a rationalistic way of thinking; the monophysitism it developed, against the background of the Platonic

---

[1] On the antidocetic character of the Gospel of John, see also Hoskyns, *Fourth Gospel,* 48–57; Lindars, *John,* 61–63; E. Schweizer, "Jesus, der Zeuge Gottes." A different opinion is voiced by Hofrichter (*Nicht aus Blut,* 155ff.). He disputes the antidocetic attitude of the Gospel of John and thinks that, against the background of 1 John, the Gospel is opposing a "dualistic baptismal theology."

[2] See Weigandt, "Doketismus," 107.

[3] See section 2.2.2.2 above.

contrast between δοκεῖν and εἶναι,[4] laid exclusive emphasis on the divinity of the Redeemer but at the same time accepted the historical appearance of Jesus of Nazareth, though in a devalued form. The paradox of the ὁ λόγος σὰρξ ἐγένετο was unthinkable for Docetists, because the Redeemer cannot enter into any real connection with matter: his "substance," in the form of his earthly appearance, is really "lack of substance." For the evangelist, on the contrary, the identity of the historical Jesus of Nazareth with the exalted Christ is connected in the most intimate way with the identity of Christian faith as a whole. Only if the Redeemer was truly human could he bring salvation to human beings. From the point of view of the fourth evangelist, it was necessary to maintain the humanity and historicity of Jesus, up to and including his death on the cross, if the kerygma was to touch human beings in their historical situation and lead them to faith. Faith is imaginable only in the form of paradox, and only at the level of anthropology is it utterable. The evangelist was thus faced with the difficult task of establishing his concept of the tension-filled union of humanity and divinity in Jesus Christ against the plausibility and attractiveness of docetic christology.

Even John's chosen genre of "gospel" must be understood as an expression of this effort. It is scarcely an accident that the evangelist composed neither a collection of sayings (cf. the *Gospel of Thomas*) nor a revelatory tract (cf. the *Acts of John*)[5] but decided on a genre whose character requires a description of the life and work of the historical Jesus of Nazareth from a post-Easter perspective. The obvious differences between the Fourth Gospel and the Synoptics should not lead us to ignore the fact that the *vita Jesu* is of fundamental importance in the Fourth Gospel as well. Within the framing concepts of preexistence and exaltation, we find depicted here the deeds and words of Jesus, from the Baptizer's witness and the call of the disciples to Jesus' death on the cross. The references to the passion that permeate the whole Gospel and the repeated emphases on Jesus' humanity[6] also show that John did not merely wish to describe a revelatory event in mythical form but wanted to depict the revelatory way of the *Incarnate One*. On the cross, revelation reaches its goal (19:30: τετέλεσται) as the course of the historical

---

[4] See Plato *Resp.* 2.361b, 362a, etc.; also Epictetus *Diss.* 2.11.15; 4.6.24. Weigandt ("Doketismus," 29ff., 148) and Grillmeier (*Jesus der Christus,* 189 n. 157) correctly emphasize the Greek background of Docetism. In particular, the Platonic conception of reality may have influenced Docetism, because for the Docetists real being is spiritual, ideal being (οὐσία, ὄντως ὄν, ὅ ἐστιν ὄν [substance, real being, that which is]), whereas the world of perceptions (which, from the docetic point of view, included the bodily existence of Jesus Christ) is subjected to appearance (δόξα, δοκεῖν). I take this position in opposition to Brox, "'Doketismus,'" 314. He thinks that early Docetism resulted from "Jewish Christian efforts to maintain [Jewish] monotheism intact."

[5] See Dunn, "Let John be John," 339.

[6] See Pokorný, "Der irdische Jesus," 221–25. This author shows that even the *ego-eimi* sayings are not at all to be interpreted throughout in the sense of a christology of glory.

Jesus comes to an end. The evangelist did not create his Gospel independently of Mark, on the basis of a supposed "semeia source" or "gospel of signs" but rather was acquainted with the "gospel"[7] genre and used it to incorporate, for the most part, heterogeneous individual traditions from the Johannine school. His purpose in doing so was to awaken and preserve faith in Jesus Christ (20:31). If it is true for the writing of gospels generally that this activity should be seen against the background of christological debates about the legitimacy of different forms of the kerygma — that is, the question of the proper understanding of Jesus[8] — that circumstance is especially pertinent in the case of the Fourth Gospel. The striking emphasis on the identity of the historical Jesus with the exalted Christ in 20:31 (ὅτι Ἰησοῦς ἐστιν ὁ Χριστός) is obviously directed against Docetists, for whom the life, suffering, and death of Jesus possess no soteriological quality. In this way, the very writing of John's Gospel represents an attempt to maintain the salvific significance of the historical Jesus and his unity with the exalted Christ.

While the docetic opponents are characterized by προάγειν [going beyond] (2 John 9), their departure from the common teaching and tradition (cf. 1 John 2:19), John uses the Gospel to document his adherence to what has been handed down.[9] A real understanding of the revelation in Christ is possible only on the basis of the tradition to whose truth and validity the Beloved Disciple witnesses. In the person of the Beloved Disciple, redactionally introduced by the evangelist, both typological and individual features combine.[10] As hermeneut for Jesus and speaker for the group of disciples, as true witness beneath the cross and legitimate successor of Jesus, the Beloved Disciple represents the type of the ideal eyewitness. This does not mean that, as a historical person, the Beloved Disciple is "a complete fiction";[11] 21:22-23 presumes his unexpected death, an event that moved the editors of the Gospel of John to insert a correction of the personal traditions about the Beloved Disciple and his relationship to Peter. Moreover, if the Beloved Disciple embodied only a type or a theological principle, his function as a recognized guarantor of tradition would not be persuasive. A more precise historical identification of the Beloved Disciple is necessarily a matter of hypothetical speculation, but two observations make it probable that we should see in the person of the Beloved Disciple the Presbyter of 2 and 3 John: (1) As the founder of the Johannine school, the πρεσβύτερος already appears

---

[7] In my opinion it is very improbable that Mark and John created the "gospel" genre independently of one another within a few decades.

[8] See Talbert, *What Is a Gospel?* 98.

[9] In addition to the traditions examined in this study, see esp. Schille, "Traditionsgut im vierten Evangelium," 77ff.; Schnackenburg, "Tradition und Interpretation im Spruchgut des Johannesevangeliums," 72ff.

[10] See Grundmann, *Zeugnis und Gestalt,* 18: "The Beloved Disciple is equally individual and type; though he dies as an individual, he subsists as a type."

[11] Kragerud, *Lieblingsjünger,* 149.

in 2 and 3 John as a special agent of tradition, which enables the evangelist to incorporate this function. (2) The Presbyter had already engaged in conflict with docetic false teachers (2 John 7),[12] so that the antidocetic witness of the Beloved Disciple (besides the idea of tradition, see esp. 19:34b-35; 20:8) is in continuity with that of the Presbyter.

If the literary figure of the Beloved Disciple conceals the Presbyter of 2 and 3 John, the evangelist, when writing the Gospel in his specific situation, endows the dominant personality of the Johannine school with the attributes that this disciple had already displayed when actively on the scene. Thus, in the figure of the Beloved Disciple, type and individual are intimately united.

In addition to the Beloved Disciple, the motif of witness also functions to confirm the dignity of the Johannine tradition. As in a legal proceeding, the witness publicly affirms what he or she saw and heard, a process that confers a special degree of truth and reliability on the matters that the witness attests.[13] The Baptizer testifies to the incarnation of the Logos (1:6-8, 15, 19-34; see also 5:33). Jesus is witness to heavenly things (3:11, 31-32), just as the Father bears witness to Jesus in his conflict with the Jews (5:31-40; 8:12-20). The Beloved Disciple testifies to the reality of Jesus' death (19:34b, 35), and in 21:24 this disciple is made the author of the Gospel, whose true witness is confirmed by the Fourth Gospel's editors. In 15:26-27 it is the Paraclete who will give testimony to Jesus. Here we see the uniqueness of the Johannine concept of tradition and witness: the Paraclete actualizes and makes present the witness of the Johannine tradition to Jesus Christ.[14] It is by no means an exhaustive description of the Gospel to call it a description of the life and death of Jesus Christ; instead, it is the expression of "Johannine theology of presence through visual recollection,"[15] which has its basis in God's revelation in Jesus Christ, as guaranteed by the Beloved Disciple and supported by the Paraclete.

The Johannine interpretation of the Christ event is accomplished at a distance in time.[16] It is conditioned by its chronological distance from the historical Jesus of Nazareth and is revealed primarily by the uniqueness of the traditions incorporated by John. The traditions fill out the temporal distance and determine both the situation and the understanding of the evangelist. Beginning from his own theological-historical situation, with the christological questions that beset him in the present, John looks back at the

---

[12] See Schnackenburg, *Johannesbriefe,* 312–13; Brown, *Johannine Epistles,* 685–86; Wengst, *Johannesbriefe,* 240. Strecker differs, interpreting ἐρχόμενον as future and thinking that the Presbyter supports a chiliastic doctrine that is rejected by the "innovators" ("Anfänge der johanneischen Schule," 35).

[13] See Blank, *Krisis,* 198ff.

[14] See Mussner, "Sehweise," 34ff.

[15] Blank, *Krisis,* 215.

[16] On the hermeneutical meaning of temporal distance, see Gadamer, *Truth and Method,* 258–67; for the Gospel of John, see Mussner, "Sehweise," 14ff.

foundation of his traditions in the life of the historical Jesus.[17] He is in possession of a fundamental proposition of faith, namely, that the pre-Easter meaning of the Jesus event is only decipherable through the post-Easter anamnesis
(see 2:22; 12:16). Thus, even for the fourth evangelist, Easter appears as the
foundation of the kerygma. It is especially true for John that the meaning of
history is recognizable only at the end of history,[18] since from the very beginning the Gospel is written from the perspective of the end (see only 1:14, 29,
36). In the Gospel there occurs a dissolution of horizons, a shrinking of the
stages of time between the post-Easter perspective and situation of the
evangelist and the past of the Christ-event, which is mediated primarily
through tradition. "The encounter with the past and with the tradition is provoked by the questions of the present."[19]

But how does the evangelist solve the problem of the temporality of
historical realities as past? What makes possible the productive interpretation
of the past in relation to the problems of the present? The Paraclete remains
with the community forever (14:16-17), teaches it and reminds it of all that
Jesus said (14:26). The Paraclete witnesses to Jesus (15:26), shares all that is
received with the community, reveals the future, and glorifies Jesus (16:13-
14). The Paraclete takes from the fullness of Jesus' revelation and gives of that
fullness to the community (16:15). The Paraclete is thus the basis for the
Johannine ability to make present what is past and is also the Spirit-enabled
interpretation of the Christ-event.[20] The Paraclete is not an agent of tradition

---

[17] See Mussner, "Sehweise," 16.

[18] See Bultmann, *Geschichte und Eschatologie*, 135.

[19] Mussner, "Sehweise," 16. On the intercalation of time, see also Wilkens, *Zeichen und Werke*, 157.

[20] Windisch has demonstrated that it is probable that the Paraclete sayings, because of their
lack of reference to their context, were introduced secondarily by the evangelist (not by a later
redactor!) among other older materials, and were inserted into their present context ("Die fünf
johanneischen Parakletsprüche," 110–23). The thoroughly Johannine linguistic character of the
Paraclete sayings, as well (Mussner, "Die johanneischen Parakletsprüche," 57–58), permits the
conclusion that it was John who first formulated them as they presently stand, in order thereby
to legitimate his witness to Christ. For the various attempts to find possible religious-historical
antecedents for the idea of the Paraclete, see Schnackenburg, *John* 3:144–50.

In the context of the present book, we can give only a few indications of the literary-
critical and tradition-critical problems in John (14)15–17. In my opinion there are three possibilities that deserve serious consideration: (1) Unprepared changes of place and abrupt transitions are not unusual in the Gospel of John (see 2:12, 13; 4:3, 43; 5:1; 7:10; 10:40; 11:54ff.),
so that the transition from 14:31 to 18:1 is not a secure criterion for literary-critical decisions.
The "farewell discourses" in chaps. (14)15–17 could then be an original part of the Gospel of
John. The evangelist would have adopted a variety of traditions from his school; see especially
Schnackenburg, *John*, vol. 3, ad loc., and Onuki, "Die johanneischen Abschiedsreden und die
synoptische Tradition." Onuki works out a connected pre-Johannine written tradition behind
John 13–17 ([a] 13:21-22, 26-27, 31-32, 33; [b] 13:34; [c] 16:1, 32; 13:36-38; [d] 12:27-28;
14:30-31; 18:11b) that was then incorporated into the Gospel. (2) The evangelist subsequently
inserted chaps. 15–17 into his work. (3) The post-Johannine redaction expanded the Gospel of

in addition to Christ but is the Johannine form of the *Christus praesens*.[21] In the Paraclete, the glorified Christ continues to work within the Johannine school, whose members regard themselves as bearers of the Spirit (see 7:39; 20:21-23). A division between the Jesus who proclaimed and the Christ who is proclaimed is thus impossible in the Fourth Gospel. "Here the real principle of the Johannine form of the Gospel is apparent; a clear separation, between the 'historical' Christ and the Christ who reveals himself through the Spirit is no longer possible. The historical Christ is the pneumatic Christ and vice versa."[22] The Paraclete makes possible a legitimate reinterpretation of the work of Jesus, because the glorified Christ speaks through the Paraclete and thereby eliminates the distance between past and present. The close combination of the testimony that makes present what is past with the fiction of historical eyewitness is not a contradiction; through the Paraclete, the time horizons are dissolved into a unity. The material occasion for this dissolution of horizons—for the emphasis on the unity of the preexistent, present, and glorified Jesus Christ—is the Docetists' attempt to eliminate that unity in favor of a christology of glory. The Johannine form of the Gospel, on the other hand, emphatically protects the identity of the historical Jesus with the glorified Christ, by making no further distinction between the two.

This is expressed with particular clarity in the miracle stories, through the evangelist's introduction of the idea of *doxa* (2:11; 11:4, 40). As deeds of the historical Jesus, the miracles have revelatory character. In them, the one *doxa* of the Preexistent, Present, and Exalted One is visible. Jesus' concrete action is an epiphany of the Logos. At the same time, the greatness of the miracles witnesses to Jesus' divinity and humanity. In their extraordinary dimensions, these deeds divert all eyes to the miracle worker, who can only come from God. At the same time, their unmistakable reality reveals Jesus' humanity, for they occur in space and time and are accomplished on behalf of concrete persons. The miracles are an expression of the revelation's concern for the world, because their purpose is the alleviation of individual suffering.

As real works of the Revealer in the world, the Johannine miracle stories carry an antidocetic accent. It is scarcely accidental that Jesus' miracles are missing from gnostic writings![23] At the same time, the miracles preserve the visibility of the revelation, in that they guard against a radical reduction of christology to the level of soteriology in the sense of an individual decision

---

John by adding chaps. 15–17, which stemmed from the evangelist or from the Johannine school.

I think preference should be given to the first-mentioned possibility; the "Johannine" character of chaps. 14–17 cannot be seriously denied, and it is the task of a redaction-critical analysis of these chapters to trace the traditions that arose within the Johannine school, their relationship to the Synoptics, and the redactional activity of the evangelist.

21 See especially Schnackenburg, "Präsenz," 55ff.

22 Blank, *Krisis,* 331 n. 46.

23 See E. Schweizer, *Ego Eimi,* 140; Schottroff, *Der Glaubende,* 267–68.

for faith.[24] Precisely in the miracles it is not only the "that" but in equal measure the "what" of the revelation that is conveyed.[25] Through the tension-filled interaction of divinity and humanity, the miracles also speak of the nature and activity of the Revealer. The story of Jesus Christ is not to be reduced to the historicity of faith! When the Johannine kerygma summons to belief in the preexistent, crucified, and exalted Son of God, it at the same time develops the basis for such a faith.

The sacramental practice of the Johannine school witnesses emphatically to the identity of the historical Jesus of Nazareth with the glorified Christ. Baptism, as a constitutive ritual of initiation, is traced to Jesus' baptizing, and it is through this continuity that it is endowed with dignity (3:22, 25, 30; 4:1). As baptism ἐξ ὕδατος καὶ πνεύματος [from water and spirit], it effects a new creation of humanity, whose solid basis is the glorification of Jesus as precondition for the gift of the Spirit (7:39). The eucharistic celebration of the Johannine school is rooted in the death of Jesus (6:51c). As the locus of the saving presence of the Incarnate, Crucified, and Glorified One, only the Lord's Supper bestows on believers the gift of eternal life. In the realistic depiction of the sacramental event, and in the claim to exclusivity expressed in 6:53b, the antidocetic purpose of the Johannine conception of the Eucharist is fully evident.

It is precisely in the sacraments that the unity of the Johannine image of Christ is most evident; the sacraments are founded on the life and death of the historical Jesus of Nazareth, and at the same time, as something occurring in space and time, they preserve the saving gifts of the new creation and eternal life. Thus they are a visible expression of the real activity of God in history, which endures beyond Jesus' earthly life.

In the prologue, John gives an indication of his understanding of the Christ-event at the very beginning of his Gospel. As a programmatic introductory text, the prologue emphasizes, with an antidocetic accent, both the reality of the incarnation of the preexistent Logos and the community's vision of the one *doxa* of the Preexistent, Incarnate, and Glorified One. In exemplary fashion, 1:1-18 expresses the unity of the historical Jesus with the glorified Christ and thus predetermines the understanding of the whole Gospel. The Gospel will develop the history of that incarnate Logos, Jesus Christ, of whom the prologue has spoken.

Johannine theology of the cross should also be regarded as an attempt to preserve the identity of the earthly Jesus with the Exalted and Glorified One. The numerous references to the passion (see only 1:29, 36; 2:4, 14-22; 3:14; 7:1-12; 8:21; 11:16, 50-51; 12:24) in themselves make the Fourth Gospel

---

[24] Against Bultmann, "Christology of the New Testament," 281–82; idem, *John,* 35. For a critique of Bultmann, see Schnackenburg, "Das Johannesevangelium als hermeneutische Frage," 203ff.; Brown, "Kerygma," 392ff.

[25] Against Bultmann, *Theology* 2:66: "John, that is, in his Gospel presents only the fact (*das Daß*) of the Revelation without describing its content (*ihr Was*)."

appear to be a passion story "with an extended introduction."[26] The notion of Jesus' representative sacrificial death (10:11, 17; 11:51-52; 13:35; 15:13) was not merely adopted by the evangelist as a relic of tradition that is not precisely understood.[27] Instead, it is a consciously antidocetic form in which to express the saving importance of Jesus' death, because the idea of the mediation of salvation through the death of the Revealer was unacceptable to Docetists.[28] Moreover, the specific interest in the fact of Jesus' death (19:34b, 35) and in the verifiable correspondence of the Crucified with the Risen One (20:24-29) is, like the realism of the Johannine passion story as a whole, antidocetic in motivation. For John, the cross is not only a necessary stage on the route to glorification; it is a part of revelation. Finally, in the Johannine conception of the cross as exaltation and glorification (see 3:14; 8:28; 12:23, 32-34) the dissolution of temporal and material horizons in the Fourth Gospel becomes evident again. As the cross is drawn into the process of exaltation and glorification, the result is a concentration of the saving event, in which the individual aspects become transparent to one another and can no longer be temporally or materially distinguished. In this process, the cross is by no means devalued: instead, it is precisely here that the exalted and glorified Revealer is seen to be no other than the crucified Jesus of Nazareth.[29]

The Gospel of John constitutes the high point and conclusion of the literature that arose in the Johannine school and has been handed on to us. Although there are hints in 2 and 3 John, the oldest writings of the Johannine school, of the conflict with the docetic opponents (2 John 7), by the time of 1 John that quarrel is in full fury, and the Gospel of John represents an attempt to meet, in comprehensive fashion, the challenge of a docetic christology, while at the same time incorporating the specific traditions that had arisen in the context of the Johannine school. The unknown author of the Fourth Gospel has developed a christocentrically conceived and kerygmatically intended depiction of the saving event, rooted "in an earthly-human-historical event, in the earthly life and death of Jesus of Nazareth, both in its theological intention and in its content."[30] This history is not merely the

---

[26] Kähler, *Der sogenannte historische Jesus,* 60. Wilkens is also accurate in remarking (*Zeichen und Werke,* 151): "The first principal section of the Fourth Gospel is constitutively a Passion story." On the fundamental importance of theology of the cross for the Johannine form of the Gospel, see also Ibuki, "Offene Fragen," 118–27.

[27] Against Bultmann, *John,* 96–97, and elsewhere.

[28] See Fischer, "Der johanneische Christus," 262ff.

[29] In particular, 8:28 makes this connection clear, because the active interpretation of ὑψοῦν [lift up] points to Jesus' being delivered up to death on the cross by the Jews (see 19:11, 16).

[30] Hegermann, "Er kam in sein Eigentum," 127; see also Walter, who correctly emphasizes that "even after Easter, faith remains bound to him [sc. Jesus] as a person of this earth" ("Glaube und irdischer Jesus," 547). See also von der Osten-Sacken, "Leistung und Grenze," 163; Schnackenburg, "Präsenz," 51; Weder, "Menschwerdung Gottes," 352ff. Weder speaks of an incarnational christology in John.

necessary "scenery and window dressing"[31] of an action that really takes place outside of time, but is constitutive of salvation, to the extent that the historical Jesus of Nazareth and the historical datum of the cross also have salvific meaning in John's Gospel. The acknowledgment of Jesus Christ cannot be divorced from his history. Thus, Johannine christology, as an independent explication of the basis and content of the Christ-event, acquires an eminently hermeneutical function. While the Docetists empty Jesus' earthly life of its historicity, the evangelist opposes them with an image of Jesus' earthly activity, a picture that retains the individual features of the Revealer and at the same time is transparent toward its end. In his own way, John invites his community to a correct understanding of the Christ-event. It is precisely the union of earthly Jesus and exalted Christ that enables the evangelist to incorporate the manifold traditions of the Johannine school, some of which were also susceptible to a docetic interpretation. But he embeds these traditions in an antidocetic context. In doing so, he does not follow source documents, but instead he consciously takes up heterogeneous individual traditions of the Johannine school that serve his purpose. The historical and theological standpoint of the fourth evangelist is to be sought in the discussions and conflicts within the Johannine school, and not in a dialogue with contemporary Judaism or with gnostic groups. John did not compose his work as an apology against the Jews, the disciples of the Baptizer, or the Samaritans; nor did "gnostic teachings about salvation enter the canon"[32] through John's Gospel. Instead, the Fourth Gospel must be regarded, for many reasons, as the original product of the Johannine school: it was composed in reaction to a christological controversy within that school; its author was evidently a prominent theologian of that school; and the individual traditions it incorporates arose mainly within that school. The Gospel is directed both inward and outward!

There is still need for more detailed investigation of the position of the Johannine school, and particularly the fourth evangelist, within the history of early Christianity. The labeling of Johannine Christianity as a marginal group, which one so often reads, is probably not accurate, for sectarian flight from the world is far from the intention of the evangelist (see only 17:15, 18, 20; 20:21-22). Moreover, the high level of its theological reflection, as well as its connections to the Synoptics and especially to Pauline Christianity,[33] make the Fourth Gospel appear rather to be located at the center of the theological history of earliest Christianity, at a point where important currents in developing Christian theology converged.

---

[31] Käsemann, *Jesu letzter Wille,* 80.

[32] Schottroff, *Der Glaubende,* 295.

[33] The long-neglected relationship between Paul and John is apparently a renewed subject of interest in recent scholarship: see Schnackenburg, "Paulinische und johanneische Christologie"; Zeller, "Paulus und Johannes."

Bibliography

Primary sources, handbooks, encyclopedia articles, monographs, periodical articles, and commentaries are not listed individually, but are placed alphabetically under the names of the authors or editors. Abbreviations follow the format used in the *TRE* and *EWNT*. I also abbreviate as follows: GJ=Gospel of John; joh.=Johannine. In the notes, the literature is cited in abbreviated form using the author's name and a key word from the title.

Aland, Barbara. "Marcion." *ZThK* 70 (1973): 420–47.

Aland, Kurt. *Neutestamentliche Entwürfe.* TB 63. Munich, 1979. Includes: "Zur Vorgeschichte der christlichen Taufe," 183–97.
"Über die Bedeutung eines Punktes—Eine Untersuchung zu Joh 1,3.4," 351–91.

Appel, Heinrich. *Einleitung in das Neue Testament.* Leipzig, 1922.

Appold, Mark L. *The Oneness Motif in the Fourth Gospel.* WUNT, ser. 2, no. 1. Tübingen, 1976.

Ashton, John. "The Transformation of Wisdom." *NTS* 32 (1986): 161–86.

Aune, David E. "Orthodoxy in First Century Judaism." *JSJ* 7 (1976): 1–10.

Avi-Yonah, Michael. *Geschichte der Juden im Zeitalter des Talmud in den Tagen von Rom und Byzanz.* Berlin, 1962. Translated and adapted by the author under the title *The Jews under Roman and Byzantine Rule: A Political History of Palestine from the Bar Kokhba War to the Arab Conquest.* New York and Jerusalem [1984], ©1976.

Baldensperger, Guillaume. *Der Prolog des vierten Evangeliums.* Freiburg, 1898.

Balz, Horst R. "Die Johannesbriefe." In *Die "katholische" Briefe: Die Briefe des Jakobus, Petrus, Johannes und Judas.* Übersetzt und erklärt von Horst Balz und Wolfgang Schrage, 156–222. NTD 10. 2nd ed. Göttingen, 1980.

———. "κόσμος." *EWNT* 2:765–73.

Barrett, Charles Kingsley. "Zweck des 4. Evangeliums." *ZSTh* 22 (1953): 257–73.

———. *The Prologue of St. John's Gospel.* London, 1971.

———. *The Gospel according to St. John.* 2nd ed. Philadelphia, 1978.

———. "Jews and Judaizers in the Epistles of Ignatius." In his *Essays on John*, 133–58. Philadelphia, 1982.

Barth, Gerhard. *Die Taufe in frühchristlicher Zeit.* BThSt 4. Neukirchen, 1981.

Bauer, Walter. *Das Leben Jesu im Zeitalter der neutestamentlichen Apokryphen.* Tübingen, 1909. Reprint, Darmstadt, 1967.

———. *Die Briefe des Ignatius von Antiochia und der Polykarpbrief.* HNT Ergänzungs-Bd. 2. Tübingen, 1920.

———. *Das Johannesevangelium.* HNT 6. 3rd ed. Tübingen, 1933.

———. *Griechisch-deutsches Wörterbuch zu den Schriften des Neuen Testaments und der übrigen urchristlichen Literatur.* 5th ed. Berlin and New York, 1958; many editions. Translated and adapted from the 4th rev. and augmented ed. by William F. Arndt and F. Wilbur Gingrich as *A Greek-English Lexicon of the New Testament and Other Early Christian Literature.* Chicago, 1958. 2nd ed. revised and augmented by F. Wilbur Gingrich and Frederick W. Danker from Walter Bauer's 5th ed. Chicago, ©1979.

———. *Rechtgläubigkeit und Ketzerei im ältesten Christentum,* mit einem Nachtrag hg. v. G. Strecker. BHTh 10. 2nd ed. Tübingen, 1964. Translated by a team from the Philadelphia Seminar on Christian Origins, and edited by Robert A. Kraft and Gerhard Krodel, under the title *Orthodoxy and Heresy in Earliest Christianity.* Philadelphia, 1971.

Bauer, Walter, and H. Paulsen, eds. *Die Briefe des Ignatius von Antiochia und der Polykarpbrief.* HNT 18/2. Tübingen, 1985.

Baumbach, Günther. "Gemeinde und Welt im Johannesevangelium." *Kairos* 14 (1972): 121–36.

Baur, Ferdinand Christian. *Ueber die Composition und den Charakter des johanneischen Evangeliums I.* ThJb 3 (1844): 1–191.

———. *Kritische Untersuchungen über die kanonischen Evangelien, ihr Verhältnis zu einander, ihren Charakter und Ursprung.* Tübingen, 1847.

Becker, Johannes. "Wunder und Christologie." *NTS* 16 (1969–70): 130–48.

———. *Johannes der Täufer und Jesus von Nazareth.* BSt 63. Neukirchen, 1972.

———. "Joh 3,1-21 als Reflex johanneischer Schuldiskussion." In *Das Wort und die Wörter: Festschrift für G. Friedrich,* edited by Horst Balz and Siegfried Schulz, 85–95. Stuttgart, 1973.

———. *Das Evangelium nach Johannes.* 2 vols. ÖTK 4/1, 4/2. Gütersloh, 1979, 1981.

———. "Aus der Literatur zum Johannesevangelium." *ThR* 47 (1982): 279–301, 305–47.

———. "Ich bin die Auferstehung und das Leben." *ThZ* 39 (1983): 138–51.

Berger, Klaus. *Die Amen-Worte Jesu.* BZNW 39. Berlin, 1970.

——. *Exegese des Neuen Testaments.* Heidelberg, 1977.

——. "Die impliziten Gegner." In *Kirche: Festschrift für G. Bornkamm,* edited by Dieter Lührmann and Georg Strecker, 373–400. Tübingen, 1980.

Bergmeier, Roland. *Glaube als Gabe nach Johannes.* BWANT 112. Stuttgart, 1980.

Bernard, John Henry. *A Critical and Exegetical Commentary on the Gospel according to St. John.* ICC 29. 2 vols. Edinburgh, 1928; new ed. 1953.

Betz, Hans Dieter. "Gottmensch II." *RAC* 12:234–312.

Betz, Otto. "Das Problem des Wunders bei Flavius Josephus im Vergleich zum Wunderproblem bei den Rabbinen und im Johannesevangelium." In *Josephus-Studien: Festschrift für O. Michel,* edited by Otto Betz, Klaus Haacker, and Martin Hengel, 23–44. Göttingen, 1974.

——. "σημεῖον." *EWNT* 3:569–75.

Betz, Otto, and Werner Grimm. *Wesen und Wirklichkeit der Wunder Jesu.* ANTI 2. Frankfurt, 1977.

Bieler, Ludwig. Θεῖος ἀνήρ. 1935–36. Reprint, Darmstadt, 1976.

Billerbeck, Paul. *Kommentar zum Neuen Testament aus Talmud und Midrasch.* 6 vols. 3rd ed. Munich, 1961–63.

Blank, Josef. *Krisis: Untersuchungen zur Johanneischen Christologie und Eschatologie.* Freiburg, 1964.

——. "Die johanneische Brotrede." *BiLe* 7 (1966): 193–207.

——. *Das Evangelium nach Johannes.* Geistliche Schriftlesung 4/1a. Düsseldorf, 1981.

——. "Die Irrlehrer des ersten Johannesbriefes." *Kairos* 26 (1984): 166–93.

Blass, Friedrich, and Albert Debrunner. *Grammatik des neutestamentlichen Griechisch,* bearbeitet von Friedrich Rehkopf. 15th ed. Göttingen, 1979. See also Robert W. Funk. *A Greek Grammar of the New Testament and Other Early Christian Literature [by] F. Blass and A. Debrunner.* A translation and revision of the 9th-10th German ed., incorporating supplementary notes of A. Debrunner. Chicago, 1961.

Bleek, Friedrich. *Einleitung in das Neue Testament.* 2nd ed. Berlin, 1865–66. Translated from the German of the 2nd ed. by William Urwick under the title *An Introduction to the New Testament.* Edited by Johannes Friedrich Bleek. Edinburgh, 1873.

Blinzler, Josef. *Johannes und die Synoptiker.* SBS 5. Stuttgart, 1965.

Bogart, John. *Orthodox and Heretical Perfectionism in the Johannine Community as Evident in the First Epistle of John.* SBL DS 33. Missoula, 1977.

Boismard, Marie Émile, and A. Lamouille. *Synopse des Quatre Évangiles en Français 3: L'Évangile de Jean.* Paris, 1977.

Borgen, Peder. "Der Logos war das wahre Licht." In *Theologie aus dem Norden.* SNTU A/2, 99–117. Linz, 1976. For an English translation, see his *Logos was the True Light, and other Essays on the Gospel of John.* Trondheim, 1983.

————. *Bread from Heaven*. Nt.S 10. 1965. 2nd ed. Leiden, 1981.

Bornkamm, Günther. *Geschichte und Glaube* 1. (*Gesammelte Aufsätze* 3). BEvTh 48. Munich, 1968. Includes:
"Die Eucharistische Rede im Johannes-Evangelium," 60–67.
"Der Paraklet im Johannes-Evangelium," 68–89.
"Zur Interpretation des Johannes-Evangeliums," 104–21.

————. *Geschichte und Glaube* 2 (*Gesammelte Aufsätze* 4). BEvTh 53. Munich, 1971. Includes:
"Vorjohanneische Tradition oder nachjohanneische Bearbeitung in der eucharistischen Rede Johannes 6?" 51–64.
"Die Heilung des Blindgeborenen," 65–72.

————. "πρέσβυς." *TDNT* 6: 651–83.

Bousset, Wilhelm. *Jüdisch-christlicher Schulbetrieb in Alexandria und Rom.* FRLANT 6. Göttingen, 1915.

————. *Kyrios Christos. Geschichte des Christusglaubens von den Anfängen des Christentums bis Irenaeus.* FRLANT 21. 6th ed. Göttingen, 1967. Translated by John E. Steely under the title *Kyrios Christos: A History of the Belief in Christ from the Beginnings of Christianity to Irenaeus.* Nashville, 1970.

————. *Die Offenbarung Johannis.* KEK 16. 6th ed. Göttingen, 1906.

Brandenburger, Egon. *Fleisch und Geist: Paulus und die dualistische Weisheit.* WMANT 29. Neukirchen, 1968.

Broer, Ingo. "Noch einmal: Zur religionsgeschichtlichen 'Ableitung' von Joh 2,1-11." SNTU A/8, 103–23. Linz, 1983.

Brooke, Alan England. *A Critical and Exegetical Commentary on the Johannine Epistles.* ICC 43. New York, 1912. Reprint Edinburgh, 1948.

Brooks, Oscar S. "The Johannine Eucharist," *JBL* 82 (1963): 293–300.

Brown, Raymond E. "The Kerygma of the Gospel according to John." *Interpretation* 21 (1967): 387–400.

————. *The Gospel according to John.* 2 vols. AncB 29, 29A. Garden City, New York, 1966, 1970.

————. *The Community of the Beloved Disciple.* New York and London, 1979.

————. *Ringen um die Gemeinde.* Salzburg, 1982.

————. *The Epistles of John.* AncB 30. Garden City, New York, 1982.

Brown, Raymond E., Karl P. Donfried, and John Reumann, eds. *Peter in the New Testament: A Collaborative Assessment by Protestant and Roman Catholic Scholars.* New York, Toronto, and Minneapolis, 1973. [German: *Der Petrus der Bibel,* Stuttgart, 1976.]

Brox, Norbert. "'Doketismus'—eine Problemanzeige." *ZKG* 95 (1984): 301–14.

Büchsel, Friedrich. *Die Johannesbriefe.* ThHK 17. Leipzig, 1933.

Bühner, Jan-Adolf. *Der Gesandte und sein Weg im 4. Evangelium.* WUNT, ser. 2, no. 2. Tübingen, 1977.

——. "Denkstrukturen im Johannesevangelium." *ThBeitr.* 13 (1982): 224–31.

Bultmann, Rudolf. *Exegetica: Aufsätze zur Erforschung des Neuen Testaments.* Edited by Erich Dinkler. Tübingen, 1967. Includes: "Der religionsgeschichtliche Hintergrund des Prologs zum Johannes-Evangelium," 10–35.
"Die Bedeutung der neuerschlossenen mandäischen und manichäischen Quellen für das Verständnis des Johannesevangeliums," 55–104.

——. "Das Johannesevangelium in der neuesten Forschung." *ChrW* 41 (1927): 502–11.

——. "Hirschs Auslegung des Johannes-Evangeliums," *EvTh* 4 (1937): 115–42.

——. "Die Christologie des Neuen Testaments." In his *Glauben und Verstehen: Gesammelte Aufsätze* 1, 245–67. 8th ed. Tübingen, 1980. Translated by Louise Pettibone Smith under the title *Faith and Understanding* 1, edited with an introduction by Robert W. Funk. New York, 1969.

——. *Das Evangelium des Johannes.* KEK 2. 19th ed. Göttingen, 1968 (Ergänzungsheft 1968). Translated from the 1964 edition with the supplement of 1966 by G. R. Beasley-Murray, general editor, R. W. N. Hoare, and J. K. Riches, under the title *The Gospel of John: A Commentary.* Philadelphia, 3rd printing 1976.

——. *Die drei Johannesbriefe.* KEK XIV. 2nd ed. Göttingen, 1969. Translated from the 2nd German edition by R. Philip O'Hara with Lane C. McGaughy and Robert W. Funk and edited by Robert W. Funk under the title *The Johannine Epistles.* Hermeneia. Philadelphia, 1973.

——. *Die Geschichte der synoptischen Tradition.* FRLANT 29. 8th ed. Göttingen, 1970. Translated by John Marsh under the title *History of the Synoptic Tradition.* New York, ©1963.

——. *Theologie des Neuen Testaments.* Edited by Otto Merk. 7th ed. Tübingen, 1977. Translated by Kendrick Grobel under the title *Theology of the New Testament.* 2 vols. New York, 1951, 1955.

——. *Geschichte und Eschatologie.* 3rd ed. Tübingen, 1979. German translation by Eva Krafft of *History and Eschatology.* Gifford Lectures, 1955. Edinburgh, 1957; New York, 1962.

Burchard, Christoph. "εἰ nach einem Ausdruck des Wissens oder Nichtwissens." ZNW 52 (1961): 73–82.

——. *Untersuchungen zu Joseph und Aseneth.* WUNT 8. Tübingen, 1965.

——. *Joseph und Aseneth.* JSHRZ 2/4. Gütersloh, 1983.

Busse, Ulrich. *Die Wunder des Propheten Jesus: Die Rezeption, Komposition und Interpretation der Wundertradition im Evangelium des Lukas.* FzB 24. Stuttgart and Würzburg, 1977.

Carson, D. A. "Current Source Criticism of the Fourth Gospel: Some Methodological Questions." *JBL* 97 (1978): 411–29.

——. "Understanding Misunderstanding in the Fourth Gospel." *TynB* 33 (1982): 59–91.

Cassem, N. H. "A Grammatical and Contextual Inventory of the Use of κόσμος in the Johannine Corpus with some Implications for a Johannine Cosmic Theology." *NTS* 19 (1972–73): 81–91.

Charlesworth, J. H. "A Prolegomenon to a New Study of the Jewish Background of the Hymns and Prayers in the New Testament." *JJS* 33 (1982): 265–85.

Clark, Douglas K. "Signs in Wisdom and John." *CBQ* 45 (1983): 201–9.

Clemen, Carl C. *Religionsgeschichtliche Erklärung des Neuen Testaments.* 1st ed. 1909. 2nd rev. ed. 1924. Berlin, 1973.

Colpe, Carsten, "υἱὸς τοῦ ἀνθρώπου." *TDNT* 8:401–77.

Colwell, Ernest C. *The Greek of the Fourth Gospel.* Chicago, 1931.

Conzelmann, Hans. *Die Mitte der Zeit.* BHTh 17. 6th ed. Tübingen, 1977. Translated by Geoffrey Buswell under the title *The Theology of St. Luke.* Philadelphia, 1982.

——. *Grundriß der Theologie des Neuen Testaments.* 2nd ed. Munich, 1968. Translated into English as *An Outline of the Theology of the New Testament.* New York, 1969.

——. "φῶς." *TDNT* 9: 310–58.

——. *Theologie als Schriftauslegung: Aufsätze zum Neuen Testament.* BEvTh 65. Munich, 1974. Includes: "Paulus und die Weisheit," 177–90. "'Was von Anfang war,'" 207–14.

——. "Die Schule des Paulus." In *Theologia Crucis, Signum Crucis: Festschrift für Erich Dinkler,* edited by Carl Andresen and Günter Klein, 85–96. Tübingen, 1979.

——. *Heiden—Juden—Christen.* BHTh 62. Tübingen, 1981.

Corsani, Bruno. *I miracoli di Gesù nel quarto vangelo.* Studi Biblici 65. Brescia, ©1983.

Coseriu, E. *Synchronie, Diachronie und Geschichte.* Internationale Bibliothek für allgemeine Linguistik 3. Munich, 1974.

Cullmann, Oscar. *Urchristentum und Gottesdienst.* AThANT 3. 4th ed. Zurich, 1962. Translated by A. Stewart Todd and James B. Torrance under the title *Early Christian Worship.* London and Chicago, 1953.

——. "Der johanneische Gebrauch doppeldeutiger Ausdrücke als Schlüssel zum Verständnis des vierten Evangeliums." In his *Vorträge und Aufsätze, 1925–1962,* edited by Karlfried Fröhlich, 176–86. Tübingen and Zurich, 1966.

——. *Die Christologie des Neuen Testaments.* 5th ed. Tübingen, 1975. Translated by Shirley C. Guthrie and Charles A. M. Hall under the title *The Christology of the New Testament.* 1959. Rev. ed. Philadelphia, 1963.

——. *Der johanneische Kreis*. Tübingen, 1975. Translated by John Bowden under the title *The Johannine Circle*. London and Philadelphia, 1976.

Culpepper, R. Alan. *The Johannine School*. SBL DS 26. Missoula, 1975.

——. "The Pivot of John's Prologue." *NTS* 27 (1981): 1–31.

——. *The Anatomy of the Fourth Gospel*. Philadelphia, 1983.

Dalman, Gustaf H. *Orte und Wege Jesu*. BFChTh, 2nd ser., no. 1. 2nd ed. Gütersloh, 1921. Translated by Paul P. Levertoff, D.D., under the title *Sacred Sites and Ways: Studies in the Topography of the Gospels*. New York, 1935.

Dauer, Anton. *Die Passionsgeschichte im Johannesevangelium*. StANT 30. Munich, 1972.

——. "Zur Herkunft der Thomas-Perikope Joh 20, 24-29." In *Biblische Randbemerkungen: Festschrift für R. Schnackenburg*, edited by Helmut Merklein and Joachim Lange, 56–76. 2nd ed. Würzburg, 1974.

——. *Johannes und Lukas*. FzB 50. Würzburg, 1984.

Deichgräber, Reinhard. *Gotteshymnus und Christushymnus in der frühen Christenheit*. SUNT 5. Göttingen, 1967.

Deissmann, Gustav Adolf. *Licht vom Osten: Das Neue Testament und die neuentdeckten Texte der hellenistisch-römischen Welt*. 4th ed. Tübingen, 1923. Translated by Lionel R. M. Strachan under the title *Light from the Ancient East*. New York, 1927.

de Jonge, Marinus. "Signs and Works in the Fourth Gospel." In *Miscellanea Neotestamentica*, edited by T. Baarda, A. F. J. Klijn, and W. C. van Unnik, 2:107–25. Nt.S 47–48. 2 vols. Leiden, 1978.

——. "The Beloved Disciple and the Date of the Gospel of John." In *Text and Interpretation: Festschrift for Matthew Black*, edited by Ernest Best and Robert McL. Wilson, 99–114. Cambridge, 1979.

Dekker, Cornelis. "Grundschrift und Redaktion im Johannesevangelium." *NTS* 13 (1966–67): 66–80.

de la Potterie, Ignace de. "'Naître de l'aut et naître de l'Esprit.'" *ScEc* 14 (1962): 417–43.

——. "Structure du Prologue de Saint Jean." *NTS* 30 (1984): 354–81.

Delling, Gerhard. "Wunder—Allegorie—Mythus bei Philon von Alexandreia." In his *Studien zum Neuen Testament und zum hellenistischen Judentum: Gesammelte Aufsätze 1950–1968*, 72–129. Berlin, 1970.

Demke, Christoph. "Der sogenannte Logos-Hymnus im johanneischen Prolog." *ZNW* 58 (1967): 45–68.

Denker, Jürgen. *Die theologiegeschichtliche Stellung des Petrusevangeliums: Ein Beitrag zur Frühgeschichte des Doketismus*. EHS, ser. 23: Theologie, vol. 36. Frankfurt, 1975.

Dibelius, Martin. "Johannesbriefe." *RGG²* 3:346–49.

——. "Joh 15,13." In *Festgabe für A. Deissmann*, 168–86. Tübingen, 1927.

——. "Zur Formgeschichte der Evangelien." *ThR* n.s. 1 (1929): 185–216.

———. "Ein neuer Kommentar zum Johannes-Evangelium." *ThLZ* 67 (1942): 258–64.

———. "Die alttestamentlichen Motive in der Leidensgeschichte des Petrus- und des Johannes-Evangeliums." In his *Botschaft und Geschichte: Gesammelte Aufsätze* 1, 221–47. Tübingen, 1953.

———. *Die Formgeschichte des Evangeliums.* 6th ed. Tübingen, 1971. Translated from the rev. 2nd ed. by Bertram Lee Woolf, in collaboration with the author, under the title *From Tradition to Gospel.* 1935. New York, 1965.

Dinkler, Erich. "Die Taufaussagen des Neuen Testaments." In *Zu Karl Barths Lehre von der Taufe,* edited by Fritz Viering, 60–153. 2nd ed. Gütersloh, 1972.

Dodd, Charles Harold. *The Johannine Epistles.* 2nd ed. London, 1947.

———. *The Interpretation of the Fourth Gospel.* 1953. Cambridge, 1978.

———. *Historical Tradition in the Fourth Gospel.* 1963. Cambridge, 1979.

Dunn, James D. G. "Joh VI—an eucharistic discourse?" *NTS* 17 (1970–71): 328–38.

———. "Let John be John." In *Das Evangelium und die Evangelien,* edited by Peter Stuhlmacher, 309–39. Tübingen, 1983. Published in English as *The Gospel and the Gospels.* Grand Rapids, Michigan, ©1990.

Eltester, Walther. "Der Logos und sein Prophet." In *Apophoreta: Festschrift für E. Haenchen,* 109–34. BZNW 30. Berlin, 1964.

Epiphanius. *Panarion.* Edited by K. Holl. GCS 25, 31, 37. Leipzig, 1915, 1922, 1933.

Esser, Dietrich. "Formgeschichtliche Studien zur hellenistischen und frühchristlichen Literatur unter besonderer Berücksichtigung der vita Apollonii des Philostrat und der Evangelien." Diss. theol. Bonn, 1969.

Fascher, Erich. Προφήτης: *Eine sprach- und religionsgeschichtliche Untersuchung.* Giessen, 1927.

Faure, Alexander. "Die alttestamentlichen Zitate im 4. Evangelium und die Quellenscheidungshypothese." *ZNW* 21 (1922): 99–121.

Fischer, Joseph Anton. *Die Apostolischen Väter.* SUC 1. 7th ed. Darmstadt, 1976.

Fischer, Karl Martin. "Der johanneische Christus und der gnostische Erlöser." In *Gnosis und Neues Testament,* edited by Karl-Wolfgang Tröger, 245–66. Gütersloh, 1973.

———. *Tendenz und Absicht des Epheserbriefes.* FRLANT 111. Göttingen, 1973.

———. *Das Urchristentum.* Berlin, 1985.

Flusser, David. "Das Schisma zwischen Judentum und Christentum." *EvTh* 40 (1980): 214–39.

Fortna, Robert T. *The Gospel of Signs.* MSSNTS 11. Cambridge, 1970.

———. "Source and Redaction in the Fourth Gospel's Portrayal of Jesus' Signs." *JBL* 89 (1970): 151–66.

——. "Christology in the Fourth Gospel: Redaction-Critical Perspectives." *NTS* 21 (1975): 489–504.

Freed, Edwin D. "Theological Prelude to the Prologue of John's Gospel." *SJTh* 32 (1979): 257–69.

Freed, Edwin D., and Russell B. Hunt. "Fortna's Signs-Source in John." *JBL* 94 (1975): 563–79.

Friedländer, Moriz. *Die religiösen Bewegungen innerhalb des Judentums im Zeitalter Jesu*. Berlin, 1905.

Fuller, Reginald H. "The 'Jews' in the Fourth Gospel." *Dialog* 16 (1977): 31–37.

——. *Interpreting the Miracles*. Philadelphia and London, 1963.

Gadamer, Hans Georg. *Wahrheit und Methode*. 4th ed. Tübingen, 1975. Translated by Joel Weinsheimer and Donald Marshall under the title *Truth and Method*. New York, ©1975; rev. 3rd ed. 1988.

Gärtner, Bertil. *John 6 and the Jewish Passover*. CNT 17. Lund, 1959.

Gese, Hartmut. "Der Johannesprolog." In his *Zur biblischen Theologie*, 152–201. BEvTh 78. Munich, 1977.

Gnilka, Joachim. "Zur Christologie des Johannesevangeliums." In *Christologische Schwerpunkte*, edited by Walter Kasper, 92–107. Düsseldorf, 1980.

——. *Das Evangelium nach Markus* 1. EKK 2/1. Neukirchen, 1978.

——. *Das Johannesevangelium*. Die neue Echter Bibel 4. Würzburg, 1983.

Goodspeed, Edgar J., ed. *Die ältesten Apologeten*. 1914. Göttingen, 1984.

Grässer, Erich J. "Die antijüdische Polemik im Johannesevangelium." *NTS* 11 (1964–65): 74–90.

Grillmeier, Alois. *Jesus der Christus im Glauben der Kirche* 1. 2nd ed. Freiburg, 1982. Translated by John Bowden under the title *Christ in Christian Tradition, from the Apostolic Age to Chalcedon (451)*. New York, 1965. 2nd rev. ed. Atlanta, 1975.

Grundmann, Walter. "Verständnis und Bewegung des Glaubens im Johannesevangelium." *KuD* 6 (1960): 131–54.

——. *Zeugnis und Gestalt des Johannes-Evangeliums*. AzTh 7. Stuttgart, 1961.

——. *Das Evangelium nach Markus*. ThHK 2. 8th ed. Berlin, 1980.

——. *Der Zeuge der Wahrheit*. Berlin, 1985.

Gutbrod, Walter. "νόμος." *TDNT* 4: 1022–91.

Haacker, Klaus. *Die Stiftung des Heils*. AzTh, ser. 1, no. 47. Stuttgart, 1972.

Haenchen, Ernst. "Aus der Literatur zum Johannesevangelium." *ThR* 23 (1955): 295–335.

——. *Der Weg Jesu*. Berlin, 2nd rev. ed. Berlin, 1968.

——. *Gott und Mensch: Gesammelte Aufsätze* 1. Tübingen, 1965. Includes: "'Der Vater, der mich gesandt hat,'" 68–77.

"Johanneische Probleme," 78–113.

"Probleme des johanneischen 'Prologs,'" 114–43.

——. *Die Bibel und wir: Gesammelte Aufsätze* 2. Tübingen, 1968. Includes: "Das Johannesevangelium und sein Kommentar," 208–34. "Neuere Literatur zu den Johannesbriefen," 235–311.

——. "Historie und Geschichte in den johanneischen Passionsberichten." In Hans Conzelmann, et al. *Zur Bedeutung des Todes Jesu: Exegetische Beiträge,* 55–78. 3rd ed. Gütersloh, 1968.

——. "Vom Wandel des Jesusbildes in der frühen Gemeinde." In *Verborum Veritas: Festschrift für G. Stählin,* edited by Otto Böcher and Klaus Haacker, 3–14. Wuppertal, 1970.

——. *Das Johannesevangelium.* Tübingen, 1980. Translated by Robert W. Funk, and edited by Robert W. Funk with Ulrich Busse, under the title *John: A Commentary on the Gospel of John.* 2 vols. Hermeneia. Philadelphia, 1984.

Hahn, Ferdinand. *Christologische Hoheitstitel.* FRLANT 83. 4th ed. Göttingen, 1974.

——. "Der Prozeß Jesu nach dem Johannesevangelium." *EKK* 5/2, 23–96. Zurich, 1970.

——. "Sehen und Glauben im Johannesevangelium." In *Neues Testament und Geschichte: Festschrift für O. Cullmann,* edited by H. Baltensweiler and B. Reicke, 125–41. Zurich and Tübingen, 1972.

——. "Die Jüngerberufung Joh 1,35-51." In *Neues Testament und Kirche: Festschrift für R. Schnackenburg,* edited by Joachim Gnilka, 172–90. Freiburg, 1974.

——. "'Die Juden' im Johannesevangelium." In *Kontinuität und Einheit: Festschrift für F. Mussner,* edited by Paul-Gerhard Müller and Werner Stenger, 430–38. Freiburg, 1981.

——. "υἱός." *EWNT* 3:912–37.

——. "Das Glaubensverständnis im Johannesevangelium." In *Glaube und Eschatologie: Festschrift für W. G. Kümmel,* edited by Erich Grässer and Otto Merk, 51–69. Tübingen, 1985.

Hamerton-Kelly, Robert. *Pre-Existence, Wisdom, and the Son of Man.* MSSNTS 21. Cambridge, 1973.

Hare, Douglas R. A. *The Theme of Jewish Persecution of Christians in the Gospel according to St Matthew.* MSSNTS 6. Cambridge, 1967.

Harnack, Adolf v. "Über das Verhältnis des Prologs des vierten Evangeliums zum ganzen Werk." *ZThK* 2 (1892): 189–231.

——. "Das 'Wir' in den Johanneischen Schriften." In his *Kleine Schriften zur Alten Kirche.* Opuscula 9/2, 626–43. 1923. Leipzig, 1980.

——. *Lehrbuch der Dogmengeschichte* 1. 5th ed. Tübingen, 1931. Translated by Neil Buchanan from the 3rd German ed., under the title *History of Dogma* 1. New York, 1958.

——. *Marcion: Das Evangelium vom fremden Gott.* 2nd ed. Berlin, 1924. Reprint Darmstadt, 1960. Translated by John E. Steely and Lyle D. Bierma under the title *Marcion: The Gospel of the Alien God*. Durham, North Carolina, 1990.

Hartke, Wilhelm. *Vier urchristliche Parteien und ihre Vereinigung zur Apostolischen Kirche* 1. Berlin, 1961.

Hartmann, Gert. "Die Vorlage der Osterberichte in Joh 20." *ZNW 55* (1964): 197–220.

Hauschild, Wolf-Dieter. "Christologie und Humanismus bei dem 'Gnostiker' Basilides." *ZNW* 68 (1977): 67–92.

Heekerens, Hans-Peter. "Die Zeichen-Quelle der johanneischen Redaktion: Ein Beitrag zur Entstehungsgeschichte des vierten Evangeliums." Diss. theol., Heidelberg, 1978.

———. *Die Zeichen-Quelle der johanneischen Redaktion*. SBS 113. Stuttgart, 1984.

Hegermann, H. "δόξα." *EWNT* 1:832–41.

———. "Er kam in sein Eigentum." In *Der Ruf Jesu und die Antwort der Gemeinde: Festschrift für J. Jeremias*, edited by Eduard Lohse, Christoph Burchard, and Berndt Schaller, 112–31. Göttingen, 1970.

Heil, John Paul. *Jesus Walking on the Sea*. AB 87. Rome, 1981.

Heiligenthal, Roman. *Werke als Zeichen*. WUNT 2/9. Tübingen, 1983.

Heising, Johannes Alkuin. *Die Botschaft der Brotvermehrung*. SBS 15. Stuttgart, 1966.

Heitmüller, Wilhelm. *Das Johannes-Evangelium*. SNT 4, 9–184. 3rd ed. Göttingen, 1920.

———. "Zur Johannes-Tradition." *ZNW* 15 (1914): 189–209.

Hennecke, Edgar, and Wilhelm Schneemelcher. *Neutestamentliche Apokryphen*. Tübingen, vol. 1, 4th ed. 1968; vol. 2, 4th ed. 1971. Translated by A. J. B. Higgins and others, and edited by Robert McL. Wilson, under the title *New Testament Apocrypha*. 2 vols. Philadelphia, 1963–66.

Hilgenfeld, Adolf. *Einleitung in das Neue Testament*. Leipzig, 1875.

Hippolytus. *Refutatio omnium haeresium*. Edited by P. Wendland. GCS 26. Leipzig, 1916.

Hirsch, Emanuel. *Das vierte Evangelium in seiner ursprünglichen Gestalt, verdeutscht und erklärt*. Tübingen, 1936.

———. *Studien zum vierten Evangelium*. BHTh 11. Tübingen, 1936.

———. *Die Auferstehungsgeschichten und der christliche Glaube*. Tübingen, 1940.

Hoeferkamp, Robert T. *The relationship between sēmeia and Believing in the Fourth Gospel*. Diss. theol., St. Louis and Ann Arbor, 1978.

Hoennicke, Gustav. *Das Judenchristentum im ersten und zweiten Jahrhundert*. Berlin, 1908.

Hofbeck, S. *Semeion*. Münsterschwarzach, 1966.

Hoffmann, Paul. "Auferstehung," II/1. *TRE* 4:478–513.

Hofrichter, Peter. *Nicht aus Blut, sondern monogen aus Gott geboren: Text-*

kritische, dogmengeschichtliche und exegetische Untersuchung zu Joh 1,13–14. FzB 31. Würzburg, 1978.

——. "'Egeneto anthropos.' Text und Zusätze im Johannesprolog." *ZNW* 70 (1979): 214–37.

——. *Im Anfang war der "Johannesprolog."* BU 17. Regensburg, 1986.

Holtzmann, Heinrich Julius. "Das Problem des ersten johanneischen Briefes in seinem Verhältnis zum Evangelium." I: *JPTh* 7 (1881): 690–707. II: *JPTh* 8 (1882): 128–43.

——. *Johannes.* 2: "Briefe und Offenbarung des Johannes," 233–74. HC 4. 2nd ed. Freiburg, 1893.

——. *Lehrbuch der Neutestamentlichen Theologie* II. 2nd ed. Tübingen, 1911.

Holtzmann, Oskar. *Das Johannesevangelium untersucht und erklärt.* Darmstadt, 1887.

Horbury, W. "The Benediction of the Minim and early Jewish-Christian Controversy." *JThS* 33 (1982): 19–61.

Horn, Friedrich W. *Glaube und Handeln in der Theologie des Lukas.* GTA 26. 2nd ed. Göttingen, 1986.

Hoskyns, Edwyn C. *The Fourth Gospel.* Edited by Francis N. Davey. 2nd rev. ed. London, 1947.

Houlden, James L. *A Commentary on the Johannine Epistles.* HNTC. New York, 1973.

Howard, Wilbert F. *The Fourth Gospel in Recent Criticism and Interpretation.* Revised by C. K. Barrett. 4th ed. London, 1955.

Hübner, Hans. "νόμος." *EWNT* 2:1158–72.

Huck, Albert, and Heinrich Greeven. *Synopse der drei ersten Evangelien.* Tübingen, 1981.

Huther, Johann Eduard. *Kritisch exegetisches Handbuch über die drei Briefe des Apostel Johannes.* KEK 14. 4th rev. ed. Göttingen, 1880.

Ibuki, Yu. "Lobhymnus und Fleischwerdung." *AJBI* 3 (1977): 132–56.

——. "Gedankenaufbau und Hintergrund des 3. Kapitels des Johannesevangeliums." *Bulletin of Sekei University* 14 (1978): 9–33.

——. "Offene Fragen zur Aufnahme des Logoshymnus in das vierte Evangelium." *AJBI* 5 (1979): 105–32.

Irenaeus. *Libros quinque adversus haereses.* Edited by W. W. Harvey. 2 vols. Cambridge, 1857.

Jacoby, Adolf. "Zur Heilung des Blinden von Bethsaida." *ZNW* 10 (1909): 185–94.

Jendorff, Bernhard. *Der Logosbegriff.* EHS ser. 20, vol. 19. Frankfurt, 1976.

Jeremias, Joachim. *Jesus als Weltvollender.* BFChTh 33. Gütersloh, 1930.

——. "Johanneische Literarkritik." *ThBl* 20 (1941): 33–46.

——. Review of R. Bultmann, *Das Johannesevangelium. DLZ* 64 (1943): 414–20.

——. *Die Wiederentdeckung von Bethesda, Johannes 5,2*. FRLANT 59. Göttingen, 1949. Translated, with major revisions, under the title *The Rediscovery of Bethesda, John 5:2*. Louisville, 1966.

——. *Die Abendmahlsworte Jesu*. 4th ed. Göttingen, 1967. Translated by Norman Perrin under the title *The Eucharistic Words of Jesus*. 3rd ed. New York, 1966.

——. "Joh 6,51c-58 — redaktionell?" *ZNW* 44 (1952–53): 256f.

——. "Μωυσης." *TDNT* 4:848–73.

——. *Die Kindertaufe in den ersten vier Jahrhunderten*. Göttingen, 1958. Translated into English by David Cairns under the title *Infant Baptism in the First Four Centuries*. London, 1960.

——. *Der Prolog des Johannesevangeliums (Johannes 1,1–18)*. Calwer H 88. Stuttgart, 1967.

——. "Zum Logos-Problem." *ZNW* 59 (1968): 82–85.

——. *Neutestamentliche Theologie*. 3rd ed. Gütersloh, 1979. Translated by John Bowden under the title *New Testament Theology*. Vol. 1. London, 1971.

Jörns, Klaus-Peter. *Das hymnische Evangelium*. StNT 5. Gütersloh, 1971.

Jülicher, Adolf. *Einleitung in das Neue Testament*. 3rd and 4th eds. Tübingen, 1901.

Jülicher, Adolf, and Erich Fascher. *Einleitung in das Neue Testament*. 7th ed. Tübingen, 1931.

Junod, Eric, and Jean-Daniel Kaestli. *Acta Iohannis*. CChr SA 1, 2. Turnhout, 1983.

Kähler, M. *Der sogenannte historische Jesus und der geschichtliche, biblische Christus*. TB 2. 1892. Munich, 1953.

Käsemann, Ernst. Review of R. Bultmann, *Das Johannesevangelium*. VF 2 (1942–1946): 182–202.

——. "Ketzer und Zeuge." In his *Exegetische Versuche und Besinnungen 1*, 168–87. 6th ed. Göttingen, 1970.

——. *Exegetische Versuche und Besinnungen 2*. 3rd ed. Göttingen, 1970. Translated into English under the title *New Testament Questions of Today*. Philadelphia, 1969. Includes:
"Neutestamentliche Fragen von heute," 11–31 (English 1–22).
"Aufbau und Anliegen des johanneischen Prologs," 155–80 (English 138–67).

——. *Jesu letzter Wille nach Johannes 17*. 4th rev. ed. Tübingen, 1980. Translated into English by Gerhard Krodel under the title *The Testament of Jesus*. Philadelphia, 1968.

Katz, Steven T. "Issues in the Separation of Judaism and Christianity after 70 C.E.: A Reconsideration." *JBL* 103 (1984): 43–76.

Kautzsch, Emil F., ed. *Die Apokryphen und Pseudepigraphen des Alten Testaments*, Vols. 1 and 2. 1900. Darmstadt, 1975.

Kelber, Wilhelm. *Die Logoslehre: Von Heraklit bis Origenes.* Stuttgart, 1958.

Kertelge, Karl. *Die Wunder Jesu im Markusevangelium.* StANT 23. Munich, 1970.

Kimelman, Ronald R. "'Birkat Ha-Minim' and the Lack of Evidence for an Anti-Christian Jewish Prayer in Late Antiquity." In *Jewish and Christian Self-Definition* 2:226–44. 3 vols. to date. Vol. 2, edited by E. P. Sanders, A. J. Baumgarten, and Alan Mendelson. London, 1981.

Kippenberg, Hans G. *Garizim und Synagoge.* RVV 30. Berlin, 1971.

Kittel, Gerhard. "λέγω." *TDNT* 4:69–143.

Klaiber, Walter. "Die Aufgabe einer theologischen Interpretation des 4. Evangeliums." *ZThK* 82 (1985): 300–324.

Klauck, Hans-Josef. *Herrenmahl und hellenistischer Kult.* NTA 15. Münster, 1982.

Klausner, Joseph. *The Messianic Idea in Israel.* Translated from the 3rd Hebrew ed. by W. F. Stinespring. New York, 1955.

Klein, Günther. "'Das wahre Licht scheint schon.' Beobachtungen zur Zeit- und Geschichtserfahrung einer urchristlichen Schule." *ZThK* 68 (1971): 261–326.

Klijn, Albertus F. J., and G. J. Reinink. *Patristic Evidence for Jewish-Christian Sects.* NT.S 36. Leiden, 1973.

Klos, Herbert. *Die Sakramente im Johannesevangelium.* SBS 46. Stuttgart, 1970.

Knox, John. *The Humanity and Divinity of Christ: A Study of Pattern in Christology.* Cambridge, 1967.

Koch, Dietrich-Alex. *Die Bedeutung der Wundererzählungen für die Christologie des Markusevangeliums.* BZNW 42. Berlin and New York, 1975.

Koester, Helmut. "Ein Jesus und vier ursprüngliche Evangeliumsgattungen." In Helmut Koester and J. M. Robinson, *Entwicklungslinien durch die Welt des frühen Christentums,* 147–90. Tübingen, 1971. Published in English as "One Jesus and Four Primitive Gospels." In H. Koester and J. M. Robinson, *Trajectories through Early Christianity,* 158–204. Philadelphia, 1971.

———. *Einführung in das Neue Testament.* Berlin, 1980. Translated into English by the author under the title *Introduction to the New Testament,* Vol. 1, *History, Culture, and Religion of the Hellenistic Age.* Vol. 2, *History and Literature of Early Christianity.* Philadelphia, Berlin, and New York, 1982.

Körtner, Ulrich. *Papias von Hierapolis.* FRLANT 133. Göttingen, 1983.

Kohler, Herbert. *Kreuz und Menschwerdung im Johannesevangelium.* Diss. theol., Zurich, 1986. Revised and published under the same title in the series AThANT 72. Zurich, 1987.

Kragerud, Alv. *Der Lieblingsjünger im Johannesevangelium.* Oslo, 1959.

Kramer, Werner. *Christos Kyrios Gottessohn.* AThANT 44. Zurich and Stuttgart, 1963. Translated into English by Brian Hardy under the title *Christ, Lord, Son of God.* Studies in Biblical Theology 50. Naperville, Illinois, 1966.

Kremer, Jacob. *Lazarus: Die Geschichte einer Auferstehung.* Stuttgart, 1985.

Kuhli, Horst. "Ἰουδαῖος." *EWNT* 2:472–82.

Kuhn, Heinz-Wolfgang. *Ältere Sammlungen im Markusevangelium.* SUNT 8. Göttingen, 1971.

Kuhn, Karl Georg. *Achtzehngebet und Vaterunser und der Reim.* WUNT 1. Tübingen, 1950.

———. "Giljonim und sifre minim." In *Judentum, Urchristentum, Kirche: Festschrift für J. Jeremias,* edited by Walther Eltester, 24–61. BZNW 26. Berlin, 1960.

Kümmel, Werner Georg. *Einleitung in das Neue Testament.* 19th rev. ed. Heidelberg, 1978. Translated into English by Howard Clark Kee under the title *Introduction to the New Testament.* Rev. 3rd ed. Nashville, 1975.

Kundzins, Karlis. *Topologische Überlieferungsstoffe im Johannes-Evangelium.* FRLANT 39. Göttingen, 1925.

Kysar, Robert. "The Source Analysis of the Fourth Gospel—a Growing Consensus?" *NT* 15 (1973): 134–52.

———. *The Fourth Evangelist and His Gospel.* Minneapolis, 1975.

———. *John, the Maverick Gospel.* Atlanta, 1976.

———. "Community and Gospel: Vectors in Fourth Gospel Criticism." *Interpretation* 31 (1977): 355–65.

Lagrange, Marie Joseph. *L'Évangile selon S. Jean.* EtB. 8th ed. Paris, 1948.

Lammers, Klaus. *Hören, Sehen und Glauben im Neuen Testament.* SBS 11. Stuttgart, 1966.

Langbrandtner, W. *Weltferner Gott oder Gott der Liebe.* BET 6. Frankfurt, 1977.

Larfeld, Wilhelm. "Das Zeugnis des Papias über die beiden Johannes von Ephesus." In *Johannes und sein Evangelium,* edited by K. H. Rengstorf, 381–401. Darmstadt, 1973.

Lattke, Michael. *Einheit im Wort.* StANT 41. Munich, 1975.

Leidig, Edeltraud. *Jesu Gespräch mit der Samaritanerin und weitere Gespräche im Johannesevangelium.* ThDiss. 15. Basel, 1979.

Leistner, Reinhold. *Antijudaismus im Johannesevangelium?* Theologie und Wirklichkeit 3. Frankfurt, 1974.

Léon-Dufour, Xavier. "Autour du Sēmeion Johannique." In *Die Kirche des Anfangs: Festschrift für H. Schürmann,* edited by Josef Ernst and Joachim Wanke, 363–77. Erfurter theologische Studien 38. Leipzig, 1977; Freiburg, 1978.

———. *Abendmahl und Abschiedsrede im Neuen Testament.* Stuttgart, 1983.

Leroy, Herbert. *Rätsel und Mißverständnis: Ein Beitrag zur Formgeschichte des Johannesevangeliums.* BBB 30. Bonn, 1968.

————. "Das johanneische Mißverständnis als literarische Form." *BiLe* 9 (1968): 196–207.

————. "Βηθεσδά." *EWNT* 1:512–13.

Liddell, Henry George, and Robert Scott. *A Greek-English Lexicon*. Vol. 1. Oxford, 1925.

Lietzmann, Hans. *Geschichte der alten Kirche*. Vol. 2. 2nd ed. Berlin, 1953. Translated into English by Bertram Lee Woolf under the title: *A History of the Early Church*, Vol. 2, *The Founding of the Church Universal*. Cleveland, 1961.

Lightfoot, Robert Henry. *St. John's Gospel, a Commentary*. Edited by C. F. Evans. Oxford, 1956.

Lindars, Barnabas. *Behind the Fourth Gospel*. London, 1971.

————. *The Gospel of John*. NCeB. London, 1972.

————. "Word and Sacrament in the Fourth Gospel." *SJTh* 29 (1976): 49–63.

————. "John and the Synoptic Gospels: A Test Case." *NTS* 27 (1981): 287–94.

Lindemann, Andreas. "Gemeinde und Welt im Johannesevangelium." In *Kirche: Festschrift für G. Bornkamm,* edited by Dieter Lührmann and Georg Strecker, 133–61. Tübingen, 1980.

Linnemann, Eta. "Die Hochzeit zu Kana und Dionysos." *NTS* 20 (1974): 408–18.

Lipsius, Richard A., and Maximilian Bonnet. *Acta Apostolorum Apocrypha* 2/1. Leipzig, 1898. Reprint, Hildesheim, 1959.

Loader, William R. G. "The Central Structure of Johannine Christology." *NTS* 30 (1984): 188–216.

Lohmeyer, Ernst. "Über Aufbau und Gliederung des vierten Evangeliums." *ZNW* 27 (1928): 11–36.

————. *Das Evangelium des Markus*. KEK 1/2. 12th ed. Göttingen, 1953; 17th ed. 1967.

Lohse, Eduard. "Wunder III. Im Judentum." *RGG*³ 6:1834.

————. "Wort und Sakrament im Johannesevangelium." In his *Die Einheit des Neuen Testaments,* 193–208. 2nd ed. Göttingen, 1973.

————. "Miracles in the Fourth Gospel." In his *Die Vielfalt des Neuen Testaments,* 45–56. Göttingen, 1982.

————. *Die Entstehung des Neuen Testaments*. 4th ed. Stuttgart, 1983. Translated into English from the 3rd German ed. by M. Eugene Boring under the title *The Formation of the New Testament*. Nashville, ©1981.

Loisy, Alfred F. *Le quatrième Évangile; les épîtres dites de Jean*. 2nd ed. Paris, 1921.

Lona, Horacio E. "Glaube und Sprache des Glaubens im Johannesevangelium." *BZ* 28 (1984): 168–84.

Lorenzen, Thorwald. *Der Lieblingsjünger im Johannesevangelium*. SBS 55. Stuttgart, 1971.

Lüdemann, Gerd. *Untersuchungen zur simonianischen Gnosis.* GTA 1. Göttingen, 1975.

———. *Paulus, der Heidenapostel,* II, *Antipaulismus im frühen Christentum.* FRLANT 130. Göttingen, 1983. Translated into English by M. Eugene Boring under the title *Opposition to Paul in Jewish Christianity.* Minneapolis, 1989.

Lührmann, Dieter. "Glaube." *RAC* 11:48–122.

Luz, Ulrich. "Erwägungen zur sachgemäßen Interpretation neutestamentlicher Texte." *EvTh* 42 (1982): 493–518.

Luz, Ulrich, and Rudolf Smend, *Gesetz.* Stuttgart, 1981.

Mack, Burton L. *Logos und Sophia: Untersuchungen zur Weisheitstheologie im hellenistischen Judentum.* SUNT 10. Göttingen, 1973.

Maier, Johann. *Jüdische Auseinandersetzung mit dem Christentum in der Antike.* EdF 177. Darmstadt, 1982.

Malatesta, Edward. *St. John's Gospel: 1920–1965.* AB 32. Rome, 1967.

Martyn, J. Louis. *History and Theology in the Fourth Gospel.* 2nd rev. ed. Nashville, 1979.

———. "Source Criticism and Religionsgeschichte in the Fourth Gospel." In *Jesus and Man's Hope* 1:247–73. Pittsburgh, 1970.

———. "Glimpses into the History of the Johannine Community." In his *The Gospel of John in Christian History,* 90–121. New York, 1978.

Marxsen, Willi. *Der Evangelist Markus.* FRLANT 67. Göttingen, 1956; 2nd ed. 1959. Translated into English by James Boyce, Donald Juel, and William Poehlmann, with Roy Harrisville, under the title *Mark the Evangelist.* Nashville, 1969.

———. *Einleitung in das Neue Testament: Eine Einführung in ihre Probleme.* 4th rev. ed. Gütersloh, 1978. Translated into English by G. Buswell under the title *Introduction to the New Testament: An Approach to Its Problems.* Philadelphia, 1968.

Mead, A. H. "The βασιλικός in John 4,46-53." *JSNT* 23 (1985): 69–72.

Meeks, Wayne A. *The Prophet-King: Moses Traditions and the Johannine Christology.* NT.S 14. Leiden, 1967.

———. "Die Funktion des vom Himmel herabgestiegenen Offenbarers für das Selbstverständnis der johanneischen Gemeinde." In *Zur Soziologie des Urchristentums,* edited by W. A. Meeks, 245–83. TB 62. Munich, 1979. (Selected articles previously published in various journals.)

Menoud, Philippe H. *L'Évangile de Jean d'après les recherches récentes.* CThAP 3. Neuchâtel, 1947.

Metzger, Bruce M. *A Textual Commentary on the Greek New Testament.* London and New York, 1975.

Meyer, Eduard. *Ursprung und Anfänge des Christentums* 1/1. 1921. Stuttgart, 1983.

Meyer, Rudolf. *Der Prophet aus Galiläa.* Leipzig, 1940.

Michaelis, Wilhelm. *Die Sakramente im Johannesevangelium.* Bern, 1946.

——. *Einleitung in das Neue Testament.* Bern, 1946.

Michel, Otto. "Der Anfang der Zeichen Jesu." In *Die Leibhaftigkeit des Wortes: Festschrift für A. Köberle,* edited by Otto Michel and Ulrich Mann, 15–22. Hamburg, 1958.

Minear, Paul S. "The Idea of Incarnation in First John." *Interpretation* 24 (1970): 291–302.

——. "The Original Functions of John 21." *JBL* 102 (1983): 85–98.

Miranda, José P. *Der Vater, der mich gesandt hat.* EHS.T 7. Frankfurt, 1972.

——. *Die Sendung Jesu im vierten Evangelium.* SBS 87. Stuttgart, 1977.

Mohr, Till A. *Markus- und Johannespassion.* AThANT 70. Zurich, 1982.

Müller, Ulrich B. *Die Geschichte der Christologie in der johanneischen Gemeinde.* SBS 77. Stuttgart, 1975.

——. "Die Bedeutung des Kreuzestodes Jesu im Johannesevangelium." *KuD* 21 (1975): 49–71.

——. *Die Offenbarung des Johannes.* ÖTK 19. Gütersloh, 1984.

Mussner, Franz. *ΖΩΗ. Die Anschauung vom "Leben" im vierten Evangelium.* MThS 1/5. Munich, 1952.

——. "Die johanneischen Parakletsprüche und die apostolische Tradition." *BZ* 5 (1961): 56–70.

——. *Die johanneische Sehweise.* QD 28. Freiburg, 1965.

——. "'Kultische' Aspekte im johanneischen Christusbild." In his *Praesentia salutis,* 133–45. Düsseldorf, 1967.

——. *Traktat über die Juden.* Munich, 1979.

Nauck, Wolfgang. *Die Tradition und der Charakter des ersten Johannesbriefes.* WUNT 3. Tübingen, 1957.

Neirynck, Frans. "John and the Synoptics." In *L'Évangile de Jean,* edited by M. de Jonge, 73–106. BEThL 44. Louvain, 1977.

——. *Jean et les synoptiques.* BEThL 49. Louvain, 1979.

Nestle, Eberhard, Erwin Nestle, and Kurt Aland. *Novum Testamentum Graece.* 26th ed. Stuttgart, 1979.

Neugebauer, Fritz. *Die Entstehung des Johannesevangeliums.* AzTh 1/36. Stuttgart, 1968.

Nicol, W. *The Semeia in the Fourth Gospel.* NT.S 32. Leiden, 1972.

Noack, Bent. *Zur johanneischen Tradition.* LSSK.T 3. Copenhagen, 1954.

Noetzel, Heinz. *Christus und Dionysos: Bemerkungen zum religionsgeschichtlichen Hintergrund von Johannes 2, 1–11.* Aufsätze und Vorträge zur Theologie und Religionswissenschaft 11. Stuttgart, 1960.

Norden, Eduard. *Agnostos Theos: Untersuchungen zur Formengeschichte religiöser Rede.* 6th ed. Darmstadt, 1974.

Odeberg, Hugo. *The Fourth Gospel: Interpreted in Its Relation to Contemporaneous Religious Currents in Palestine and the Hellenistic-Oriental World.* 1929. Amsterdam, 1960.

Oepke, Albrecht. "ἕλκω." *TDNT* 2:503–4.

Olsson, Birger. *Structure and Meaning in the Fourth Gospel.* CB. NT 6. Lund, 1974.

Onuki, Takashi. "Die johanneischen Abschiedsreden und die synoptische Tradition." *AJBI* 3 (1977): 157–268.

———. *Gemeinde und Welt im Johannesevangelium.* WMANT 56. Neukirchen, 1984.

Orbe, Antonio. *Christología Gnóstica.* 2 vols. Madrid, 1976.

Overbeck, Franz. *Das Johannesevangelium.* Tübingen, 1911.

Painter, John. "Christology and the History of the Johannine Community in the Prologue of the Fourth Gospel." *NTS* 30 (1984): 460–74.

———. "The 'Opponents' in 1 John." *NTS* 32 (1986): 48–71.

Pancaro, Severino. *The Law in the Fourth Gospel.* NT.S 42. Leiden, 1975.

Patsch, Hermann. "Abendmahlsterminologie außerhalb der Einsetzungsberichte." *ZNW* 62 (1971): 210–31.

———. "εὐχαριστεῖν." *EWNT* 2:219–21.

Pesch, Rudolf. "'Ihr müßt von oben geboren werden.' Eine Auslegung von Joh 3,1-12." *BiLe* 7 (1966): 208–19.

———. *Der reiche Fischfang: Lk 5,1-11/Joh 21,1-14.* Düsseldorf, 1969.

Petzke, Gerd. *Die Traditionen über Apollonius von Tyana und das Neue Testament.* StCH 1. Leiden, 1970.

Pfleiderer, Otto. "Beleuchtung der neuesten Johannes-Hypothese." *ZWTh* 12 (1869): 394–421.

Philo. *Opera I–VII.* Edited by Leopold Cohn and Paul Wendland. 7 vols. in 8. Berlin, 1896–1930.

Philostratus, Flavius. *Vita Apollonii.* Edited by V. Mumprecht. Munich, 1983.

Pohlenz, Max. "Paulus und die Stoa." In *Das Paulusbild in der neueren deutschen Forschung,* edited by Karl H. Rengstorf and Ulrich Luck, 521–64. WdF 24. 2nd ed. Darmstadt, 1969.

Pokorný, Petr. "Der irdische Jesus im Johannesevangelium." *NTS* 30 (1984): 217–28.

Porsch, Felix. *Pneuma und Wort.* FTS 16. Frankfurt, 1974.

Rahlfs, Alfred, ed. *Septuaginta.* 2 vols. 8th ed. Stuttgart, 1965.

Ratschow, Carl H. *Die eine christliche Taufe.* Gütersloh, 1972.

Reim, Günter. *Studien zum alttestamentlichen Hintergrund des Johannesevangeliums.* MSSNTS 22. Cambridge, 1974.

———. "Johannes 21—Ein Anhang?" In *Studies in New Testament Language and Text: Essays in honour of George D. Kilpatrick,* edited by James K. Elliott, 330–37. NT.S 44. Leiden, 1976.

———. "Joh 9—Tradition und zeitgenössische messianische Diskussion." *BZ* 22 (1978): 245–53.

Reitzenstein, Richard. *Hellenistische Wundererzählungen.* 1906. Darmstadt, 1963.

Rengstorf, Karl H. *Die Anfänge der Auseinandersetzung zwischen Christus-glaube und Asklepiosfrömmigkeit.* Schriften zur Förderung der Westfäli-schen Landesuniversität zu Münster 30. Münster, 1953.

——. "σημεῖον." *TDNT* 7:200–269.

Richter, Georg. *Studien zum Johannesevangelium.* BU 13. Regensburg, 1977. Includes:

"'Bist du Elias?' (Joh 1,21)," 1–41.

"Zur Formgeschichte und literarischen Einheit von Joh 6,31-58," 88–119.

"Blut und Wasser aus der durchbohrten Seite Jesu (Joh 19,34b)," 120–42.

"Die Fleischwerdung des Logos im Johannesevangelium," 149–98.

"Die alttestamentlichen Zitate in der Rede vom Himmelsbrot Joh 6,26-51a," 199–265.

"Der Vater und Gott Jesu und seiner Brüder in Joh 20,17. Ein Beitrag zur Christologie im Johannesevangelium," 266–80.

"Zur sogenannten Semeia-Quelle des Johannesevangeliums," 281–87.

"Zum sogenannten Tauftext Joh 3,5," 327–45.

"Präsentische und futurische Eschatologie im 4. Evangelium," 346–82.

"Zum gemeindebildenden Element in den johanneischen Schriften," 383–414.

Ridderbos, H. "The Structure and Scope of the Prologue to the Gospel of John," *NT* 8 (1966): 180–201.

Riedl, J. *Das Heilswerk Jesu nach Johannes.* FThSt 93. Freiburg, 1973.

Riesenfeld, Hermann. "Zu den johanneischen ἵνα-Sätzen." *StTh* 19 (1965): 213–220.

——. "τηρέω." *TDNT* 8:140–51.

Riga, Peter. "Signs of Glory." *Interpretation* 17 (1963): 402–24.

Rissi, Mathias. "Die Hochzeit in Kana." In *Oikonomia: Festschrift für O. Cullmann,* edited by Felix Christ, 76–92. Hamburg, 1967.

——. "Die Logoslieder im Prolog des vierten Evangeliums." *ThZ* 31 (1975): 321–36.

——. "Der Aufbau des vierten Evangeliums." *NTS* 29 (1983): 48–54.

Robinson, James M. "Die johanneische Entwicklungslinie." In H. Koester and J. M. Robinson, *Entwicklungslinien durch die Welt des frühen Chris-tentums,* 216–50. Tübingen, 1971. English version entitled "The Johan-nine Trajectory." In H. Koester and J. M. Robinson, *Trajectories through Early Christianity,* 232–68. Philadelphia, 1971.

——, ed. *The Nag Hammadi Library in English.* Leiden, 1977; 3rd ed. San Francisco, 1988.

——. "Sethians and Johannine Thought. The Trimorphic Protennoia and the Prologue of the Gospel of John." In *The Rediscovery of Gnosticism,* edited by Bentley Layton, 2:643–70. SHR 41. Leiden, 1980–1981.

Rohde, Joachim. *Die redaktionsgeschichtliche Methode.* Hamburg, 1966. Translated into English by Dorothea M. Barton under the title *Redis-*

covering the Teaching of the Evangelists. New edition, with revisions and additional material by the author. Philadelphia, 1968.

———. "Häresie und Schisma im Ersten Clemensbrief und in den Ignatius-Briefen." *NT* 10 (1968): 217–33.

Roloff, Jürgen. "Der johanneische 'Lieblingsjünger' und der Lehrer der Gerechtigkeit." *NTS* 15 (1968): 129–51.

———. *Die Offenbarung des Johannes.* ZBK NT 18. Zurich, 1984.

Ruckstuhl, Eugen. *Die literarische Einheit des Johannesevangeliums.* SF n.s. 3. Freiburg, 1951.

———. "Wesen und Kraft der Eucharistie in der Sicht des Johannesevangeliums." In *Das Opfer der Kirche* 1:47–90. Luzerner Theologische Studien. Lucerne, 1954.

———. "Zur Aussage und Botschaft von Joh 21." In *Die Kirche des Anfangs: Festschrift für H. Schürmann,* edited by Rudolf Schnackenburg, Josef Ernst, and Joachim Wanke, 339–62. Freiburg, 1978.

———. "Johannine Language and Style." In *L'Évangile de Jean,* edited by M. de Jonge, 125–47. BEThL 44. Louvain, 1977.

———. "Kritische Arbeit am Johannesprolog." In *The New Testament Age: Essays in Honor of B. Reicke,* edited by William C. Weinrich, 2:443–54. Macon, Georgia, 1984.

Rudolph, Kurt. *Die Gnosis: Wesen und Geschichte einer spätantiken Religion.* 2nd ed. Göttingen, 1980. Translated and edited by R. McL. Wilson under the title *Gnosis, the Nature and History of Gnosticism.* San Francisco, 1983.

Saito, Tadashi. *Die Mosevorstellungen im Neuen Testament.* EHS ser. 23, vol. 100. Bern and Las Vegas, 1977.

Sanders, Jack T. *The New Testament Christological Hymns.* MSSNTS 15. Cambridge, 1971.

Sänger, Dieter. *Antikes Judentum und die Mysterien.* WUNT ser. 2, vol. 5. Tübingen, 1980.

Saß, Gerhard. *Die Auferweckung des Lazarus.* BSt 51. Neukirchen, 1967.

Schäfer, Peter. "Die sogenannte Synode von Jabne." *Jud.* 31 (1975): 54–64, 116–24.

———. *Geschichte der Juden in der Antike.* Stuttgart and Neukirchen, 1983.

Schäferdiek, Knut. "Herkunft und Interesse der alten Johannesakten." *ZNW* 74 (1983): 247–67.

Schenke, H. M. "Die neutestamentliche Christologie und der gnostische Erlöser." In *Gnosis und Neues Testament,* edited by K. W. Tröger, 205–29. Berlin, 1973.

Schenke, H. M., and K. M. Fischer. *Einleitung in die Schriften des Neuen Testaments* II. Berlin, 1979.

Schenke, Ludger. *Die Wundererzählungen des Markusevangeliums.* SBB. Stuttgart, 1974.

———. "Die formale und gedankliche Struktur von Joh 6,26-58." *BZ* 24 (1980): 21–41.

———. "Die literarische Vorgeschichte von Joh 6,26-58." *BZ* 29 (1985): 68–89.

———. "Das Szenarium von Joh 6,1-25." *TThZ* 92 (1983): 191–203.

Schille, Gottfried. "Traditionsgut im vierten Evangelium." *TheolVers* 12 (Berlin, 1981): 77–89.

Schlatter, Adolf. "Die Sprache und Heimat des vierten Evangelisten." In *Johannes und sein Evangelium,* edited by Karl H. Rengstorf, 28–201. Darmstadt, 1973.

———. *Der Evangelist Johannes.* 4th ed. Stuttgart, 1975.

Schlier, Heinrich. "Johannes 6 und das johanneische Verständnis der Eucharistie." In his *Das Ende der Zeit,* 102–23. Freiburg, 1971.

———. "Im Anfang war das Wort.—Zum Prolog des Johannesevangeliums." In his *Die Zeit der Kirche,* 274–87. Freiburg, 1956.

Schmidt, Karl Ludwig. "Der johanneische Charakter der Erzählung vom Hochzeitswunder in Kana." In *Harnack-Ehrung,* 32–43. Leipzig, 1921.

Schmithals, Walter. "Der Prolog des Johannesevangeliums." *ZNW* 70 (1979): 16–43.

Schnackenburg, Rudolf. "Logos-Hymnus und johanneischer Prolog." *BZ* n.s. 1 (1957): 69–109.

———. "Die Erwartung des 'Propheten' nach dem Neuen Testament und den Qumran-Texten." *Studia Evangelica* 1:622–39. TU 73. Berlin, 1959.

———. "Zur Traditionsgeschichte von Joh 4,46-54." *BZ* n.s. 8 (1964): 5–88.

———. "Das Johannesevangelium als hermeneutische Frage." *NTS* 13 (1966–67): 197–210.

———. *Das Johannesevangelium.* 3 vols. HThK IV, 1–3. Freiburg, 1965–1984. Translated into English by Kevin Smyth under the title *The Gospel According to St. John.* 3 vols. New York, 1982.

———. *Die Johannesbriefe.* HThK XIII, 3. 6th ed. Freiburg, 1979.

———. *Das Johannesevangelium: Ergänzende Auslegungen und Exkurse.* HThK IV, 4. Freiburg, 1984. Includes:
"Entwicklung und Stand der johanneischen Forschung seit 1955," 9–32.
"Die johanneische Gemeinde und ihre Geisterfahrung," 33–58.
"Tradition und Interpretation im Spruchgut des Johannesevangeliums," 72–89.
"Zur Redaktionsgeschichte des Johannesevangeliums," 90–102.
"Paulinische und johanneische Christologie," 102–18.
"Das Brot des Lebens (Joh 6)," 119–31.

———. "Die bleibende Präsenz Jesu Christi nach Johannes." In *Praesentia Christi: Festschrift für J. Betz,* edited by Lothar Lies, 50–63. Düsseldorf, 1984.

Schneider, Gerhard. "Βηθανία." *EWNT* 1:511–12.

Schneider, Johannes. "Zur Frage der Komposition von Joh 6, 17–58(59)." In *In memoriam Ernst Lohmeyer,* edited by Werner Schmauch, 132–42. Stuttgart, 1951.

——. *1. Johannesbrief.* NTD 10:137–88. 9th ed. Göttingen, 1961.

——. *Das Evangelium nach Johannes.* ThHK, Sonderband. 2nd ed. Berlin, 1978.

Schnelle, Udo. *Gerechtigkeit und Christusgegenwart: Vorpaulinische und paulinische Tauftheologie.* GTA 24. 2nd ed. Göttingen, 1986.

Schnider, Franz, and Werner Stenger. *Johannes und die Synoptiker.* BH 9. Munich, 1971.

Schoedel, William R. *Ignatius of Antioch.* Hermeneia. Philadelphia, 1985.

Schottroff, Luise. "Heil als innerweltliche Entweltlichung." *NT* 11 (1969): 294–317.

——. *Der Glaubende und die feindliche Welt.* WMANT 37. Neukirchen, 1970.

——. "ζῶ." *EWNT* 2:261–71.

Schrage, Wolfgang. "ἀποσυνάγωγος." *TDNT* 7:848–52.

——. "τυφλός." *TDNT* 8:270–94.

——. *Ethik des Neuen Testaments.* GNT 4. Göttingen, 1982. Translated into English by David E. Green under the title *The Ethics of the New Testament.* Philadelphia, 1987.

Schram, T. L. "The Use of Ioudaios in the Fourth Gospel." Diss. theol. Utrecht, 1974.

Schreiber, Johannes. *Theologie des Vertrauens.* Hamburg, 1967.

Schulz, Siegfried. *Untersuchungen zur Menschensohn-Christologie im Johannesevangelium.* Göttingen, 1957.

——. *Komposition und Herkunft der Johanneischen Reden.* BWANT 5/1. Stuttgart, 1960.

——. *Das Evangelium nach Johannes.* NTD 4. Göttingen, 1972.; 5th ed. 1987.

——. *Q: Die Spruchquelle der Evangelisten.* Zurich, 1972.

Schunack, Gerd. *Die Briefe des Johannes.* ZBK NT 17. Zurich, 1982.

Schürer, Emil. "Über den gegenwärtigen Stand der johanneischen Frage." In *Johannes und sein Evangelium,* edited by Karl H. Rengstorf, 1–27. Darmstadt, 1973.

——. *Geschichte des Jüdischen Volkes im Zeitalter Jesu Christi.* 2 vols. Leipzig, 5th ed. 1920, 4th ed. 1907. Translated into English by T. A. Burkill et al. under the title *A History of the Jewish People in the Age of Jesus Christ.* Revised and edited by Geza Vermes and Fergus Millar. 3 vols. in 4. Edinburgh, 1973–1987.

Schürmann, Heinz. *Ursprung und Gestalt.* Düsseldorf, 1970. Includes: "Jesu letzte Weisung. Joh 19,26-27a," 13–28. "Joh 6,51c—Ein Schlüssel zur großen johanneischen Brotrede," 151–66.

"Die Eucharistie als Repräsentation und Applikation des Heilsgeschehens nach Joh 6,53-58," 167–87.

Schwartz, Eduard. *Aporien im vierten Evangelium.* NGWG.PH (1907), 342–72; (1908), 115–48, 149–88, 497–560.

Schweitzer, Albert. *Die Mystik des Apostels Paulus.* 2nd ed. Tübingen, 1954.

Schweizer, A. *Das Evangelium Johannes nach seinem innern Werthe und seiner Bedeutung für das Leben Jesu kritisch untersucht.* Leipzig, 1841.

Schweizer, Eduard. *Ego Eimi.* FRLANT 56. 2nd ed. Göttingen, 1965.

——. *Neotestamentica.* Zurich, 1963. Includes:
"Der Kirchenbegriff im Evangelium und den Briefen des Johannes," 254–71.
"Das johanneische Zeugnis vom Herrenmahl," 371–96.
"Die Heilung des Aussätzigen," 407–15.

——. "πνεῦμα." *TDNT* 6:332–455.

——. "Zum religionsgeschichtlichen Hintergrund der 'Sendungsformel' Gal 4,4f., Röm 8,3f., Joh 3,16f.; 1Joh 4,9." In his *Beiträge zur Theologie des Neuen Testaments,* 83–95. Zurich, 1970.

——. *Jesus Christus im vielfältigen Zeugnis des Neuen Testaments.* Munich, 1968. Translated into English by David E. Green under the title *Jesus.* Richmond, 1971.

——. *Das Evangelium nach Markus.* NTD 1. 4th ed. Göttingen, 1975. Translated into English by Donald H. Madvig under the title *The Good News according to Mark.* Richmond, 1970.

——. "Jesus der Zeuge Gottes: Zum Problem des Doketismus im Johannesevangelium." In *Studies in John: Essays in honor of J. N. Sevenster,* 161–68. NT.S 24. Leiden, 1970.

Slusser, Michael. "Docetism: A Historical Definition." *The Second Century* 1 (1981): 163–72.

Smalley, Stephen S. *John, Evangelist and Interpreter.* 1978. Exeter, 1983.

Smith, Dwight Moody. *The Composition and Order of the Fourth Gospel.* New Haven, 1965.

——. "Johannine Christianity: Some Reflections on its Character and Delineation." *NTS* 21 (1975): 222–48.

——. "The Milieu of the Johannine Miracle Source: A Proposal." In *Jews, Greeks and Christians: Essays in honor of W. D. Davies,* edited by Robert Hamerton-Kelly and Robin Scroggs, 164–80. Leiden, 1976.

Spitta, Friedrich. *Das Johannesevangelium als Quelle der Geschichte Jesu.* Göttingen, 1910.

Stählin, Gustav. "Zum Problem der johanneischen Eschatologie." *ZNW* 33 (1934): 225–59.

——. "φιλέω." *TDNT* 9:113–71.

Stauffer, Ethelbert. Review of R. Bultmann. *ZKG* 62 (1943): 347–52.

Stegemann, Hartmut. Review of Pierre Prigent, *Les Testimonia dans le Christianisme primitif.* *ZKG* 73 (1962): 142–53.

Stemberger, Günter. "Die sogenannte 'Synode von Jabne' und das frühe Christentum." *Kairos* 19 (1977): 14–21.

———. *Das klassische Judentum.* Munich, 1979.

Stenger, Werner. "Die Auferweckung des Lazarus." *TThZ* 83 (1974): 17–37.

Stolz, Fritz. "Zeichen und Wunder." *ZThK* 69 (1972): 125–44.

Strathmann, Hermann. *Das Evangelium nach Johannes.* NTD 4. 4th ed. Göttingen, 1959.

———. "Johannesbriefe." *EKL* 2:363–65.

Strecker, Georg. *Das Judenchristentum in den Pseudoklementinen.* TU 70. 2nd ed. Berlin, 1981.

———. *Der Weg der Gerechtigkeit.* FRLANT 82. 3rd ed. Göttingen, 1971.

———. *Eschaton und Historie: Aufsätze.* Göttingen, 1979. Includes: "Redaktionsgeschichte als Aufgabe der Synoptikerexegese," 9–32. "Die Makarismen der Bergpredigt," 108–31.

———. "μακάριος." *EWNT* 2:925–32.

———. "Judenchristentum und Gnosis." In *Altes Testament, Frühjudentum, Gnosis,* edited by Karl-Wolfgang Tröger, 261–82. Gütersloh, 1980.

———. "Die Anfänge der johanneischen Schule." *NTS* 32 (1986): 31–47.

Strecker, Georg, and Udo Schnelle. *Einführung in die neutestamentliche Exegese.* 2nd ed. Göttingen, 1985.

Streeter, Burnett Hillman. *The Four Gospels.* New York, 1925.

Talbert, Charles H. *What Is a Gospel?* Philadelphia, 1977.

Teeple, Howard M. *The Literary Origin of the Gospel of John.* Evanston, 1974.

Temple, Sydney. "A Key to the Composition of the Fourth Gospel." *JBL* 80 (1961): 220–32.

Tertullian. *Adversus Marcionem.* Edited by A. Kroymann. CSEL 47. Leipzig, 1906.

Theissen, Gerd. *Urchristliche Wundergeschichten.* StNT 8. Gütersloh, 1974. Translated into English by Francis McDonagh under the title *The Miracle Stories of the Early Christian Tradition.* Edited by John Riches. Philadelphia, 1983.

Theobald, Michael. "Der Primat der Synchronie vor der Diachronie als Grundaxiom der Literarkritik." *BZ* 22 (1978): 161–86.

———. *Im Anfang war das Wort.* SBS 106. Stuttgart, 1983.

Thompson, J. M. "The Structure of the Fourth Gospel." *Exp* 10 (1915): 512–26.

Thraede, Klaus. "Untersuchungen zum Ursprung und zur Geschichte der christlichen Poesie I." *JAC* 4 (1961): 108–27.

Thüsing, Wilhelm. *Die Erhöhung und Verherrlichung Jesu im Johannesevangelium.* NTA 21:1, 2. Münster, 1960.

Thyen, Hartwig. "Johannes 13 und die 'Kirchliche Redaktion' des vierten Evangeliums." In *Tradition und Glaube: Festschrift für K. G. Kuhn,* edited by Gert Jeremias, Heinz-Wolfgang Kuhn, and Hartmut Stegemann, 343–56. Göttingen, 1971.

———. "Aus der Literatur zum Johannesevangelium." *ThR* 39 (1974): 1–69, 222–52, 289–330; *ThR* 42 (1977): 211–70; *ThR* 43 (1978): 328–59; *ThR* 44 (1979): 97–134.

———. " '. . . denn wir lieben die Brüder' (1 Joh 3,14)." In *Rechtfertigung: Festschrift für E. Käsemann,* edited by Johannes Friedrich, Wolfgang Pöhlmann, and Peter Stuhlmacher, 527–42. Tübingen, 1976.

———. "Entwicklungen innerhalb der johanneischen Theologie und Kirche im Spiegel von Joh 21 und der Lieblingsjüngertexte des Evangeliums." In *L'Évangile de Jean,* edited by M. de Jonge, 259–99. BEThL 44. Louvain, 1977.

———. " 'Niemand hat größere Liebe als die, daß er sein Leben für seine Freunde hingibt.' " In *Theologia Crucis — Signum Crucis: Festschrift für E. Dinkler,* edited by Carl Andresen and Günter Klein, 467–81. Tübingen, 1979.

———. " 'Das Heil kommt von den Juden.' " In *Kirche: Festschrift für G. Bornkamm,* edited by Dieter Lührmann and Georg Strecker, 163–84. Tübingen, 1980.

Tiede, David L. *The Charismatic Figure as Miracle Worker.* SBL DS 1. Missoula, 1972.

Trilling, Wolfgang. "Gegner Jesu — Widersacher der Gemeinde — Repräsentanten der 'Welt.' Das Johannesevangelium und die Juden." In *Gottesverächter und Menschenfeinde?* edited by Horst Goldstein, 190–210. Düsseldorf, 1979.

Tröger, Karl-Wolfgang. "Ja oder Nein zur Welt: War der Evangelist Johannes Christ oder Gnostiker?" *TheolVers* 7 (Berlin, 1976): 61–80.

———. "Doketische Christologie in Nag-Hammadi-Texten." *Kairos* 19 (1977): 45–52.

Urbach, Efraim E. "Self-Isolation or Self-Affirmation in Judaism in the First Three Centuries: Theory and Practice." In *Jewish and Christian Self-Definition,* edited by E. P. Sanders, A. J. Baumgarten, and Alan Mendelson, 2:269–98. London, 1981.

van Belle, Gilbert. *De semeia-Bron in het vierde Evangelie.* Studiorum Novi Testamenti Auxilia 10. Louvain, 1975.

van der Loos, H. *The Miracles of Jesus.* Translated by T. S. Preston. NT.S 9. Leiden, 1965.

Venetz, Hermann-Josef. " 'Durch Wasser und Blut gekommen.' Exegetische Überlegungen zu 1 Joh 5,6." In *Die Mitte des Neuen Testaments: Festschrift für E. Schweizer,* edited by Ulrich Luz and Hans Weder, 345–61. Göttingen, 1983.

Vielhauer, Philipp. "Erwägungen zur Christologie des Markusevangeliums." In his *Aufsätze zum Neuen Testament,* 199–214. TB 31. Munich, 1965.

———. *Geschichte der urchristlichen Literatur.* Berlin and New York, 1975.

Volz, Paul. *Die Eschatologie der jüdischen Gemeinde.* Tübingen, 1934. Reprint, Hildesheim, 1966.

von Campenhausen, Hans. *Die Entstehung der christlichen Bibel.* Tübingen, 1968. Translated by J. A. Baker under the title *The Formation of the Christian Bible.* Philadelphia, 1972.

von der Osten-Sacken, Peter. "Der erste Christ. Johannes d. T. als Schlüssel zum Prolog des vierten Evangeliums." *ThViat* 13 (1975–76): 155–73.

———. "Leistung und Grenze der johanneischen theologia crucis." *EvTh* 36 (1976): 154–76.

von Wahlde, Urban C. "The Johannine 'Jews': A Critical Survey." *NTS* 28 (1982): 33–60.

Walter, Nikolaus. "Die Auslegung überlieferter Wundererzählungen im Johannes-Evangelium." *TheolVers* 2 (Berlin, 1970): 93–107.

———. "Glaube und irdischer Jesus im Johannesevangelium." *StEv* 7 (Berlin, 1982): 547–52.

Weder, Hans. "Die Menschwerdung Gottes." *ZThK* 82 (1985): 325–60.

Wegner, Uwe. *Der Hauptmann von Kafarnaum.* WUNT ser. 2, vol. 14. Tübingen, 1985.

Weigandt, P. "Der Doketismus im Urchristentum und in der theologischen Entwicklung des zweiten Jahrhunderts." Diss. theol. Heidelberg, 1961.

Weinreich, Otto. *Antike Heilungswunder.* RVV 8,1. Giessen, 1909.

Weiss, Bernhard. *Die drei Briefe des Apostels Johannes.* KEK 14. 6th ed. Göttingen, 1899.

Weiß, Konrad. "Die 'Gnosis' im Hintergrund und im Spiegel der Johannes-briefe." In *Gnosis und Neues Testament,* edited by Karl-Wolfgang Tröger, 341–56. Berlin, 1973.

Wellhausen, Julius. *Erweiterungen und Änderungen im vierten Evangelium.* Berlin, 1907.

———. *Das Evangelium Johannis.* Berlin, 1908.

Wendt, Hans Hinrich. *Das Johannesevangelium.* Göttingen, 1900. Translated into English by Edward Lummis, M.A., under the title *The Gospel According to St. John.* Edinburgh, 1902.

———. *Die Schichten im vierten Evangelium.* Göttingen, 1911.

———. "Der 'Anfang' am Beginne des 1. Johannesbriefes." *ZNW* 21 (1922): 38–42.

———. "Die Beziehung unseres ersten Johannesbriefes auf den zweiten." *ZNW* 21 (1922): 140–46.

———. *Die Johannesbriefe und das johanneische Christentum.* Halle, 1925.

Wengst, Klaus. *Tradition und Theologie des Barnabasbriefes.* AKG 42. Berlin, 1971.

———. *Christologische Formeln und Lieder des Urchristentums.* StNT 7. Gütersloh, 1972.

———. *Häresie und Orthodoxie im Spiegel des ersten Johannesbriefes.* Gütersloh, 1976.

——. *Der erste, zweite und dritte Brief des Johannes.* ÖTK 16. Gütersloh, 1978.

——. *Bedrängte Gemeinde und verherrlichter Christus.* BThSt 5. 2nd ed. Neukirchen, 1983.

——. *Didache. Barnabasbrief. Zweiter Klemensbrief. Schrift an Diognet.* SUC 2. Darmstadt, 1984.

Wenz, Helmut. "Sehen und Glauben bei Johannes." *ThZ* 17 (1961): 17–25.

Wetter, Gillis Petersson. *"Der Sohn Gottes."* FRLANT 26. Göttingen, 1916.

Wettstein, Johann Jakob. *Novum Testamentum Graecum.* 2 vols. 1751–1752. Graz, 1962.

Whitacre, Rodney A. *Johannine Polemic: The Role of Tradition and Theology.* SBL DS 67. Chico, 1982.

Whittaker, Molly. "'Signs and Wonders': The Pagan Background." *StEv* 5 (Berlin, 1968): 155–58.

Wiefel, Wolfgang. "Die Scheidung von Gemeinde und Welt im Johannesevangelium auf dem Hintergrund der Trennung von Kirche und Synagoge." *ThZ* 35 (1979): 213–27.

Wikenhauser, Alfred. *Das Evangelium nach Johannes.* RNT 4. 3rd ed. Regensburg, 1961.

Wikenhauser, Alfred, and Josef Schmid. *Einleitung in das Neue Testament.* 6th ed. Freiburg, 1973.

Wilckens, Ulrich. "Der eucharistische Abschnitt der johanneischen Rede vom Lebensbrot (Joh 6,51c-58)." In *Neues Testament und Kirche: Festschrift für R. Schnackenburg,* edited by Joachim Gnilka, 220–48. Freiburg, 1974.

——. "Der Paraklet und die Kirche." In *Kirche: Festschrift für G. Bornkamm,* edited by Dieter Lührmann and Georg Strecker, 185–203. Tübingen, 1980.

——. *Auferstehung.* 2nd ed. Gütersloh, 1977. Translated into English by A. M. Stewart under the title *Resurrection: Biblical Testimony to the Resurrection.* Atlanta, 1978.

Wilkens, Wilhelm. *Die Entstehungsgeschichte des vierten Evangeliums.* Zollikon, 1958.

——. "Das Abendmahlszeugnis im vierten Evangelium." *EvTh* 18 (1958): 354–70.

——. "Die Erweckung des Lazarus." *ThZ* 15 (1959): 22–39.

——. "Evangelist und Tradition im Johannesevangelium." *ThZ* 16 (1960): 81–90.

——. *Zeichen und Werke.* AThANT 55. Zürich, 1969.

Windisch, Hans. "Die johanneische Weinregel." *ZNW* 14 (1913): 248–57.

——. "Der johanneische Erzählungsstil." In *Eucharisterion II: Festschrift für H. Gunkel,* edited by Hans Schmidt, 174–213. Göttingen, 1923.

——. *Johannes und die Synoptiker.* Leipzig, 1926.

———. "Die fünf johanneischen Parakletsprüche." In *Festgabe für A. Jülicher,* edited by Hans von Soden and Rudolf Bultmann, 110–37. Tübingen, 1927.

———. *Johannesbriefe.* HNT 15: 106–44. 3rd ed. Tübingen, 1951.

Wrede, Wilhelm. *Charakter und Tendenz des Johannesevangeliums.* SGV 37. 2nd ed. Tübingen, 1933.

Zahn, Theodor. *Einleitung in das Neue Testament* II. 2nd ed. Leipzig, 1900.

———. *Das Evangelium des Johannes.* KNT 4. 5th and 6th eds. Leipzig, 1921.

Zeller, Dieter. "Paulus und Johannes." *BZ* 27 (1983): 167–82.

Zenger, Erich. "Die späte Weisheit und das Gesetz." In *Literatur und Religion des Frühjudentums,* edited by Johann Maier and Josef Schreiner, 43–56. Würzburg, 1973.

Zimmermann, Heinrich. "Christushymnus und johanneischer Prolog." In *NT und Kirche: Festschrift für R. Schnackenburg,* edited by Joachim Gnilka, 249–65. Freiburg, 1974.

Index

Selected New Testament Writings

Modern Authors